W9-ADI-837

# Integrated Risk Management for Leisure Services

Robert B. Kauffman, PhD
Frostburg State University

Merry Lynn Moiseichik, ReD, JD
University of Arkansas

Human Kinetics

**Library of Congress Cataloging-in-Publication Data**

Kauffman, Robert B.
Integrated risk management for leisure services / Robert B. Kauffman, Merry Lynn Moiseichik.
p. cm.
Includes bibliographical references and index.
1. Leisure industry. 2. Recreation industry. 3. Risk management. I. Moiseichik, Merry Lynn. II. Title.
GV188.K38 2013
790.06'9--dc23
2012031190

ISBN-10: 0-7360-9565-9 (print)
ISBN-13: 978-0-7360-9565-5 (print)



The web addresses cited in this text were current as of August 2012, unless otherwise noted.

**Acquisitions Editor:** Gayle Kassing, PhD; **Developmental Editor:** Melissa Feld; **Assistant Editor:** Rachel Brito; **Copyeditor:** Amanda Eastin-Allen; **Indexer:** Alisha Jeddeloh; **Permissions Manager:** Dalene Reeder; **Graphic Designer:** Joe Buck; **Graphic Artist:** Kathleen Boudreau-Fuoss; **Cover Designer:** Keith Blomberg; **Photographs (interior):** © Human Kinetics, unless otherwise noted; **Photo Asset Manager:** Laura Fitch; **Visual Production Assistant:** Joyce Brumfield; **Photo Production Manager:** Jason Allen; **Art Manager:** Kelly Hendren; **Associate Art Manager:** Alan L. Wilborn; **Illustrations:** © Human Kinetics, unless otherwise noted; **Printer:** Sheridan Books

Printed in the United States of America 10 9 8 7 6 5 4 3 2 1

The paper in this book is certified under a sustainable forestry program.

**Human Kinetics**
Website: www.HumanKinetics.com
*United States:* Human Kinetics
P.O. Box 5076
Champaign, IL 61825-5076
800-747-4457
e-mail: humank@hkusa.com

*Canada:* Human Kinetics
475 Devonshire Road Unit 100
Windsor, ON N8Y 2L5
800-465-7301 (in Canada only)
e-mail: info@hkcanada.com

*Europe:* Human Kinetics
107 Bradford Road
Stanningley
Leeds LS28 6AT, United Kingdom
+44 (0) 113 255 5665
e-mail: hk@hkeurope.com

*Australia:* Human Kinetics
57A Price Avenue
Lower Mitcham, South Australia 5062
08 8372 0999
e-mail: info@hkaustralia.com

*New Zealand:* Human Kinetics
P.O. Box 80
Torrens Park, South Australia 5062
0800 222 062
e-mail: info@hknewzealand.com

E5188

This book is dedicated to the memory of Betty van der Smissen, a pioneer and leader in the field.

Her contribution to the field is well known. She wrote several books on legal liability and numerous articles that bear testimony to her groundbreaking work in the field. Dr. Kauffman is her former student and Dr. Moiseichik was mentored by her. It is difficult to fully document her contribution as a mentor and instructor. She had a considerable impact on both authors, and that alone is a sufficient reason to dedicate this book to her. Her profound contribution to the recreation and park discipline is in part reflected by the current emphasis on legal liability in the recreation and parks curricula. Just as her work spurred the field in a new direction toward legal liability, the authors hope that this book, which builds on her foundational work in the risk management field, will spur the field in new directions regarding risk management and the accident process. If this book is successful, this new direction is, in part, attributable to her pioneering efforts in legal liability and risk management.

# Contents

# Preface

The purpose of risk management is to manage, reduce, or eliminate risks in order to make recreation and park activities safer. In the recreation and park field, risk management has traditionally been associated with the legal profession and case law. This is due in large part to the pioneering efforts of Betty van der Smissen, to whom this book is dedicated. Under her tutelage, risk management in the recreation and park field grew significantly and tended to have a legal focus. The focus that evolved is a tribute to her influence and contribution to the field.

It is important to have some understanding of legal liability. The question is, how much does a professional really need to know about case law? The role of an organization's legal assistant or legal counsel is to fully understand the law and its ramifications regarding the organization and its recreation programs. Hence, the objective is for a recreation and park professional to have enough knowledge regarding legal liability and negligence to communicate with the legal staff or counsel. This text provides a basic understanding of the principles associated with negligence. In a litigious society, the importance of focusing on legal liability and negligence cannot be understated.

Are there risk management approaches that the recreation and park field has not yet embraced and incorporated? The answer is a resounding yes. Barrier analysis, energy transfer, tree analysis, and the ripple effect are several examples of new or little-known content areas that need to be integrated into the risk management thoughts of recreation and park leaders and organizations. This text provides this integration.

The fundamental question that most students ask is "I don't want to be sued. What can I do to prevent an accident?" A second question that can be almost as important as the first is "Now that an accident has occurred, can I do anything to prevent being sued or to reduce the likelihood of having a similar accident occur again?" New content areas and schools of thought provide practical methods and procedures for reducing the likelihood of accidents occurring.

The integrated risk management model (figure P.1) reflects the integration of these new content areas as well as the more traditional emphasis on legal liability. The model presents four complementary schools of thought in risk management. The common element in the schools of thought is injury, damage, or loss. The first school of thought focuses on negligence from a legal perspective. The second school of thought focuses on accident causation and safety management. If no accident occurs, there is no injury, damage, or loss and therefore little or no grounds for a legal suit. Hence, preventing the accident potentially prevents the lawsuit. Complementing this approach is the risk management plan, the third school of thought, which one uses to identify risks that can lead to injury, damage, or loss and to develop a strategy that best deals with the risks. The last school of thought focuses on what to do to mitigate the effects on all concerned after an accident or incident resulting in injury, damage, or loss occurs.

## OVERVIEW OF THE CHAPTERS

This text reinforces good programming and leadership principles and practices by using a broad-based approach to risk management. The four major schools of thought represented in the integrated risk management model form the structure of the four main parts of this text. Part I presents the first school of thought, which focuses on legal liability and negligence. Understanding negligence (chapters 1 and 2) and understanding the defenses against negligence (chapter 3) helps reduce the likelihood of injury, damage, or loss. Part I provides a primer on negligence that will help recreation and park professionals understand the legal principles of negligence and will help them communicate with legal counsel. The

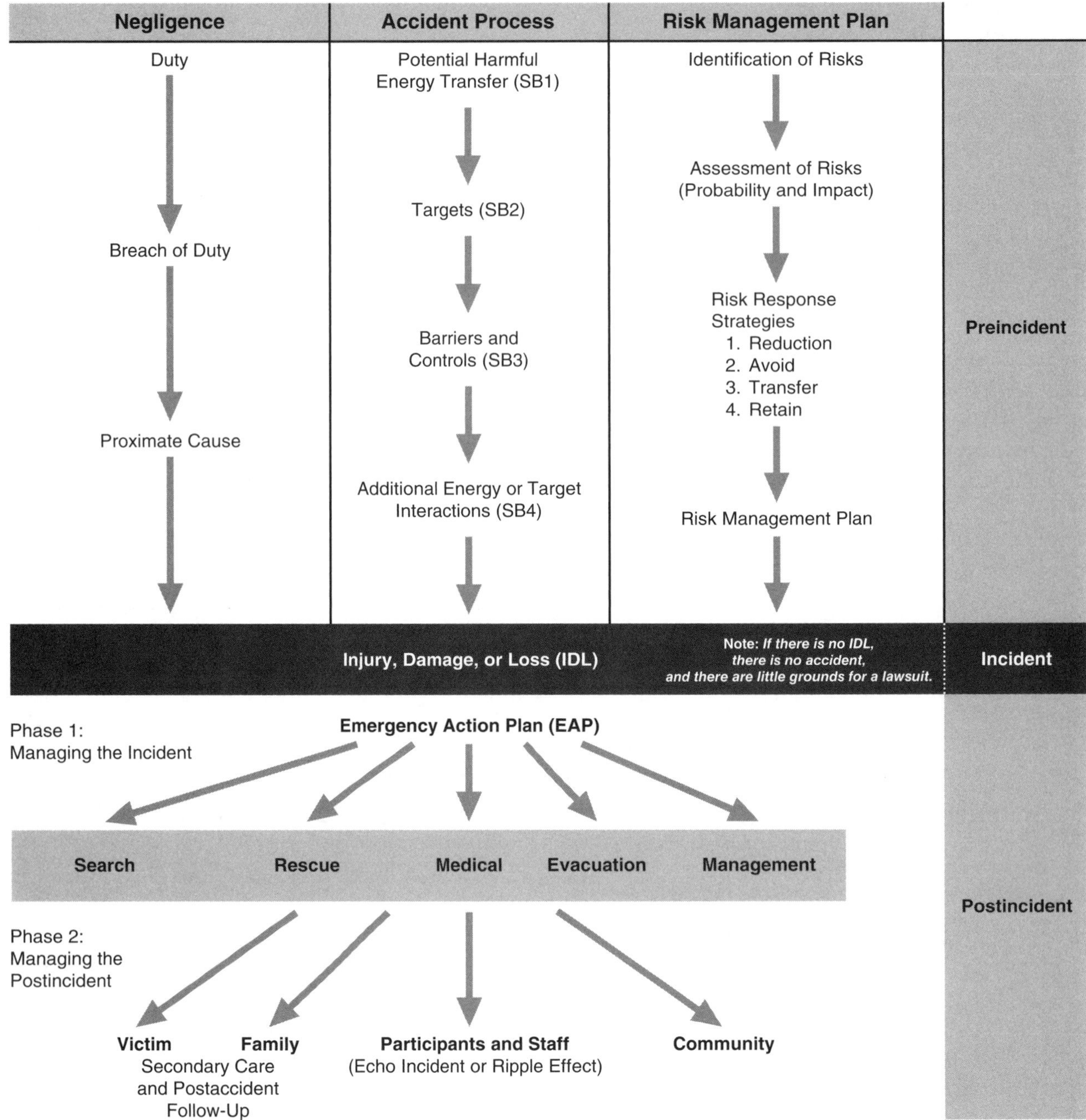


**Figure P.1** The integrated risk management model, which integrates four schools of thought toward risk management, provides the foundation for this text.

information in part I provides a frame for the rest of the parts in the text.

Part II presents the second school of thought, which focuses on accident causation and safety management. Understanding accident causation and safety management enables programmers and leaders to take measures that help prevent the accident from happening in the first place. Within this school of thought, there are several conceptual and historical threads that significantly impact the adaption of this material to the recreation and parks field.

The first thread focuses on the fact that historically most models are implemented at the organizational level by a safety manager hired by the organization. This is an underlying proposition in most of the models discussed in chapters 4 and 5. It is evident in Frederick Heinrich's domino theory, one of the earliest models developed, which is discussed in chapter 4. Also, it is evident in the analytical tree models discussed in chapter 5. In the recreation and parks field dominated by leadership and programming, the outdoor field has a history of developing accident causation models that emphasize the leader and programmer. Chapter 6 presents these traditional models and incorporates the discussions in chapters 4 and 5.

A second thread focuses on the adaption of models developed for large complex systems to the recreation and parks field. Most of the analytical tree models presented in chapter 5 involve large complex systems associated with the Atomic Energy Commission, the Strategic Air Command, and the National Aeronautics and Space Administration (NASA). The question for the recreation and parks field is "Are the principles developed for large complex systems also adaptable to a recreation and parks field dominated at the leadership and programmer level?" The answer is yes. Barrier analysis, energy transfer, fault tree analysis, and positive tree analysis are easily adaptable to the recreation and parks field. In addition, the concepts of barrier analysis and energy transfer discussed in chapter 5, along with the basic factors discussed in the domino model in chapter 4, are directly incorporated into the existing outdoor models discussed in chapter 6.

A third thread is that the recreation and parks field—and in particular the outdoor field—has embraced risk as a potentially important component in its activities and programs. Conceptually, this is anathema to traditional accident causation and safety management approaches. This issue needs to be addressed and reconciled. Chapter 7 addresses the issue of programming for risk.

Part III, comprising chapter 8, presents the third school of thought, which focuses on the risk management plan. The risk management plan is an organizational plan instituted and implemented by the organization's safety manager. The Commission for Accreditation of Park and Recreation Agencies recommends having a plan, which is normally considered a common practice or even an industry standard for any recreation and park agency. Although a safety manager normally creates risk management plans, principles involving the risk management plan carry over to the recreation leader or programmer, who must consider what she can do to reduce the likelihood of an accident occurring in the first place. Chapter 8 also presents a practical risk management approach that can be utilized either at the organizational level or the leader and programmer levels.

Part IV presents the fourth school of thought, which focuses on what to do after an accident or incident occurs. Evidence shows that how a person handles events after an accident occurs can directly influence whether that person is sued. Once an incident occurs, events move quickly. Chapter 9 presents an emergency action plan that will help a leader or organization react quickly once an incident occurs. Chapter 10 focuses on managing the scene of the incident. Chapter 11 focuses on crisis management. Chapter 12 focuses on developing a relationship with the victim and the victim's family in order to redirect their anger and help prevent a lawsuit.

Chapter 13 focuses on the ripple effects of the original incident. An accident can devastate the foundations of an organization. Staff members seek other jobs or leave the profession because they do not want to be associated with the tragedy, and the community can lose confidence in the agency. If the agency is not careful, it can go out of business.

Chapter 14 focuses on how to perform an investigation of the accident or incident that occurred. Determining the underlying causes of the accident helps a recreation provider improve operations and prevent the accident from happening in the future. An investigation shows that a recreation provider was following the common practices of the activity or industry and provides important feedback to improve operations without admitting culpability. The process comes full circle.

In addition, there are several appendixes included in the text. The material included in the appendixes serves two purposes. First, they provide examples that complement the discussion of concepts and principles in the chapters. For example, appendix C contains the script of *Cold, Wet, and Alive*. The script provides an account of David's river trip that is used in the discussion of the accident process. Second, the materials in the appendixes provide source material for many of the chapter exercises.

## ACCIDENT VERSUS INCIDENT

Depending on the literature reviewed, there has been a recent trend toward using the term *incident* rather than the term *accident*. Most people consider an accident to be an incident that results in an injury, damage, or loss to the victim. In addition, the term *accident* implies that something happened by chance and was unexpected and uncontrolled. Herein lies the problem. The safety-management field has advanced the notion that everything involving an accident can be controlled. When the definition implies that not everything can be controlled, the field seeks a new definition. Incident is the proposed replacement term for *accident*. It is a neutral term. Again, herein lies the problem. Although it has meaning to professionals in the safety-management field, it lacks real meaning to the public.

When the Coast Guard became actively involved in recreational boating, they sought to change the term *life jacket* to the term *personal flotation device*. A life jacket was defined as the life jacket that passengers wear when a ship goes down. Conversely, personal flotation devices were subdivided into five categories. Thirty years later, after lack of public acceptance, the Coast Guard has returned to referring to life jackets as life jackets because the public perceives all life jackets as life jackets. The term *personal flotation device* has not been abandoned, but it has been replaced once again by the term *life jacket*. The use of the term *life jacket* has gone full circle.

Conversely, the use of *incident* instead of *accident* has not yet gone full circle. It might not. It remains to be seen whether the public will abandon the use of the term *accident* in favor of the term *incident*. For example, when someone says they had an automobile accident, it makes perfect sense. In contrast, if someone says they had an automobile incident, it sounds awkward. For most of the public, an automobile incident is somewhat meaningless. If and when the term *automobile incident* has the same meaning to the public as the term *automobile accident*, incident will most likely replace accident as the operative term used to describe accidents. Until that time, and in terms of this text, unless otherwise stated, *accident* and *incident* are used fairly interchangeably. It should be noted that in some cases, incidents can also include events that do not involve injury, damage, or loss.

## INJURY, DAMAGE, OR LOSS

The integrated risk management model uses the terms *injury*, *damage*, and *loss*. Connotative differences exist between the terms. Injury normally refers to bodily harm. Damage normally involves property loss. Loss generally connotes financial loss. There is some movement in the safety-management field toward using the term *loss*, although it is relatively bland and lacks effect. The insurance industry uses these three terms but arranges the terms in a different order. No uniformity exists in the terminology either within or between the different industries involved in risk management and safety management.

Regardless of the term used, an important aspect of this book is to eliminate and reduce injuries, property damages, and losses in the recreation and park field and in general. In this respect, this book sets a new course by integrating new schools of thought into the recreation and park mainstream. More important, it gives students the tools and techniques that can make the delivery of recreation and park activities and programs safer.

## BENEFITS OF THIS TEXT

As suggested in the title of this book and of the integrated risk management model, this text provides a broader approach to risk management than is traditionally covered in other books. Much of the content in this text is new to the recreation and park field.

This text reviews legal liability, and negligence in particular, in the context of a litigious society and in terms techniques that can help prevent a person from being sued. This discussion sets the context for the rest of the book, which answers the question "What can the organization do, and what specifically can I do, to reduce the likelihood of injury, damage, or loss from occurring and, hence, the likelihood of being sued?"

This text also emphasizes that risk management is not optional, but rather is part of normal programming and leadership activities. It involves correctly selecting an activity that matches participants' skills and sought experience with the challenges and experience provided. It is knowing when to stop or postpone the activity. It involves understanding the common practices and following them, and knowing what other professionals are doing in similar situations elsewhere.

This text integrates content areas that traditionally have not been addressed in the recreation and park field but should be included. Barrier analysis, energy transfer, tree analysis, and the outdoor models are new content areas that can easily be infused into the mainstream of risk management thought in the recreation and park field and can easily be adapted to the needs of the leader or programmer. Similarly, much of the content in part IV (e.g., the ripple effect, and how to proceed after an accident occurs in order to avoid a legal suit) has not yet permeated the mainstream thought of recreation.

In the safety-management field it is often assumed that the safety-management officer is responsible for overseeing the safety-management efforts. People often interpret this to mean that safety is someone else's job. However, one goal of this text is to answer the question "What can I do to prevent accidents?" For example, in barrier analysis, the question for the leader or programmer becomes "How can I place administrative or physical barriers [handrail] between the potential hazards identified [potential fall] and the target [the participant]?" The domino model or Curtis' accident models help answer the question "How do I balance or compensate for the human, environmental, and equipment factors that can lead to accidents in the activities and programs that I provide?" An emphasis in this text is to provide risk management tools that a recreation leader or organization can use in activities and programs as well at an administrative level.

This textbook can be used as a stand-alone text for a course in risk management. This text includes enough content and activities to complete a semester course in risk management. The textbook can also supplement the risk management needs of courses in leadership, programming, or administration. Or, relevant parts of this text can be applied to specialized courses in the curriculum.

The role of recreation engineering is to build experiences in the hearts and minds of the participants. A recreation engineer cannot guarantee safety. She can, however, create an environment that reduces the likelihood of injury, damage, or loss when creating the desired experience for the participant. She can seek to provide experiences that match participants' skills, abilities, and capabilities with the challenges and risks they seek. This text provides practical risk management tools to use in activities and programs to make them safer, more enjoyable experiences.

# Acknowledgments

Any good collaboration maximizes the strengths of those involved and minimizes their weaknesses. The result is often greater than the sum of its parts. Each of the three collaborators helped to strengthen the content and provide a new direction in the recreation and parks field.

A great deal of the credit for this book goes to Gayle Kassing, acquisitions editor at Human Kinetics. Her vision was to create a book on risk management with a new direction. Gayle provided considerable input on the content. Without her initial vision, this book would not have materialized.

I (Robert Kauffman) would like to acknowledge coauthor Merry Moiseichik, one of only a handful of people in the recreation and parks field with a law degree. Her legal perspective significantly strengthened and refined the entire text. I also acknowledge the support of our faculty at Frostburg State University. Although they didn't contribute directly to the content, they provided the continued support I needed in order to complete the project: Diane Blankenship, Veronica Hill, Maureen Dougherty, Susan Gray, Natalia Buta, and Ken Witmer and Clarence Golden, our deans. Also, I thank our graduate assistants, Heather Niederberger, Molly Downey, and Jessica Leer. I extend my appreciation to our administrative assistant, Karen Frink, who reviewed the manuscript and assisted in the hard task of obtaining permissions. I thank Virgil Chambers and Pam Dillon, who have assisted me throughout my career in boating safety and helped to provide me with opportunities that made this book possible. Finally, I thank my wife, Sally. Without her support, this book would not exist.

I (Merry Moiseichik) thank my coauthor, Robert Kauffman. His experience as an expert witness and his 30-plus years of involvement in boating safety and safety education bring significant merit to this text. Robert has developed accident models and incorporated the accident process into the safety videos that he cowrote and produced. His diverse experiences enabled him to expand on Gayle's vision, develop the integrated risk management model, and link together seemingly divergent strands of risk management into a textbook with a new direction. I also thank my friend and colleague, Jean Hughes, who discussed many ideas with me over the years and especially during the writing of this book. I thank my children, Sky Moiseichik and Shenan Boit, who have always supported me. I also thank my mother, Phoebe Jay, who supported me financially and encouraged me to make it through law school.

*Robert B. Kauffman*
*Merry Moiseichik*

# PART I

# Principles of Negligence

The first leg in the integrated risk management model focuses on negligence (figure I.1). Four components are necessary for negligence to occur: a duty; a breach of standard of care; proximate cause or a relationship between the breach of standard of care; and the injury, damage, or loss.

In a litigious society, people and operations are continually concerned about being sued and preventing lawsuits. The issue is not necessarily winning or losing the suit; rather, it is the cost of litigation in both real and indirect costs. Indirect costs include revenue that is lost because participants go elsewhere, the time and energy that people put into a defense that they could put into conducting programs, and ripple effects (discussed in chapter 13), where the secondary effects of an accident can devastate staff and the business. The real costs, either compensative or punitive, often seem minor compared with the indirect costs. Litigation is a serious problem.

By preventing injury, damage, or loss, one will prevent being sued. Part I introduces the concept of negligence, what is necessary for negligence to occur, and some defenses that will help one avoid negligence and prevent being sued. Chapter 1 discusses the four components of negligence and the standard of care as it applies to recreational leadership and programming. Chapter 2 focuses on the standard of care as it applies to landowners and facilities. Chapter 3 focuses on defenses against negligence, including legal doctrines and transfer strategies.

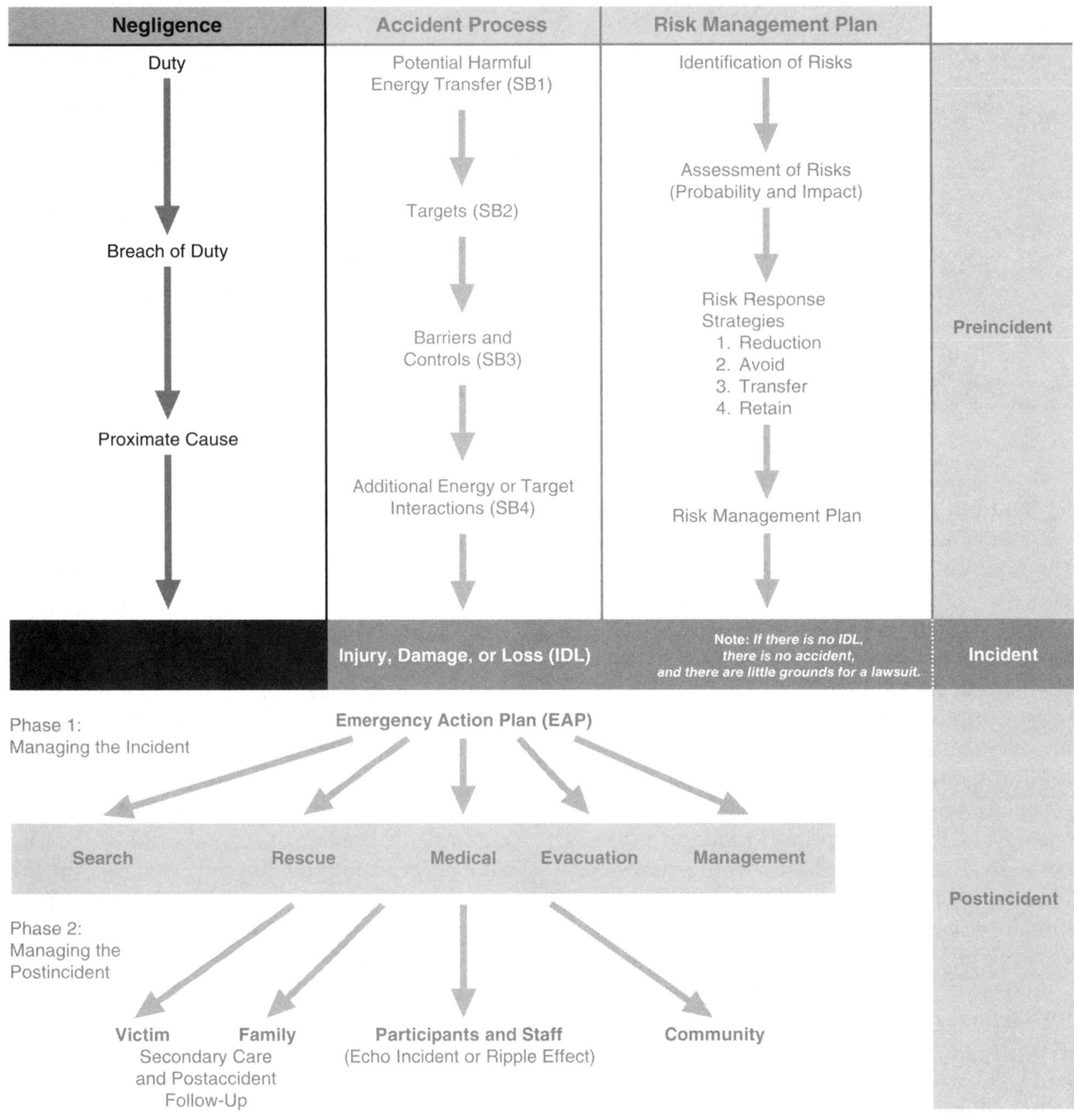


**Figure I.1** Negligence as part of the risk management model.

Chapter 1

# Negligence

Contemporary American society is highly litigious. The proportion of lawyers in the workforce nearly doubled between 1970 and 2000. It seems as though everyone is suing everyone else over everything and anything (Will, 2009), and many people fear being sued. This chapter introduces the concept of negligence—the laws under which a person who is injured by another citizen gains compensation for his injury—and the four components required to prove negligence in order to collect compensation. This chapter also discusses how high-quality leadership and program-planning skills will potentially protect a person if he or she is sued.

## GENERAL LEGAL PRINCIPLES

Before discussing negligence, it is important to learn a little about the three types of law. Legislated law, which people are most familiar with, is the law passed down from the legislature, state, and even city that identifies what people can and cannot do. If a person breaks a law, he can be prosecuted and punished. Regulatory law comprises rules and regulations that are created, with permission from the legislature, by an agency (e.g., the health department). An individual or organization that does not follow these rules may be fined or closed due to lack of compliance. Examples of such rules include day-care regulations, pool requirements, and food-safety regulations in restaurants. Common law is law created by precedence (past findings) of the courts. When the court makes a decision a certain way, the court must continue to judge future cases with similar facts in the same way, unless a higher court overturns the decision. For example, a court found that warning labels are necessary on helmets. Even though no legislation was passed on the issue, all helmets must now include a warning label.

The two main types of courts are criminal court and civil court. A person who breaks a law would go before a criminal court. A person who hurts another citizen can be brought into civil court by the injured party. Civil means between citizens. One cannot be brought before the same court twice for the same crime. However, this does not mean that one cannot be tried twice for the same wrongdoing. The case must be tried in a different court. A person can be tried in criminal court for hurting someone and be found innocent. The same person can be brought to civil court and be tried again and found guilty. The criminal court would put the person behind bars, whereas the civil court makes the person pay damages. In the criminal court a much higher level of proof ("beyond a shadow of a doubt") is used, whereas in civil court a lower standard of proof (preponderance of evidence) is used.

Different issues are filed in different courts. In addition to criminal and civil courts, there are federal and state courts. Federal laws, such as freedom of speech as granted by the U.S. Constitution, are tried in a federal court.

State laws are filed in a state court. If the issue crosses state lines, it can be brought in a federal court. The most important thing to understand is that a state law will most likely be tried in state court. Recreation professionals should be aware of which laws are state laws because those laws can vary from state to state. Laws dealing with negligence are state laws. The variations in laws from state to state make a big difference in whether someone suing for negligence is successful.

## FOUR WINDOWS OF NEGLIGENCE

Negligence is a part of tort law. A tort is a civil wrong or wrongful act, whether intentional or accidental, that results in injury to another. A tort is an injury that occurs between two citizens. The plaintiff is the injured citizen. The defendant is the citizen who has allegedly committed the harm. Negligence is a type of tort or wrongdoing in which a person unintentionally injures another by not acting with reasonable care. Negligence falls under state law, so it usually is filed in a state court. Although each state is a little different, the general concepts are the same. While all states have the same definition for negligence, each state may differ in how long you can wait to file the suit (called statute of limitations), what kinds of exceptions they might have in who can sue or be sued, or what kinds of defenses can be used.

**negligence**—The failure to exercise the standard of care that a reasonably prudent person would have exercised in a similar situation.

Four components must be present to prove negligence: duty; breach of standard of care; proximate cause; and injury, damage, or loss. No matter how complex the situation, it is framed within the context of these four elements. Each component of negligence is like a window. In order for the plaintiff or the injured party who is bringing the suit to win, all four windows must be kept open. The defendant's attorney seeks to close any one of the four windows to remove one of the elements necessary for negligence.

To illustrate the four points of negligence and the concept of windows, a portion of Thomas Ebro's deposition is provided in figure 1.1. In this portion, Ebro's lawyer, Mr. Lombardi, seeks to determine the common practices or industry standards of handling an injury on the Lehigh River. Generally, focusing on inadequate or faulty equipment is a quick way to prove negligence. His opinion regarding the incident provides a concise illustration of the principles involved.

### Duty

The first element required for negligence is duty—a responsibility, obligation, or relationship—to the injured party. The duty can be formal or it can be assumed. A recreation leader has a responsibility or duty to his participants.

Figure 1.2 presents three related case studies that ask whether a lifeguard has a duty to an injured party. In terms of duty owed, scenario 1 is fairly clear. Because the lifeguard is an employee of the agency, he has a duty to act. Scenario 2 suggests that although the lifeguard may have a moral duty to rescue the victim, he does not have a legal duty to perform a rescue—that is, unless he assumes the duty. In scenario 3, the lifeguard assumes the duty of the rescue. It is questionable whether there would be a lawsuit filed against him if the rescuer aborted the rescue after walking into the water and finding that it was cold. Nevertheless, the lifeguard could be negligent because someone else who was qualified may have been discouraged from taking action or responsibility when the lifeguard acted first.

Employment creates duty. The head of a senior center has a relationship with, and therefore a duty to, all the seniors. Situation can create duty. A parent or a relative has a relationship and therefore a duty. A person who acts as though he has a duty, like the lifeguard who moves to make a rescue, has the responsibility to finish the act because, as stated previously, the act may stop someone else from taking on the responsibility. The law does not create duty where none exists. For example, if someone is drowning

## Percheski Case: Negligence Factors and Wetsuit Booties

Thomas Ebro was an expert witness for the plaintiff. The portion of his deposition presented here is his description of the incident based on the materials that he reviewed. In terms of the four components, Ebro's argument essentially goes as follows.

1. Duty: The rafting company has a duty. A relationship was created because Percheski was on their raft.
2. Breach of standard of care: A standard of care exists that requires the rafting company to provide appropriate equipment. According to Ebro, they need to provide wetsuit booties with holes in them. The holes allow water to drain from the booties and prevent ballooning, which occurs when the bootie fills with water, allowing the foot to slide around. According to Ebro, the booties should have had holes in them to allow drainage, but they did not (omission).
3. Proximate cause: Percheski blew out his knee (injury, damage, or loss) because the wetsuit booties did not have holes to allow the water to drain out (breach of standard of care). According to Ebro, the injury seems to be related to the breach.
4. Injury, damage, or loss: Percheski blew out his knee, which required surgery (injury).

Two comments regarding Ebro's statement: First, in lines 21 through 25, note how he contends that splashing activity is encouraged and is considered a normal activity for rafters. Second, no one in the whitewater community is familiar with the need to put holes in wetsuit booties to drain water. This point, although not evident in this passage, becomes fairly evident in the more than 200 pages of the deposition. Regardless, Ebro makes a very good statement illustrating the four points of negligence.

Q: Mr. Lombardi (plaintiff's lawyer)

A: Thomas Ebro (expert witness)

Page 56

Q Can you describe for me what your
understanding is as to how the accident happened?

A Very well. Mr. Percheski was a member of a four
person group in a raft. There was an encouraged water
splashing activity ongoing during the course of their
time on the river.
Everyone, including the guides themselves, were
engaging in that practice. Buckets had been provided

Page 57

in each raft for that purpose.
Mr. Percheski in one of those episodes of
reaching over, filling a bucket, standing up to deliver
the bucket's contents toward another occupant of
another boat, experienced his foot sliding from

*(continued)*

**Figure 1.1** This excerpt from a deposition illustrates the four windows of negligence.

Thomas Ebro, John M. Percheski and Fern C. Percheski, his spouse, per quod, versus Lehigh River Rafting, LTD. et al., Superior Court of New Jersey Law Division – Middlesex County Docket No. W-001468-89, April 19, p. 65-67.

the sole portion of his bootie onto the vertical or the wall portion, a very common occurrence, and I've experienced and every diver has when you slip inside your bootie.

The bootie itself had an opportunity to draw into the loose cavity or space inside of water, and there were no holes in Mr. Percheski's boots to relieve that balloon like condition. So during that instance when Mr. Percheski was delivering the bucket full or water towards another rafter, his reliance on traction failed in that he lost traction, his foot slipped inside the bootie, which caused the bootie to climb up on the instep, and in that process of slippage he severely injured his knee and portions of his foot.

He screamed in pain. He drew the attention of others. Ultimately, he was helped ashore by members of his group. There was no first aid kit available. There was no first aid administered by the members of the Leigh staff. There was no rapid manifestation of help, in that there was no communication other than a

page 58

fellow running to summon help.

Q All right. I don't want to be rude.

A I'm sorry.

Q I will get into that aspect later. I'm only talking about the actual happening of the accident. You've told me everything as to the happening of the accident.

A Right.

Q Do you have any ideas, based upon what you've read, as to how far a distance his foot slipped in the boot?

A I don't have the—I haven't made that measure, but it's one that can be made. I would estimate it slipped about five inches.

Q Is this boot large enough that his foot can slip five inches to one side or the other?

A My testimony a moment ago when I described the slippage was that there is a—well, to give you the explanation. Let me describe the boot....

**Figure 1.1** *(continued)*

## Baywatch: Does the Lifeguard Have a Duty?

In the following three scenarios consider whether the lifeguard has a duty—a legal duty, not a moral duty—to perform a rescue.

**Scenario 1:** A Baywatch lifeguard is on duty at the beach. A swimmer in front of him proceeds to drown.

1. Does the lifeguard have a duty to the drowning person?
2. If the person drowns, is there a breach of standard of care?
3. Did an injury, damage, or loss occur?
4. Was there proximate cause?
5. Is the lifeguard negligent?

**Scenario 2:** A Baywatch lifeguard is visiting a beach in a jurisdiction that is not his own. He is sitting on a blanket enjoying the rays when he notices a swimmer in front of him drowning. He waves goodbye to the victim as she proceeds to drown.

1. Does the lifeguard have a duty to the drowning person?
2. If the person drowns, is there a breach of standard of care?
3. Did an injury, damage, or loss occur?
4. Was there proximate cause?
5. Is the lifeguard negligent?

**Scenario 3:** A Baywatch lifeguard is visiting a beach in a jurisdiction that is not his own. He is sitting on a blanket enjoying the rays when he notices a swimmer in front of him drowning. Because no lifeguard is on duty, he announces to everyone that he is a lifeguard. He proceeds into the water to perform a rescue. He gets a few steps into the water and exclaims, "This water is cold!" He turns around, sits back down on the blanket, and continues to enjoy the rays.

1. Does the lifeguard have a duty to the drowning person?
2. If the person drowns, is there a breach of standard of care?
3. Did an injury, damage, or loss occur?
4. Was there proximate cause?
5. Is the lifeguard negligent?

Answers

Scenario A: 1) yes, 2) yes (omission), 3) yes, 4) yes, 5) yes

Scenario B: 1) no, 2) no, 3) yes, 4) no, 5) no

Scenario C: 1) yes (the lifeguard assumed it), 2) yes, 3) yes, 4) yes, 5) yes (potentially)

**Figure 1.2** These scenarios explore the various concepts of duty.

in front of a beach full of people, who has the duty to save the victim if no guard is present? The law indicates that no one is responsible. How would one decide who is responsible if no guard, friend, or relative is present? Because it is not fair to choose someone randomly and assign duty, no one is responsible. The victim's estate cannot sue everyone on the beach.

### Respondeat Superior

Respondeat superior is Latin for "let the master answer." This principle means that an employer is responsible for the actions of an employee. A plaintiff seeks to sue whoever has the deepest pockets financially, which is usually the organization. This principle allows the plaintiff to move up the organizational chain of command and to include the supervisor and the organization in their suit. It can also include the board of directors that makes the policy decisions. The employee responsible for the injury is not off the hook just because the plaintiff moves up the ladder to get to the deep pockets. In the lifeguard example, the plaintiff would sue the lifeguard as well as the organization that hired the lifeguard.

The law allows the plaintiff to get to the supervisors and the organization because the agency or organization is responsible for hiring a person of maturity, for ensuring that that person is trained, and for supervising the person to ensure that he follows appropriate policies and procedures. Because the agency is responsible for the actions of the employee, it too can be sued.

This principle has significant implications because an employee's actions affect her superiors in the chain of command and because an organization becomes responsible for the actions of an employee. Organizations have reason to examine what employees do on behalf of the organization. Even though a programmer is responsible for putting on the activity, the agency is held responsible for the programmer's actions and decisions.

### Ultra Vires Act

Sometimes employees do things that they do not have permission to do, that go against their training, or that break policy. The law does not give responsibility to the superiors when the employee acts outside the scope of her employment or commits ultra vires acts. *Ultra vires* is Latin for "beyond powers," or acting outside of authority.

**ultra vires**—Unauthorized; beyond the scope of power allowed or granted by a corporate charter or by law.

The potential connection between ultra vires and respondeat superior is evident in the definition of respondeat superior, which includes wrongful acts committed within the scope of the employment or agency. Essentially, the organization and those higher in the chain of command are responsible for only those things within the scope of an employee's duties.

From an employee's perspective, the principle of ultra vires has two implications. First, an employee must follow procedures and complete appropriate paperwork to record her actions. For example, if an employee fills out a travel form, it reflects that she is following agency policy and procedures. Second, an employee must understand the nature of her job and make sure that she is operating within the scope of her duties. To not do so is to potentially suggest an ultra vires act for which she will be responsible.

## Breach of Standard of Care

Once the first element of negligence—who has the duty, or responsibility—is defined, the court looks to the second element of negligence, which is whether the person responsible followed or breached the standard of care of the industry. A breach of standard of care is committed when a person does not do something that he should be doing or when a person does something that he should be doing but does it incorrectly. Generally, there are two types of breaches: omission and commission.

**standard of care**—The watchfulness, attention, caution, and prudence that a reasonable person in the circumstances would exercise. If a person's actions do not meet this standard of care, then the acts fail to meet the standard of care that all people (supposedly) have toward others. Failure to meet the standard is negligence, and any damages resulting therefrom may be claimed in a lawsuit by the injured party. The problem is that the standard is often a subjective issue on which reasonable people can differ.

## Omission

Omission, sometimes referred to as nonfeasance, is committed when a person should have done something (standard of care) but did not do it. For example, a swimmer drowns because the lifeguard on duty is socializing with a friend and, distracted, does not perform a rescue. The fact that the lifeguard has a duty and did not perform a rescue is potentially an act of omission. It is also a breach of standard of care. The window of negligence remains open for the plaintiff.

In well-established industries, lawyers may determine the common practices using books, manuals, course outlines, or expert witnesses. The role of an expert witness is to explain to the court the common practices or industry standards of an activity or industry. Considerable disagreement often exists between experts for the plaintiff and those for the defense.

For example, a programmer conducting a Senior Olympics event for local seniors takes the normal precautions to create a safe environment for participants. She has participants fill out a basic health form to identify any health conditions, selects age-appropriate activities, monitors the weather, and has an ambulance with qualified personnel on call at the event. Most programmers would agree that these are commonly accepted practices in the activity and industry.

However, during the Senior Olympics event, the ambulance does not show up. One of the participants suffers heat exhaustion, collapses, and dies before reaching the hospital. If a group of programmers serving as expert witnesses is asked whether the programmer should have provided an ambulance, most of them would answer yes. The programmer should have had an ambulance on site but did not. This is an act of omission. It would most likely be considered a breach of standard of care.

A portion of Thomas Ebro's deposition in the Percheski case is provided in figure 1.1. Ebro suggests that the rafting company needed to provide wetsuit booties with holes to allow water to drain from the booties and to prevent ballooning, where the bootie fills with water and allows the foot to slide around inside. Ebro sought to keep the window of breach of standard of care open by suggesting that by not supplying wetsuit booties with holes in them, the rafting company did not provide the standard of care.

In contrast, the defense sought to close the window of breach of standard of care. In more than 200 pages of Ebro's deposition not included here, the defense sought to show that common industry practice does not include placing holes in wetsuit booties to let the water drain and, hence, the rafting company did not breach standard of care by not placing holes in the wetsuit booties. The defense argued that no omission occurred because no such standard of care exists.

## Commission

Commission occurs when a person does something he is supposed to do but does it incorrectly. For example, a lifeguard on duty attempts to rescue a person who is drowning. While rescuing the victim, the lifeguard chokes the victim with the hold used. The victim's windpipe collapses and she dies. The victim's estate sues the lifeguard because, although he performed a rescue, he did it incorrectly. The plaintiff shows a textbook photo of how to hold a victim. A bystander on the beach took a picture of the rescue. The lifeguard's hold on the victim is significantly different from the hold pictured in the textbook. The plaintiff suggests that although the lifeguard performed a rescue, he did it incorrectly, and that his potential breach of standard of care was an act of commission. For the plaintiff, the window of breach of standard of care most likely remains open. Returning to the Percheski case (figure 1.1), had Ebro argued that the company had put holes in the wetsuit booties but that the holes were the wrong size, his argument would be one of commission.

## Proximate Cause

The third element of negligence is proximate cause. Some connection or relationship must exist between the breach of standard of care and the injury, damage, or loss (covered in the next section). In the lifeguard examples, the lifeguard's inattention or incorrect hold on the victim resulted in the injury, damage, or loss to the victim. In both of the lifeguard examples the breach of standard of care relates to the injury, damage, or loss and the window of proximate cause most likely remains open for the plaintiff. However, if the victim was attacked by a shark and the lifeguard could not have saved the victim even if the lifeguard had been paying attention, the proximate cause would be the shark rather than talking to his friend. In this case, the window of proximate cause closes.

In the Senior Olympics example, one of the participants dies from heat exhaustion before being transported to the hospital. The plaintiff's attorney would argue that an ambulance, had it been present at the event, could have transported the victim to the hospital and prevented the fatality. The attorney would argue that a direct relationship existed or that there was proximate cause between the breach of standard of care and the injury, damage, or loss that resulted. Again, for the plaintiff, the window most likely remains open.

Proximate cause requires a relationship between the breach of standard of care and the injury, damage, or loss that results. The relationship has to be causal in that the breach of standard of care is both necessary and sufficient to cause the injury damage or loss. Necessary means that the injury would not have happened if the action had not happened. Sufficient means that the action was significant enough to create the injury. For example, when taking a group on a hike, a recreation leader takes the group off the path and the group members step in a hive of yellow jackets. A person gets stung and dies. Would deviating from the path be the proximate cause? The plaintiff would try to show that, yes, that was the necessary element. But was the bee sting sufficient to cause death? The defendant would try to show that something unrelated to the deviation off the path may have caused the death.

Returning to the lifeguard example, during an investigation the plaintiff discovers that the lifeguard has an invalid driver's license on his driving record and was once ticketed for driving while intoxicated (DWI). Are these two facts proximate cause between the breach of standard of care (i.e., the lifeguard held the drowning victim incorrectly or missed performing the rescue) and the injury, damage, or loss (i.e., the person drowned)? They are not connected. Having an invalid driver's license did not contribute in any way to the drowning, nor did the DWI, unless the lifeguard was drinking on the job. However, the plaintiff's attorney will still try to make the connection that the lifeguard's poor judgment regarding the invalid driver's license and DWI is symptomatic of the poor judgment he exhibited in performing the rescue incorrectly.

Figure 1.3 includes an excerpt from a report about the near drowning of Adam Dzialo. This case illustrates many principles discussed throughout this text. Dzialo caught his foot in a foot entrapment during a river rescue exercise and nearly drowned. In the excerpt, Charles Walbridge, who wrote the report, asserts that helmets are at best optional on this type of river. He then makes the point that even if one could argue that the participants should have worn helmets, wearing or not wearing a helmet had nothing to do with the foot entrapment. His argument goes directly to proximate cause.

Returning to the Percheski case (figure 1.1), Percheski blew out his knee (injury, damage, or loss) because the wetsuit booties had no holes to allow the water to drain from them (breach of standard of care). According to Ebro, the injury is related to the breach. He seeks to keep the window of negligence open. The defense argued that Percheski had a predisposition to blow out his knee, as evidenced by previous injuries, and that this predisposition rather than the wetsuit bootie was the cause of his

## Dzialo Case: Breach of Standard of Care and Proximate Cause

In the Adam Dzialo case, Greenfield Community College hired Charlie Walbridge as an external investigator to investigate the near drowning of Adam Dzialo. The college performed a popular swimming activity at this site. The following passage demonstrates two things. First, the standard of care is determined by the practices within an activity and industry. What does Charlie Walbridge suggest is the standard of care for helmets? Second, in the professional opinion of Charlie Walbridge, did not wearing a helmet (possible breach of standard of care) contribute (possible proximate cause) to the near drowning (injury, damage, or loss)?

### Helmets

"Adam Dzialo was not wearing a helmet during his swim. Although helmets are required for commercial rafting on the Fife Brook section of the Deerfield, this exceeds the usual standard of care in the rafting industry. This section of the river is rated class I-II with one drop of class III. Helmets are not used on the Nantahala in North Carolina (class II-III) or the Lehigh in Eastern Pennsylvania (class I-II+) or the Youghiogheny in Western Pennsylvania (class II-III+). This latter run is significantly harder than the Fife Brook section of the Deerfield.

"Adam's father tells me his son showed no signs of head injury, so wearing a helmet would have made absolutely no difference in this case. Although some outfitters may choose to issue helmets on easier runs, I see no reason to recommend helmets for swimming class I-II rapids except as an extra, added precaution." (p. 14)

**Figure 1.3** An example of the examination of standard of care.

From C. Walbridge, 1998, Report on Adam Dzialo's near drowning (Greenfield, Massachusetts: Board of Trustees). November 2.

injury. With this argument, the defense seeks to close the window of proximate cause.

Professionals in park and recreation are responsible for knowing the industry standards and, thus, for foreseeing all things that might occur and preparing for them. However, they are not expected to see events that are unforeseeable. The operative term in the definition of foreseeability is *anticipation*. Foreseeability is an element of proximate cause.

**foreseeability**—The quality of being reasonably anticipatable. Foreseeability, along with actual causation, is an element of proximate cause in tort law.

In part, foreseeable events are defined by the common practices of an activity and industry. At a beach, which of the following are normally foreseeable events: sharks, riptides, jellyfish, storm surges, and hypothermia? The issue is whether these issues are found at the beach and whether one has reason to expect finding them there. If dangerous sharks are not native to the beach, and if they have never been seen there or at nearby beaches, the first shark attack at the beach would likely be considered unforeseeable. The attack was not anticipatable. In contrast, the second attack would most likely be considered foreseeable because one shark attack had already occurred.

In the Dzialo case on the Deerfield River, most professionals who examined the site agreed that it was an ideal site for the swimming and rescue activity (figure 1.4). The bottom was cobble, which normally does not lend itself to foot entrapments. The suitability of the site is revealed in the investigative report of Dzialo's near drowning (figure 1.5). In the general sense, any site can potentially contain a foot entrapment. In the general sense, foot entrapment is always foreseeable. However, most experts would agree that a foot entrapment at this site was unlikely and that a foot entrapment was not foreseeable at this site.

## Injury, Damage, or Loss

The fourth element required for negligence is that an injury, damage, or loss must occur. Bodily harm, mental duress, property damage, or loss of life are examples of injury, damage, or loss. Injury, damage, or loss must be presented in terms of money. A fatality results in the lost income of the person over his or her lifetime. An automobile accident includes the damages to the vehicle and any bodily damages resulting from the accident. The loss of a young person can be significant because it can include the lost wages of a lifetime of working.

If no injury, damage, or loss occurs, there is no negligence. In the lifeguard example, if someone else rescues the victim or if the victim rescues herself, no injury, damage, or loss occurs. The lifeguard may lose his job or receive a reprimand for his conduct, but there would be no negligence. However, the plaintiff may still try to keep the window open by claiming a different injury (e.g., mental damages). If the plaintiff can make the case, there might be an injury, damage, or loss.

In the Senior Olympics example, the programmer may follow normal first aid procedures, give the victim water, and quickly transport the victim to the hospital. The victim recovers. No injury, damage, or loss occurs and, most likely, there was no negligence. The defense notes this point in an attempt to close the window of negligence. This does not erase a reprimand for not having an ambulance present on site.

This example brings up two important issues. The first issue is the initial heat exhaustion and collapse, which raises the question of whether the programmer should have recognized the symptoms and taken action. The second issue is the transportation. Even though a standard of care was potentially breached by not having an

Photo courtesy of Robert B. Kauffman.

**Figure 1.4** The cobble bottom, large eddies, and good visibility of the entire site make this an ideal site for a group-swimming activity. This is the actual site of the near drowning of Adam Dzialo.

## Dzialo Case: Foreseeability

In the Adam Dzialo case, Greenfield Community College hired Charlie Walbridge as an external investigator to investigate the near drowning of Adam Dzialo. The college performed a popular swimming activity at this site. The following passage, which is a portion of the site survey, explains the activity and describes the site. Based on the information provided in the following report, was the incident foreseeable in the opinion of Charlie Walbridge?

### Site Suitability: Site Survey

"Although we warn against standing up in rapids, many people do so every year without injury. The odds are against a dangerous crevice being present in a class I cobble rapid. That Adam's foot would find this crevice, which is smaller than a catcher's mitt, is also an incredible piece of bad luck. Had he touched bottom a few inches to either side there would have been no problem. This [is] an unfortunate example of the random element of uncontrolled risk that exists in all outdoor activities.

"I then swam the rapid several times after the release arrived. The swims were uneventful, and I believe that I would have chosen to use the site myself. I could use the site today after placing a rock in the crevice and warning my students, as always, to keep their feet up." (p. 10)

**Figure 1.5** The concept of foreseeability is examined in this excerpt from the report on the near drowning of Adam Dzialo.

From C. Walbridge, 1998, Report on Adam Dzialo's near drowning (Greenfield, Massachusetts: Board of Trustees). November 2.

ambulance present, was there proximate cause? Did the lack of an ambulance contribute further to the heat exhaustion and collapse? The answer is not necessarily. The condition of the patient improved and the patient fully recovered. This may seem like a fine distinction. Even simple examples can quickly become complex.

On the same note, the plaintiff might bring up why the heat exhaustion occurred in the first place. The plaintiff may claim that the venue lacked shaded areas and that few hydration options were available. Then the negligence arguments start again. Was there a duty? Yes, it was the programmer's event. Did a breach of standard of care occur? To answer the question, one would have to consider what a normal, prudent person would do under the circumstances of weather, number of expected guests, and type of guests that were visiting and use expert witnesses and literature. If it is determined that a breach occurred, did that breach create the heat exhaustion or was it caused by something the senior did or did not do? For example, although the witness says that not enough water was available, perhaps the victim turned down water twice, so lack of water was not the proximate cause. The injury could be pain and suffering from the heat exhaustion and the cost of the hospital visit. A lot must be considered in order to prove negligence.

In the Percheski case, after Percheski blew out his knee, the raft guides left him unattended on the shore until help arrived (figure 1.1, p. 57, lines 21-25). Although this does not make the rafting company look good, leaving the client on the shore unattended most likely did not cause any further damage. In terms of the four windows, the plaintiff needs to show that leaving Percheski on the shore unattended contributed to his injury or made it worse. No further injury, damage, or loss was associated with leaving him on the shore. Therefore, the window is closed for this specific issue.

Recreation professionals need to identify potentially hazardous situations and reengineer them to make the experiences safer. In the Percheski example, should the company have recognized the potential danger in using 5-gallon buckets and substituted something different, such as a water gun? A gallon of water weighs approximately 8 pounds. A 5-gallon bucket of water that is half full weighs about 20 pounds. That a person standing in an unstable raft tried to throw 20 pounds of water at someone in another raft may better explain the cause of Percheski's injury than the lack of drainage holes in his wetsuit booties. For the recreation programmer, the issue is how to create water-splashing or water-battle activities that reduce the likelihood of injuries like the one Percheski received.

### Levels of Negligence

Recreation professionals should be aware of three levels of negligence: ordinary negligence, gross negligence, and willful and wanton negligence. *Ordinary negligence* refers to what an ordinary, prudent person (the law thinks this is the perfect person, one who never makes a mistake) would do in the same or similar circumstances. In ordinary negligence, an injury was caused by a mistake that the perfect person would not make. As the law sees it, if a person follows the standard of care perfectly, no injury should occur. If a mistake is made and thus an injury occurs, there is ordinary negligence.

*Gross negligence* is what a reckless person would do in the same or similar circumstances. Recklessness is worse than a mistake because the negligence occurs when a person is not paying attention to what she is doing. If the person had been paying attention, she likely would not have committed the negligent act. *Willful and wanton negligence* is more than reckless—it is intentional. Each level is worse than the one before.

For example, a maintenance person working in a park is told to fix the drinking fountain. He goes to the fountain, opens the manhole, and climbs down and fixes the pipe. When he finishes, he climbs back out of the manhole, thinking about his next chore. He picks up his tools and leaves without closing the cover. Some might label this a mistake. It would likely be considered ordinary negligence. In the same scenario, the man climbs out of the manhole and a group of children is standing around the open manhole. Their presence should remind him to cover the hole. To not close it would be considered reckless and fall under gross negligence. In the same scenario, if the man climbs out of the manhole and pushes a child into the hole, he has committed willful and wanton negligence. These distinctions are important when discussing typical protections used for negligence (e.g., waivers and insurance) because although these protections cover ordinary negligence, they do not cover gross or willful and wanton negligence.

## PROFESSIONAL CONDUCT

The standard of care is normally defined as what a reasonable and prudent person would do in a similar situation. A professional in the recreation and park field is expected to know and apply the common practices of the activity or industry. However, standards are often subjective. The role of an expert witness is to provide testimony regarding the common practices in the activity or industry or regarding what a professional should have done. For example, in Charlie Walbridge's section on helmets in figure 1.3, he quotes the practices on other rivers. His purpose is to suggest the common practices for wearing helmets during river swimming activities. He even uses the term standard of care.

### Prudent Professional

In discussing the standard of care, van der Smissen (1975) expands the concept of a reasonable and prudent person to suggest that one needs to be a reasonable and prudent professional. This is a higher standard of care than that of a lay person. A reasonable and prudent professional knows what the standard of care is for the activity that he or she is conducting. If a lawsuit occurs, a recreation leader will be held to the common practices or the industry standards of a professional conducting the activity.

In an activity such as a standardized first aid course, the standard of care is relatively easy to determine. One simply opens the first aid book and compares what he did with what he was supposed to do. However, in most activities that are not as well delineated, lawyers will call on a group of experts, who will indicate the common practices in the field. Ebro's deposition in figure 1.1 is an example of an expert witness giving his opinion. A lot of discrepancy can exist between expert opinions on the standard of care.

What is the standard of care that a professional needs to provide? If one conducts a pottery class, one needs to know the common practices of other professionals who are also conducting pottery classes, such as how to operate the potter's wheel and kiln properly and safely. If one teaches a climbing activity, one needs to know how to top rope, belay, tie knots, and anything else that is a common practice in climbing activities. If a recreation leader uses a bowline and everyone else uses a figure-eight knot, the leader may have a problem if the knot fails and someone becomes injured.

Also, the standard of care defines the common practices a prudent professional should not be doing. After numerous playground injuries and lawsuits, the Giant Stride has been phased out of most playgrounds (figure 1.6). A Giant Stride on a playground invites an eventual accident and lawsuit. The recreation professional acting as a prudent professional will be called into question since Giant Strides on playgrounds go against the common practice of the industry.

Photo courtesy of Robert B. Kauffman.

**Figure 1.6** The Giant Stride has led to numerous playground injuries. Although they are still produced today, most playground providers have phased them out or removed them from playgrounds.

In a lawsuit or deposition, a lawyer seeks to determine what the common practices or industry standards are in an activity or industry. Figure 1.7 provides an example. The plaintiff's lawyer, Mr. Lombardi, seeks to find out what the common practices or industry standards are when he asks Thomas Mills, the trip leader, about the standard operating procedure. Mr. Mills testifies that the standard operating procedure on a raft trip with 70 guests and 3 guides is for 1 guide to go to the take-out for help, for the remaining 2 guides to continue down the river with the trip, and for the victim to wait unattended on the shore for help to arrive.

This raises an interesting question for future recreation and park professionals. The raft trip has 70 guests in 15 to 20 rafts, and 3 guides. This is a guide-to-guest ratio of 1:14. Some in the adventure experience industry believe that the ratio should be 1:5 or 1:6. Assume that the common practice is for 1 guide to stay with the group, for 1 guide to run to the take-out for help, for 1 guide to run to the put-in for help (not stated here), and to leave the victim with a blown-out knee on the shore by himself in growing darkness. Is something wrong with this picture? The result is a policy of leaving the victim on the shore alone and leaving the remainder of the raft trip understaffed with only 2 guides.

The issue for the future professional in the recreation and park field is whether the administrative practices and policies of the company put the trip leader and the guides in a compromised position. Do they really have adequate supervision on the trip to handle this or, for

## Percheski Case: Common Practices and Industry Standards

In this portion of the deposition, the plaintiff's lawyer, Mr. Lombardi, seeks to determine the common practices on the Lehigh River regarding handling an injury (see specifically line 22). As noted in this passage, Percheski engaged in a water battle with other passengers and dislocated his knee. Thomas Mills, the trip leader for the raft trip, is being questioned by Lombardi. It is evident that Lombardi's line of questioning seeks to determine these common practices so he can compare what was actually done with the standards.

Q: Mr. Lombardi (plaintiff's lawyer)

A: Thomas Mills (trip leader)

Page 65

Q Did you ask Mr. Percheski what happened to him?

A I did not have an opportunity to talk to Mr. Percheski at all. He was removed from the river by my guides and I believe some of his friends that were on the trip. I had gained this information upon the end of the trip, talking to my guides. I never saw Mr. Percheski at all from the accident. I remained with the rest of the trip and he was removed from the gorge.

Q Is that standard operating procedure, that when an accident occurs on the river one of the guides is to remain with the group?

A Yes, you would have to, absolutely.

Page 66

Q In this case, the trip leader?

A Yes. Which was myself.

Q The guides on the Romanowski group, to my understanding, was George Munro and Marylou Mylett?

A That is correct.

[deleted section on where they currently lived]

After the incident occurred, Tom, did you have an opportunity to speak with either or both Marylou and George Munro as to what happened to Mr. Percheski?

A I did eventually have an opportunity to discuss

*(continued)*

**Figure 1.7** This passage asks for reflection on the standard of care that a prudent professional should provide.

Thomas Mills, John M. Percheski and Fern C. Percheski, his spouse, per quod, versus Lehigh River Rafting, LTD. et al., Superior Court of New Jersey Law Division – Middlesex County Docket No. W-001468-89, January 18, p. 65-67.

Page 67

the specifics with them at the end of the trip.

Q What do you recall?

A From my understanding, what had happened was Mr.
Percheski was standing up in the raft, threw a bucket
of water and dislocated his knee. At that point
Marylou and George administered first aid, put the
gentleman in a splint and I believe George after they
hauled him up the bank, George ran down to Rockport,
which is our designated take out spot, and notified
DER [Department of Environmental Resources].
I know he was removed, I'm not sure if it was by
ambulance or by a DER truck. I don't recall.

Q Your investigation of the accident
occurred after the rafting trip?

A Yes.

Q Again, the reason why you did not remain
with Mr. Percheski was as a trip leader your
responsibility was to the remainder of the group?

A That is correct. I knew I had qualified guides
who were certified in CPR and my responsibility was
the safety for the rest of the trip.

**Figure 1.7** *(continued)*

that matter, any situation? The trip leader does not sound professional and does not sound like he knew what was going on during his trip. However, is the problem actually structural rather than the fault of the trip leader or guide? Is this the type of situation in which a recreation professional would want to work? The victim in this case had a blown-out knee. Would it be different if it had been a fatality?

The bottom line is that a recreation professional will be held to a standard of care that represents the common practices or industry standards for the activity he is conducting. Therefore, he must know what these common practices are. How does one learn or become informed regarding what others are doing in similar activities with similar participants? The following strategies will help recreation professionals become familiar with the common practices or industry standards for the types of activities or programs that they may deliver (Kauffman, 2010).

- **Check With Published Industry Standards.** Many organizations, such as the Council for Accreditation of Park and Recreation Agencies (CAPRA), the American Camping Association, and the Association of Experiential Educators, publish accreditation standards or other professional practices. The purpose of these accreditation standards is to provide commonly accepted practices of what people in the field should be doing. For example, section 9 of the CAPRA standards, which is included in chapter 9, focuses on risk management.

An important issue is whether an organization needs to become accredited or whether it just needs to practice the standards. Normally, following the practices suggested in the standard is more important than being accredited. If an organization is accredited, it will have a risk management plan in order to comply with section 9 of the CAPRA standards (CAPRA, 2009). However, an organization can have a risk management plan without being accredited.

- **Join a Trade Organization.** General professional organizations, such as the National Recreation and Parks Association, or state organizations are often sufficient to provide interaction with other professionals to know what they are doing in a given activity area. However, a professional might find that a more specialized trade organization, such as Professional Paddlesports Association, is helpful in providing the necessary information regarding a specific activity (Kauffman and Councill, 2005b).

- **Attend Conferences.** Attending professional conferences goes hand in hand with joining a trade organization. Conferences provide the opportunity to meet other professionals, discuss with them what they are doing, and network. This is a good opportunity to discuss problems or concerns with others and to determine how others handle similar situations.

- **Become Certified.** Certification suggests that a professional possesses the knowledge and skill involved in the certification. In a legal case a person will be judged by his or her actions. Having a certification merely suggests that the professional has been exposed to the knowledge and has developed the skill to do what is appropriate. The professional must remember to practice what she has learned because if a case ever goes to trial, the other attorney will question her on the content of the certification and whether she applied it to what she was doing.

- **Take a Course, Workshop, or In-Service Training.** Often no certification is available, particularly at the administrative level. Many professional organizations offer courses, workshops, in-service training, and seminars that help people train in the professional practices of their activity. These are excellent ways to help determine the common practices of an activity or industry.

It is worth restating what these measures will and will not do. A professional who follows any or all of these suggestions has no guarantee against being negligent. However, a professional who becomes certified or participates in workshops and in-service training will become familiar with the common practices and the standard of care for his activity or industry. This provides good protection against negligence because it increases the probability that his actions will be in line with the common practices of his activity or industry.

Along with her daughter, Janice Cody owned and operated a canoe livery, Winding River Canoe Rentals, on the Clinton River near Detroit, Michigan. At two different times, a year apart, Janice rented boats to people whose trips down the river ended in tragedy; a kayak flipped in fast water and one of the kayakers got caught in a strainer and drowned. As is evident in the passage from her deposition in figure 1.8, she did virtually nothing to learn about the common practices of her industry during the time between the two fatalities. She went out of business shortly after the second fatality occurred. A leader and programmer must know and apply the common practices of an activity or industry. By Cody's own admission in her deposition, she did not know the common practices, nor did she make an attempt to learn them.

## Supervision

Supervision has three components: provision (i.e., how many people are supervising and what type of supervision), qualifications and understanding of the activity and the skills needed to supervise a specific activity, and first aid and rescue skills for the environment in which the activity takes place in the event that something goes wrong.

Supervision is a critical element in many lawsuits. There are three types of supervision: general, specific, and transitional. *General supervision* means that the leader must be in the activity area and overseeing the activity, like a police officer watching the crowd at a concert. *Specific supervision* means that the leader has hands-on involvement in the activity, like a police officer providing directions to a patron. *Transitional supervision* occurs when the leader moves from general to specific supervision or

## Janice Cody's Deposition

The following transcript is from a deposition given under oath by Janice Cody, the owner and operator of Winding River Canoe Rentals. Had Janice Cody done a simple investigation of the hazards present on the Clinton River outside of Detroit, Michigan, Melanie Carlson might be alive today. Along with other passages from her deposition, this passage suggests that she had little understanding of the canoe rental business.

Page 14

Q Between the death of Joe Miranda on July 3 of 1999
and Melanie Carlson on July 4, 2000 did you take
any classes to possibly obtain or hone your skills
in white water boating?

A No.

Q Did you do anything as far as reading any materials
between those two time periods to learn more about
boating or renting a boat livery?

A No.

Q Did you at any time after 1999 contact any boating

Page 15

association to find out if maybe you could improve
the way the livery was run?

A No.

Q Did you do anything after 1999 to find out the
difference in handling characteristics of a
canoe or a kayak?

A No.

Q Did you do anything after 1999 that dealt with
knowing more about what might be appropriate
equipment for customers?

A No.

**Figure 1.8** Janice Cody's failure to become knowledgeable of the common practices in her own industry likely resulted in the death of Melanie Carlson.

Estate of Melanie Carlson v. Janice Cody d/b/a Winding River Canoe Rentals and Dawne Kabold. (2002). Deposition of Janice Cody. Circuit Court of Macomb, Michigan. Case No: 02-3319 NO, 1-94.

from specific to general. When a police officer switches from watching everyone to moving to take care of a problem, transitional supervision is the time after he stops watching everyone in order to take care of the problem and before he actually makes contact.

A leader overseeing a playground sees two groups forming and it looks like a fight is brewing. The leader needs to move from general supervision by approaching the groups (transitional supervision), separating the groups, and calming the waters (specific supervision).

A leader supervising gymnastics practice watches the different stations where participants are practicing (general supervision). A student on the high bar wants to practice a new and potentially difficult dismount. The leader moves in (transitional supervision) and spots the person during the dismount (specific supervision). In both of these examples the leader in general supervision is systematically reviewing the site and has access to everyone if needed. As the situation changes, the supervisor moves into a specific supervision situation. When she does so, she is no longer in a general supervision situation. During the time she is moving between general and specific, she is in transitional supervision, which actually is no supervision.

The following example shows why this concept is important. When a lifeguard is in the chair scanning for problems, he is in general supervision. He sees a swimmer in trouble and leaves the chair to help the person. The guard is no longer in general supervision because he is watching just one swimmer, and he is not in specific supervision because no contact has occurred yet. The guard enters the water and heads to the troubled swimmer. If he is the only guard and another swimmer gets in trouble at this time, there would truly be a problem because the guard would not even see the other swimmer. To alleviate this problem, it is a standard of care to always have two guards on duty. When the guard sees the swimmer in trouble, he can alert the second guard. That guard usually clears the pool while the first guard, in transitional supervision, enters the water to make the rescue. The second guard remains in general supervision and the first guard reaches the swimmer and is then in specific supervision.

The first component of supervision has to do with standard of care. What type of supervision is needed and how many lifeguards? In the swimming pool, the standard is a minimum of 2 guards or a 1:25 ratio, whichever is largest. Therefore, there are 2 guards needed until there are 51 swimmers in the pool. The guards provide general supervision until specific supervision is needed.

The second component of supervision is appreciation of the activity. A good synonym for appreciation is experience. As a general rule, participants with more experience have more appreciation for the activity in which they participate and assume more risks for themselves. The experience helps participants understand the dangers of the activities and appreciate all the possible areas of risks. A leader or programmer who has a good appreciation of an activity will provide their participants with a progression of the activity. Every activity is taught starting at a beginning level and progressing through skill levels. Standard of care plays a role here as well. Expectations of what the supervisors should know in terms of skills and what they should do while on duty for many activities are defined by the industry.

The third component of supervision is first aid and rescue. No matter how well prepared and well trained one feels, a possibility always exists that something may go wrong. Supervisors are responsible for being prepared for the worst and for being able to react to a situation and handle an emergency. That means that the proper equipment and supplies for first aid or rescue must be available and the supervisors must know what to do and react quickly and efficiently.

Returning to the Percheski case, Ebro indicated in figure 1.1 that none of the guides rendered first aid and that they left Percheski sitting on the shore without supervision while a guide ran for help and the other guides continued on with the trip. As previously noted, this was not good form. If the plaintiff can show that not rendering first aid contributed further to Percheski's injuries, bad form becomes a potential breach of standard of care, contributing to additional injury and possible negligence on the part of the rafting company.

## Conduct of the Activity

Conducting an activity has three components: adequacy of progression, maturity and condition of the participants, and safety equipment and environmental conditions. Adequacy of progression refers to the steps a participant must take to be involved in an activity. In an activity such as boxing, where the objective of the sport is to knock down an opponent, one does not immediately start in the ring with another boxer. An activity begins with participants learning the necessary skills and becoming familiar with the equipment. Adequacy of progression is closely linked with appreciation because a student gains understanding, appreciation, and experience with progression of activity. Appreciation means that the participant becomes aware of what can happen, how significant an injury may be, and ways to prevent the injury. For example, as the boxer learns where to put his hands to fend off punches, he also learns what happens when he does not keep his hands up.

Next, the instructor or leader must be alert to the maturity and the physical and psychological condition of the participants. For example, the leader must note fatigue in participants and modify or end the activity before injury occurs. The boxer learns to warm up, to move quickly, and to keep his guard up. He learns to protect himself and how to lift weights to get stronger. The leader must be aware of the condition of the boxer and his changing needs at every practice. The exercises in chapters 4 and 6 that use the videos *Cold, Wet, and Alive* and *Decide to Return* echo this theme and are excellent examples of how failing to note changing conditions in participants can lead to injury, damage, or loss.

Finally, a leader must provide safety equipment and ensure that it works properly. When a group plays baseball, the leader must provide appropriate helmets to batters and safety equipment for the catcher. Defective equipment is usually a cause for a quick settlement in a lawsuit. A missing safety guard on a potter's wheel could be problematic if an injury occurs. A leader must also monitor environmental conditions and their effect on the activity. If high winds, thunderstorms, flash floods, or a change in temperature occur, the leader should modify, change, or end the activity to meet the changing situation. This concept is discussed in detail in chapters 4 through 6.

## SUMMARY

One cannot entirely eliminate the possibility of being sued because the plaintiff chooses whether to sue. One can, however, take precautions to minimize the success of the plaintiff if he chooses to sue. Four components are necessary for negligence to occur: a duty; breach of standard of care; proximate cause; and injury, damage, or loss. If any window closes or any component is missing, negligence does not occur. If one does everything that he or she should do and does it correctly, there should be no breach of standard of care. If a breach of standard of care does not occur and if there is no proximate cause, there most likely will not be any injury, damage, or loss. If injury, damage, or loss does occur, it is not attributable to negligence.

A recreation leader is held to a standard of care of a reasonable and prudent professional. This means that a leader is expected to know and understand, and has a duty to perform, the common practices of her activity or industry. Ignorance of these common practices is not an excuse. Many leaders join professional organizations, take classes, become certified, and attend conferences in order to expand their professional knowledge. A leader who does not know or apply the common practices of her activity or industry potentially sets herself up for a breach of standard of care. A leader must also create a safe environment through supervision and conduct of the activity and by providing safety equipment.

## EXERCISES

### Exercise 1: *White Mile*

The purpose of this exercise is to view the video *White Mile* (2004) and to analyze the components of negligence that are present. *White Mile* depicts an actual rafting trip as well as the courtroom proceedings that follow it.

1. Analyze the events in the video in terms of the four elements necessary for negligence. Were all the elements present?
2. Was the fatality foreseeable?
3. Does respondeat superior apply between Dan Cutler, who was responsible for the outing, and his parent company DDB Needham Worldwide, or was his outing a case of ultra vires?
4. Do you agree with the verdict?

### Exercise 2: Hawk Mountain Trip and Ultra Vires

The purpose of this exercise is to explore ultra vires. On a field trip, a camp counselor is driving a group of campers to Hawk Mountain, a unique natural resource. The counselor filed his travel request and followed the normal camp procedures associated with preparing for trips like this.

The trip to Hawk Mountain is 30 miles. On the way to Hawk Mountain, the counselor decides to take a side trip for a personal matter. He did not note his side trip on the travel form. His destination is 3 miles one way off the normal direct route to Hawk Mountain.

Unfortunately, he has an accident while on this portion of the trip. One of the campers on the trip decides to sue him for damages. In accordance with respondeat superior, she sues the camp as well. She claims that the accident occurred during the camp field trip.

The camp director discusses the matter with the camp's legal representative. On close examination, they conclude that the leader of the trip was on an unauthorized field trip. They claim ultra vires and make a motion to exclude the camp from the suit. They indicate that the leader was not on a direct route to Hawk Mountain, that he was on a personal errand, that he had not indicated that he was going on a side trip as part of the field trip, and that the side trip was outside of his authority.

Who is right? What lessons, if any, can be taken away from this example?

### Exercise 3: General and Specific Supervision in the Percheski Case

The purpose of this exercise is to help you understand how specific and general supervision affect risk management and the need to plan for how many supervisors are needed and where they need to be during the course of a program.

In the Percheski case, there were 15 to 20 rafts on the trip and 3 guides. The rafts on the trip became fairly strung out on the river. The sweep raft, which brings up the rear of the trip, normally carries the first aid kit because it has access to everyone on the river. Assume that Ebro's account of the incident is accurate (figure 1.6). Review Thomas Mills' account of his involvement in the incident (figure 1.1). Read between the lines. As trip leader, did he have general supervision of the trip, let alone specific supervision of the incident once it occurred? Being so far down river prevented him from transitioning from general to specific supervision. Should he have had specific supervision of the incident once it occurred? Plugging this into the general negligence model, did Thomas Mills' lack of supervision (either general or specific) contribute to Percheski's injuries, or was it simply bad form on his part that he did not know the full details of what happened until the end of the trip?

## Exercise 4: Programming Implications

The purpose of this exercise is to show how the principles of negligence interact with good programming principles. A recreation leader or programmer, or even resource manager, must consider the relationship between the two. In the Percheski case, depicted in figure 1.1, Thomas Ebro notes that splashing activities are a normal part of the rafting experience. A gallon of water weighs approximately 8 pounds. A 5-gallon bucket of water that is half full weighs approximately 20 pounds. Could this have anything to do with Percheski blowing out his knee? Splashing and water battles are normal activities among rafters. Consider the following questions.

1. Should rules exist regarding splashing activities? Suggest some.
2. Do a quick Internet search for the terms *water gun* and *super soaker*. Would these provide a better alternative to the use of 5-gallon buckets?

Chapter 2

# Standard of Care

As discussed in chapter 1, standard of care is the experience that one expects a reasonable and prudent recreation professional to provide to a participant. Standard of care also applies to facilities and landowners. Three categories of visitors exist: invitee, licensee, and trespasser. This chapter discusses the levels of care an individual or organization owes a visitor according to the category in which the visitor falls. This chapter also reviews recreational land use statutes and attractive nuisance, two key concepts that affect recreational use of outdoor resources.

## VISITOR CATEGORIES

Visitors fall into three categories: invitee, licensee, and trespasser. The duty an individual or organization owes a visitor is based on visitor status, or on the visitor's relationship with the individual or organization. Standard of care varies among visitor categories.

### Invitee

An invitee receives the highest standard of care. An invitee enters another's premises for the purpose of doing business in the facility or on the land. The invitee (visitor) and the inviter (owner) both benefit from the presence of the invitee. A public invitee is an invitee who enters and remains on another's property for a purpose for which the property is open to the public.

**invitee**—A person who has an express or implied invitation to enter or use another's premises, such as a business visitor or a member of the public for whom the premises are held open. The occupier has a duty to inspect the premises and to warn the invitee of dangerous conditions.

For example, a club member enters a health club and, when going down the stairs, leans on a faulty railing. The railing breaks, injuring the member. The member is considered an invitee and would be offered the highest level of care. If a guest of the member enters the health club, leans on the faulty railing, and is injured, the guest would be offered the same level of care as the member. The guest has an implied and most likely an expressed invitation to enter the premises. Even when no money changes hands, the visitor is still an invitee because he sees what the business has to offer and may come back another time to do business.

As another example, a park has a basketball court. Local youths play basketball on the court during the park's open hours. A player trips in a pothole in the court and is injured. The youths are considered invitees because they are at the park for the express purpose of the premises: to play basketball. Therefore, the duty (relationship) is of the highest level and the invitee deserves the highest level of standard of care. The premises should be kept as risk-free as possible, and warnings should be issued where risks do exist.

## Licensee

A licensee enters another's property with permission but without any benefit to the landowner. The visitor is there for his own purposes (e.g., to hunt). Although the owner provides consent for the visitor to be on the land, the owner does not charge the visitor and therefore does not benefit. Consent includes implied consent, where the owner knows from past behavior that the visitor is frequenting the property and does not take action to prevent it. Also, in business terms, no consideration (an agreement with exchange negotiated between the two parties) exists between the landowner and visitor. The standard of care owed the visitor is a warning of known danger. The landowner is not required to make upgrades to the land or inspect it for a licensee.

**licensee**—One who has permission to enter or use another's premises, but only for one's own purposes and not for the occupier's benefit. The occupier has a duty to warn the licensee of any dangerous conditions known to the occupier but unknown to the licensee.

For example, Whiting's Neck Cave is on a farmer's property. The cave is used by the public. The entrance to the short trail leading to the cave is in clear view of the farmer's house on the overlooking hill. Users park their cars up the road in a parking area. Clearly, cavers enter the land for their own purposes. The landowner knows that people visit the cave and that they have been doing so for years. The farmer receives no reimbursement for use of the cave. One could argue that by his actions, or in this case lack of action, the farmer consents to cavers using the cave. The relationship is one of licensee, and the standard of care is only to warn the visitors of the dangers the landowner knows are there. The farmer is not required to fix the danger, as he would for an invitee, but is required to warn visitors of its existence. If the farmer keeps a bull in the field, he would most likely need to warn cavers of the bull's presence if the bull poses a threat, or he might move the fence so that the bull cannot interact with the cavers walking to the entrance of the cave. This standard of care would arise from the farmer's knowledge that cavers use his property.

## Trespasser

A trespasser enters another's premises intentionally and without the consent of the owner. The trespasser is on the property illegally. The standard of care a landowner owes a trespasser is not to intentionally harm the trespasser.

**trespasser**—One who commits a trespass; one who intentionally and without consent or privilege enters another's property. In tort law, a landowner owes no duty to unforeseeable trespassers.

A landowner owes no duty to unforeseeable trespassers. Unforeseeable means that the landowner had no reason to know that people are on the property. He does not see them enter, he did not give them permission to be there, and he made some sort of statement that they are unwelcome. "No trespassing" signs or locked gates that are difficult to transverse are examples of statements that no one should enter the premises.

For example, a landowner owns several acres, and on the land is a mine shaft. The landowner is unaware of its existence—that is, until a trespasser accidently falls through the rotting timbers covering the entrance and dies. Everyone else is just as surprised as the landowner is regarding the presence of the mine shaft. The trespasser's estate sues the landowner. Is the landowner negligent? Probably not. She did not know about the mine shaft and had no reason to expect that it was there. Normally, one does not have a duty to protect a trespasser.

However, change some of the elements of this example and the landowner would most likely be considered negligent. After traversing the property and coming across the mine shaft, the landowner's friend sends her an e-mail notifying the landowner that the mine shaft is there and describes where it is located on the property. The landowner now knows that people are entering her property. If she takes no action to stop them, they become licensees.

Photo courtesy of Robert B. Kauffman.

Students entering one of the two entrances at Whiting's Neck Cave. What is the standard of care that the land owner needs to provide cavers accessing this popular cave in western Maryland?

The landowner takes no immediate action to repair the mine shaft. Two months later, another person accidently falls through the rotting timbers and dies in the mine shaft and his estate sues the landowner. Unlike in the first example, the landowner is probably negligent. Was the person a licensee or a trespasser? The e-mail indicates that the landowner knew that people were crossing the land and did not more clearly mark it with "no trespassing" signs, thus creating implied consent. The licensee is owed a warning of foreseeable dangers, and this accident was foreseeable because the landowner knew about the hazard. Also, most people would consider two months to be a reasonable period of time to place warning signs or to secure the entrance of the mine shaft.

If the landowner had posted obvious "no trespassing" signs, then she would not need to warn of the hazard on the land. However, she must enforce the no trespassing rule and stop people when she sees them on her land. If she sees them and does not stop them, they become licensees who require a higher level of standard of care.

The duty of a landowner can change because of the landowner's behavior. For example, behind the local park and recreation center is an outdoor basketball court. A group of teenagers sneaks in and plays a game of midnight basketball on Wednesday and Friday evenings. The director of the center has police reports, and maintenance has found some trash by the court in the morning. The director leaves on the lights that illuminate the court. He even stays late one evening so that he can meet with the teenagers. He requests that they put their trash in the nearby dumpster. What is the relationship: invitee, licensee, or trespasser?

In this case, the teenagers are invitees. The park is public and the director has acknowledged the presence of the teens. They deserve the same sort of warnings, inspections, and maintenance as do people playing basketball during the day. If the teens can prove that the director knew they were there, they are there with his permission and thus, because they are there for the purposes of the agency, they are invitees. On the other hand, if the director realizes that the teens are there and requests that the police warn them that they are trespassing and run them off, the director does not owe them the same level of care that he would owe invitees. The public is invited to the park only when it is open.

If the park was private property and the director knew that the teens were there, they would be licensees because they are on the property with implied permission. If the director does not collect fees from the teens for using the space, the required standard of care is only to warn of known dangers. Finally, if the closing of the park was enforced and the teens knew they were not supposed to be there because they had been kicked off or given citations, they would be trespassers. The director owes them no duty except to not create a danger that would injure them.

This example illustrates a dilemma for park and recreation professionals. If a professional allows an activity such as basketball after the park is closed, then he needs to provide the standard of care that he would normally provide for that activity at that time. For example, lighting needs to meet the industry standards for outdoor basketball courts, and supervision needs to be consistent with normal supervision found during the day. Otherwise, the professional needs to extinguish the activity or discourage the activity with posted signs and periodic police patrols of the area.

Photodisc/Getty Images

A professional needs to provide the same standard of care for a basketball court when the court is open as when it's closed.

## RECREATIONAL LAND USE STATUTES

All states have enacted recreational land use liability statutes that encourage recreational use on private lands while protecting landowners from negligence. Generally, the statute limits the rights of the plaintiff to collect damages from the landowner. It does not, however, allow for gross or willful and wanton negligence. In addition, the landowner needs to be careful to not take remuneration from the user because this could negate the statute and elevate the standard of care to that of an invitee. The duty is that owed to a licensee, and the standard of care is to warn visitors of known dangers but does not require inspection of the property to find dangers.

Although the recreational land use statute has been adopted by every state, the statute can vary significantly from state to state. Some states list very specific outdoor activities that are protected, some states include all landowners (including public landowners), and some states exclude special groups. For example, New Jersey limits application of the law to only those landowners enrolled in specific state programs, and Oklahoma excludes farm and ranch lands. Some states limit the protection to natural areas only, whereas others open it to any recreational areas, including ball fields and swimming pools. See figure 2.1 for an example statute from the state of Vermont.

Recreational land use statutes are passed because of the limiting factor of many outdoor activities: the available resource. Any outdoor activity—equestrian, hiking, biking, whitewater, climbing, hunting, fishing, and so on—is potentially limited by the availability of outdoor resources. Without the outdoor resource, the user has no place to perform the activity. Manufacturers produce and sell outdoor equipment. Consumers buy the equipment. Both the manufacturer and the consumer turn to someone else, usually the state, to provide the outdoor resource for the activity. However, not enough public land is available to meet the needs of all outdoor participants.

Recreational land use statutes assist in making private lands available for recreational use. A quick Internet search using the term *recreational land use statutes* reveals that land use is a topic that interests many outdoor-oriented organizations that need to provide outdoor resources or a place to perform their activity. Recreational land use statutes serve an important function. The statute helps make private lands available to outdoor users by addressing landowners' worry about being sued if someone gets hurt on their land.

For the owner of Whiting's Neck Cave, the land use statute would potentially lower the standard of care to which he would be held. A more accurate interpretation is that the land use statute would classify the standard of care as that owed a trespasser. If the owner relocated a fence to protect users, it would not change his standard of care; it would still be that owed to a trespasser. For the landowner, this is reassuring and it will most likely entice him to keep his land open to the cavers.

## ATTRACTIVE NUISANCE

A landowner has an extra duty to protect children from manmade items or conditions on his property that may foreseeably lure children to trespass. This duty is covered under the attractive-nuisance doctrine. In essence, the owner's duty is to protect the children from injuring themselves.

**attractive-nuisance doctrine**—The rule that a person who owns property on which there is a dangerous thing or condition that will foreseeably lure children to trespass has a duty to protect those children from the danger.

For example, an abandoned farmhouse sits on a landowner's property. The windows are boarded up, the doors are locked, and the house is reasonably secure. However, like any old farmhouse that is abandoned and boarded up, local youths will likely try to break in and explore it. The farmhouse qualifies as an attractive nuisance because it is manmade and its attractiveness to children is foreseeable.

The landowner's options are as follows. First, she can secure the building by boarding it up and periodically patrolling it to ensure that children are not playing inside. If she finds signs of children playing in the building, she needs to take corrective action. Second, she can repair the house and make it livable. If someone lives in the building, it is no longer an attractive nuisance. Third, she can raze the building and eliminate it as an attractive nuisance. Although recreational land use statutes protect landowners from adults trespassing, it does not protect them from children trespassing, especially if something the children are lured to on the land be something that interests them. The law treats children different than adults, partially because children have less appreciation for danger.

## SUMMARY

Providing outdoor recreational activities is contingent on land resources, but possible litigation against the landowner is a major deterrent to the use of private lands for outdoor recreation purposes. Recreational land use statutes help provide the outdoor resources for these activities. Many of the professional organizations that provide these outdoor activities are keenly

## Vermont's Recreational Land Use Statute

### Statute, Status, and Description

The Vermont limited liability statute is found in title 12 (Court Procedure), chapter 203 (Limitations to Landowner Liability), sections 5791-5795. It was substantially revised in 1997.

12 V.S.A. § 5791 (2006)

**§ 5791. Purpose**

The purpose of this chapter is to encourage owners to make their land and water available to the public for no consideration for recreational uses by clearly establishing a rule that an owner shall have no greater duty of care to a person who, without consideration, enters or goes upon the owner's land for a recreational use than the owner would have to a trespasser.

**§ 5792. Definitions**

As used in this chapter:

(1) "Consideration" means a price, fee, or other charge paid to or received by the owner in return for the permission to enter upon or to travel across the owner's land for recreational use.

Consideration shall not include

(A) compensation paid to or a tax benefit received by the owner for granting a permanent recreational use easement,

(B) payment or provision for compensation to be paid to the owner for damage caused by recreational use, or

(C) contributions in services or other consideration paid to the owner to offset or insure against damages sustained by an owner from the recreational use or to compensate the owner for damages from recreational use.

(2) (A) "Land" means

(i) open and undeveloped land, including paths and trails;

(ii) water, including springs, streams, rivers, ponds, lakes, and other water courses;

(iii) fences; or

(iv) structures and fixtures used to enter or go upon land, including bridges and walkways.

(B) "Land" does not include

(i) areas developed for commercial recreational uses;

(ii) equipment, machinery, or personal property; or

(iii) structures and fixtures not described in subdivision (2)(a)(iii) or (iv) of this section.

(3) "Owner" means a person who owns, leases, licenses, or otherwise controls ownership or use of land, and any employee or agent of that person.

(4) "Recreational use" means an activity undertaken for recreational, educational, or conservation purposes, and includes hunting, fishing, trapping, guiding, camping, biking, in-line skating, jogging, skiing, swimming, diving, water sports, rock climbing, hang gliding, caving, boating, hiking, riding an animal or a vehicle, picking wild or cultivated plants, picnicking, gleaning, rock collecting, nature study, outdoor sports, visiting or enjoying archeological,

*(continued)*

**Figure 2.1** Vermont's recreational land use statute is representative of other state statutes. Residents in other states should check the specifics of the statute in their state. Residents of Vermont should check their current statute.

Reprinted from the Vermont Statutes Annotated Title 12 Sections 5791-5795.

scenic, natural, or scientific sites, or other similar activities. "Recreational use" also means any noncommercial activity undertaken without consideration to create, protect, preserve, rehabilitate, or maintain the land for recreational uses.

**§ 5793. Liability limited**

(a) Land. An owner shall not be liable for property damage or personal injury sustained by a person who, without consideration, enters or goes upon the owner's land for a recreational use unless the damage or injury is the result of the willful or wanton misconduct of the owner.

(b) Equipment, fixtures, machinery, or personal property.

(1) Unless the damage or injury is the result of the willful or wanton misconduct of the owner, an owner shall not be liable for property damage or personal injury sustained by a person who, without consideration and without actual permission of the owner, enters or goes upon the owner's land for a recreational use and proceeds to enter upon or use.

(A) equipment, machinery, or personal property; or

(B) structures or fixtures not described in subdivision 5792(2)(a)(iii) or (iv) of this title.

(2) Permission to enter or go upon an owner's land shall not, by itself, include permission to enter or go upon structures or to go upon or use equipment, fixtures, machinery, or personal property.

**§ 5794. Landowner protection**

(a) The fact that an owner has made land available without consideration for recreational uses shall not be construed to

(1) limit the property rights of owners;

(2) limit the ability of an owner and a recreational user of the land to enter into agreements for the recreational use of the land to vary or supplement the duties and limitations created in this chapter;

(3) support or create any claim or right of eminent domain, adverse possession, or other prescriptive right or easement or any other land use restriction;

(4) alter, modify, or supersede the rights and responsibilities under chapters 191, animal control, and 193, domestic pet or wolf-hybrid control, of title 20; under chapters 29, snowmobiles, and 31, all-terrain vehicles, of title 23; under chapter 23, bicycle routes, of title 19; and under chapter 20, Vermont trail system, of title 10;

(5) extend any assurance that the land is safe for recreational uses or create any duty on an owner to inspect the land to discover dangerous conditions; or

(6) relieve a person making recreational use of land from the obligation the person may have in the absence of this chapter to exercise due care for the person's own safety in the recreational use of the land.

(b) Nothing in this chapter shall create any presumption or inference of permission or consent to enter upon an owner's land for any purpose.

(c) For the purposes of protecting landowners who make land available for recreational use to members of the public for no consideration pursuant to this chapter, the presence of one or more of the following on land does not by itself preclude the land from being "open and undeveloped": posting of the land, fences, or agricultural or forestry-related structures.

**§ 5795. Exceptions**

This chapter shall not apply to lands owned by a municipality or the state.

**Figure 2.1** *(continued)*

aware of this statute and its importance for maintaining the future viability of outdoor pursuits. Reducing the liability of the landowner is the key to making private lands available for public use.

The standard of care provided to people using a natural resource depends on the relationship between the landowner and the user. If the landowner is in the business of using the natural resource to provide an activity and if the user is there for that purpose, the standard of care is most likely that of an invitee. The landowner has the highest level of duty and therefore must provide the highest level of standard of care. The premises must be inspected and maintained.

If the user is there for her own purpose and if she is there without the consent of the landowner, the user is most likely a trespasser. Trespassers are afforded the lowest level of standard of care. A landowner is not required to inspect or maintain the property for trespassers; however, a landowner cannot create dangers that would harm them.

In between the invitee and the trespasser is the licensee. The user is there for her own purposes and the landowner consents to her being there. Normally, a reasonable and prudent landowner should provide a standard of care commensurate with the needs of the user. However, this may not be the case when taking into account the recreational land use statute. In an effort to provide a public good (i.e., recreational use), the statute protects landowners by classifying the standard of care at the lower level of trespasser. The standard of care comes full circle when balance is present among the needs of the visitor, the rights and requirements of the landowner, and the public good.

## EXERCISES

### Exercise 1: The Backyard Swing Set

The purpose of the first three exercises is to explore the standard of care afforded a visitor. The swing set in your back yard is the envy of your neighbors. Your neighbor does not use your swing set when you are present. However, you suspect that he uses it when you are not present because of the telltale signs left behind and because of his comments that inadvertently refer to using the swing set. You have no real evidence that he is using your swing set. You have not given him permission to use your swing set.

1. Is the neighbor using the swing set for his own purposes?
2. Did you give consent (actual or implied) for the neighbor to use the swing set?
3. Is the swing set your business or did you receive payment for the use of your swing set?
4. Is the standard of care that of an invitee, licensee, or trespasser?
5. Would the swing set be considered an attractive nuisance?
6. What is your responsibility?

### Exercise 2: The Apple Pies and the Backyard Swing Set

The swing set in your back yard is the envy of your neighbors. The family next door uses your swing set in your presence. The family periodically gives you an apple pie to show their appreciation.

1. Are the neighbors using the swing set for their own purposes?
2. Did you give consent (actual or implied) for the neighbors to use the swing set?

3. Is the swing set your business or did you receive payment for the use of your swing set?
4. Is the standard of care that of an invitee, licensee, or trespasser?
5. What is your responsibility?

### Exercise 3: The Friendly Neighbors and the Backyard Swing Set

The swing set in your back yard is the envy of your neighbors. Your neighbor uses your swing set in your presence and with your consent. You do not receive payment from the neighbor.

1. Is the neighbor using the swing set for her own purpose?
2. Did you give consent (actual or implied) for the neighbor to use the swing set?
3. Is the swing set your business or did you receive payment for the use of your swing set?
4. Is the standard of care that of an invitee, licensee, or trespasser?
5. What is your responsibility?

### Exercise 4: Recreational Land Use Statutes

The purpose of this exercise is to analyze a typical recreational use statute in terms of its provisions. The questions in this exercise refer to the Vermont statute example in figure 2.1.

**1.** A hunter pays a landowner $50 in exchange for being allowed to hunt on the landowner's property. Would this statute apply to the hunter if the hunter is injured on the property while hunting? If the hunter gives the landowner two homemade cherry pies before hunting on the property, would this statute still apply?

**2.** Referring to § 5793, assume that the landowner places a wire across the trail at approximately head height to discourage unwanted mountain bikers from using his property. Would the statute waive the right of a mountain biker (plaintiff) who runs into the wire and is injured (near decapitation) by the wire?

**3.** A recreational user under this statute enters a cabin on the landowner's property. The landowner has the recreational user arrested for breaking and entering. Is the recreational user covered under this statute?

**4.** Section 5795 excludes the recreational use statute from municipality- and state-owned lands. Why might they be excluded?

### Exercise 5: Attractive Nuisance: The Upgraded Swimming Hole

The purpose of this exercise is to explore the underpinning of attractive nuisance. On your park land is a deep hole filled with water. A group of youths goes swimming here on a regular basis. They have tied a rope to the limb of a tree that hangs over the hole so that they can swing out into the water, and they have built stone steps so that they can exit the water. They increased the height of the water by damming the hole. They even lashed a table out of logs so that they can eat lunch and converse.

1. Are children using the attraction?
2. Are they trespassing?

3. Is this a manmade attraction?
4. Is this an attractive nuisance?

### Exercise 6: Attractive Nuisance: The Natural Swimming Hole

The purpose of this exercise is to explore the underpinning of attractive nuisance. On your park land is a deep hole filled with water. Next to the hole is a large tree. A group of youths goes swimming here on a regular basis. They have not altered the site in any way.

1. Are children using the attraction?
2. Are they trespassing?
3. Is this a manmade attraction?
4. Is this an attractive nuisance?

Chapter 3

# Defenses Against Negligence

Chapters 1 and 2 explored negligence and the four elements necessary for negligence to occur. This chapter discusses some traditional defenses against negligence, including legal doctrines that limit liability, and transfer strategies such as assumption of risk, waivers, insurance, and contracting. Individuals and organizations should develop a mix of risk reduction and avoidance strategies, legal strategies, and risk transfer strategies to best defend against negligence.

The programmatic strategies fall under risk management. Risk is the possible loss of money. Risk management involves identifying where risk might occur and trying to minimize or eliminate that loss. Generally, four risk management strategies exist: reduction (of possible injuries), avoidance (of injury by not offering an activity), transfer of the cost of injury to another party, and retention (accepting that some injury might occur). Of these strategies, reduction and avoidance tend to be programmatic since they affect programs and how they are conducted. Programmatic has to do with how programs are managed or operated as opposed to passing the risk to another party or just accepting them without making changes. An example of programmatic strategy might be using an extra mat when practicing a new gymnastics move or increasing instructor spotting until one learns the move. These strategies are the primary focus of this text. The integrated risk management model emphasizes the risk management approach of reduction. This approach includes administrative and programmatic procedures and practices. The strategy is simple: Reducing the likelihood of injury, damage, or loss reduces the chance of negligence. In terms of negligence, the risk management strategies used can focus on one or more of the four components necessary for negligence to occur: duty; breach of standard of care; proximate cause; and injury, damage, or loss. If any of the four windows of negligence are closed, negligence does not occur.

## LEGAL DOCTRINES THAT LIMIT LIABILITY

Several legal doctrines can be useful in defending against negligence: sovereign or governmental immunity, recreational land use statutes, hazardous recreation statutes, statute of limitations, and comparative negligence. These doctrines, often the interface between potentially conflicting philosophies and interests, create a balance by providing recreational opportunities for the greater good while protecting the rights of the individual. For example, governmental immunity limits an injured citizen's right to sue a governmental entity for an injury in exchange for the greater good of the government providing a service. Recreational land use statutes sacrifice the individual's right to sue a landowner in order to provide the greater public good of increased access to the land. As discussed in the following sections, although these strategies are important, the scope and potential effectiveness of these legal defenses are often limited.

## Sovereign Immunity

Governmental or sovereign immunity, which originates from English common law, states that no governmental body can be sued unless it gives permission. It is based, in part, on the concept that the king is the sovereign and the king can do no wrong. In the United States, after the Revolutionary War when the sovereign no longer existed, sovereign immunity transferred to the individual states and later to the federal government. Over time, in many jurisdictions, this doctrine fell out of use. If a mistake was made by a governmental agent with sovereign immunity, the injured citizen had to bear all the costs. Some states found this unfair; the government, like other citizens, should pay for their mistakes. In those states sovereign immunity was dropped in an effort to balance a citizen's right to collect on harms done to them by the state. In other states, sovereign immunity has been maintained because of the state's need to protect its coffers for the best interest of its community.

Individual states have handled the issue of governmental immunity differently. Seven states have waived immunity altogether, and eight states have placed limits on the amount an individual can collect in the event of negligence. The remaining 35 states use many different methods to protect governments from lawsuits for negligence, especially in recreational settings.

**governmental immunity**—The doctrine from English common law that no governmental body can be sued unless it gives permission. This protection resulted in injustices because public hospitals, government drivers, and other employees could be negligent but be free from judgment. The Federal Tort Claims Act and state waivers of immunity (with specific claims systems) have negated this rule in many states, which stemmed from the days when kings set prerogatives.

Eleven states have strong immunity laws. The Arkansas immunity statute is one of the strongest in the country and is typical of these laws. The Arkansas state constitution states, "The government shall not be a defendant in her courts," meaning that no one can sue a governmental entity in Arkansas for negligence. This includes any tax-supported entity and anyone related to the entity. It includes schools, city and state governments and their employees, volunteers, and board members.

However, even the Arkansas statute has exceptions. The first exception is that if the government has liability insurance, it can be sued up to the amount of the insurance and the insurance company will pay the loss. However, if a state has this exception, most of the governmental entities will not purchase insurance because being insured is an invitation to be sued. Instead, the governmental entities insure themselves by putting aside money or identifying where they will get the money in the event that one of the other exceptions is met.

Transportation is a second exception. The government can be sued if the negligence occurs in a vehicle or on a roadway. The states that have this exception allow for insurance to be purchased separately for these types of accidents.

The third exception is gross or willful and wanton negligence (discussed in chapter 1). Gross or willful and wanton negligence is not covered by immunity or by insurance and is never waived. If an individual is reckless or creates an injury on purpose, the courts make the individual responsible for the costs of the injury.

Finally, if a person feels she has been significantly wronged, she can appeal to the state legislature to permit the state to be sued. A special court is in place to assist in this process. Many states changed their immunity laws because state legislatures were being inundated with so many appeals for the right to sue that they were having trouble taking care of state business. The states simply eliminated immunity by deciding that the state government would be treated like a citizen in cases of negligence.

Potential injustices or abuses have resulted from the doctrine of sovereign immunity. The fatal drowning of five innercity youths on the Meramec River in Castlewood State Park near St. Louis, Missouri, exemplifies this issue. (This case is discussed in greater depth in chapter 5.) The state park had a drop-off where, without warning, the water depth in the river went from 1.5 feet to more than 5 feet in a span of 5 feet. However, because of sovereign immunity, the state park could not be included as a second defendant in the lawsuit. Was the park guilty of negligence for not warning beach users of the drop-off? Possibly. However, one cannot state definitively that the park was negligent because the case never went to trial. Whether a state has sovereign immunity or not is a balancing act between providing a greater public good—in this case, a public swimming area for the citizens of St. Louis—and the loss resulting from the drownings, assuming that negligent behavior occurred.

## Recreational Land Use Statutes

The following expands the discussion of recreational land use statutes (see chapter 2) to include the public sector under the statute. When governmental immunity was waived, recreation and parks departments looked for methods to protect themselves from lawsuit. One of the methods used was to go back to the protection the private landowners had. Municipalities were offering recreation on land they owned. If a recreational land use statute was vague about the type of land the statute applied to (private or public), the government began using the recreational land use statutes as a defense. When cases ensued on land that was provided by the state or city and where no fee was charged, many state courts determined that because the law states that the government would be treated like a citizen and that citizens have immunity from negligence for opening their land to the public, the government should have the same immunity. Outdoor recreational activities that often take place in parks were also considered to be immune. Eleven states have legislated expanded recreational land use statutes and added public entities to the list of those who receive such immunity.

As explained in chapter 2, exceptions exist, and these exceptions apply to the government unless it has expanded its law to include improved lands. Nebraska is a case in point. The law did not specify what type of land (private or public) or what types of recreational purposes were covered. Therefore, the Nebraska government was allowed to use the statute to protect the parks.

*Bronson v. Dawes County, NB* (2006) indicates how nuanced the law can be and how significant a seemingly simple ruling can be. In this case the use of recreational land use legislation by governmental entities was ultimately struck down. The plaintiff, Bronson, attended a concert, for which no fee was charged, on the courthouse lawn. Bronson stepped in a hole and injured her ankle, and she sued the county. The county argued that they had immunity because Bronson was at the courthouse for a recreational activity, and the county won. However, on appeal the court decided that was not right or fair that a person coming to the courthouse for business should be treated differently than one coming for a recreational reason. They should both be treated the same and negligence could not be determined based on why a person is on the land. The court pointed out that the intent of the statute was to protect private landowners. Therefore, the court determined that public land was not included in the statute, and Bronson won.

The result of this decision was major. Almost immediately, skateboard parks and BMX trails were closed due to fear of lawsuits. Parks closed sledding hills in the winter. People in the state were upset and pushed for the recreational statutes to include public land. Although it did not get enacted as a recreational user statute, a new section that gave protection back to the providers of public recreation facilities was added to the Tort Claims Act in May of 2007 (Political Subdivision Tort Claims Act, 2012, section 13-910).

Recreational land use or recreational user statutes, when expanded to include governmental entities, often come with many stipulations and are different for every state. Some states include only natural areas whereas others include swimming pools and ball fields. Each individual should become familiar with the laws in his own state. The Nebraska statute states

> The purpose of sections 37-729 to 37-736 is to encourage owners of land to make available to the public land and water areas for recreational purposes by limiting their liability toward persons entering thereon and toward persons who may be injured or otherwise damaged by the acts or omissions of persons entering thereon. (Political Subdivision Tort Claims Act, 2012, section 37-729)

## Hazardous Recreation Statutes

Hazardous recreation statutes are laws written specifically to encourage governments to provide the activities listed, often skateboarding. California has a comprehensive statute (see figure 3.1). At least six states depend on these statutes to protect governmental entities from negligence when providing recreational activities deemed hazardous.

As with all tort law, these statutes are state specific. For example, Florida requires that if a municipality offers a specific activity, anyone under the age of 17 must have permission from a parent to participate in that activity. This means that governmental recreation programs

Galina Barskaya/fotolia.com

Recreational land use statutes help municipalities avoid lawsuits due to injuries that can take place at skateboard parks.

## Hazardous Recreational Land Use Statute of California

(a) Neither a public entity nor a public employee is liable to any person who participates in a hazardous recreational activity, including any person who assists the participant, or to any spectator who knew or reasonably should have known that the hazardous recreational activity created a substantial risk of injury to himself or herself and was voluntarily in the place of risk, or having the ability to do so failed to leave, for any damage or injury to property or persons arising out of that hazardous recreational activity.

(b) As used in this section, "hazardous recreational activity" means a recreational activity conducted on property of a public entity that creates a substantial (as distinguished from a minor, trivial, or insignificant) risk of injury to a participant or a spectator.

"Hazardous recreational activity" also means the following:

(1) Water contact activities, except diving, in places where or at a time when lifeguards are not provided and reasonable warning thereof has been given or the injured party should reasonably have known that there was no lifeguard provided at the time.

(2) Any form of diving into water from other than a diving board or diving platform, or at any place or from any structure where diving is prohibited and reasonable warning thereof has been given.

(3) Animal riding (including equestrian competition), archery, bicycle racing or jumping, mountain bicycling, boating, cross-country and downhill skiing, hang gliding, kayaking, motorized vehicle racing, off-road motorcycling or four-wheel driving of any kind, orienteering, pistol and rifle shooting, rock climbing, rocketeering, rodeo, spelunking, sky diving, sport parachuting, paragliding, body contact sports (i.e., sports in which it is reasonably foreseeable that there will be rough bodily contact with one or more participants), surfing, trampolining, tree climbing, tree rope swinging, waterskiing, white-water rafting, and windsurfing. For the purposes of this subdivision, "mountain bicycling" does not include riding a bicycle on paved pathways, roadways, or sidewalks.

(c) Notwithstanding the provisions of subdivision (a), this section does not limit liability that would otherwise exist for any of the following:

(1) Failure of the public entity or employee to guard or warn of a known dangerous condition or of another hazardous recreational activity known to the public entity or employee that is not reasonably assumed by the participant as inherently a part of the hazardous recreational activity out of which the damage or injury arose.

(2) Damage or injury suffered in any case where permission to participate in the hazardous recreational activity was granted for a specific fee. For the purpose of this paragraph, a "specific fee" does not include a fee or consideration charged for a general purpose such as a general park admission charge, a vehicle entry or parking fee, or an administrative or group use application or permit fee, as distinguished from a specific fee charged for participation in the specific hazardous recreational activity out of which the damage or injury arose.

(3) Injury suffered to the extent proximately caused by the negligent failure of the public entity or public employee to properly construct or maintain in good repair any structure,

*(continued)*

**Figure 3.1** An example of California's code protecting publicly offered programs.

Reprinted from California Department of Parks and Recreation.

recreational equipment or machinery, or substantial work of improvement utilized in the hazardous recreational activity out of which the damage or injury arose.

(4) Damage or injury suffered in any case where the public entity or employee recklessly or with gross negligence promoted the participation in or observance of a hazardous recreational activity. For purposes of this paragraph, promotional literature or a public announcement or advertisement that merely describes the available facilities and services on the property does not in itself constitute a reckless or grossly negligent promotion.

(5) An act of gross negligence by a public entity or a public employee that is the proximate cause of the injury. Nothing in this subdivision creates a duty of care or basis of liability for personal injury or for damage to personal property.

(d) Nothing in this section shall limit the liability of an independent concessionaire, or any person or organization other than the public entity, whether or not the person or organization has a contractual relationship with the public entity to use the public property, for injuries or damages suffered in any case as a result of the operation of a hazardous recreational activity on public property by the concessionaire, person, or organization.

**Figure 3.1** *(continued)*

in Florida must devise a method for obtaining the signatures and must enforce the rule of no participation for those who do not provide signatures. Each individual should become familiar with the laws in his own state and note any special restrictions.

## Statute of Limitations

Statute of limitations states that the victim (plaintiff) needs to file the lawsuit within a certain period of time. If he does not file the lawsuit within that time period, he forfeits his right to sue. Normally, the statute of limitations ranges from one to six years, although the period of time varies from state to state. The date of the statute of limitations may be extended due to the date that the injury is found. Rhode Island usually has a 10-year limitation, and California has a period of 1 to 2 years. However, it can range from 5 to 25 years depending on circumstances. For example, children generally have the number of years of the statute of limitations past the age of majority (18 years of age in most states) to file a suit (Law.com, 2012). If a child is 6 years old when an injury from negligence occurs and the statute of limitations is 3 years, the parents have 3 years from the date when they realize an injury exists to file on behalf of themselves or the child. However, the child has until 3 years past her 18th birthday to file a suit.

Limitations, extensions, exclusions, and qualifications for this doctrine exist, and they are different for every state. Recreation professionals should check with their legal counsel regarding the statute of limitations in their state because it affects the nature of an incident and how long they should keep incident reports on file. The statute of limitations has limited applicability because most people identify an injury and decide to sue in the allotted period of time.

## Comparative Negligence

Comparative negligence is a doctrine in which the amount of contribution toward the negligence becomes the basis for determining the amount of the settlement between the two parties. For example, Eddie Leadfoot, the driver of one car, is speeding. Rudy Airhead, the driver of an oncoming car, fails to signal and, incorrectly judging Leadfoot's speed, starts to turn left. A crash ensues and Airhead is hurt. Airhead's damage recovery will be reduced by the percentage that his failure to judge Leadfoot's speed contributed to or caused the accident. If it is judged to be 10 percent, Leadfoot is responsible for 90 percent of the cost of the injury. The problem with comparative negligence is that it is often difficult to determine the contribution of each party to the negligence, particularly in more complex cases, and the formulas used to figure out, attribute, and compare negligence often make assessment of damages problematic and possibly subjective. Not all states use comparative negligence (California is a fairly recent convert to using it), and some states still use contributory negligence, which denies recovery to any party whose negligence added to the cause of the accident in any way. Contributory negligence is often so unfair that juries tend to ignore it.

**comparative negligence**—A plaintiff's own negligence that proportionally reduces the damages recoverable from a defendant.

Three types of comparative negligence exist. The definition of each type varies by state. The first type is pure comparative. Pure comparative negligence means that the defendant will pay the percentage of the award the court relegates to her. If she is 30 percent at fault, she will be required to pay 30 percent of the cost of the injury as determined by the court. In the Eddie Leadfoot example, the jury determines the contribution of each party and Eddie pays his share of the damages (i.e., 90 percent). Under the second type of comparative negligence, the plaintiff must have less fault than the defendant in order to collect. In the example, Rudy Airhead (the plaintiff) could collect damages because he contributed less than Eddie Leadfoot. Under this interpretation, had the jury concluded that Rudy contributed 50 percent or more of the accident, he would not have collected anything. Under the third type of comparative negligence, the plaintiff could collect even if the jury determined that the parties were equally at fault (50 percent each); but not if he was 51 percent at fault.

Again, comparative negligence is state specific. In some states, the plaintiff collects as much money as the judgment says is not his fault. If the plaintiff is 90 percent at fault, he collects 10 percent of the judgment. Other states have decided that if the plaintiff is more at fault, or equally at fault, he cannot collect anything. The idea is that one who has a part in creating his own injury should not collect.

## TRANSFER STRATEGIES

An individual or organization uses transfer strategies to transfer to someone else any or all of the four components of negligence or the cost of the injury, damage, or loss. An organization can seek to transfer the injury, damage, or loss through assumption of risk doctrines, or can even seek to transfer their negligence to participants though waivers and hold harmless clauses.

### Assumption of Risk

Under the doctrine of assumption of risk, the participant takes or assumes the risk associated with the danger of the activity. Assumption of risk is used particularly in adventure activities such as skydiving, whitewater, mountain biking, and hiking, or sports where injury is a high probability such as football or gymnastics. Organizations use the assumption of risk doctrine as an affirmative defense. In other words, if a person takes part in an activity that he knows is dangerous, he assumes or takes on the risk that is inherent in the activity and cannot sue if he gets hurt by such risk. For example, if a person rides a mountain bike through the woods, he knows that the terrain is not smooth and that an inherent risk of falling exists. He knows that if he falls, he might break a bone or get a head injury. If a person plays football, he knows that he might get hurt when he gets tackled. It is more difficult for a person to win a negligence suit for an injury that occurs when he knows that the possibility of injury is part of the activity. If one took the inherent risk out of the activity, the activity would no longer exist. Inherent risk is part of the sport. If you take tackling out of football, it is no longer tackle football.

Assumption of risk comprises three elements: the participant knows that the risk exists, the participant understands how serious that risk could be, and the participant chooses to take part in the activity even with that understanding. Going back to the mountain biking example, the leader should warn participants that dangers exist and that there is no way to ensure safety. If a person rides a bike down a hill that may have rocks and roots, she might fall and hurt herself. If she understands that and participates anyway, she is assuming the risk. If she then gets hurt by that inherent risk, the courts will not let her collect for her injuries from the agency that provided the trail.

An agency can prove that participants assumed the risk by having them sign an assumption of risk form or a warning. An assumption of risk form lists the possible injuries that could occur and the precautions the participant should take to avoid those injuries. Participants sign the form to affirm that they understand the risks and are participating voluntarily. The form is often used in place of a waiver when a waiver is inappropriate.

**assumption of risk**—The act or an instance of a prospective plaintiff taking on the risk of loss. Also, the principle that one who takes on the risk of loss, injury, or damage cannot maintain an action against a party that causes the loss, injury, or damage.

The first paragraph of the waiver in figure 3.2 is an example of an assumption of risk clause. It lists all the elements of the activity and the types of injuries that might occur. An assumption of risk clause should indicate how the participant can minimize the risk.

## Waivers

A waiver is a contract between two entities in which one entity, in order to participate in an activity, relinquishes the right to sue for negligence that may result in injury. From a risk management viewpoint, the purpose of waivers is to transfer injury, damage, or loss to the participant even if the agency is negligent. For recreation leaders and programmers, waivers have become a way of life. In eight states, waivers are either outlawed or have not held

If a person takes part in an activity that he knows is dangerous, he assumes or takes on the risk that is inherent in the activity and cannot sue if he gets hurt by such risk.

Anytown Recreation Center
235 Schole Road
Anytown, AP 55512

## Participation Waiver Form

I HEREBY ASSUME ALL OF THE RISKS OF PARTICIPATING IN THIS ACTIVITY OR EVENT, including by way of example and not limitation, any risks that may arise from negligence or carelessness on the part of the persons or entities being released, from dangerous or defective equipment or property owned, maintained, or controlled by them, or because of their possible liability without fault.

I certify that I am physically fit, have sufficiently prepared or trained for participation in the activity or event, and have not been advised to not participate by a qualified medical professional. I certify that there are no health-related reasons or problems that preclude my participation in this activity or event.

I acknowledge that this accident waiver and release of liability form will be used by the event holders, sponsors, and organizers of the activity or event in which I may participate, and that it will govern my actions and responsibilities at said activity or event.

In consideration of my application and permitting me to participate in this event, I hereby take action for myself, my executors, administrators, heirs, next of kin, successors, and assigns as follows:

(A) I WAIVE, RELEASE, AND DISCHARGE from any and all liability, including but not limited to liability arising from the negligence or fault of the entities or persons released, for my death, disability, personal injury, property damage, property theft, or actions of any kind that may hereafter occur to me, including my traveling to and from this event, THE FOLLOWING ENTITIES OR PERSONS: [*sponsoring organization*] and their directors, officers, employees, volunteers, representatives, and agents; the activity or event holders; activity or event sponsors; activity or event volunteers.

(B) I INDEMNIFY, HOLD HARMLESS, AND PROMISE NOT TO SUE the entities or persons mentioned in this paragraph from any and all liabilities or claims made as a result of participation in this activity or event, whether caused by the negligence of release or otherwise.

I acknowledge that [*sponsoring organization*] and their directors, officers, volunteers, representatives, and agents are NOT responsible for the errors, omissions, acts, or failures to act of any party or entity conducting a specific event or activity on behalf of [*sponsoring organization*].

I acknowledge that this activity or event may involve a test of a person's physical and mental limits and may carry with it the potential for death, serious injury, and property loss. The risks may include, but are not limited to, those caused by terrain; facilities; temperature; weather; condition of participants; equipment; vehicular traffic; actions of other people, including but not limited to participants, volunteers, spectators, coaches, event officials, event monitors, and producers of the event; and lack of hydration. These risks are not only inherent to participants, but are also present for volunteers.

*(continued)*

**Figure 3.2** This example includes the main components of a waiver, including assumption of risks. It can easily be modified for any recreational activity.

I hereby consent to receive medical treatment that may be deemed advisable in the event of injury, accident, and/or illness during this activity or event.

I CERTIFY THAT I HAVE READ THIS DOCUMENT AND I FULLY UNDERSTAND ITS CONTENT. I AM AWARE THAT THIS IS A RELEASE OF LIABILITY AND A CONTRACT AND I SIGN IT OF MY OWN FREE WILL.

| Print participant's name | Age | Parent's name (if participant is under 18 years of age) | |
|---|---|---|---|
| Participant's signature | Date | Parent's signature<br>(if participant is under 18 years of age) | Date |

I understand that at this event or related activities, I may be photographed. I agree to allow my photo, video, or film likeness to be used for any legitimate purpose by the event holders, producers, sponsors, organizers, and assigns. The accident waiver and release of liability shall be construed broadly to provide a release and waiver to the maximum extent permissible under applicable law.

| Print participant's name | Age | Parent's name (if participant is under 18 years of age) |
|---|---|---|
| Participant's signature | Date | Parent's signature<br>(if participant is under 18 years of age) |

**Figure 3.2** *(continued)*

up in court. However, when waivers are legal and written correctly, they are an excellent risk management strategy. A quick reading of a typical waiver (figure 3.2) reveals that the organization transfers to the participant any and all costs involved in the injury, damage, or loss.

**waiver**—The voluntary relinquishment or abandonment—express or implied—of a legal right or advantage.

A participant signs a waiver voluntarily or of his own free will. The waiver should be clear and easy to read and make obvious that the participant is giving up a right, and should include no form of coercion that nudges or forces the participant to sign the waiver and participate. An organization should ensure that its practices do not create a situation that would cause the courts to void the waiver. For example, a person reads the waiver and decides not to participate. He asks the organization to reimburse the activity fee he paid. If the organization will not reimburse his money and he decides to participate, is he really participating of his own free will? For this reason, a school that requires programs in physical education cannot have students sign waivers because the programs are not voluntary. An assumption of risk form or warning would work better in this case.

Because a waiver is a contract, the person signing it must be capable and must be allowed to sign it legally. One cannot contract with a minor. Parents, in most states, cannot sign away the rights of their child. When a parent signs a waiver, they agree that they will not sue for their losses or on behalf of their child. However, it does not take away the child's right to sue when he or she becomes of age (18 years of age in the United States). The court will not uphold a contract with someone with a mental disability or who signed the contract under the influence of alcohol or drugs. When a person signs a contract, he must be aware of what he is doing.

The person must also have appropriate conditions under which to sign the contract. He must have the ability to read the contract and time to read it before signing it. For example, if an organization holds a midnight run, it should either make sure there is enough lighting for participants to read the waiver or give out the waivers early so participants can bring the signed waivers with them. Organizations should have a translator available if a number of people who do not speak English will be signing contracts.

Several elements in the waiver help ensure that participants relinquish the right to sue. The title of the waiver should be in bold print and should clearly indicate that the participants are giving up the right to sue. The statement relinquishing the right to sue for negligence should also be in bold print. In some states, the form must include the word *negligence* so that participants clearly understand that they are giving up the right to sue for negligence in order to participate. The form should not include extraneous sections that are not related to the waiver. The waiver is not a place to request use of photos or ask for health information.

All contracts, whether for hiring employees or relinquishing rights, must follow the same rules. Because a waiver is a contract, it must follow all the rules of a contract. The next sections discuss those rules as they relate to waivers. Contracts can be complicated and can include many clauses. One should always consult a lawyer when entering into a contract.

## Waiver Clauses

Indemnity and hold harmless clauses are often used in waivers. An indemnity agreement means that the participant will pay all costs incurred if an injury or lawsuit occurs. For example, if a participant is hurt and an ambulance is called, the cost of the ambulance belongs to the participant and not to the provider of the service. The purpose of the hold harmless clause is to create a contractual relationship in which the participant agrees not to blame the provider of the activity or service for injury or loss. In figure 3.2, the waiver has an indemnification and hold harmless clause: "I indemnify, hold harmless, and promise not to sue the entities or persons mentioned in this paragraph from any and all liabilities or claims made as a result of participation in this activity or event, whether caused by the negligence of release or otherwise."

**indemnity clause**—A contractual provision in which one party agrees to answer for any specified or unspecified liability or harm that the other party might incur.

## Ancillary Items

The following are ancillary items that may be included in a waiver. Including these items may help avoid using multiple forms to address multiple purposes. Figure 3.2 includes two of these ancillary items: medical treatment and a photo release. It is recommended that there be a separate line for signing on each of these ancillary items after the signature field of the waiver to be signed by the participant, or if a minor, the minor's parent. However, one must ensure that a waiver does not become too cluttered with ancillary items. Most agencies include these items in the waiver so that people will assume that the items are part of the waiver and not ancillary to it. Anyone including ancillary items in a waiver should first check with a lawyer because in several cases a waiver was disallowed because of the presence of these clauses.

*Agreement to sue in the organization's jurisdiction.* This clause indicates that if a person decides to bring any legal action against the organization, she agrees to bring legal action in the jurisdiction of the home office of the organization. In communities where the organization's business makes a substantial contribution to the local economy, this clause can have a beneficial effect. A community is often less likely to find a business guilty if the business contributes substantially to the local economy. Conversely, if an organization is not held in high esteem in the community, its reputation can work against it.

*Photo agreement.* In a photo agreement, the participant gives the organization permission to use his photo for promotional purposes. A parent must sign this agreement if the participant is younger than 18 years of age. Because this agreement is different than the actual waiver, an organization can include it as a check item or an item that the participant initials. If the photo agreement is included as an item in the waiver, most people will simply sign the waiver. If a participant does not wish to permit the organization to use his photo, the organization can cross out the clause and initial it.

*Medical consent.* Medical consent allows the organization to provide treatment or transport to a medical facility if the participant is hurt during the event. If a participant becomes unconscious, the organization may take her to the hospital because she has granted the organization permission to act on her behalf (or, if the participant is a minor, to act on behalf of her parents). The organization must notify the participant's family of the incident in a timely manner. A statement of medical consent should define who is responsible for any medical bills incurred. Failure to indicate who is responsible for these costs can lead to a lawsuit. Some courts have decided that the person who makes the medical decision is financially responsible for incurred costs unless defined otherwise. A waiver should include a separate place for a signature for this clause in case the person signing wants to agree to one clause and not others.

## Insurance

Insurance transfers the costs of an injury, damage, or loss to a third party: the insurance company (Dorfman, 2008). Insurance is a pool that combines all of the potential losses and then transfers the cost of the predicted losses to those exposed. An insurance company promises to pay for the agreed-on losses in exchange for the cost of the policy, or the premium, which reflects the potential for that loss. The premiums collected are usually more than the predicted losses. This enables the insurance company to pay claims, pay operation costs, develop a pool against unexpected losses, and earn money on its investments. Insurance companies themselves have insurance against unexpected losses. This practice is known as *reinsurance.*

In the insurance industry, loss is an undesirable or unplanned reduction of economic value. The term *economic value* suggests that one can place monetary value on injury, damage, or loss. *Direct losses* are losses that result from the cause of the loss, called the peril. If a recreation center burns to the ground, the fire is the peril that results in the direct loss of the center. In contrast, *indirect losses* are secondary impacts. After the fire, the recreation agency may need to rent a facility in order to conduct its programs. The need to rent the facility represents an expense and is a secondary impact of the fire. Another indirect loss is the money lost in memberships or money that the agency would have received if it had a facility. Insurance can cover both direct and indirect losses.

A *hazard* is a condition that can lead to a peril. Building in a flood plain is a hazard that can result in a flood (peril) that creates loss. The chance of loss is the probability that the peril will happen. Building in a 100-year flood plain suggests that the probability of flooding loss is low. Generally, two types of insurance coverage exist: specified peril and open peril. *Specified-peril* policies list specific items that are covered by the policy. An *open-peril* policy covers all items except those that are specifically excluded.

In order for insurance to cover a loss, proximate cause must exist between the cause of the loss and the insured peril. For example, it makes a difference whether the recreation center is destroyed by a fire (a covered peril) or by a flood (an excluded peril). This distinction can be important in determining coverage when concurrent causes exist. If a flood (an excluded peril) causes a circuit breaker box to short, which causes a fire (an included peril), is the loss of the recreation center covered or not covered by insurance? Depending on circumstances, it may be necessary for a court of law to determine the coverage of the loss.

These issues raise questions to consider when dealing with insurance providers. Kaiser (1986, p. 235) suggests some specific questions to ask when analyzing an insurance policy.

1. What events are covered?
2. What property or activities are covered?
3. What persons are covered?
4. What losses are covered?

5. What locations are covered?
6. What time period is covered?
7. What special conditions are excluded?
8. What amount of loss will the insurer pay?
9. What steps must the insured take after a loss?
10. What is the deductible (the amount the policy holder pays before the insurance company pays on the loss)? The higher the deductible, the lower the premium. For example, the owner of a fitness center may have a $100,000 fire insurance policy with a $5,000 deductible. That means that if the owner has a fire loss, she pays the first $5,000 and the insurance company pays the rest, up to $100,000. Policy holders must make sure that they have enough coverage to get back to where they started after the loss. If the owner of the fitness center has a $10,000,000 building, a $100,000 insurance policy would not help her much.

An organization can obtain liability insurance to protect itself in case it is found negligent in a lawsuit. If a lawsuit against an organization with liability insurance goes to court and the jury finds in favor of the plaintiff, the insurance company pays the cost of the award up to the limits of the policy. Because the insurance company is involved in the process as a third party, it can agree to pay a settlement before the case goes to court and before a jury makes a decision.

The insurance company is the silent third party and is not normally involved in any way in the court proceedings. However, the insurance company often decides whether the case will go to court. It bases its decision on how likely the agency is to win, how much it will cost in defense charges, public relations, and how much the payout would cost without going to court. Whereas the plaintiff pays the lawyer only if she wins, the defendant pays the lawyer regardless. If the costs of the lawyers may be higher than the settlement, the insurance company has a cost incentive to settle out of court. Public relations might be an issue. Because what occurs in court is often in the news, it may be better to settle out of court and keep it quiet. In the McDonald's scalding-coffee incident, McDonald's lost but in the end won on appeal. However, everyone remembers that McDonald's lost. It may have been better to settle out of court and pay the injury cost. The insurance company looks at the costs and benefits of taking a case to court and makes a decision after talking to the plaintiff's lawyers. Ninety-eight percent of cases are settled out of court. If either side decides it will not settle and other alternative dispute resolutions such as arbitration do not work, the case is taken to court.

Two types of damages can be awarded: compensatory and punitive. *Compensatory damages* award the plaintiff for his actual and future losses. For example, if an adolescent drowns in municipal swimming pool and the municipality is found negligent, compensation can include the potential earnings of the adolescent over his lifetime. This can amount to several million dollars of lost potential earnings. *Punitive damages* award the plaintiff as a means to punish the defendant for the defendant's gross negligence or outrageous behavior. Insurance can cover both of these losses. However, 25 states do not allow for coverage of punitive damages and in most states liability insurance does not cover more than ordinary negligence.

The case against Winding River Canoe Rentals (see chapter 1) was settled out of court. Therefore, Janice Cody was not proven negligent by a jury. One can infer from the portion of her deposition in figure 1.8 what the jury might have concluded regarding her negligence had the case gone to trial. However, the outcome of a jury decision is an uncertainty. It was to the insurance company's advantage to pay the settlement amount because doing so cut the company's potential losses, particularly if punitive damages would have been awarded, and it saved on the court costs.

In this case, settlement was a three-way win. The plaintiff received compensation, although perhaps less than if the case went to trial and the plaintiff won. However, a settlement in hand is better than the possibility of receiving nothing if the jury were to decide that Winding

River Canoe Rentals was not negligent. Janice Cody wins because she is not proven negligent and her losses are covered by her insurance. She also does not receive the bad public relations she would receive if found negligent. The insurance company wins because it has a known settlement payment and the case is finished and off the table. The company also saves on defense and court costs.

## Contracting Services

An individual or organization that contracts services seeks to transfer the duty and the cost of injury, damage, or loss to another agency by contracting with that agency to provide an activity, program, or facility. Contracting the service saves the individual or organization the logistics of providing the service, including the liability. Examples of services that might be contracted include lodging or food facilities at a park, camps for a city park and recreation department, lawn mowing for a regional park, or swim lessons or exercise classes at a YMCA. Sometimes the service is contracted because the private sector can do it at a lower cost, because it is too risky, or because it is easier for someone who has the equipment or knowledge to do it.

Returning to the Janice Cody case in chapter 1, Shelby Township contracted the canoe rental business on the Clinton River near Detroit to Winding River Canoe Rentals (see figure 1.8). In doing so, Shelby Township successfully transferred all aspects of the business, including insurance and the cost of the loss in the Melanie Carlson case. Although Shelby Township did not incur any financial loss, there was still an issue of contracting the service to provide an enjoyable and safe experience for participants. The contracting agency should have some ability to determine the competency and ability—in this case Winding Rivers—to deliver the service. For example, a homeowner hires a contractor to repair a leaky roof. Even though the homeowner isn't performing the repair, the homeowner still needs to be able to determine that the repair was performed correctly. This requires some knowledge and ability on the part of the homeowner, the contractor. Although the court determined that Shelby Township didn't have a legal duty in this case, Shelby Township still has a professional responsibility to make sure that Winding River Canoe Rentals is providing a safe experience.

Kaiser (1986, p. 245) notes that leasing of facilities and contracting services has several advantages for the organization doing the leasing, or the lessor. Normally, the lessor can successfully transfer its liability to the lessee. Shelby Township successfully transferred liability to Winding Rivers Canoe Rentals. However, the lessor is responsible for correcting any hazardous conditions before lease. The lessor must also define the areas for which the lessee is responsible. For example, in an arena, the lessor may be responsible for the hallways and common areas.

Leasing and contracting of facilities and services are not without problems. It may be difficult for a recreation programmer to contract the desired experience. Also, when the contractor becomes the point of contact with the public, the public may think the experience it provides is offered by a major company. For example if a resort offers horseback riding through a contractor, the patrons may not realize it is not the resort offering the service. If the contractor does not do a good job, it reflects poorly on the resort. The Winding River Canoe Rentals example provides a glimpse of this problem. For people canoeing the Clinton River, Winding River Canoe Rentals, not Shelby Township, was the face of the experience because the people dealt with Winding River. It is not an issue if the public knows that Winding River Canoe Rental is separate from Shelby Township. If they do not see it as separate, then the reputation of one reflects on the other.

To be awarded a contract, a contractor must follow a procurement process, particularly if the agency providing the contracting possibility is a governmental agency. The typical procurement process includes five stages (see table 3.1): planning and preparation, notification and prequalification, tendering, evaluation, and contract award. Perhaps the most important and most easily overlooked phase is the planning and preparation stage. Research at this phase pays dividends later in the process.

**Table 3.1** Steps in a Typical Local Authority Procurement Process for Services or Consultancy

| Local authority | Contractor or service provider |
|---|---|
| **Planning and preparation** | |
| Consultation and market testing to insure that procurement strategy and contracting practices are conductive to securing an effective competitive response | Market analyses and business strategy<br>Focus on target sectors |
| Project definition and design including initial drafting of bid specification or terms of reference | Market intelligence for contract opportunities |
| Decision to adopt the restricted procedure | Client and project research |
| Determination of contract award criteria, weightings and quality: price ratio | Contacts with client managers |
| Appointment of assessment and selection panel | |
| Review of supplier database, registration and prequalification information | |
| **Notification and prequalification** | |
| Initial advertisement and contract notice, inviting expressions of interest | Response to contract notice |
| First stage of selection: assessment panel filters received expressions of interest and, if necessary, reduces list to a manageable total for second stage of selection | Preparation and submission of expression of interest |
| Second stage of selection: a more detailed assessment of prospective bidders, possibly including interviews and visits | |
| Definition of shortlist—say, four to six selected tenderers | |
| **Tendering** | |
| Finalization of work specifications | |
| Issue of proposal invitations and accompanying documentation | Acknowledgement of invitation<br>Decision to bid<br>Confirmation of intention to submit a proposal |
| Decisions on evaluation approach | Analysis of work specification<br>Preparation of proposal |
| Arrangements for dealing with clarification requests | Request for clarification |
| Formal site visits or briefings, if appropriate | Briefing or meeting with client, if appropriate |
| Receipt of proposal | Submission of proposal |
| **Evaluation** | |
| Formal tender opening and checks for compliance | |
| Proposal evaluation—quality and price | |
| Arrangements for presentations by lead contractors | Preparation of presentation |
| Preparation of format and key questions for presentations | Delivery of presentations |
| Further clarification of contract issues, if appropriate, through negotiation | Further clarification of contract issues, if appropriate, through negotiation |
| Selection of the most economical advantageous tender | |
| **Contract award** | |
| Notification to successful bidder, including any conditions to be discussed at a further contract negotiation stage | |
| Notification to unsuccessful bidders, including placing a reserve or hold on the bidder ranked second in case contract negotiations with the first-ranked bidder fail | |

Reprinted, by permission, from H. Lewis, 2007, *Bids, tenders and proposals: Winning business through best practice,* 2nd ed. (Philadelphia: Kogan Press), 24.

As the saying goes, "If you don't know where you want to go, you won't know when you get there." Good preplanning and preparation helps determine where one is going and how to get there.

During the planning and preparation process, an agency needs to determine exactly what it wants the contractor to provide. Everything that follows, including the final experience provided, is predicated on the specifications that an agency develops in this phase of the procurement process.

What should the agency include in the request for proposal (RFP)? One approach is for the agency to adapt the specifications of the RFP to those who will submit proposals and eventually provide the service. Using this approach, the agency would incorporate specifications that requesters for a proposal and providers of the service agree should be included and avoid specifications that would deter providers from responding to the RFP. If the request for proposal does not specify the service, they may get a highball bid, in which the bidder gives a bid on the RFP that makes it worth his while to do the service. A third approach is for the agency to include specifications that require the bidder to stretch or that the bidder may not like but that do not make the RFP unacceptable to those who will eventually submit proposals. The agency needs to work with potential vendors to provide specifications that are acceptable to both parties and with their attorneys.

Generally, the specifications need to be broad enough so that anyone in the industry can meet them. Agencies must maintain ethics and be careful not to create a sweetheart deal, in which an agency's RFP favors one vendor only. For example, if the owner of a swimming pool wants to contract lifeguarding to an outside agency but knows little about lifeguarding services, how does the owner know what to include in the RFP? Who knows what to provide better than the potential provider of the service? Providers often have bidding specifications and sample contracts where they need to only insert the name of organization. This practice is convenient and provides both parties with an acceptable delineation of responsibilities. In many service areas that are well defined, this is done all the time. However, an agency must always be careful when using the contract or bidding specifications of a potential service provider because providers tend to write specifications that favor what they provide. How an agency defines the specifications may result in the agency unintentionally favoring one group over another or excluding some vendors that may give a more favorable bid.

The agency should consider some crucial items when creating a RFP. How long should the contract last? If the contractor will have to make significant investments to complete the project, such as building a hotel, the lease needs to be longer in order to provide a reasonable return on investment for the firm building and

When contracting lifeguarding to an outside agency, the owner of the swimming pool should be careful that the RFP doesn't favor the bidding agency.

operating the hotel. No one will build a hotel if it has only five years to pay for itself. On the other hand, if a contract is too long, the agency may be making a commitment that will be difficult to alter if its mission or policies change. The agency must also determine who is liable for what. For example, the agency should be listed as a third party insured to protect itself from negligence in case of a lawsuit, in which the plaintiff will name everyone connected with the situation. The agency should also put standards of doing business in the RFP, including the quality of service, hours of operation, quality of goods sold, and so on. Even if the owners of the facility are not doing the operations, they have their name on it and they need to make sure their reputation is protected.

Finally, when an organization does research and develops the specifications in the RFP, it should consider how it will evaluate the specifications near the end of the procurement process. Again, as the saying goes, "If you don't know where you want to go, you won't know when you get there." Evaluating the specifications when developing them will help the agency know when it "gets there."

## REDUCTION STRATEGIES

In contrast with transfer strategies, reduction strategies seek to reduce the likelihood of injury, damage, or loss. These are the strategies of accident prevention, safety management, and risk management plans. Traditionally, reduction strategies include reduction and avoidance. They focus on how the recreation professional does the activity and program. In contrast, the strategies discussed in this chapter seek to transfer the cost of a loss to someone else or seek legal doctrines that can prevent the injured party from suing.

Philosophically, most recreation and parks professionals eventually come to the conclusion that the best defense against negligence is to reduce or avoid the likelihood of the incident or accident from occurring in the first place. For a recreation and park professional in the business of doing activities and programs, reduction becomes the logical strategy. Usually, reduction means doing the activity or program more safely. This is the focus of the remainder of this text.

## SUMMARY

Risk reduction strategies, as discussed in chapters 1 and 2, are the most effective strategies because they reduce the likelihood that an accident or incident will occur in the first place. However, not all risk reduction methods will eliminate all accidents all of the time. For this reason, in order to defend against possible negligence, individuals and organizations must be familiar with legal doctrines (assumption of risk, immunity statutes, and comparative negligence) that limit liability and with transfer strategies (waivers, insurance, and contracting programs to others) that help protect organizations from being found negligent or that limit their liability.

Because legal strategies (assumption of risk, immunity statutes, or comparative negligence) are potentially limited in usefulness and impact in light of state laws, recreation and park professionals should not rely on them alone to prevent negligence and lawsuits. Individuals and organizations should develop a mix of risk reduction and avoidance strategies, legal strategies, and risk transfer strategies to defend against negligence. Lastly, for recreation and park professionals in the business of providing recreation and park services, reducing the likelihood of the incident or accident becomes the logical strategy and defense against negligence, which is the focus of the following sections in this book.

## EXERCISES

### Exercise 1: Negligence

The purpose of this exercise is to help determine the statutes that affect you in your state. Using the Internet or a local lawyer, explore the negligence statutes in your state. Do the statutes mentioned in the chapter apply in your state? If yes, discuss what is included in them such as negligence and its statute of limitations. Do any other restrictions exist?

### Exercise 2: Searching for the Bulletproof Waiver

Search the Internet for activity waivers, or ask people in your industry for a copy of their activity waivers.

1. Collect at least five waivers.
2. Rank the waivers in terms of your perception of their effectiveness.
3. Examine each waiver for the following elements.
   - Does it contain an assumption of risk clause?
   - Does it include hold harmless and indemnity clauses?
   - Does it include a statement in which the participant waives his rights?
   - Has the language been expanded to include everyone who might be involved on both sides?
   - Has the language been expanded to include all ancillary activities?
   - Is the signature placed at the end of the waiver and does it not pertain to clauses that are not part of the waiver?
   - Is the organization responsible for any risks? If yes, which risks?
   - Is the participant responsible for any risks? If yes, which risks?
4. In your estimation, which waiver is the most bulletproof? Why?
5. In your estimation, which waiver is the least bulletproof? Why?
6. Which waiver would you most likely use? Why?

# PART II

# The Accident Process and Safety Management

The second leg in the integrated risk management model focuses on reducing injury, damage, or loss (figure II.1). The thesis of this section is fairly straightforward: If one can prevent an accident from occurring, no injury, damage, or loss occurs and there are no grounds for a lawsuit. Part II provides specific models and approaches that are directly applicable to leadership and programming roles in the recreation and park profession as well as the overall organization. These tools can reduce the likelihood of an accident occurring.

Although accident causation and safety management are not new schools of thought, they are relatively new areas in the recreation and park field. When integrated into the mainstream, they can make a valuable contribution to recreation leadership and programming. Part II explains these new concepts—many of which build on each other—and how they can reduce risk within the recreation and park field.

Chapter 4 covers the history of accident prevention and summarizes nearly 100 years of accident-prevention thought. Emphasis is on the evolution of Heinrich's domino theory of causation. Chapter 5 reviews the analytical tree models surrounding the management oversight and risk tree, which was developed in 1973 to address the needs of the nuclear industry. Highly complex, it spawned a series of concepts—the accident sequence, barrier analysis, and fault tree analysis—that directly apply to the recreation and park profession. These models also contribute to modifying the attitudes of leaders in the recreation and park profession and their approach to their leadership and programming roles.

The model in figure II.1 lists four components involved in accident causation. As part of the MORT (management oversight and risk tree) and barrier analysis, these four components have been identified as necessary (causal) for the accident process. The first factor, potential harmful energy transfer (SB1), results from the basic causes, underlying factors, or conditions that facilitate the incident. Essentially, potential harmful energy transfers are the normal byproduct of performing an activity or program. Next, the targets (SB2) are the vulnerable people or objects being protected from the potential energy transfer due to a less than adequate (LTA) barrier or control. The barriers and controls (SB3) include the hard (physical) and soft (administrative) barriers designed to reduce or eliminate potential unwanted energy transfers from occurring. Last, there may be more than one contributing energy or target interaction that results in the accident. SB4 merely accounts for this possibility. These factors are discussed in more depth in chapter 5.

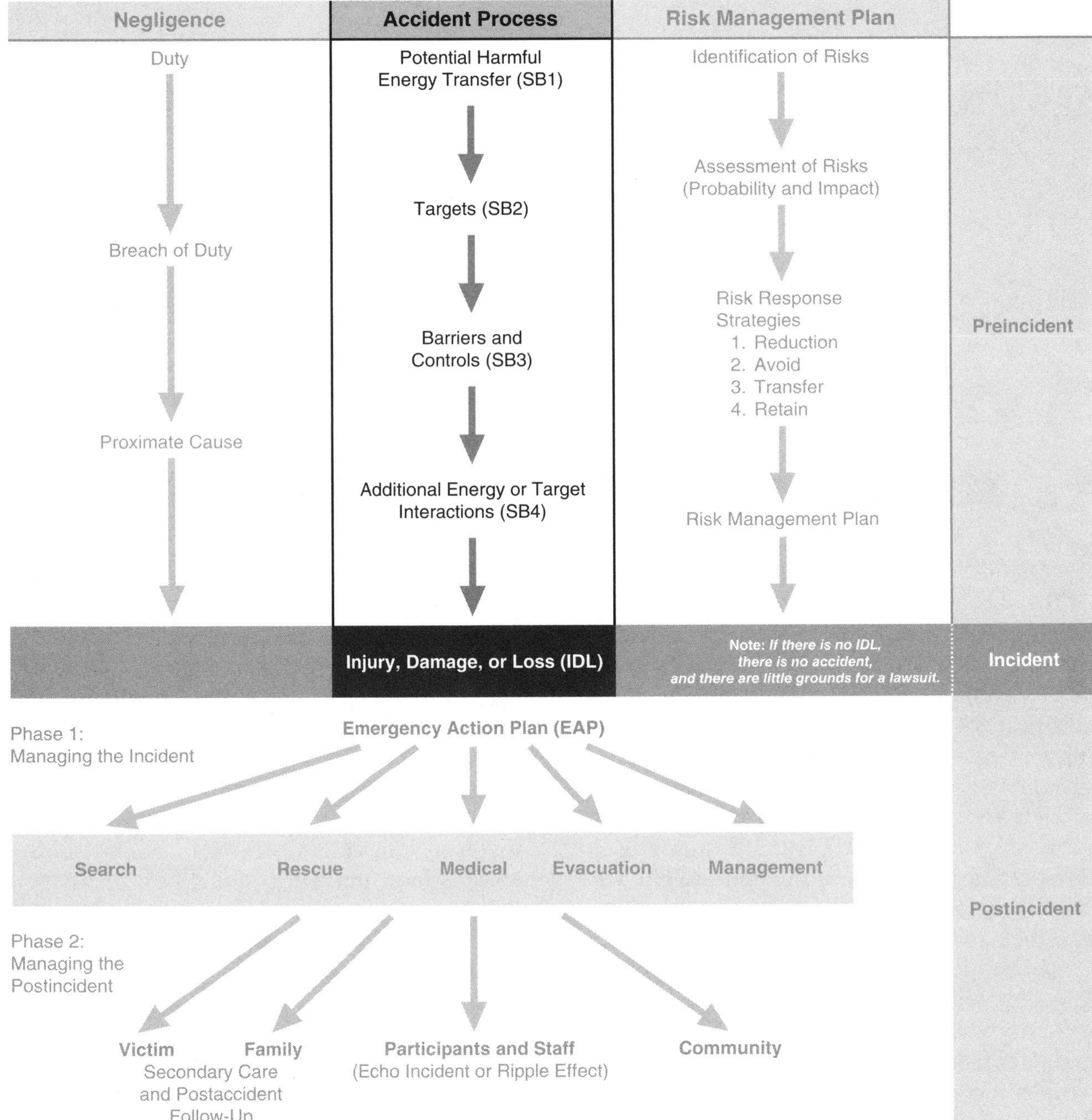


**Figure II.1** The accident process and safety management as part of the risk management model.

Chapter 6 covers the models of the outdoor adventure area, which has been continuously involved in addressing the accident process. In contrast with the mainstream models in chapters 4 and 5 that are organization focused, the models in the outdoor area tend to be leader focused. This gives these models considerable utility because they involve what a leader or programmer can do to reduce incidents and accidents. In addition, these models can easily benefit from the infusion of the concepts discussed in chapters 4 and 5 and can be significantly upgraded. For example, the domino model, which incorporates energy transfer and barrier analysis, is a hands-on model that a leader or programmer can use to actively reduce the likelihood of accidents.

Chapter 7 addresses the issue of programming for risk. In the safety-management field risks are an anathema. Every effort is made to reduce or eliminate all risks. In contrast, in the recreation and park field, and particularly in the outdoor adventure area, risks are viewed as an important part of the recreational experience. A potential conflict exists between the recreation and park field and everyone else. Chapter 7 presents an alternative view in which the outdoor field considers risks to be an integral part of outdoor activities. This view is presented after the outdoor models because, historically, the two have been interrelated programmatically.

Chapter 4

# Accident Causation and Safety Management

This chapter provides a background of the safety management field and discusses 90 years of principles and concepts relating to accident theories discussed in this and the next chapter. Although all models have weaknesses or methodological concerns, they are powerful tools that will help a person focus on preventing accidents before they happen and will change how a person approaches programs in the future. Also, this chapter introduces highly reliable organizations (HRO), which is an innovative approach where safety systems are developed in reaction to an environment where there are numerous hazards present and the possibility of accidents is commonplace. These models and innovations are presented in the context of the recreation and park field.

## HISTORICAL OVERVIEW OF SAFETY MANAGEMENT

The field of safety management has a long history, and the development of accident models is not new. Heinrich et al. (1980) explain the domino theory of accident causation, which has been around since the mid-1920s. He developed a series of theorems, which are defined and explained in the following chapter and illustrated by the "domino sequence." These theorems show the following: industrial injuries result only from accidents, accidents are caused directly only by unsafe acts of people or exposure to unsafe mechanical conditions, unsafe actions and conditions are caused only by faults of persons, and faults of people are created by environment or acquired by inheritance.

As much as things change, they also stay the same. For nearly 100 years, the underlying principles of the accident process have been known. One principle is the concept of causation. Accidents cause injury, damage, or loss. By understanding the accident process and breaking the accident chain by incorporating appropriate management practices, people can prevent accidents and thereby prevent injury, damage, or loss. Another principle is that both *unsafe acts* (i.e., actions and decisions) and *unsafe conditions* (i.e., environment and equipment) are the result of the actions of people. Unsafe conditions are the result of poor maintenance or design or poor or incorrect decisions regarding environmental conditions. An example of poor maintenance is insufficient mulch beneath playground equipment, and an example of poor design is not maintaining a proper fall zone. An example of poor decisions regarding environmental conditions is a mountaineering group traversing across a ravine that is avalanche prone and subsequently getting caught in an avalanche.

Heinrich et al. (1980, p. 9) suggest a five-step approach to accident prevention (see figure 4.1). This model is a forerunner to the traditional research model of collecting data, analyzing it, and making recommendations based on it. The model is depicted as a ladder built on a base of individual and organizational philosophy regarding accident prevention. The first rung on the ladder is the organization, including the safety director or safety engineer, who collects data through surveys, inspections, observations, and incident investigations (the second rung). In the third, fourth, and fifth rungs of the ladder, the safety director or engineer analyzes the data, selects remedies, and applies remedies, respectively. Figure 4.1 emphasizes the importance of the safety engineer in the organization.

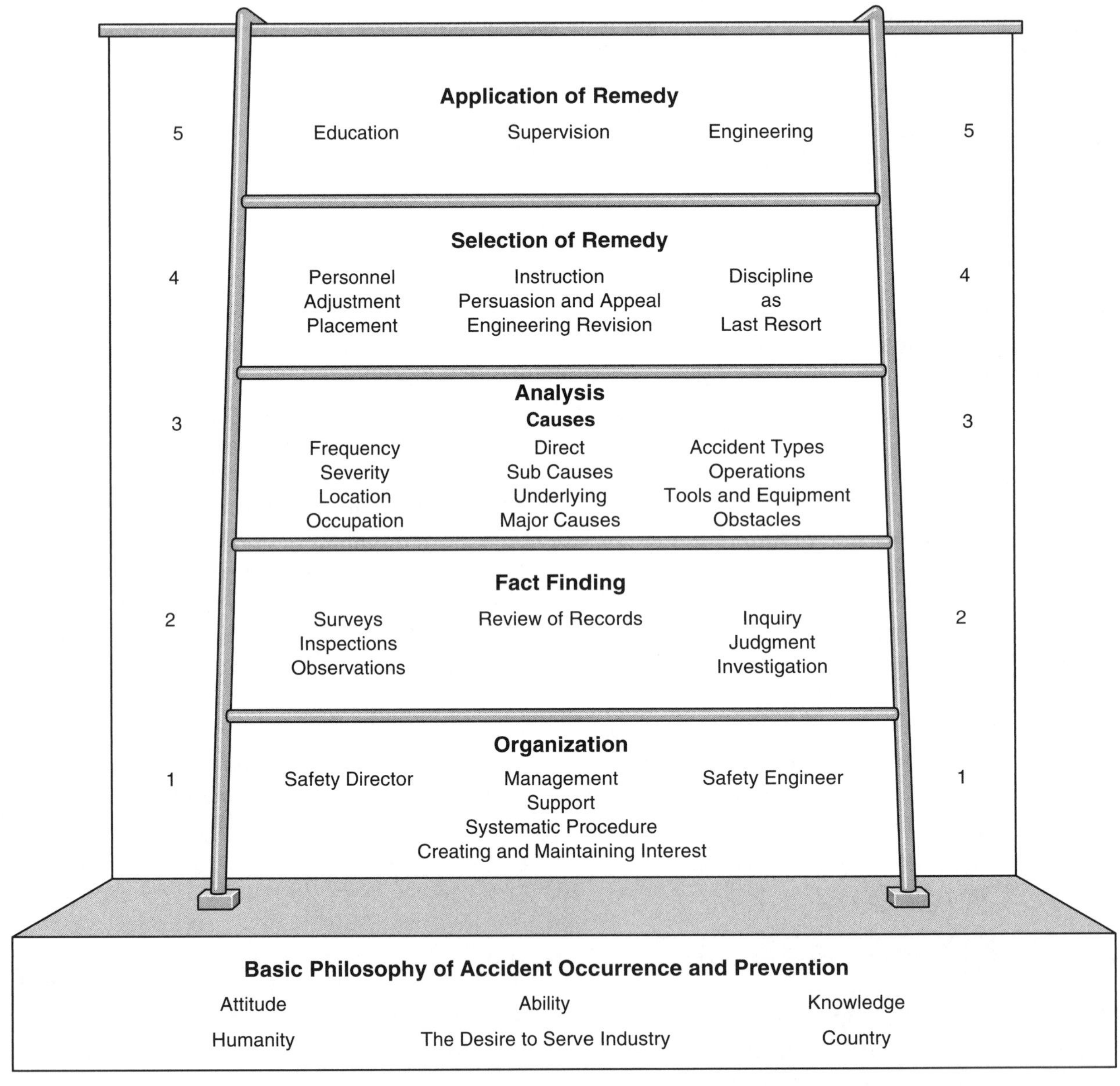


**Figure 4.1** Heinrich's ladder depicts the research process as built on a philosophical foundation. Later models retained most of the components but reorganized them into different configurations.

Reprinted, by permission, from H.W. Heinrich, D. Petersen, N.R. Roos, 1980, *Industrial accident prevention: A safety management approach* (New York: McGraw-Hill Companies), 9.

Safety management, which includes the knowledge and skills that the safety engineer brings to the work environment, is built on a philosophy of accident prevention. The safety engineer conducts surveys, analyzes systems, and determines areas of study. He collects data, analyzes it, recommends remedies, and implements and monitors the remedy. Over time, Heinrich's ladder transformed into a model that lists the factors in more circular patterns in which the monitoring phase feeds back into the data-collection phase.

## Accident Ratio Study

In terms of preventing accidents, the accident ratio study of Bird and Germain (1985) justified the need for and assisted in the creation of safety management programs in industrial settings. The accident ratio principle was stated as one of several axioms by Heinrich. Bird and Germain conducted a study that analyzed 1,753,498 accidents reported from 297 companies from 21 industrial groups (Bird and Germain, 1985, p. 20; Oakley, 2003, p. 16). This study represents more than 3 billion work hours and more than 1,750,000 employees. The accident pyramid (figure 4.2) is derived from their study. They found that for every serious or major injury, there were 10 minor injuries, 30 property-damage accidents, and 600 near misses or close calls in which no visible injury, damage, or loss occurred.

Bird and Germain (1985, p. 21) suggest that it is important to study more than just the major incidents that result in serious injury, damage, or loss. Major incidents are comparatively rare. Although this is a good thing, it means that data are not always available for analysis. Also, one must study the underlying factors that lead to the loss or mishap. Organizations need to systematically study and investigate the work environment to effect accident prevention. The accident ratio study helped organizations justify employing safety managers.

The study also suggested that incidents that result in no visible injury or damage are precursors to serious or major injuries. Organizations can prevent accidents that result in serious or major injuries by studying and addressing minor incidents. This principle is an underlying theme in most of the accident models discussed in this chapter.

## Accident Sequence

The domino model (figure 4.3) states that injury or loss starts with an incident or accident that is created by a hazard that was caused by human error that was caused by environment,

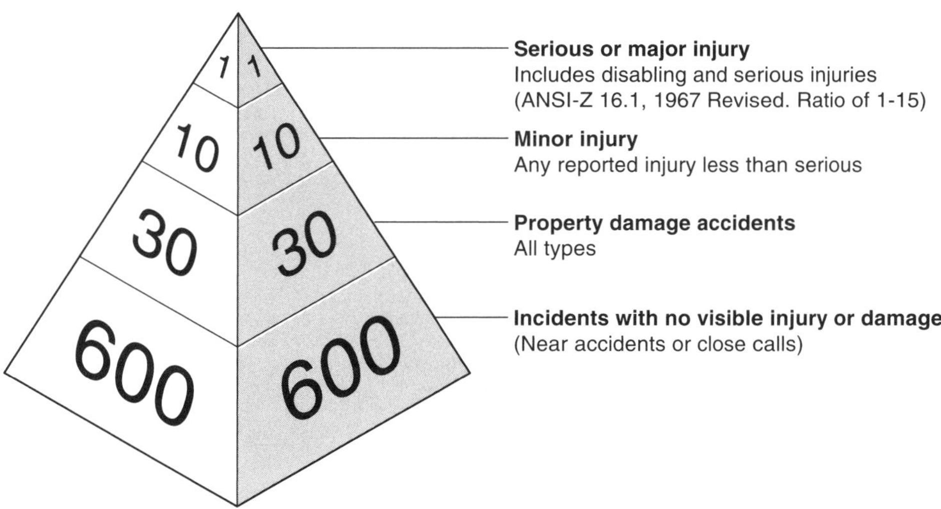


**Figure 4.2** The accident ratio study resulted in a pyramid model of accidents.

Reprinted, by permission, from F.E. Bird and G.L. Germain, 1996, *Practical loss control leadership, revised edition* (Hovik, Oslo, Norway: Det Norske Veritas).

education, or upbringing. Metaphorically, as one domino begins to fall, it hits the next domino, which hits the next one, which eventually ends in the incident and the injury. Heinrich states that risk management should focus not on the injury or incident but rather on the domino that preceded it. That accident or incident was most likely caused by human error.

## Incident or Accident: Contact

The incident or accident is defined as the event that precedes the loss. Usually, some type of contact occurs that reflects an exchange of energy. If a woman slips on a banana peel, the slip and fall (the event) precedes breaking her arm (the loss) as she hits the sidewalk (the incident). The incident or accident is an energy transfer due to the kinetic energy of the fall. The addition of energy transfer in the 1990s is an evolutionary refinement of Heinrich's earlier domino model. Energy transfer, an important concept, is discussed in more depth in chapter 5.

## Immediate Causes: Standards

Immediate causes directly precede the incident. These are the factors that almost everyone addresses in safety management practices. They are frequently categorized as unsafe acts and unsafe conditions. As discussed previously, unsafe acts involve people and the decisions that they make, and unsafe conditions involve the circumstances or environmental conditions under which the incident occurs. In the banana peel example, dropping the banana peel on the pavement is the immediate cause.

Bird and Germain (1985, p. 26) note that modern safety professionals think a little bit more broadly and often use the terms *substandard practices* and *substandard conditions*. These terms imply that a standard exists that can be measured and analyzed and that deviation from the standard can be determined. These terms also tend to mitigate the stigma associated with doing something wrong, but still imply that someone indeed did something wrong. The terms relate to negligence and the concepts of industry standards and common practices. In the banana peel example, what actions and precautions should an organization take to prevent someone from slipping? Are adequate trash cans placed throughout the facility, or is an appropriate number of custodians available to provide a quick response if banana peels are found on the floor? What would a reasonable and prudent professional in a given activity and field do to remove banana peels? Bird and Germain (1985) list typical substandard practices and substandard conditions.

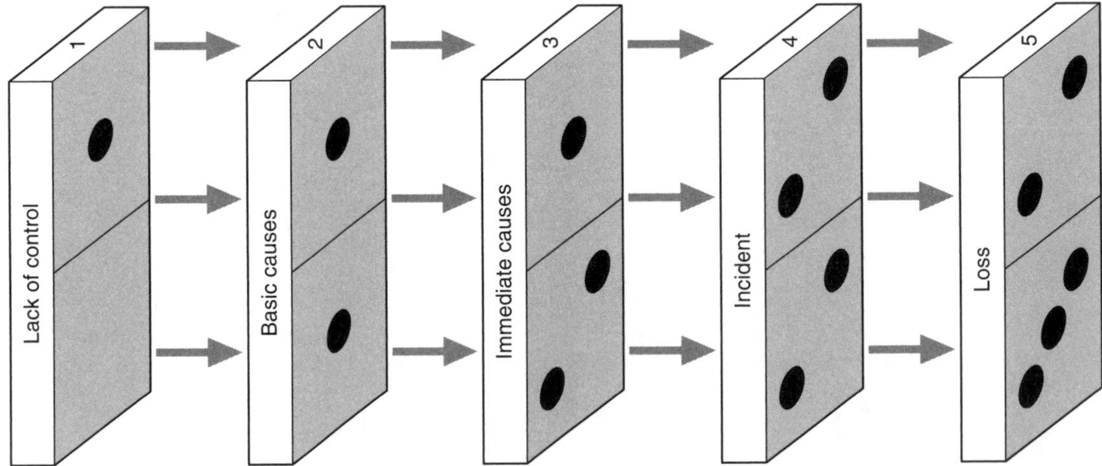


**Figure 4.3** The original domino model developed by Heinrich and refined by Bird and Germain (1985). The incident or accident resulting in a loss is the result of the immediate causes (i.e., violation of standards), basic causes (i.e., origins of the incident), and the lack of control resulting from the organizational culture.

Reprinted, by permission, from F.E. Bird and. G.L Germain, 1985, *Practical loss control leadership* (Loganville, GA: Institute Publishing), 34.

**Substandard Practices**

1. Operating equipment without authority
2. Failure to warn
3. Failure to secure
4. Operating at improper speed
5. Making safety devices inoperable
6. Removing safety devices
7. Using defective equipment
8. Using equipment improperly
9. Failing to use personal protective equipment properly
10. Improper loading
11. Improper placement
12. Improper lifting
13. Improper position for task
14. Servicing equipment in operation
15. Horseplay
16. Under the influence of alcohol or drugs [the employee]

**Substandard Conditions**

1. Inadequate guards or barriers
2. Inadequate or improper protective equipment
3. Defective tools, equipment, or materials
4. Congestion or restricted action
5. Inadequate warning system
6. Fire and explosion hazards
7. Poor housekeeping or disorderly workplace
8. Hazardous environmental conditions (gases, dust, smoke, fumes, vapors)
9. Exposure to noise
10. Exposure to radiation
11. Exposure to high or low temperatures
12. Inadequate or excessive illumination
13. Inadequate ventilation

Maintaining proper pool conditions is one of the factors that a manager of a pool facility must address to avoid unsafe conditions.

## Basic Cause: Origins

Although the immediate causes are most directly related to the incident, they are the result of the basic cause, or origin. According to Bird and Germain (1985), basic causes are the real causes of an incident, or the disease behind the symptoms. Basic causes help explain why people in an organization perform at substandard practices or allow for substandard conditions. Basic causes are influenced by the basic management practices covered in the next section, and they directly influence the immediate causes that precede the incident. By addressing and fixing the basic causes, the immediate causes will take care of themselves. Bird and Germain (1985, p. 28) divide basic causes into two categories: personal factors and job factors (table 4.1). Although the classification is somewhat arbitrary, personal factors tend to focus on the psychology, physiology, knowledge and skills, and motivation of the employee, while job factors tend to focus on the environment that influences the individual employee such as leadership and supervision, tools and equipment provided, and work standards. Obviously, the two classifications interact. For example, work standards can influence employee motivation or facilitate stress.

## Lack of Control

A prominent French industrialist, Henry Fayol, advanced his five pillars of administration—planning, organizing, command, coordination, and control—which gained prominence in organizational management. In discussing lack of control, Bird and Germain (1985) build upon this management concept. The first component is *planning,* or examining the future and drawing up a plan of action. Second is *organizing,* where management builds structure in terms of material and human resources to carry out the plan. Third is *command,* which is to instill

**Table 4.1** Basic Causes of Loss

| **Personal factors** | |
|---|---|
| Inadequate physical or physiological capability<br>• Inappropriate height, weight, size, strength, reach, and so on<br>• Restricted range of body movement<br>• Limited ability to sustain body positions<br>• Substance sensitivities or allergies<br>• Sensitivities to sensory extremes (e.g., temperature, sound)<br>• Vision deficiency<br>• Hearing deficiency<br>• Other sensory deficiency (e.g., touch, taste, smell, balance)<br>• Respiratory incapacity<br>• Other permanent physical disabilities<br>• Temporary disabilities | Mental or psychological stress<br>• Emotional overload<br>• Fatigue due to mental task load or speed<br>• Extreme judgment decision demands<br>• Routine monotony or demand for uneventful vigilance<br>• Extreme concentration perception demands<br>• "Meaningless" or "degrading" activities<br>• Confusing directions<br>• Conflicting demands<br>• Preoccupation with problems<br>• Frustration<br>• Mental illness |
| Inadequate mental or psychological capability<br>• Fears and phobias<br>• Emotional disturbance<br>• Mental illness<br>• Intelligence level<br>• Inability to comprehend<br>• Poor judgment<br>• Poor coordination<br>• Slow reaction time<br>• Low mechanical aptitude<br>• Low learning aptitude<br>• Memory failure | Lack of knowledge<br>• Lack of experience<br>• Inadequate orientation<br>• Inadequate initial training<br>• Inadequate update training<br>• Misunderstood directions<br><br>Lack of skill<br>• Inadequate initial instruction<br>• Inadequate practice<br>• Infrequent performance<br>• Lack of coaching |

**Personal factors** *(continued)*

Physical or physiological stress

- Injury or illness
- Fatigue due to task load or duration
- Fatigue due to lack of rest
- Fatigue due to sensory overload
- Exposure to health hazards
- Exposure to temperature extremes
- Oxygen deficiency
- Atmospheric pressure variation
- Constrained movement
- Blood sugar insufficiency
- Drugs

Improper motivation

- Improper performance is rewarding
- Proper performance is punishing
- Lack of incentives
- Excessive frustration
- Inappropriate aggression
- Improper attempt to save time or effort
- Improper attempt to avoid discomfort
- Improper attempt to gain attention
- Inappropriate peer pressure
- Improper supervisory example
- Inadequate performance feedback
- Inadequate reinforcement of proper behavior
- Improper production incentives

**Job factors**

Inadequate leadership and supervision

- Unclear or conflicting reporting relationships
- Unclear or conflicting assignment of responsibility
- Improper or insufficient delegation
- Giving inadequate policy, procedure, practices, or guidelines
- Giving conflicting objectives, goals, or standards
- Inadequate work planning or programming
- Inadequate instructions, orientation, and training
- Providing inadequate reference documents, directives, and guidance publications
- Inadequate identification and evaluation of loss exposures
- Lack of supervisory or management knowledge
- Inadequate matching of individual qualifications and job or task requirements
- Inadequate performance measurement and evaluation
- Inadequate or incorrect performance feedback

Inadequate tools and equipment

- Inadequate assessment of needs and risks
- Inadequate human factors or ergonomics considerations
- Inadequate standards or specifications
- Inadequate availability
- Inadequate adjustment, repair, or maintenance
- Inadequate salvage and reclamation
- Inadequate removal and replacement of unsuitable items

Inadequate engineering

- Inadequate assessment of loss exposures
- Inadequate consideration of human factors or ergonomics
- Inadequate standards, specifications, and design criteria
- Inadequate monitoring of construction
- Inadequate assessment of operational readiness
- Inadequate monitoring of initial operation
- Inadequate evaluation of changes

Inadequate work standards

- Inadequate development of standards
  - Inventory and evaluation of exposures and needs
  - Coordination with process design
  - Employee involvement
  - Inconsistent standards, procedures, or rules
- Inadequate communication of standards
  - Publication
  - Distribution
  - Translation to appropriate languages
  - Training
  - Reinforcing with signs, color codes, and job aids
- Inadequate maintenance of standards
  - Tracking of work flow
  - Updating
  - Monitoring use of standards, procedures, and rules

*(continued)*

**Table 4.1** *(continued)*

| **Job factors** *(continued)* | |
|---|---|
| Inadequate purchasing<br>• Inadequate specifications on requisitions<br>• Inadequate research on materials or equipment<br>• Inadequate specifications to vendors<br>• Inadequate mode or route of shipment<br>• Inadequate receiving inspection and acceptance<br>• Inadequate communication of safety and health data<br>• Improper handling of materials<br>• Improper storage of materials<br>• Improper transporting of materials<br>• Inadequate identification of hazardous items<br>• Improper salvage and waste disposal | Wear and tear<br>• Inadequate planning of use<br>• Improper extension of service life<br>• Inadequate inspection and monitoring<br>• Improper loading or rate of use<br>• Inadequate maintenance<br>• Use by unqualified or untrained people<br>• Use for wrong purpose |
| Inadequate maintenance<br>• Inadequate preventive<br>  • Assessment of needs<br>  • Lubrication and servicing<br>  • Adjustment or assembly<br>  • Cleaning or resurfacing<br>• Inadequate reparative<br>  • Communication of needs<br>  • Scheduling of work<br>  • Examination of units<br>  • Part substitution | Abuse or misuse<br>• Condoned by supervision<br>  • Intentional<br>  • Unintentional<br>• Not condoned by supervision<br>  • Intentional<br>  • Unintentional |

Reprinted, by permission, from F.E. Bird and. G.L Germain, 1985, *Practical loss control leadership* (Loganville, GA: Institute Publishing), 29.

initiative and maintain activity among personnel. Fourth is the *coordination* of resources and activity to implement the plan. Last is *control,* which is to verify that the plan is being implemented and the instructions are being followed.

These five components define the management culture, which in turn influences the other components in their domino model. For example, poor administrative planning can result in an organizational culture in which people become harried. This in turn affects multiple basic causes, including "physical and physiological stress," resulting from "fatigue due to sensory overload." Because the worker is harried and suffering from fatigue, a result of doing too much, he cuts corners and "fails to use personal protection properly" (immediate cause). The result is an incident resulting in injury damage or loss. It could be an automobile accident, a chainsaw injury, a drowning, or a playground injury.

Conversely, Bird and Germain make the point that the safety manager needs to analyze the dominoes in reverse order to determine and correct the basic causes of loss, as well as change and modify the management culture to be safer. In the previous example, failure to wear chaps, a helmet, and other protective equipment was the immediate cause of the chainsaw accident. Looking deeper, the safety manager would conclude that the accident was really caused by a management culture that resulted in the worker becoming harried and cutting corners. The safety manager would seek to modify the factors at each level (domino) in their model. In the end, accidents are caused by lack of control over the management culture.

Bird and Germain (1985) suggest three common reasons for lack of control: inadequate programs, inadequate program standards, and inadequate compliance with the standards. Recreation and park programs may be inadequate because the safety manager is focusing her energy elsewhere or because she has not developed programs to assess and monitor recreational activities. Often, standards are inadequate when an activity is small in size and scope and does not warrant much attention. This is the situation in the whitewater rafting industry, where quantifying industry standards is difficult. In contrast, the pool-management literature is vast and numerous standards exist.

In terms of organizational management and lack of control, Heinrich et al. (1980), suggest that "Four basic methods are available for preventing accidents—engineering revision, persuasion and appeal, personnel adjustment, and discipline" (p. 21). These four methods permeate the planning, organizing, command, coordination, and control functions within the organization. A safety manager or recreation and park professional uses these four methods to address the organizational control and prevent lack of control. The latter three options relate to managing the culture of the organization.

Managing the culture in any organization in terms of safety is not always easy. It is worth noting that in many organizations employees are encouraged to keep things running smoothly and to not rock the boat. If an employee reports an error or mishap, he can be labeled an obstructionist or not a team player. To management, the employee becomes the problem rather than the actual problem that needs to be corrected. For a counterpoint to this traditional approach of managing the culture, see the section on highly reliable organizations later in this chapter.

**Engineering Revision** Engineering revision can involve redesigning equipment and facilities. For example, after observing children playing on play equipment, a recreation and park professional might wish to redesign the play equipment to make it safer. He could redesign the play structure to remove trip hazards or to allow proper spacing. Or he might provide surfaces with different textures to provide visual cues for users, as is often done on interpretive trails.

Engineering revisions can also include soft systems or administrative changes. In the playground example, administrative changes could include implementing rules about the kinds of play actions allowed on the play structure. Redesigning lifeguard shifts at the swimming

Rules about the kinds of play allowed could be considered a soft engineering revision.

pool to reduce the length of time a lifeguard is in the chair is another example of a soft-system engineering revision.

**Persuasion and Appeal** Most people seek to do what is right, appropriate, and safe. If the organization seeks to create a safe environment, most people working there will seek to conform to the safety-conscious culture. Employers can educate and inform workers of safe practices through both formal and informal methods while following the normal practices in leadership training. Formal courses can include in-service training, such as courses in van driving and seminars on preventing sexual harassment. Informal training includes training initiated by the worker, such as attending conferences and workshops and maintaining continuing education units for certification. Persuasion and appeal can involve a systematic review and evaluation of programs and activities offered by the agency. In the following example, a simple review of the activity by this author on a three-day canoe trip for a group of New York middle school youths resulted in persuasion of the safeties regarding how to act more safely. This author recommended that they should periodically turn around in their canoes and look at the trip behind them because this simple act increased the sphere of supervision twofold. The suggestion was simple and the idea made perfect sense to the safeties once they were told about it.

**Personnel Adjustment** Four options exist regarding personnel adjustment: hiring, continuation, transfer, or termination. Once hired, continuation of employment requires the employer to persuade and educate the employee to change their behavior, in this case to act more safely. If the employee does not conform, the employer can transfer or terminate the employee. Transferring the employee to another area may solve the problem, or it may simply transfer the problem to another unit. Termination is an option when an employee violates a significant organizational policy.

**Discipline** Discipline can include corrective action such as mandatory education programs, reassignment of duties, or termination. If an employee has several documented incidents of a similar nature and management has taken no corrective action, the organization may be in trouble if an injury, damage, or loss results from a similar incident and someone sues. An organization must take corrective action once an employee establishes a track record. Often, supervisors are quick to note deficiencies but are lax on the follow-through because they hope that the problem will correct itself or eventually go away. If an organization follows a disciplinary approach, the incident needs to be documented and management needs to follow through with corrective action.

### Summary of the Historical Overview of Safety Management

Heinrich's domino model and its continuation by Bird and Germain (1985) represent several important underlying safety management principles that permeate most of the accident process discussion in this chapter and the next. First, it provides the historical evolution of an important school of thought regarding accident prevention. Second, it suggests that the causes of accidents are multilayered (immediate causes, basic causes, lack of control), and accident prevention needs to permeate the entire operations and management culture of the organization. To effectively facilitate safety, management needs to address the planning, organizing, coordination, command, and control functions in the organization. Third, there needs to be a safety manager to carry out the process of implementing safety within the organization. Last, the principles developed by Heinrich percolate into the other models presented in this and the next chapter. In some cases, it helps to explain the differences in approach taken by other schools of thought toward the accident process and safety management.

## BEHAVIORAL MODELS

Behavioral models state that major changes and uncertainties in a person's life tend to lead to accidents, injury, and illness. One of the more interesting behavioral models that illustrates this concept is life change unit theory. Table 4.2 presents the table of life change and the stress units associated with each life change. The changes are ranked in terms of the corresponding stress score. A total score of more than 300 indicates that the person is extremely susceptible to an accident (or injury, illness, and so on). A score between 200 and 299 indicates that the person is still in a crisis situation, only slightly less so. A score between 150 and 199 indicates that the person is moderately susceptible.

It is easy to see how these life-changing factors could make a person more prone to an accident. Many of the factors included in the life change unit theory are similar to the human factors in the domino model (e.g., physical or physiological capabilities or stress, mental or psychological capabilities or stress, and motivation factors in table 4.1).

**Table 4.2** Life Change Units

| Rank | Life event | Mean value |
|---|---|---|
| 1 | Death of spouse | 100 |
| 2 | Divorce | 73 |
| 3 | Marital separation | 65 |
| 4 | Jail term | 63 |
| 5 | Death of close family member | 63 |
| 6 | Personal injury or illness | 53 |
| 7 | Marriage | 50 |
| 8 | Fired at work | 47 |
| 9 | Marital reconciliation | 45 |
| 10 | Retirement | 45 |
| 11 | Changes in family member's health | 44 |
| 12 | Pregnancy | 40 |
| 13 | Sex difficulties | 39 |
| 14 | Gain of new family member | 39 |
| 15 | Business readjustment | 39 |
| 16 | Change in financial state | 38 |
| 17 | Death of a close friend | 37 |
| 18 | Change to different line of work | 36 |
| 19 | Change in number of arguments with spouse | 35 |
| 20 | Mortgage greater than $__________ | 31 |
| 21 | Foreclosure of mortgage or loan | 30 |
| 22 | Change in work responsibilities | 29 |
| 23 | Son or daughter leaving home | 29 |
| 24 | Trouble with in-laws | 29 |
| 25 | Outstanding personal achievement | 28 |
| 26 | Wife begins or stops work | 26 |
| 27 | Begin or end school | 26 |
| 28 | Change in living conditions | 25 |
| 29 | Revision of personal habits | 24 |
| 30 | Trouble with boss | 23 |
| 31 | Change in work hours, conditions | 20 |
| 32 | Change in residence | 20 |
| 33 | Change in schools | 20 |
| 34 | Change in recreation | 19 |
| 35 | Change in church activities | 19 |
| 36 | Change in social activities | 18 |
| 37 | Mortgage or loan less than $________ | 17 |
| 38 | Change in sleeping habits | 16 |
| 39 | Change in number of family get-togethers | 15 |
| 40 | Change in eating habits | 15 |
| 41 | Vacation | 13 |
| 42 | Christmas | 12 |
| 43 | Minor violations of the law | 11 |

Reprinted from *Journal of Psychosomatic Research*, Vol. 11, No. 2, T.H. Holmes and R.H. Rahe, "The social readjustment rating scale," pgs. 213-221, copyright 1967, with permission of Elsevier.

## EPIDEMIOLOGICAL MODELS

Epidemiology is the study of the disease process. According to Heinrich et al. (1980), in the 1970s and 1980s practitioners in the health and medical fields began applying the model to the study of accidents. The epidemiological triangle model (figure 4.4) includes three main components in the model: the agent, the host, and the environment. Some models also include time as the fourth element.

The first component of the triangle, the *agent*, is what causes the disease. The agent is usually thought of, but not always, as a microbe. For example, when injected into the human host by the mosquito, eukaryotic protists (the agent) cause malaria (the disease).

The second component of the triangle, the *host*, is who harbors the agent. The host is usually human or animal. When exposed to the disease, the host may or may not show the symptoms of the disease. In the case of malaria, one host (man) shows the symptoms of the disease whereas the other host (mosquito) does not. Because the mosquito does not get sick, it is often referred to as the carrier of the disease.

The third component of the triangle, the *environment*, is the place or the conditions under which the disease occurs. The environment

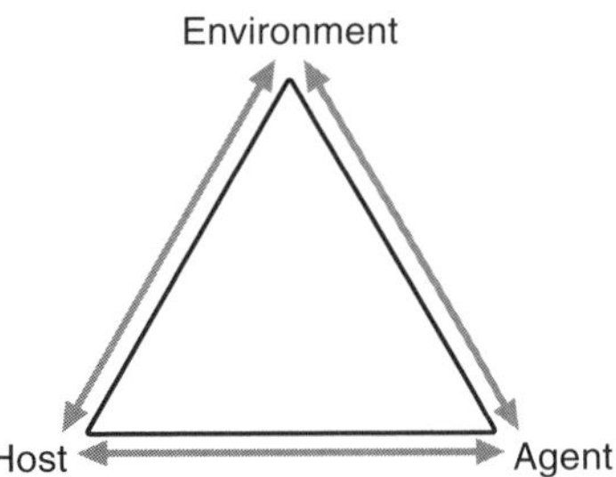


**Figure 4.4** The epidemiological triangle includes the agent (what caused the accident), the host (who harbored the agent), and the environment (where the accident occurred or the conditions under which it occurred).

includes the favorable conditions that enable the host to transmit the disease. Generally, these conditions are external to the host. The most important environmental factor in the transmission of malaria is the stagnant water where the mosquitoes breed.

Some models include *time* as a fourth component. In this example, time is the incubation period between infection and when the disease symptoms appear. In the model, the first three components (agent, host, and environment) are causal (both necessary and sufficient) for the disease or in this case the accident to occur. In contrast, although the time factor in the form of an incubation period is usually present, it is more descriptive of the process and is not really a necessary component for the disease process to occur.

The epidemiological triangle model has been applied to the accident process (Oakley, 2003; Robertson, 1998). The host is the injured person; the agent is what injured the person; and the environment, vehicle, or vector is what conveyed the injury. For example, on a playground, a child slides down a metal slide that is directly facing the rays of the sun. The child receives second-degree burns. The child is the host, or the victim. The thermal energy from the slide is the agent, or what caused the injury. The metal slide is the environment, or the place where the injury occurred. If time is included in the example, it reflects the time between going down the slide and getting burned and when the blisters appear.

Dekker (2006) notes that the epidemiological model "sees accidents as related to latent failures that hide in everything from management decisions to procedures to equipment design. These 'pathogens' do not normally wreak havoc unless they are activated by other factors" (p. 81). He

In the epidemiological triangle model, the metal slide is the environment, or the place where the injury occurred.

notes that the model sees accidents as the combination of active errors and latent errors. Active errors are unsafe acts or human-related errors, and latent errors are unsafe conditions that lie dormant in an organization until some event triggers them to create an accident. He also notes that because accidents tend to result from long-term deficiencies caused by unsafe conditions, the use of epidemiological models tends to shift the emphasis away from human errors. Although the epidemiological model has been useful in the study of diseases, it is generally considered too narrow in scope for studying accidents given the other models available. In addition, thinking of accidents as a disease is not generally intuitive for the lay public.

## HUMAN ERROR MANAGEMENT

Under the human error management approach, developed by Reason (1990), human error is viewed as the symptom of deeper trouble in an organization rather than the immediate cause of the accident. Hence, the focus is on the organization, its systems, and its management culture. Under this approach, organizations that develop good systems and a good safety culture develop an environment that is less likely to produce accidents. Conceptually, this dovetails with dominoes of basic causes and lack of control (Heinrich et al., 1980).

Reason calls the designers and managers who create the climate of an organization the "blunt end" of the system. Reason refers to factors such as the management culture, working conditions, and the equipment used as *latent factors* or latent conditions. Latent factors or conditions set the tone for the environment in which the worker operates. For example, if the management culture expects all employees to work double overtime, the organization is facilitating a climate in which the worker is more likely to make a mistake.

Reason calls the *active errors* made by people that directly caused the accident the "sharp end" of the system. For example, if a person working double overtime has an injury due to fatigue, is the injury really attributable to the error or is it attributable to the management policy that demands double overtime? Although Reason notes that it is easy to blame the individual for his mistake, he notes that in this model the management culture is really to blame.

Many models tend to place blame on human error. In contrast, the human error management model emphasizes the latent factors in the accident process. For example, figure 1.7 includes a portion of a deposition from Thomas Mills, who was a trip leader on a rafting trip on the Lehigh River. The trip was supervised by the trip leader and two guides, and there were roughly 70 guests in 15 to 20 rafts. In his deposition, Mills indicates that he did not have general supervision, let alone specific supervision, of the group during an accident in which Mr. Percheski blew out his knee, and he did not know the details of what happened until the end of the trip. Mills was doing his job. He was acting in good faith and any errors he made were most likely unintentional. Was his lack of supervision (active error) really his fault, or was it really management's fault given that the raft company ran trips with inadequate supervision (latent error)? One can make an excellent case that the management culture and practices created a work environment that set Mills up for supervision failure. This becomes obvious from reading between the lines in his deposition. Because latent factors usually facilitate the active factors, the human error management approach focuses on the latent errors in the organization.

The human error management approach is often represented by two models. The Swiss cheese model (figure 4.5) focuses on the accident process in terms of the latent and active factors. The Swiss cheese represents the actions an organization takes to reduce the likelihood that an accident will occur. The holes in the cheese represent both active and latent factors. In the double overtime example, a latent error (and hole in the Swiss cheese) is associated with the informal management policy that condones and encourages double overtime. Choosing to work double overtime and the resulting fatigue are active factors, or additional holes in the Swiss cheese. An accident can potentially occur when the metaphorical holes in the cheese line up with each other, in this case an informal management culture that encourages double overtime, the workers choice to do so, and the resulting fatigue. An accident will not always occur simply because the holes line up. The double overtime policy by itself does not cause an accident. However, the latent error in the system is always waiting for an active error to occur. Together, a latent error and an active error can result in an accident. In the double overtime example, the worker is more likely to have an accident occur.

The primary emphasis of the human error management approach is on filling the holes. Not all holes can be eliminated. An organization can manage, control, or reduce these holes by implementing safety measures (represented by the solid portion of another slice of Swiss cheese). In the case of Thomas Mills, the rafting company may realize that the trips require additional supervision and hire more guides. In the double overtime example, management may become aware of its errant ways and change their policy regarding double overtime.

The second model (Reason, 2008, p. 17), reflects the implementation of the human error approach within the organization (figure 4.6). The model is illustrative in several ways. Conceptually, it reflects and reinforces several of the approaches to safety management previously discussed with Heinrich et al. (1980) and Bird and Germain (1985). Although the terms may be different and there may be a difference in emphasis, the underlying concepts are very similar. There are organizational factors (latent factors) that facilitate local workplace factors (basic causes), which result in unsafe acts (immediate causes). In figure 4.6, the box atop the pyramid is the Swiss cheese model (figure 4.5), in which the defenses are the slices of Swiss cheese where the holes are lined up to create a loss. As with Heinrich et al. (1980) and Bird and Germain (1985), Reason's approach is comprehensive to the organization and has an organizational emphasis.

## HUMAN ERROR MODEL

A variation of the human error management model is the human error model, developed by Betty van der Smissen. This model tends to focus on human error; however, it includes organizational and management behavior and legal and regulatory rules. It also emphasizes risk management. In order to understand risk management under the human error model,

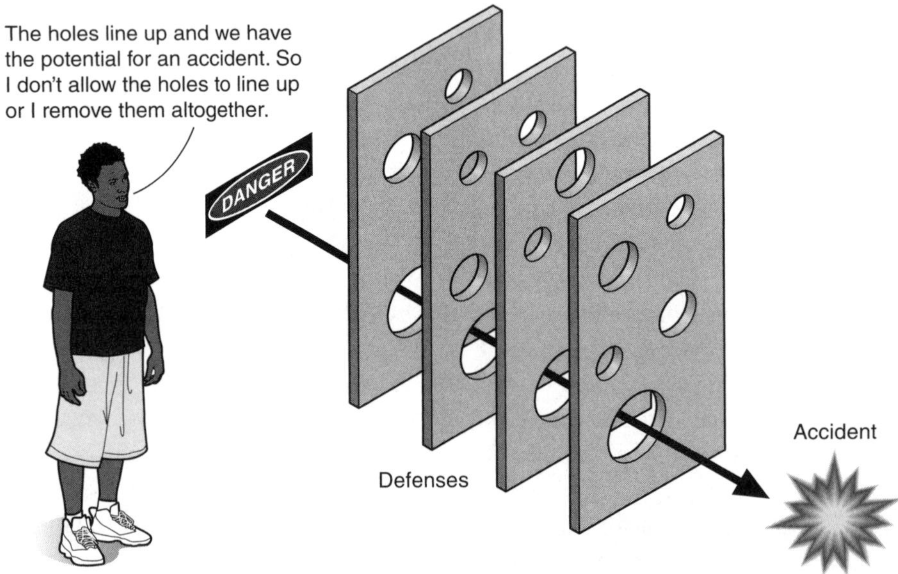


**Figure 4.5** The slices of Swiss cheese represent the actions that an organization takes to prevent accidents. The holes in the cheese represent that latent and active errors are present.

Adapted from Reason 1990.

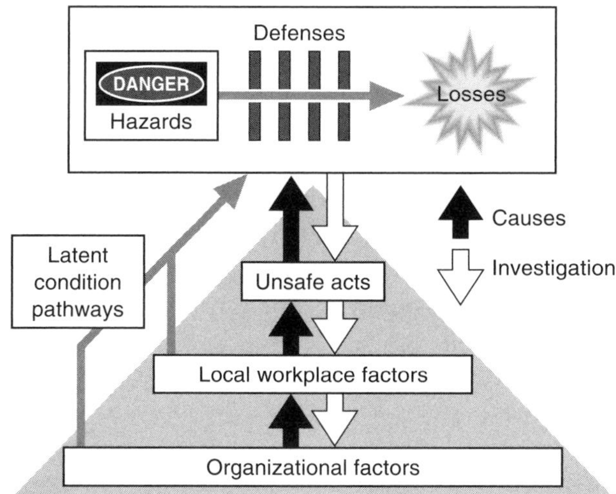


**Figure 4.6** Reason's model is the second model that represents the human error management approach.

one must understand what human error is and how behavior principles affect how a person perceives a situation.

## Human Error

Traditionally, risk management has focused on three areas: physical areas and facilities, conducting the activity, and controlling the participants. What is often not considered is the human factor and how a person's actions and thoughts lead to accidents.

Human error is a mistake or misjudgment and is the result of not focusing at the right time and the right place. Mistakes can result from a variety of issues: skills, rules, knowledge, and training. Skill-based errors occur from slips and lapses; a person forgets something she was told to do because it has not yet become second nature. Rule-based errors arise from mistake or ignorance; a person either forgets the rule or did not learn the rule. Knowledge-based errors transpire through mistakes created by lack of understanding. Improper training leads to errors created by that training or lack thereof.

The U.S. Department of Transportation (2000) states that 70 to 90 percent of accidents are attributable to the human factor. Other fields that have focused on the human factor have identified it in accident reporting. Human error has been identified as part of the cause of amusement ride, bicycle, boating, and snowmobiling accidents; product liability; health care injuries and deaths; and airline industry accidents (Strauch, 2002).

Human error is a part of risk management and should be controlled. Human error takes different forms, has different psychological origins, occurs in different parts of operational systems, and requires different management methods. The organization must develop external controls in the form of rules, regulations, and procedures. The individual must acquire internal controls through training and experience.

## Behavior Principles

To manage risks, one must understand what goes on in a person's mind regarding the situation. If one understands more about human behavior, one can analyze cause of injuries in terms of human factors and identify predictable human error. The fact is that normal people do not pay attention to everything occurring around them, have faulty perception, and forget things that have occurred in the past. They do not always act with intellect or use good judgment. People are not perfect; they make mistakes.

People are not the free agents they think they are. They are relegated to act according to experiences, perceptions, mindset, and moods that are situational in nature. People can see and act only according to the reality at the moment an event occurs.

According to Holmes (1870), "The more we examine the mechanism of thought, the more we shall see that the automatic, unconscious action of the mind enters largely into all its processes." People use experiences and biases to make sense of the world. The statement "Wow, I thought that was [longer, shorter, higher, lower] than it actually was!" illustrates bias, counterfactual thinking, fundamental attribution error, and confirmation bias of thinking, which are created by shortcuts, or cognitive frugality. Such thinking allows people to make split-second decisions without examining every detail.

Some examples of cognitive frugality are cue generalization, creation of expectations based on experience, and inattentional blindness. When a person uses cue generalizations, she takes a few cues without looking carefully to make a determination based on past experience. For example, if she sees a person with very short hair, she thinks the person is male. After taking a closer look, she may see other characteristics that indicate she is wrong. As another example, a young girl lives on the sea and her family has a dock. Her parents have told her that when the top of the dock is far from the water, it is not safe to dive because the tide is low and the water is shallow. When the water is near the top of the dock, it is safe to dive. The girl visits a park with a floating dock, and the top of the dock is always near the water. The girl sees the "no diving" sign and thinks, "That must be for when the water is not close to the top of the dock." She dives and hits the sea bottom and is severely hurt. She used past experience and generalized the cue of the standing dock to the floating dock.

As another example of this thinking, an expert snowmobiler suffered a catastrophic brain injury when he was riding on a hill and came to a significant drop (25 percent slope) at a speed of at least 45 miles per hour. The snowmobile lifted 2 to 3 feet off the ground and crashed. The snowmobiler said that no warning signs were posted on this hill even though signs had been posted on preceding hills. Surrounding level terrain created his expectation of gentle slopes. His previous experience on the trail indicated that a sign would be posted if the ground would drop suddenly.

Inattentional blindness, a fairly new concept, is when people do not see unexpected objects when they are concentrating on or attending to one type of circumstance. For example, one study asked people to pay attention to the team wearing black shirts in a basketball game. During the game, a person dressed as a gorilla walked across the court and beat his chest. When asked, only about one third of the people saw the gorilla. The results indicate that when people are attending to one thing, they may miss something else even if it is obvious (Mack and Rock, 1998). As another example, a spectator at a baseball game was hit by a foul ball. He was distracted because the dinosaur mascot was touching him with its tail. The spectator could not pay attention to both the game and the mascot. As another example, a spectator crossed his legs, leaned back, and fell backward off the bleachers, which had no back support. He forgot that no bar was behind him because his attention was directed toward the game.

Experience and maturity also factor into human error. A child on a Ferris wheel will reach out and try to hit the bars as they go by. Therefore, Ferris wheel designers make the bars too far away to reach. Children will misjudge how far they can reach on a playground or how long they can hold onto a bar. Therefore, playground designers place fall-absorbing surfaces under the play equipment.

## Risk Management and Human Error

By understanding that the human factor will affect the way people act and react, risk managers can consider human abilities, limitations, and psychological biases and anticipate human actions. Risk management procedures should provide error protection, error capturing, and error tolerance.

Error protection comes in the form of warnings and supervision. Warnings alert the public of where danger exists and where an error might occur. Warnings include posted signs (e.g., "stay back," "steep drop-off") and written and oral information. Each warning must convey the existing danger so the participant can make a decision regarding the potential hazard. "No diving" is a regulation, not a warning. "No diving—Rocks" or "No diving—Shallow water" are warnings that give the participant information about why the regulation exists. Monitoring and supervision are required because a certain amount of error is expected. Organizations should have policies and procedures in place to set parameters so that patrons do not need to make decisions. Supervisors remind or teach patrons about the rules and regulations and enforce the policies. Supervisors must be aware that young children do not have the maturity to make wise decisions and that they will likely follow a crowd even when the crowd is making a bad decision.

Children may not understand the possibilities of how they can be hurt because they have limited knowledge, experience, and skills.

Error capturing is the safety margin designed into facilities and equipment. For example, bleachers need to have railings because people pay attention to the game, not the bleachers. Facilities need buffer zones and wall mats because people have difficulty stopping once they are in motion. Recreation leaders need to enforce the use of safety equipment, especially if the equipment is uncomfortable (e.g., safety glasses or life jackets).

Error tolerance is the placement of hard and soft barriers (physical and administrative) to reduce the likelihood of an accident from occurring. It includes many of the risk management standards in place. Enforcing height limits on amusement rides ensures that the children who do not fit into the seats or are not mature enough to know where mistakes might occur do not get on the ride. Organizations often guide participants in how to handle certain situations in order to prevent an error before it occurs.

Emergencies will happen, and people may not be able to think clearly in an emergency. Organizations should write out and practice plans for how to react. When people practice a plan, the plan becomes second nature and reaction time is faster and more accurate. An organization should have a practiced plan for every type of emergency in every venue and every program or event. This is covered in more depth in chapter 9, Emergency Action Plans.

## HIGHLY RELIABLE ORGANIZATIONS

Highly reliable organizations (HRO) represents a paradigm shift in organizational culture. They have been associated with potentially dangerous situations and environments in which unexpected events can be encountered at any time. Traditionally, HRO have been associated with flight decks on aircraft carriers, nuclear power plants, emergency rooms in hospitals, air traffic control rooms, hostage negotiations, and similar settings. Because unexpected events can occur at any time in these settings, HRO develop their systems and management culture to continually address and handle these events. The practices of HRO can easily be applied to recreation and park settings, particularly the outdoor and adventure programming areas, where those in the field believe that unexpected events can occur at any time.

In order to understand the paradigm shift associated with HRO, it is necessary to understand traditional organizational culture. In contrast to HRO, most organizations and the people in them view the organizational environment as normally safe. Accidents are mishaps that occur only occasionally. Accidents carry the implication that someone did something wrong, and a stigma is often associated with having an accident. Therefore, in order to avoid blame, people have an incentive to not report accidents, let alone near misses where nothing happened but something might have under different circumstances. When injury, damage, or loss does occur, most people want to move on and have it go away. Also, the organization wants the accident to go away because it consumes time and diverts energy away from normal business. Because the belief in this organizational culture is that accidents occur infrequently, management believes that the next accident will occur far in the future when this accident is long forgotten.

The organizational culture of HRO is quite different. According to Weick and Sutcliffe (2001), HRO exhibit the following characteristics: preoccupation with failure, reluctance to accept simplification, sensitivity to operations, commitment to resilience, and deference to expertise. The following discussion of the characteristics of HRO incorporates an example that is based on the plot from the video *Cold, Wet, and Alive* (Kauffman, 2011) (see also appendix C for full script). This example is David's story of what happened on an early-spring canoe trip. The air temperature was 70 degrees, so he decided to dress for the warmer air temperature rather than the colder water temperature. He chose not to snack on food when everyone else did. He then rolled his kayak and got wet. At the lunch stop, the group discussed ending the trip and hitchhiking back to the car but decided to continue the trip. Eventually, David became hypothermic, came out of his boat, lost his boat, and was rescued by members of his group. The loss of his boat qualifies as an accident.

## Preoccupation With Failure

The first characteristic identified by Weick and Sutcliff (2001) is that HRO tend to continually look at their failures. The HRO environment encourages people to report and examine errors, including near misses. Recreation leaders, specifically outdoor leaders, constantly examine the activity and environment for things that can go wrong and seek to make adjustments before a major incident or accident can occur.

In an HRO environment, an incident report is filed when an incident occurs. The incident is then thoroughly analyzed in terms of the factors that contributed to it. Because an unexpected event can occur at any time, both the organization and its members focus on learning from the incident in order to prevent future incidents.

In terms of David's canoe trip, the group would write and file an incident report. They would analyze the factors that led to the accident (the boat loss) and they would take steps to rectify the situation and prevent similar situations from occurring again in the future. (It is worth noting that most HRO take steps that would prevent David from losing his boat in the first place.)

## Reluctance to Accept Simplifications

According to Weick and Sutcliff (2001), "HRO take deliberate steps to create more complexity and nuanced pictures. In contrast, traditional organizations tend to look at their operations as a whole rather than delving into specifics. HRO simplify less and see more" (p. 11). Simplification tends to cover up the problems rather than address them. HRO tend to look at the specifics and analyze them more because they desire to learn as much as possible.

The following is a simplification and rationalization of David's trip that might be associated with the traditional approach: "We take a lot of outdoor trips every year. Probability indicates that accidents will occur sooner or later. Risk is in integral part of activities like David's canoe trip. For the most part, these incidents are anomalies. We need to make sure that David dresses more appropriately for the trip next time." In contrast, an HRO would seek to learn more through the postincident analysis. On David's trip, he decided to dress for the warmer air temperature rather than the colder water. The following questions seek a deeper analysis of why David was dressed improperly for the activity: Why did David dress for the air temperature rather than the water temperature? What clothes should one wear for an early-spring trip? Why did he choose incorrectly? Should we institute a control or rule that one wears a wetsuit when the water temperature is below a certain temperature, or would the participants be better served with education on how to dress for cold weather? Did David take extra, dry clothing? If he did, why did he not use it? Could the group have implemented a better layering system where they added layers of clothes to keep warm? Why did David get hypothermia whereas the other trip participants did not? These questions suggest a more complex approach to learning more about what happened so that the organization can implement corrective action in the future.

## Sensitivity to Operations

Rather than waiting for an accident to occur and then doing a postincident analysis, HRO look for anomalies in their normal operations that could lead to problems. In the safety literature, the belief exists that near misses are the precursors of future accidents. This was the impetus behind Bird and Germain's (1985) accident ratio study (see figure 4.2). The question is how to effectively study not only the near misses but the anomalies in the normal operations to prevent the unexpected event and accident. HRO do this by constantly learning and reacting to what is going on in their operations and seeking better ways to do what they are already doing rather than waiting for the system to break before fixing it.

Rather than waiting for David to eventually have an accident and then completing a postincident analysis, people in an HRO environment would probe and analyze their normal operations to find the anomalies and address them. They would ask all the questions raised in the previous section and apply their findings to their operations. These little anomalies had occurred to a lesser degree on previous trips. In an HRO environment, David would not have lost his boat because most of the factors that led to his hypothermia would be engineered out of the activity before David's trip by applying prior learning.

## Commitment to Resilience

Resilience results from keeping errors and mishaps small. The process of probing, analyzing, and reacting associated with HRO is useful in addressing problems and making them manageable. In addition, a commitment to resilience involves determining through simulation activities what potentially could happen. In terms of David's trip, the scenario described in this chapter and in appendix C would be a simulation activity, not an actual trip on which he loses his boat. It would be a learning activity designed to probe, analyze, and react to what could happen. The organization would then integrate this learning into its operations.

## Deference to Expertise

In traditional management organizations, everything normally follows the chain of command in which the supervisor or the person higher on the organizational chart is responsible for all operations. In contrast, HRO seek to place the most qualified person in a position to address the unexpected event. HRO recognize that specialists, because of their specialized knowledge, need to be placed in direct command and often act independently of the normal chain of command. This is an example of pushing the decision-making process downward so that the most qualified person can focus his or her talents on the specific task at hand.

In an HRO environment, an organization analyzes incidents and takes steps in the future to prevent similar incidents from occurring such as instituting a rule that one wear a wetsuit when the water is below a certain temperature.

For example, in the outdoor adventure area or a rescue operation, the incident commander is responsible for the entire operations of the rescue. The incident commander asks the group who has the highest level or certification of medical training. That person becomes responsible for any medical situation. In essence, the incident commander indicates to everyone present that the person with the medical training supersedes the normal chain of command regarding medical problems.

The following example illustrates the differences between the two types of organizational culture as well as the importance of the organizational culture in setting the attitude toward safety management in the organization. At a recent workshop at the Association of Experiential Education conference, a prominent leader in the field was explaining his effort to create a national database that would analyze accidents in terms of their underlying factors in order to determine what causes accidents. This undertaking relied on everyone in an organization documenting and reporting all incidents and near misses. An audience member asked the following question: If a person continually reports all the near misses as well as accidents, would not the organization conclude at some point that this person was acting unsafely? This person's documentation would indeed support this conclusion. Conversely, does an incentive exist for this person not to report everything given that not reporting implies that she is acting safely? The question raised by the audience member captures the dichotomy between the traditional organizational culture toward safety management and the culture of HRO and illustrates that individuals can hold different assumptions about organizational cultures. The prominent leader presenting at the workshop believed that most organizations gravitate toward an HRO-type environment, whereas the audience member believed that most organizations gravitate toward a traditional management culture.

## A CAUTIONARY NOTE

According to Dekker (2006), several methodological issues associated with the accident process suggest caution when using accident process models. The first methodological problem is that hindsight tends to be 20/20, meaning that it is usually easy for people to deductively reach conclusions after the incident occurs. However, the correct choice is not always obvious to those going through the experience. For example, if an accident investigator reviews David's accident, it is fairly easy in the postincident analysis to determine the factors that contributed to the accident.

The second methodological problem is that people desire to analyze what went wrong, to determine where the error occurred, and to assign blame. People believe that because an accident occurred, someone must have done something wrong. If someone hadn't done something wrong, no accident would have occurred. This argument is circular. David chose to not dress properly. He chose to dress for the air temperature and not the water temperature. In addition, he didn't plan on getting wet. For him it was a perfectly logical choice. Unfortunately, it was not the best choice. It is easy to blame him for getting hypothermia. The same can be done with snacking or trip planning. In the postincident analysis, it is easy to indicate what David did wrong and to affix blame. Remember, there are many people who behave very similarly to David and never have an accident. Conversely, there are many people who do everything correctly and still have an accident.

It is also easy to suggest what he should have done to prevent the accident. This is a continuation of the previous points. If only he had done something differently. If only he had dressed properly. If only he had snacked. It almost seems as though David wanted this accident to occur. However, David did not go on this trip seeking to get hypothermia and lose his boat. As the day progressed, he applied normal decision-making behavior to specific problems that he encountered: "What should I wear today?" "Should I eat something if I'm not really hungry?" During an activity, people do not have the privilege of knowing the effect of their mundane decisions or the outcome of their actions before they occur.

## Determining Your HRO Characteristics

HRO offer an interesting approach to safety management and point out weaknesses in traditional organizational culture toward safety management. Return to the question posed to the prominent leader at the national conference. Although you may embrace HRO and practice its principles in your operations, you must consider what you do in the context of your organization and understand the overall management culture in which you are really operating. You want to avoid the situation where you think your management culture is one type when in reality it is the other. Figure 4.7 presents an abbreviated quiz to help you determine the HRO characteristics of your organization. The results will help you to assess your management culture so that you can more effectively cope with it if you are practicing HRO principles within a traditional management setting.

---

### Do You Work in a Highly Reliable Organization (HRO)?

**Directions:** Please answer the following questions and enter your response in one of the two columns on the right.

| | | |
|---|---|---|
| 1) We systematically investigate our near misses to determine how we can improve what we are doing. (PWF) | ___ No | ___ Yes |
| 2) If we report a problem or a potential problem, our administration acts as if we are *rocking the boat* or as if we are *the problem*. (PWF) | ___Yes | ___ No |
| 3) We tend to seek a more complete picture of what is going on in our activities and programs by becoming more *nuance* and detailed. We simplify less. (RTAS) | ___ No | ___ Yes |
| 4) We tend to cover up our problems rather than address them. (RTAS) | ___ Yes | ___ No |
| 5) We play the *what if game* to make our operations safer. This is where we examine what might go wrong and take corrective action before something actually goes wrong. (STO) | ___ No | ___ Yes |
| 6) We wait until we have a major incident before we make changes. (STO) | ___ Yes | ___ No |
| 7) We are **not** encouraged to probe, analyze, and report errors in our activities and programs. (CTR) | ___ Yes | ___ No |
| 8) We train for worse case scenarios with simulations and other training exercises. (CTR) | ___ No | ___ Yes |
| 9) We will often put the most qualified person or people in charge of the incident, even if they are at the bottom of the chain of command. (DTE) | ___ No | ___ Yes |
| 10) In a crisis situation, we tend to follow the hierarchal chain of command where those further up the chain tend to make most of the decisions. (DTE) | ___Yes | ___ No |
| Total the checks | _______ | _______ |

**Number of checks in second column**

8-10: HRO type organization

5-7: Traditional organization with some HRO characteristics

0-4: Traditional organization

*Note:* The abbreviations stand for the different subcharacteristics of HROs. PWF: Preoccupation with failure, RTAS: Reluctance to simplicity, STO: Sensitivity to operations, CTR: Commitment to resilience, and DTE: Deference to expertise.

---

**Figure 4.7** This simple survey helps determine whether your work environment is also an HRO environment.

Only during the postincident analysis can one clearly determine the chain of events that led to the loss.

Another methodological problem is that the actions and decisions that David made led to an accident only because postincident analysis attributed the cause of the incident to those factors. As previously noted, many people take outdoor trips similar to David's and make decisions that are similar to those he made, and they do not get hypothermia and lose their boats. The postincident analysis suggests that specific factors caused his accident. Those factors indeed caused David's accident, but those factors will not always cause accidents in similar situations.

Finally, the model a person uses tends to potentially bias the conclusions made regarding why an accident occurred. This becomes a sampling issue in which one fits the uncovered data to the model. Dekker (2006) likens this to the shopping cart approach. When a person goes to the grocery store, he can choose from many items. He puts items in his shopping cart. When he checks out, he determines what food is available in the grocery store based on the items in the shopping cart. The contents of the shopping cart do not represent the food found in the grocery store. However, the contents are an accurate reflection of what he plans to eat. Similarly, the accident model one uses determines the data one finds and selects, which determines the causes of the accident. In a sense, a person's conclusion becomes a self-fulfilling prophesy that is determined by the model he uses.

A variation of this concept is the fallacy of the checklist. For example, review the basic causes in figure 4.4 as a large checklist where you fill your shopping cart with the listed factors. Should we be surprised that our conclusion is influenced by the factors? Or, David has a checklist titled "hypothermia causes." Among several other factors, the list includes *inadequate clothing, inadequate food intake,* and *immersion in cold water.* In the postincident analysis, one would go down the checklist and mark these three items. Would it be surprising if one concludes that these items caused the accident?

The accident models discussed in this chapter and in the following chapters are susceptible to these methodological issues. These issues do not negate the use of the models. Rather, this discussion provides better insight into their use, their limitations, and the conclusions that you make using them.

## SUMMARY

Although models of accident causation and prevention are relatively new to the recreation and park field, safety management has been an active field for nearly 100 years. This chapter covers the history of the accident causation and prevention movement, beginning with Heinrich's domino theory, which is foundational for understanding the movement. This model was updated and refined by Bird and Germain (1985). This chapter also introduces the behavioral, epidemiological, human error management, and human error models and the concept of HRO. These models emphasize the important role a safety manager or safety engineer plays in an organization. These principles and concepts are easily adaptable to practitioners delivering services in the recreation and park field.

# EXERCISES

## Exercise 1: Determining the Need for Safety Management

The purpose of this exercise is to survey the nature and extent of accidents in your specialty area. If you have a specialty area, search the Internet or your governing association to determine the extent of accidents in your area. Do not be surprised if you do not find a lot of information. If possible, develop a list of the top seven causes of accidents in your discipline area.

## Exercise 2: Determining Immediate Factors

The purpose of this exercise is to relate substandard practices and substandard conditions to a specific activity or setting. The list of substandard practices and conditions in the section titled "Immediate Causes: Standards" is clearly related to industrial settings. Your task is to adapt these to your specific recreation or park setting (e.g., gymnasium, swimming pool, playground, interpretive trails, park facilities). Draw three columns on a piece of paper. In the first column list the substandard practices and conditions. In the second column, list an example related to your activity that illustrates each of the substandard practices or conditions. In the third column, "triage" the substandard practices and conditions listed in the second column based on your activity. You have three options: leave the substandard practice or condition as is, modify or change the substandard practice or condition to better meet the specifics of your setting, or eliminate the substandard practice or condition because it is not applicable.

## Exercise 3: Determining the Basic Conditions—Personal Factors

The purpose of this exercise is to personalize the basic conditions listed by Bird and Germain (1985) and Heinrich (1980) to a specific activity or setting. Choose a recreation or park setting. You will most likely choose the activity you chose in exercise 2. Draw three columns on a piece of paper. In the first column list the seven personal factors listed in table 4.1. In the second column, provide an example illustrating one of the subfactors listed under each of the personal factors. In the third column, "triage" the factors listed in the second column based on your activity. You have three options: leave the factor as is, modify or change the factor to better meet the specifics of your setting, or eliminate the factor because it is not applicable.

## Exercise 4: Controlling for the Basic Factors

The purpose of this exercise is to seek safety remedies for the factors you identified in exercise 3. In exercise 3, you identified and adapted basic conditions to your specific activity or setting. In the Heinrich (1980) and Bird and Germain (1985) models, the next step is control. Assume that you are the person in control of an organization. For each of the seven examples in exercise 3, indicate what you would do to manage the effect of each of the basic personal factors to an acceptable and safe level. When completing this exercise, you may find it convenient to simply create a fourth column for the control factor on your work from exercise 3.

*Note:* By completing exercises 2 through 4, you are performing the functions of a safety manager in seeking out potential problems and developing solutions to reduce incidents. You are also creating a process for analyzing your work environment in order to reduce accidents.

Chapter 5

# Analytical Trees

In the early 1970s, William Johnson (Johnson, 1973) developed for the U.S. Department of Energy an approach that emphasized the development of fault tree analysis and that analyzed accidents as a series of events. His approach became known as the management oversight and risk tree (MORT). It is used primarily in accident investigations to analyze accidents.

This chapter discusses MORT as well as the numerous analytical tree models spawned by the creation of MORT, including event and causal factor analysis, energy transfer, barrier analysis, and fault tree analysis. These models are quite useful because they address the accident process as well as accident investigation. This chapter also explores barrier analysis and the concept of energy transfer. Although historically linked to MORT and the other analytical tree models, these two stand-alone approaches can easily be integrated into the models presented in chapters 4 and 6. The concepts of barrier analysis and energy transfer should change a person's approach to recreation leadership and programming.

Historically, most of the models presented in this chapter have been associated with large, complex, and multifaceted systems of organizations such as the U.S. Department of Defense, the Atomic Energy Commission, or the National Aeronautics and Space Administration. This can be an important consideration when adapting these techniques from one type of setting to an entirely different discipline and setting such as recreation and parks. Although the historical lineage affects the use of the models, the models can and do change to meet different situations. The analytical tree models discussed in this chapter represent a significant contribution to the recreation and park field.

## EVENT AND CAUSAL FACTOR ANALYSIS

Event and causal factor analysis is a technique that graphically charts the chain of events in the accident process. This process is foundational in accident investigation and prevention techniques because other methods (i.e., barrier analysis, fault tree analysis, and MORT) incorporate these basic charting principles (Buys and Clark, 1995; Oakley, 2003). Event and causal factor analysis is used to record the events and conditions involved in an accident and to establish a time sequence of events, which can be helpful in validating and verifying facts. Because it documents events, it can be useful in determining multiple causes of an accident.

Buys and Clark (1995) recommend the following conventions in charting events and in conducting the causal analysis (figure 5.3). Events are normally enclosed in rectangles and are connected with other events using solid arrows. Conditions are normally enclosed in ovals and are connected to other conditions or to events using dashed arrows. Events or conditions based on factual evidence are enclosed in solid lines, and events or conditions based

## Meramec River Incident

Many of the examples in this chapter refer to the Meramec River incident. The three parties in the incident are Joyce Meyer Ministries, the Missouri state parks, and the victims. Most of the examples in this chapter are viewed from the perspective of the state parks rather than from the perspective of Joyce Meyer Ministries, which would likely approach this incident differently.

On July 9, 2006, approximately 40 innercity youths participated in a Church Appreciation Day picnic at Castlewood State Park on the Meramec River near St. Louis, Missouri. The youths were from the St. Louis Dream Center, part of the Joyce Meyer Ministries that works with innercity youths. They arrived on site at 3:30 p.m. and proceeded to shelter 2, which is a pavilion with a picnic table. Shortly after arriving, the group went swimming at the public beach in the park on the Meramec River.

The swimming area is a sand and gravel beach (figure 5.1). In the beach area, the water depth varies from 4 to 5 feet at the deepest spots in the river. Based on an engineering study performed at the site, the water flows from 1 to slightly more than 3 miles per hour. The current is consistent and subtle. It tends to continuously move people downstream, but it is not overwhelming. Other than the drop-off, no real hazards were identified in the beach area.

The topology of the site contributes to the creation of a hazard just downstream of the beach area. A slight bend in the river results in a slight constriction at the bottom of the beach area where the effective channel narrows. In the constricted area, the depth of the river decreases to about 1.5 feet. In accordance with Bernoulli's principle, as water constricts and becomes shallower, its speed increases. As the water speed in the river increases from 1 to 3 miles per hour, its ability to carry sediment also increases. This is noted in the engineer's report. As the water enters the pool on the next bend, the current slows and the sediment drops, forming a drop-off in the river. In a span of 3 or 4 feet, the river depth goes from less than 2 feet to more than 4 to 5 feet.

Photo courtesy of Robert B. Kauffman.

**Figure 5.1** Entrance to the sandy beach area on the Meramec River in Castlewood State Park.

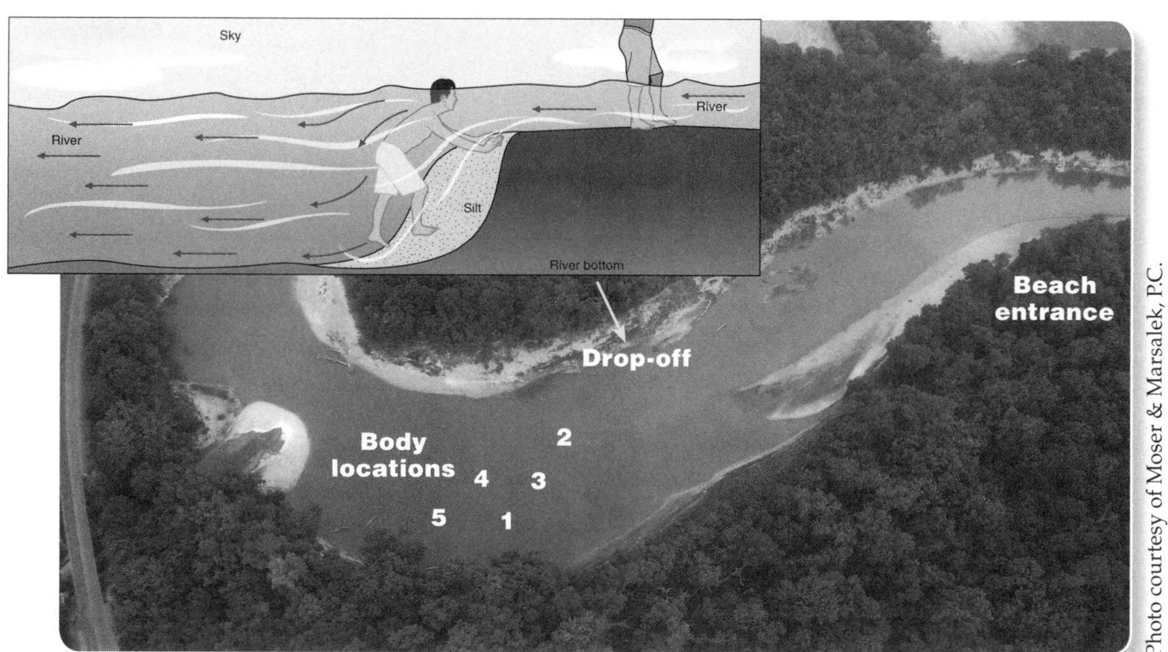


**Figure 5.2** This photo shows both the beach entrance and the drop-off. Moving from right to left, the gentle current tends to move swimmers downstream toward the drop-off. As depicted in the insert, the depth of the river goes from 1.5 feet to more than 4 to 5 feet. The victims' bodies were found downstream of the drop-off.

Figure 5.2, an overhead photo taken shortly after the incident, clearly shows the drop-off, which is made of loose gravel. The gravel makes it nearly impossible to climb back up to the shallow area before the drop-off, and the slow current tends to move objects downstream into the deeper water.

Anyone who is familiar with river currents and has some swimming ability can easily swim to the shore on a diagonal. However, the drop-off is a hazard for nonswimmers, who can panic when they are suddenly in water that is over their heads. This can easily result in a drowning.

Six youths went off the drop-off one after another. One victim was pulled from the river bottom and was resuscitated. The five other victims drowned. Their bodies were recovered downstream in approximately 10 feet of water.

on presumptive information are enclosed in dashed lines.

The primary events are those events that specifically lead to the incident. Each event should describe in a short sentence a single, discrete occurrence (e.g., "The victim stepped off the drop-off in the river" rather than "The drop-off was in the river"). If the sentence includes the word *and*, the sentence can be split into two events. For example, "The victim stepped off the drop-off in the river, drifted downstream, and drowned" can be split into two events: "The victim stepped off the drop-off in the river" and "The victim drifted 20 feet downstream from the drop-off and drowned." When possible, the event should be quantified. In the previous example, "The victim drifted 20 feet downstream from the drop-off and drowned" quantifies the distance traveled.

Using these charting techniques, the Meramec River incident was charted in figure 5.4 using the information presented in figures 5.1 and 5.2. Regarding the primary events, the group went swimming, six participants became

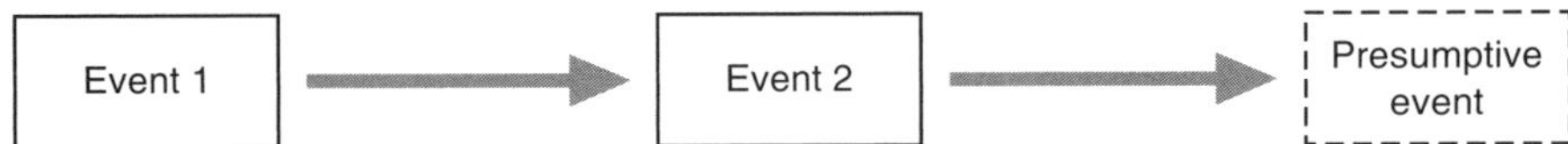


1. Events are normally enclosed in rectangles. They are connected with solid lines. The primary sequence of events is depicted chronologically in a straight horizontal line beginning on the left and ending on the right. Presumptive events are outlined or enclosed with a dashed line.

2. Conditions are normally enclosed in ovals. They are connected with events or other conditions using dashed lines. Presumptive events are outlined or enclosed with a dashed line.

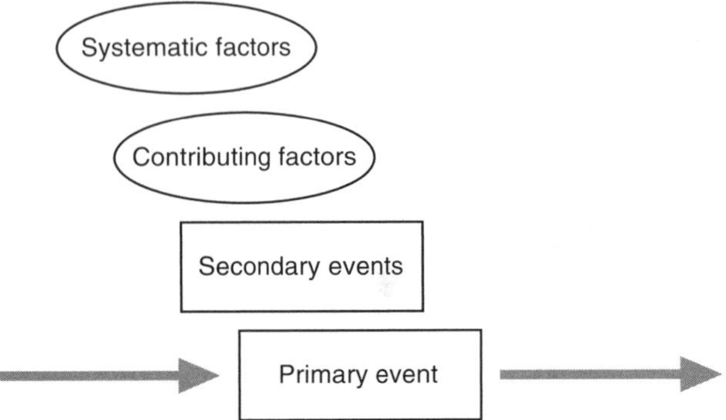


3. Secondary event sequences, contributing factors, and systematic factors are depicted using horizontal sequences at different levels.

**Figure 5.3** Basic charting techniques used in accident investigation and prevention techniques.

Reprinted, by permission, from J. Buys and J. Clark, 1995, *Event and causal factors analysis* (Idaho Falls, Idaho: Technical Research and Analysis Center, SCIENTECH, Inc.).

separated, an incident occurred, and five victims drowned while one was resuscitated. Some sources depict the specific incident (they stepped off the gravel ledge) with a diamond as done here, and other sources simply depict it as another event with a rectangle. Either approach is satisfactory. If possible, the primary events should be posted with date and time.

Secondary events, contributing factors, and systematic factors are plotted outward vertically from the primary events. Secondary events are those that are ancillary to the primary events. In this case, they include those events that occurred prior to going swimming or wading. Those relating to Joyce Meyer Ministries are plotted on the top, and those relating to Castlewood State Park are listed on the bottom. It wouldn't make any difference if Joyce Meyer Ministries was plotted on the bottom and Castlewood State Park was plotted on the top. In general, they are plotted sequentially also.

Conditions describe a state or circumstance rather than something that happened (an event). Contributing and systematic factors are considered conditions. In contrast to events, conditions describe a state or circumstance. Conditions are written in the passive rather than the active form. When applicable, those conditions that were less than adequate (LTA) are identified also. In figure 5.4, the state park was unaware of the hazard, and their assessment of the hazards as part of their risk management plan was less than adequate (LTA). The *Buddy system ineffective in swimming rescue* condition was circled with a dashed line because it was presumptive and a conclusion rather than a fact. In contrast, the *Participants not wearing life jackets* condition is factual and circled with a solid line.

Systematic factors include those underlying factors in the organization. In figure 5.4, the risk management plan for the state park and

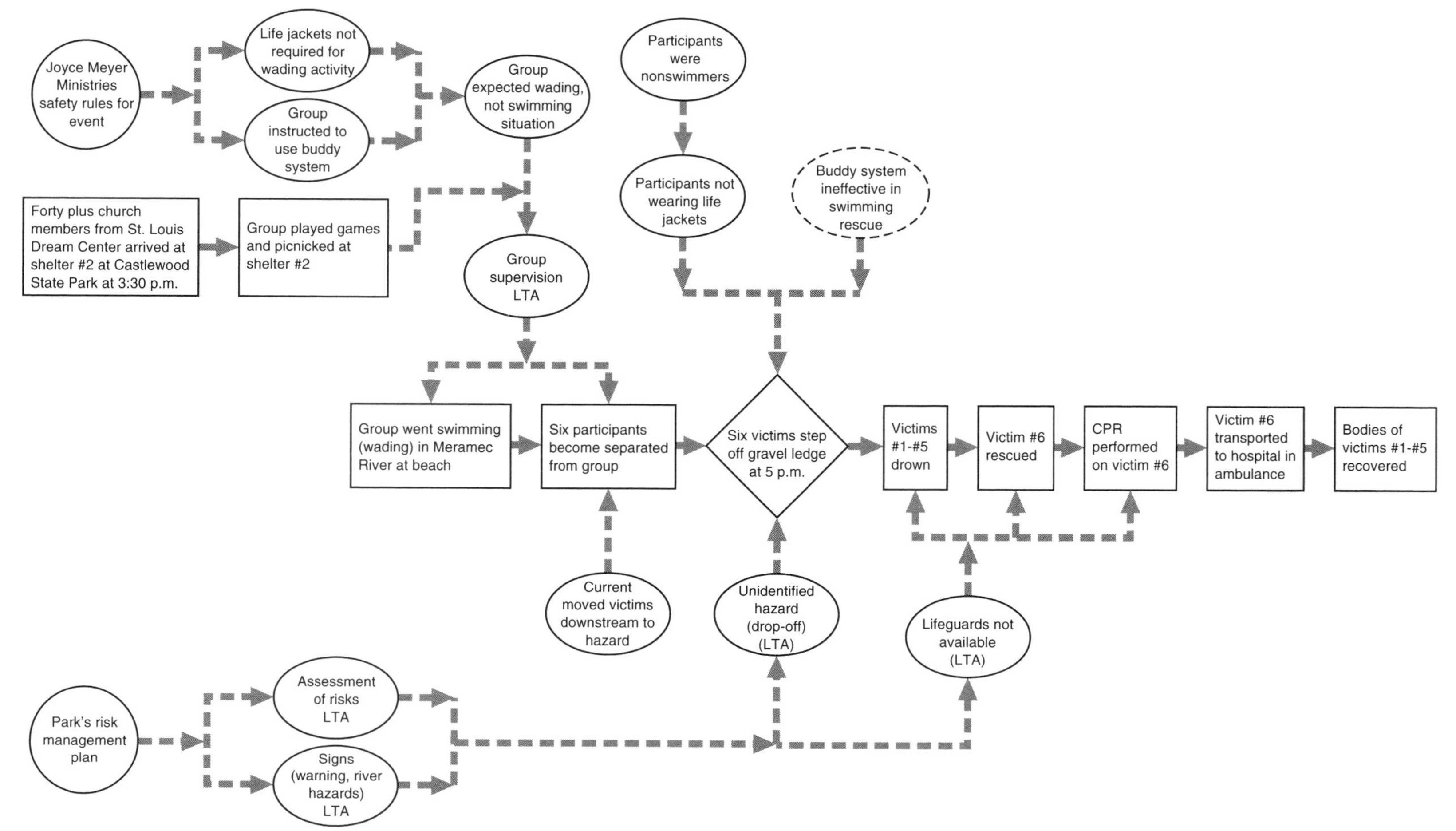


**Figure 5.4** The Meramec River incident charted using the basic charting techniques of event and causal factor analysis.

the safety rules for Joyce Meyer Ministries are systematic factors.

When creating a chart, one should consider writing events and conditions on repositionable notes so that items can be easily added and moved as needed. Think of each event or condition in figure 5.4 as a note on the wall or bulletin board. When possible, each note should include the date, the time the event occurred, and the source. The source is very important because it allows one to validate the event and to backtrack sources if a question arises.

Although the sequence of events moves from left to right, it is easier to read the chart from right to left. It is like reading the conclusion in a book and then seeing how the plot leads to the conclusion. As you read the chart from right to left, see if you agree with the chart making the following conclusion regarding the causes in the Joyce Meyer Ministries incident. First, the state park was unaware of the hazard (drop-off) at the bottom of the normal beach area. Perhaps they should have been aware of the hazard. Second, Joyce Meyer Ministries and its participants expected a swimming experience that was really a wading experience where the water was not over anyone's head. It is as if some of the participants wound up in the deep end of a swimming pool when they expected to be in the shallow end. In conclusion, the experience being provided at the beach was not the experience expected by the visitors because of the hazard. In laying out the events and conditions, does the chart in figure 5.4 spatially make this conclusion? If so, the basic purpose of event charting was successful.

## BARRIER ANALYSIS

Barrier analysis is a conceptual cornerstone of the accident process and accident prevention. Although it is an important component within the management oversight and risk tree (MORT), it is a stand-alone analysis that is useful in the accident process and accident prevention. Using the analysis to identify barriers prior to the occurrence of an accident makes barrier analysis a useful tool in accident prevention. This section explains barrier analysis and provides a simple approach to applying it in a recreation and parks setting. The following section is adapted from a technical paper titled *Barrier Analysis* by the Technical Research and Analysis Center (Trost and Nertney, 1995).

The objective of barrier analysis is to place barriers between the target (people or objects) and the potential hazard in order to prevent the transfer of unwanted energy (figure 5.5). If the barrier is less than adequate (LTA), the unwanted energy transfer can result in an incident or accident. In MORT analysis, an incident is defined as an event in which a transfer of energy occurs, and an accident is defined as an incident that results in adverse consequences. Two graphic representations of barrier analysis are provided. Figure 5.5 presents barrier analysis in a cartoon format, and figure 5.6 presents it more formally as an accident triangle.

In the models, a *hazard* is anything that can cause an energy transfer that might cause injury, damage, or loss to the target. The *target* is the person or object that can potentially be harmed by an energy transfer from the hazard. A *barrier* is anything that separates the target from the energy flow emanating from the hazard. Barriers include both hard and soft barriers. *Hard barriers* are physical barriers (handrails, fences). *Soft barriers* are administrative barriers (policies, protocols, rules, regulations). If the barrier is *less than adequate (LTA)*, either all or part of the energy transfer reaches the target.

Some of the traditional energy forms are kinetic, chemical and biological, thermal, electrical, and ionizing and nonionizing radiation. Examples of energy transfer are commonplace, although not always obvious, in the recreation and park field. Examples of kinetic energy include falling from playground equipment, bicycles, and climbing walls or tripping and falling to the ground in sport or recreation activities. Chemical energy includes the chlorine used in swimming pools or herbicides and insecticides used in park management. Heat exhaustion, dehydration, and hypothermia result from a thermal exchange. Lightning striking a golfer on a golf course is an example of electric energy.

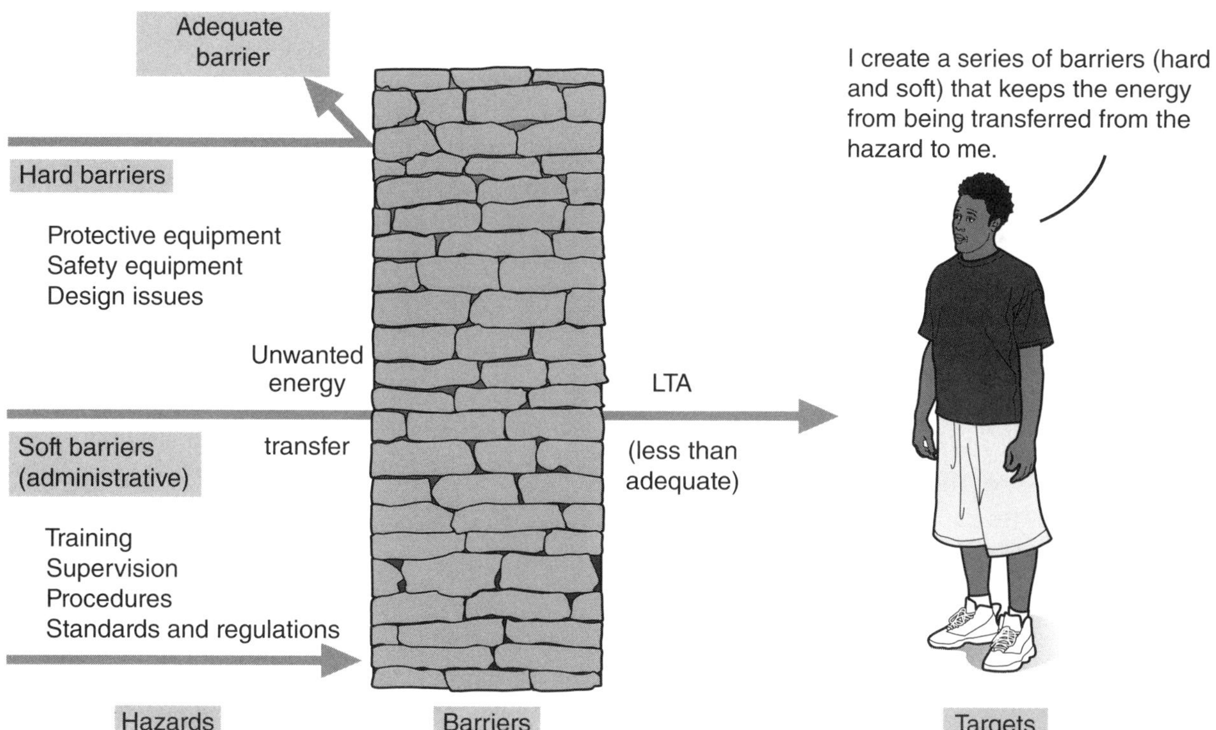


**Figure 5.5** The objective of barrier analysis is to place hard (physical) and soft (administrative) barriers between the target (the participant) and the hazard. If the barrier is less than adequate, there is a transfer of energy and injury, damage, or loss (an accident) can occur.

Adapted, by permission, from J. Reason, 1990, *Human error* (Cambridge, UK: Cambridge University Press), 173.

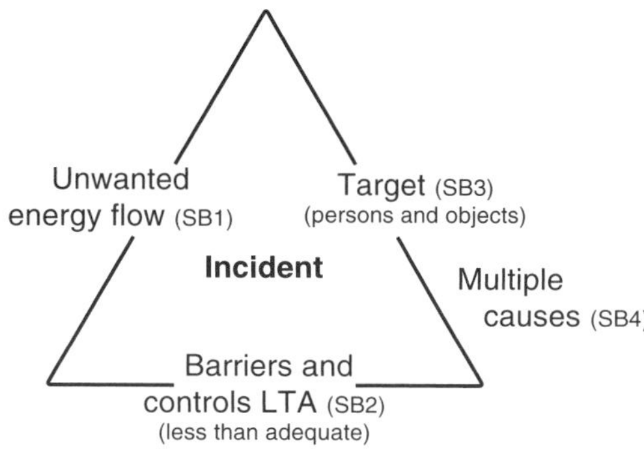


**Figure 5.6** The accident triangle formally states barrier analysis in terms of its three component parts. In this example, if the camper took less than adequate protection measures, the spilled boiling water is the unwanted energy that will burn the target (the camper) and create an accident.

Adapted from Stephenson 1991.

Energy transfer is classified as either wanted (controlled or functional) or unwanted (uncontrolled or nonfunctional). Usually, *wanted energy transfer* is associated with the work being performed and is necessary to accomplish the work. *Unwanted energy transfer* is usually not desired and can lead to a mishap. For example, a camper uses a gas stove to boil a pot of water. The energy transfer is controlled and desired and accomplishes the task of boiling the water. Boiling the water is a wanted energy transfer. The camper accidentally knocks over the stove and the pot of boiling water. An unwanted energy transfer occurs as the boiling water spills onto everything. Unwanted energy transfer may also result from the open flame on the stove. In this situation, the water can either hit the earth harmlessly (an incident) or burn the cook (an accident). In this example, barrier analysis focuses on placing barriers between the hazards (stove and boiling water) and the target (camper).

Four components are *necessary* for an accident to occur:

1. potential harmful energy transfer or environmental condition (basic causes,

underlying factors, or conditions that facilitate the incident) (SB1);
2. vulnerable people or objects (target) (SB2);
3. barriers and controls (physical and administrative) (SB3); and
4. events and energy transfers leading to an accident (additional contributing energy or target interactions, multiple causes) (SB4).

The SB code refers to the tree branch and its level in the MORT analysis (see figures 5.7 and 5.17) The S stands for the specific control factors tree branch and the B indicates the second level (1, 2, 3, or 4) of the tree.

These four components are significant for several reasons. First, they reflect the concept of the transfer of energy from the hazard to the target. Second, a causal relationship exists among the components in that if any one of the elements is not present, an accident does not occur. Third, the causal relationship is a component of MORT tree analysis (see figures 5.7 and 5.17), which is considered one of the premiere accident investigation tools. Finally, the components are the basis of barrier analysis.

## Energy Transfer

Energy transfer is applicable to most of the accident models discussed in this text, including accident models that do not explicitly acknowledge energy transfer. By definition, when an incident or accident occurs, energy transfer also occurs. The only issue is whether the energy transfer is sufficient to cause injury, damage, or loss or simply cause a near miss. It can determine whether, after slipping on a banana peel, a woman breaks her arm or brushes the dirt off her arm from the fall and walks away.

The concept of energy transfer builds on the work of Haddon (1973). He developed the concept that the energy transfer leading to a harmful event can be controlled by one or more barriers or measures, which he referred to as energy barriers. *Hard energy barriers* are physical barriers, whereas *soft energy barriers* are administrative practices, procedures, and protocols that are often intangible. His 10 steps for reducing or preventing energy transfer are as follows.

1. Prevent the marshaling (do not produce or manufacture the energy).

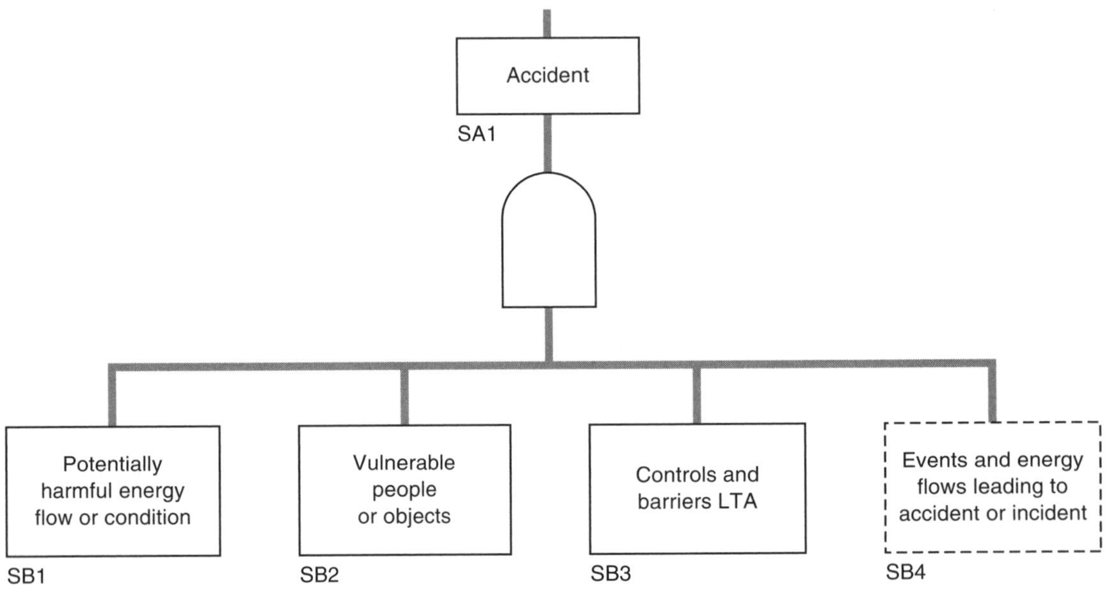


**Figure 5.7** The elements presented in this tree are a portion of the total MORT tree analysis (see figure 5.17). The four components are necessary for an accident (injury, damage, or loss) to occur.

Reprinted, by permission, from J. Kingston et al., 2009, *NRI MORT user's manual—For use with the management oversight and risk tree analytical logic diagram* (AG Delft, Netherlands: The Noordwijk Risk Initiative Foundation), xii.

2. Reduce the amount (e.g., voltages, fuel storage).
3. Prevent the release of energy (e.g., strengthen the energy containment).
4. Modify the rate of release (e.g., slow down burning rate, speed).
5. Separate in space or time (e.g., keep electric lines out of reach).
6. Interpose material barrier (e.g., insulation, guards, safety glasses).
7. Modify shock-concentration surfaces (e.g., round off, make soft).
8. Strengthen the target (e.g., earthquake-proof structures).
9. Limit the damage (e.g., prompt signals and action, sprinklers).
10. Rehabilitate persons and objects.

The concept of energy transfer may seem foreign to the recreation and park field, but it is really quite applicable. In terms of Haddon's principles, examine the construction and use of the bouldering rock in figures 5.8, *a* and *b*. Those familiar with playground safety standards will note their application (e.g., fall zones, surfacing, warning signs) to the bouldering area in the figure.

Using Haddon's 10 steps, a designer could erect multiple barriers on the bouldering boulder to protect a target. He could remove the artificial boulder to prevent falls (item 1). He could reduce the amount of energy potentially transferred (item 2) by limiting the height of the structure to no more than five feet. The use of pea gravel as a surfacing material could constitute a material barrier to help protect the target by absorbing some of the force of the fall (item 6). Although impractical in this setting, a top-rope system and belay is another example of a material barrier that would protect the target (the person bouldering). Rounding off the edges of the boulder and making sure of the structural integrity of the edges is an example of modifying the surfaces (item 7). Although they may seem impractical, training the person bouldering how to properly fall and absorb energy when hitting the pea gravel or having the boulderer wear protective gear are examples of strengthening the target (item 8). The pea gravel surface is an example of seeking to limit damage (item 9). Signs indicating how to boulder or providing pointers would be helpful for rehabilitation (item 10). In this example, one can put numerous systems in place as barriers to prevent several types of energy transfer resulting from a fall.

Creating barriers relating to all 10 steps is not always possible, necessary, or practical. In the boulder example, preventing the release of energy (item 3) is not practical. Additionally, using a belay system to modify the rate of release

Photos courtesy of Robert B. Kauffman.

**Figure 5.8** *(a)* A bouldering boulder and a boulderer using it for practice. Playground safety standards include an adequate fall zone, pea gravel surfacing, and warning signs. *(b)* Children playing on the boulder in an unintended manner. Designers need to consider unintended uses when designing play equipment.

(item 4) is not viable because belay systems do not work effectively at low heights. Similarly, separating the source in terms of space from the target (item 5) is not practical given that vertical height is a normal part of bouldering.

Returning to the Meramec River incident, one potential management alternative that would be illustrative of Haddon's energy transfer would be to require all waders and swimmers at the beach to wear life jackets. In terms of Haddon's energy transfer, this management alternative would reduce or control several types of energy transfer (assuming that everyone wears a life jacket and that the state park can properly enforce the rule). Mandatory life jackets would reduce the amount of energy released (item 4) because people would float after stepping off the drop-off. In addition, life jackets could be a material barrier (item 6) between the energy source (drop-off) and the target (wader or swimmer). Life jackets strengthen the target (item 8) by making waders and swimmers more resilient to the effects of stepping off the drop-off. Also, mandatory life jackets potentially limit damage (item 9) by keeping people afloat.

## Barrier Classification

Barrier classification is a process of preventing or reducing the energy transfer from the hazard to the target. Trost and Nertney (1995) classified barriers by type, location, and function (figure 5.9). The following is a discussion of each of these classifications.

### Type

Barriers by type include design (e.g., equipment and facilities); physical barriers; warning devices; procedures, processes, and protocols; knowledge and skill; attitude; and supervision. These barrier types are discussed below.

Historically, the safety industry has focused mainly on *design of equipment and facilities* to control hazards. Most people are familiar with the concept of automobile safety. In general, automobile safety comprises three parts: the highway, the automobile, and the driver. On the highway, Jersey barriers prevent head-on crashes and guardrails prevent cars from hitting bridge abutments or running into ravines. Inside the automobile, seat belts, air bags, and crumble zones increase driver and passenger safety. With some exceptions such as playground safety and challenge courses, the recreation and park field traditionally has not focused on design solutions to control hazards. In such a field that relies heavily on leadership and programming skills, design solutions may be less important than the soft skills involving developing procedures, policies, common practices, and protocols.

*Physical barriers* are barriers that are placed between the hazard and target to modify or limit the behavior of the target. Physical bar-

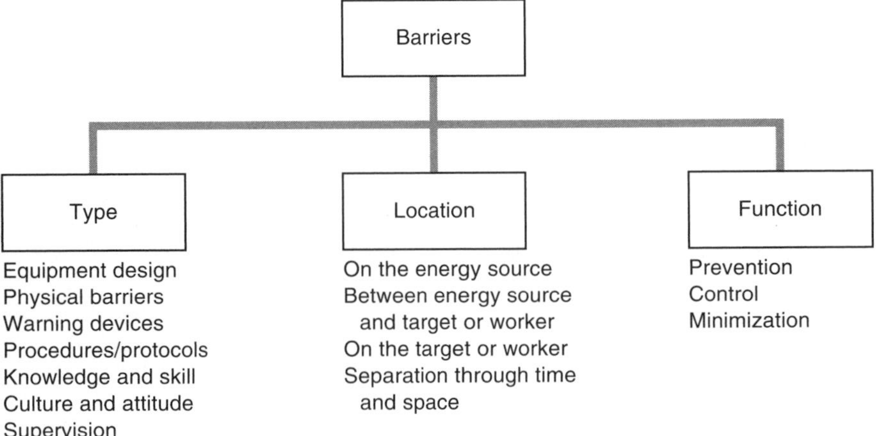


**Figure 5.9** In general, barriers can be classified by their type, location, or function.

Reprinted, by permission, from W. Trost and R. Nertney, 1995, *Barrier analysis* (Idaho Falls, ID: Technical Research and Analysis Center), 11.

riers include guardrails, walls, or temporary barriers. In the recreation and park field, plantings are frequently used to effectively create physical barriers. For example, a hedge that is 30 inches high creates a physical barrier; most people will walk around the barrier rather than step over it or walk through it. A hedge is more effective as a barrier when it is backed up with a fence of the same height (Carpenter et al., 1975).

*Warning devices* warn people of the hazard. The familiar yellow caution sign warns people that they could slip on a wet floor. Other warning devices include plaques on playground equipment that convey age appropriateness or the line on the frame of playground equipment that indicates how high the mulch level should be. In the Meramec River example, the park could have considered placing a series of buoys above the drop-off in the river. After the accident, they placed a "swim at your own risk" sign. The problem with the sign is that it did not warn people of the hazard or of the things that could transfer energy. Rather, it attempted only to transfer legal responsibility to the individual. It is equivalent to placing a "drive at your own risk" sign on a highway in an attempt to warn people that a bridge is out down the road. Both signs are general warnings; people need specific warnings. An interpretive warning device warns people by educating or providing them with the necessary information regarding the activity environment. People from an innercity environment visiting a seemingly benign flowing river simply do not know of the dangers that drop-offs and currents pose. An interpretive sign at the beach entrance is a barrier that informs people of the potential hazards. The information places a barrier between the hazard (the drop-off) and the target (waders and swimmers).

*Procedures and protocols* are administrative practices that create safety barriers. Requiring that at least one person on a trip be certified in first aid and CPR, requiring a minimum of two leaders, or establishing a leader-to-participant ratio are examples of providing barriers between potential hazards and the target. Requiring an on-call ambulance during a special event is another example of a barrier. Creating administrative or protocol barriers may also include placing restrictions on when one can conduct an activity due to weather extremes (high or low temperatures) or adverse weather condition (thunderstorm, tornado, hurricane, flash flood, or snowstorm). In the Meramec River example, the state operations manual described and classified the types of swimming areas, and the classification determined whether lifeguards were needed on site. The presence of lifeguards could be a partial barrier because they could supervise the site and prevent waders and swimmers from reaching the drop-off in the river. In addition, they could educate and inform waders and swimmers of the hazard. The purpose of this example is to show that procedures and protocols can be used to create barriers to protect the target (in this case, waders and swimmers).

Increasing the *knowledge and skill of the target* can place a barrier between the hazard and the target. Armed with the proper knowledge, most people will modify their behavior to avoid a hazard. For example, installing interpretive signs at the entrance to the Meramec River swimming area would possibly create a barrier between the hazard and the targets by increasing the knowledge of waders and swimmers.

*Organizational culture and worker attitudes* are an extension of procedures and protocols. In the management literature, an adage states, "Manage the culture, manage the organization." The culture is the collective attitudes and practices of the organization. For example, chapter 4 discusses highly reliable organizations, which are normally found in seemingly dangerous environments. Because the environment is so dangerous, these organizations develop a culture that addresses how everyone should behave in that environment. For example, the organization may institute a policy where it is the duty of employees to report near misses.

*Supervision* refers to barriers at both the administrative and leadership levels. In the recreations and park field, supervision relates to park administrators and how they implement park policies and procedures. It also relates to park rangers and interpreters and how they communicate and inform the public of existing hazards.

### Location

Location refers to where the barrier is placed. A barrier can be placed on the energy source, on the target, or between the target and the hazard. The barrier can be physical, such as a guardrail or a fence around a swimming pool, or it can be administrative (see figure 5.3). People often use time and space in an effort to separate the hazard from the target. For example, if accidents occur during the heat of late afternoon, one could separate the target (participants) from the hazard (heat) by conducting the activity early in the day. If a foul ball (hazard) from an adjacent baseball field narrowly misses a group (target) playing next to the field, the group could move the activity to another area (separation by space) or wait until the game is over before returning to the field (separation by time).

In the Meramec River example, placing an interpretive sign explaining river hazards at the beach entrance is an example of placing a barrier between the target (waders and swimmers) and the hazard (the drop-off). Separating the target from the hazard by closing the swimming area or moving it to another location is an example of separation by space.

### Function

In general, function focuses on prevention, control, or minimization. Generally, *prevention* involves removing the hazard, *control* involves managing the hazard or target or the relationship between them, and *minimization* involves lessening the impact of the energy transfer between the hazard and the target.

In the Meramec River example, closing the swimming area or moving it to another site is an example of prevention. It would not protect the casual swimmer who ventured into the river at the site of the drop-off. The interpretive signs, rangers, lifeguards, and buoys are examples of controlling or managing the relationship between the hazard and the target. Requiring all swimmers to wear an approved life jacket or personal flotation device is an example of minimizing the energy transfer. When the target (wader or swimmer) steps off the ledge into the drop-off (hazard), he would simply float, thus minimizing energy transfer.

## Limitations of Barriers

Barriers have limitations. First, placing a barrier may not be practical. In the Meramec River example, it would not be practical to place a sign in the river noting the drop-off because water levels fluctuate. Also, placing a sign in the river might create a new hazard. Often, barriers are not practical because of economic considerations. In the Meramec River example, substantial costs are associated with hiring lifeguards and upgrading the swimming area.

Barriers can also fail, either in part or totally. Guardrails need maintenance. Policies, procedures, and protocols need review and updating to keep them current and need appropriate and rigorous enforcement. People must keep their skills and training current. For example, most people will forget half of what they learned in first aid training after six months and three fourths of what they learned after a year. People must continually review and practice training and skills.

Another limitation is that barriers may not be used because they were not provided or because of employee error. In the Meramec River example, barriers such as interpretive signs, lifeguards, and roving rangers were not used because they were not provided.

Given these limitations, no barrier is guaranteed to be totally effective. In the Meramec River example, even closing the site would not guarantee total safety. Closing the site would remove most of the targets by preventing most of the waders and swimmers from being in close proximity to the hazard. However, casual visitors could still seek out the site and go swimming. The hazard is still there. Therefore, the potential transfer of energy is still there. The possibility of energy transfer is not eliminated; it is only less likely to occur because fewer targets (people) are in close proximity to the hazard.

## Barrier Assessment Analysis

The assessment of barriers in recreation and park settings is a valuable accident prevention tool. The potential hazards and the barriers used to prevent or minimize them can be formally assessed using the instrument in figure 5.10. Even if this instrument is not used, consider it as part of the thought processes where the potential

## Barrier Identification Table

**Activity or program:** ______________________________

| Energy flow (hazard): Harmful agent, adverse environmental condition | Target: Vulnerable person or thing | Barrier and controls: Used to separate energy and target | Purpose/prevention | Limitations |
|---|---|---|---|---|
| 1. | | | | |
| 2. | | | | |
| 3. | | | | |
| 4. | | | | |
| 5. | | | | |
| 6. | | | | |

**Directions**

1. Identify the activity or program. This identifies the system level.
2. In column 1, list all the potential hazards that can affect the program.
3. In column 3, list the potential barriers or controls for each hazard. Consider the following barriers: equipment and facility, physical barriers, warning devices, procedures and protocols, knowledge and skills, attitude and culture, and supervision. (Conceptually, the flow is from column 1 through column 3. Most people will address the barriers and controls second, in response to the hazard.)
4. In column 2, identify the target, vulnerable person or thing. If you have different targets for the same hazard, consider sorting the lines so that the common targets are grouped together for the same hazard.
5. In column 4, indicate whether the barrier will prevent, control, or minimize the hazard. Indicate how.
6. In column 5, indicate any limitations to placing the barrier (e.g., cost, administrative feasibility).

**Figure 5.10** Barrier assessment analysis is an accident investigation tool.

Adapted, by permission, from J. Kingston et al., 2009, *NRI MORT user's manual—For use with the management oversight and risk tree analytical logic diagram* (AG Delft, Netherlands: The Noordwijk Risk Initiative Foundation), xx; Oakley 2003.

energy transfer from the hazard to the target and what can be done to prevent or minimize the incident from occurring is identified.

The first three columns identify the energy transfer (hazard), the target, and the barriers and controls, respectively. The basic purpose of the barrier and controls is to separate the hazard from the target. The fourth column identifies the purpose and how the barrier will prevent or minimize the energy transfer. The fifth column addresses the limitations of implementing the barrier. Not all barriers are practical or cost effective. Creating a barrier can also create a new hazard that warrants creating additional barriers. For example, placing warning buoys in a river as a barrier or safety measure potentially creates a new hazard (the warning buoys).

Figure 5.11 is an example of using barrier assessment analysis for the Meramec River incident. In the first column, the drop-off in the river is listed as the hazard or potential energy transfer. (This is only one of numerous potential hazards in the swimming area of the park that could be identified.) The third column lists most of the barriers discussed in the text. In the second column, waders and swimmers are listed as the target. The fourth column is the purpose of the barrier, or how it will prevent or reduce the impact of the energy transfer from the hazard. Think in terms of the type, location, and function classifications discussed in the previous section. The fifth column discusses the limitations or problems associated with the implementation of the potential barrier. For example, the interpretive signage is only a partial barrier, lifeguards are expensive, upstream buoys would create a potential hazard themselves, and there is an enforcement problem with the mandatory life jackets requirement.

## Barrier Identification Table

**Activity or program: Castlewood State Park, beach area**

| Energy flow (hazard): Harmful agent, adverse environmental condition | Target: Vulnerable person or thing | Barrier and controls: Used to separate energy and target | Purpose/prevention | Limitations |
|---|---|---|---|---|
| 1. Drop-off in river downstream of beach area before bend in river | Waders/ swimmers | Interpretive sign at entrance | The purpose is to warn visitors of the hazards in the river environment, including the drop-off. | It is a partial barrier. It educates the public; it does not warn of the specific hazard. |
| | Waders/ swimmers | Lifeguards | Lifeguards supervise the beach area. They also warn participants of the hazard and keep people upstream of the hazard. | Implementing lifeguards would change the classification of the beach and increase costs. |
| | Waders/ swimmers | Buoys in river before drop-off | Buoys are physical features that can be used to warn waders and swimmers of the hazard. They can be used in conjunction with interpretive signs. | Large fluctuations in water may remove the buoys. Care must be taken so that the buoys in the water do not become hazards. |
| | Waders/ swimmers | Mandatory life jackets | Mandatory life jackets remove the energy transfer by keeping people afloat after the drop-off. | The problem is enforcing the rule and making life jackets available to people who do not bring them to the beach. |
| 2. | | | | |
| 3. | | | | |

**Directions**

1. Identify the activity or program. This identifies the system level.
2. In column 1, list all the potential hazards that can affect the program.
3. In column 3, list the potential barriers or controls for each hazard. Consider the following barriers: equipment and facility, physical barriers, warning devices, procedures and protocols, knowledge and skills, attitude and culture, and supervision. (Conceptually, the flow is from column 1 through column 3. Most people will address the barriers and controls second, in response to the hazard.)
4. In column 2, identify the target, vulnerable person or thing. If you have different targets for the same hazard, consider sorting the lines so that the common targets are grouped together for the same hazard.
5. In column 4, indicate whether the barrier will prevent, control, or minimize the hazard. Indicate how.
6. In column 5, indicate any limitations to placing the barrier (e.g., cost, administrative feasibility).

**Figure 5.11** Using barrier assessment analysis for the Meramec River incident.

Adapted from Kingston et al. 2009; Oakley 2003.

# TREE ANALYSIS

Tree analysis is the development of fault trees and analytic tree analysis. One uses fault tree analysis to analyze the actual events leading up to an accident or incident. In contrast, one uses analytical trees to compare a developed tree of what happened with one that was created for the system before the accident or incident occurred. Oakley (2003) and Stephenson (1991) note that trees can be used in accident investigation, as a planning tool, for causal analysis, and for project evaluation.

Tree analysis is a process of deductive reasoning. The tree approach takes a complex event such as an accident or incident and, through systems analysis, breaks the larger event down into smaller, more understandable and manageable events (see figure 5.12). At the top is the main event. Next are the intermediate events, which can be subdivided into basic events. Basic events are the base level and are not further dividable. Using tree analysis, one starts with the main event and analyzes the event into subevents until the basic causes are determined. To relate this approach to systems analysis, the intermediate event is equivalent to the system level, the top event is the suprasystem, and the basic event is the subsystem.

Charting tree analysis builds on many of the principles of the accident sequence. Figure 5.13 presents many of the symbols used in tree analysis, including MORT. Intermediate events are enclosed in rectangles and basic events are enclosed in circles. Triangles indicate a transfer to and from or a link to somewhere else on the chart. For every transfer, a corresponding transfer from somewhere else on the chart must occur.

The tiers, or subsystems, are linked together with logical connectors, or gates. There are two gate symbols: *and* and *or.* An *and* means that all of the subsystem components must occur for the event at the higher level to occur. An *or* means that only one of the subsystem items must occur for the event at the higher level to occur. Often, the link is implied and not formally included on the chart. For example, in figure 5.7, the gate symbol is an *and,* indicating that all four elements must be present for an accident to occur.

Often, the levels are labeled. If they are not they should still follow the following basic principles. For example, in the MORT analysis each level and each item is labeled according to its spatial location. The MORT tree divides into two major branches: specific control factors and management system factors. The first letter in the MORT identification code indicates the branch. The letter S represents specific control factors and the letter M represents management systems factors. The second letter in the MORT identification code indicates the level of the item on the tree. The letter A is the first level, B is the second level, and so forth. The third item in the MORT identification code is a number. For each item on the same level, the elements are numbered consecutively from left to right. For example in figure 5.7, a MORT identification code of SB3 indicates that the intermediate event is on the *specific control factor* branch, is on the second level, and is the third item from the left. It identifies "vulnerable people or objects."

Conceptually, there are three types of tree analyses: fault tree analysis, positive tree analysis, and MORT. Both fault tree analysis and MORT are used to determine what went wrong after an accident and therefore aid in an accident investigation (see chapter 14). In contrast, the positive tree analysis can be utilized in planning and in helping to prevent accidents.

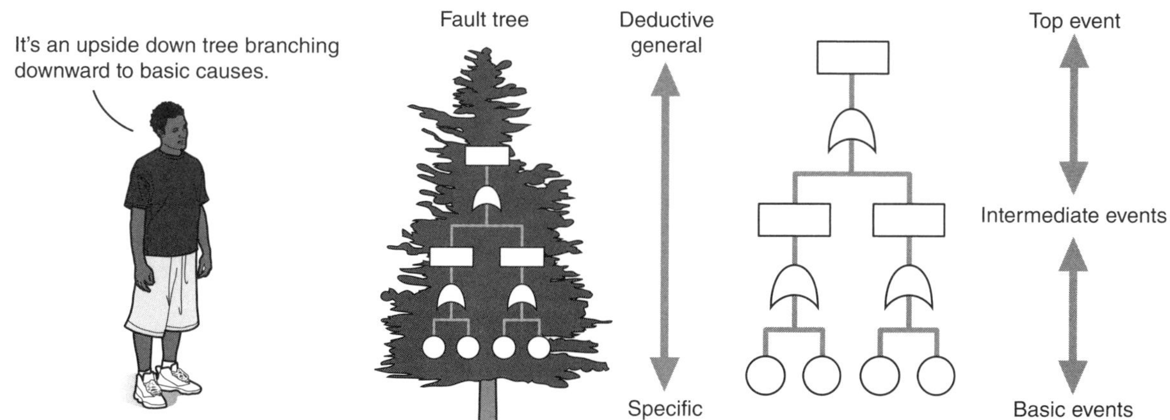


**Figure 5.12** A tree spreads out its branches as it grows. Fault tree analysis branches outward from larger events to smaller, more manageable events.

Adapted, by permission, from J. Oakley, 2003, *Accident investigation techniques* (Des Plaines, Illinois: American Society of Safety Engineers).

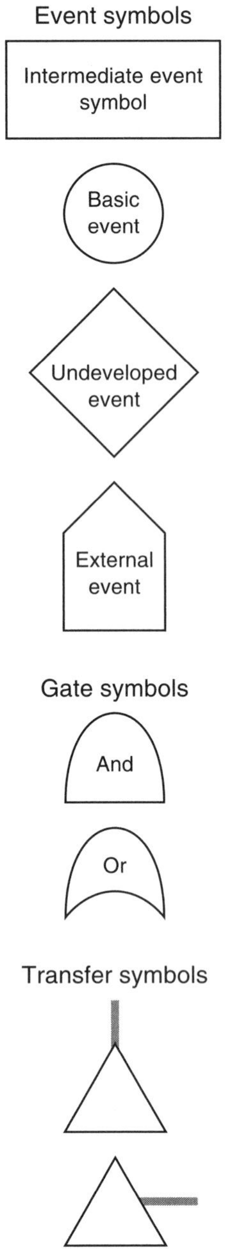

Event symbols

|  |  |
|---|---|
| Intermediate event symbol | **Intermediate event** - A fault event that occurs either at the top or at an intermediate step. Generally, the symbol is not used for a basic event. |
| Basic event | **Basic event** - The initiating event or fault that requires no further subdevelopment or subdividing. |
| Undeveloped event | **Undeveloped event** - An event that is not going to be developed further because there is insufficient information available or because it has little or no consequence to the outcome. |
| External event | **External event** - An event that normally is expected to occur. |

Gate symbols

|  |  |
|---|---|
| And | **And** - All of the items listed on the tree below the gate are necessary for the event above it to occur. |
| Or | **Or** - Only one of the items listed on the tree below the gate is necessary for the event above it to occur. |

Transfer symbols

**Transfer in** - Indicates a transfer from another page. Each transfer in must have a transfer out somewhere else.

**Transfer out** - Indicates a transfer to another page. Each transfer out must have a transfer in somewhere else.

**Figure 5.13** Basic fault tree symbols.

Adapted, by permission, from R.A. Stephans and W. Talso, 1997, *System safety analysis handbook*, 2nd ed. (Unionville, VA: The System Safety Society); Oakley 2003.

## Fault Tree Analysis

One uses fault tree analysis to determine what went wrong. Using fault tree analysis, one starts with the accident or incident and works backward to determine the causal or basic events. Stephenson (1991) and Oakley (2003, p. 105) list the following steps in the tree construction for an accident.

1. Define the top event (accident, injury, or damage).
2. Investigate the accident. (Learn about the systems, the management structure, the accident, and so on.)
3. Construct the tree. (Work from the top down, asking why the top event occurred.)

4. Develop causal factors. (The basic events—the bottom tier of the tree—are causal factors.)
5. Validate the tree. (Ensure that all information has been analyzed.)
6. Develop corrective actions. (The basic events will make corrective actions apparent.)

Figure 5.14 depicts a fault tree analysis for the Meramec River incident from the perspective of the state park. The main event—failure to prevent the drowning—is listed at the top of the chart. The main event is subdivided into two intermediate events: failure to manage waders and swimmers and failure to remove or minimize the hazard.

The first intermediate event—failure to manage waders and swimmers—is subdivided into two intermediate events. The first is a failure to provide adequate warning signs. This intermediate event comprises two basic events:

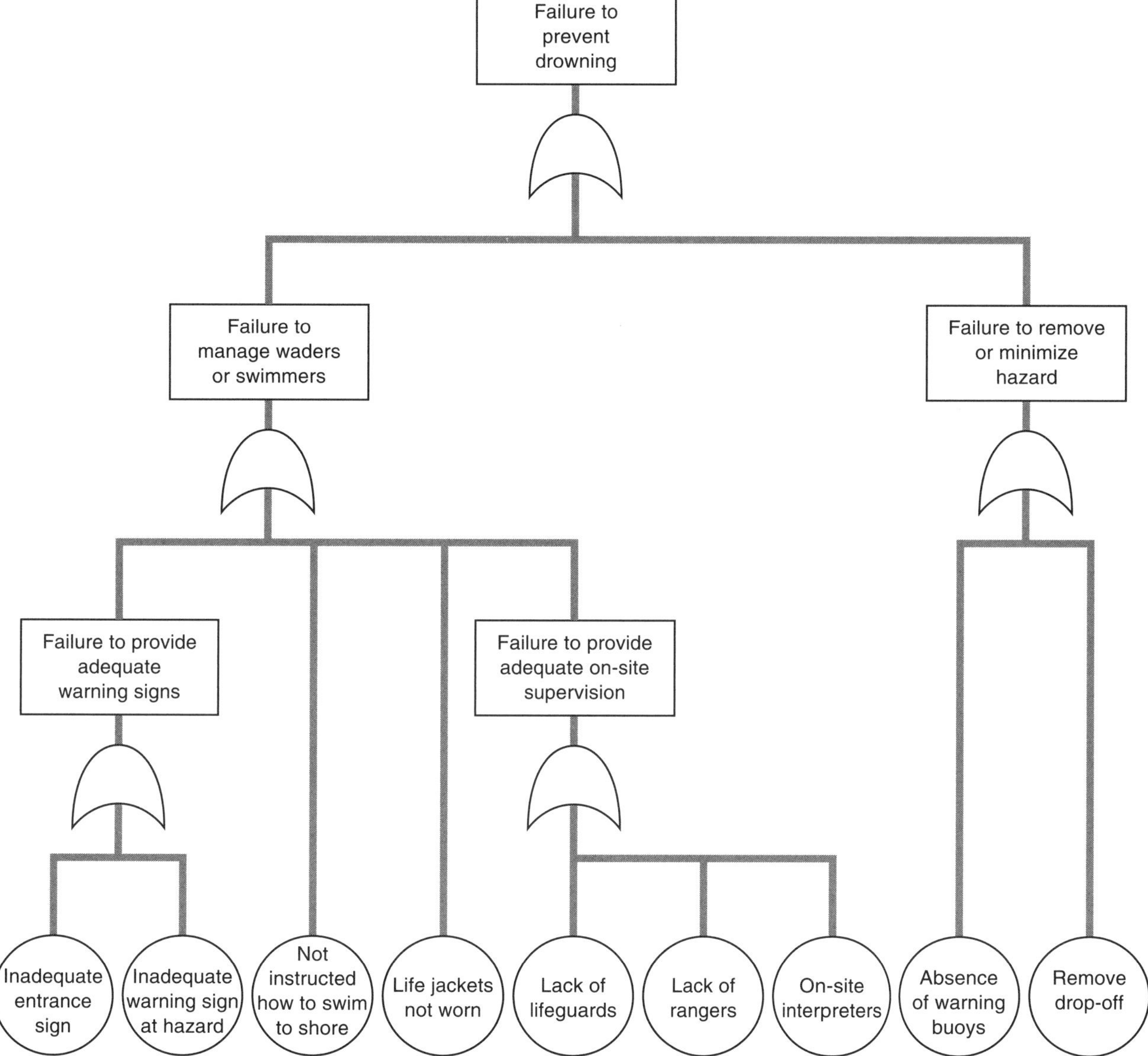


**Figure 5.14** Fault tree analysis analyzes the failure to prevent the drownings in the Meramec River incident into basic events so that management can address them using basic barrier analysis techniques (e.g., figure 5.9). The use of the *or* connector or gate symbol suggests that the basic events can be analyzed and managed independently of each other.

inadequate entrance sign and inadequate warning signs at the hazard. The second intermediate event is a failure by the park to provide adequate on-site supervision at the beach. In addition, two basic events are listed under failure to manage waders and swimmers. The first basic event is instructing waders and swimmers how to swim diagonally in the current to reach the shore; the interpretive entrance sign could include this information. The second basic event is whether waders and swimmers should be required to use life jackets and, if so, how the park would make the jackets available to the public.

The second intermediate event—failure to remove or minimize the hazard (the drop-off)—is subdivided into two basic events. Questions exist regarding the feasibility of both suggestions. First, park management could place buoys in the river before the drop-off, but they would need to exercise caution so that the buoys do not become a hazard in their own right. Second, park management could dredge the drop-off so that it gradually rather than suddenly increases in depth. This would require constant maintenance because the river would fill the drop-off back in with sediment.

A review of the basic events listed at the bottom of the fault tree analysis in figure 5.14 reveals a plethora of alternatives that park management could implement to prevent future drowning at this site. The park could evaluate each of the alternatives in terms of costs, feasibility, and viability in order to prevent or reduce future drownings at this site. They could use the barrier analysis identification instrument in figure 5.9 to help do their analysis.

## Positive Tree Analysis

In contrast to fault tree analysis, positive tree analysis uses systems analysis to break complex events down into simpler and more manageable steps. Its purpose is to determine how existing systems function. One can use positive tree analysis for comparison with other methods when an incident occurs. For example, compare the positive tree analysis in figure 5.15 for beach safety (prior to the incident) with the fault tree analysis (postincident analysis) in figure 5.14 for possible discrepancies or missing components.

Figure 5.15 presents a positive tree analysis for beach safety on the Meramec River at Castlewood State Park. Fault tree analysis starts with a known hazard or incident and works backward to determine the causal events; positive tree analysis works in the opposite direction. Because the park was not necessarily aware of the drop-off in the river before the actual accident and because the effect of the hazard on the eventual fatalities is not yet known, the approach of the positive tree analysis is more generic. For this reason, the top event is simply listed as "beach safety."

When developing the positive tree analysis, one normally lists administrative categories such as information management, supervision and staff, maintenance and inspections, and policies as the intermediate steps. Other categories may be used such as the "content of work" and "process."

From this step, one lists the basic events under each intermediate event that can be addressed. These basic events should be generic because the effect of hazards most likely has not yet been identified. In the Meramec River example, the interpretive sign at the entrance is an important management tool used to increase safety on the beach regardless of the drop-off because it educates visitors about potential hazards that they may encounter on the river.

## MORT Analysis

MORT is a highly disciplined method of analyzing accidents using the logic tree approach. It is indirectly related to fault tree analysis, barrier analysis, and the accident sequence. Unfortunately, MORT is often too complex and time consuming for use in analyzing minor accidents; this is evident from the following passage from the original manual. However, the technique is often quoted and it has spawned simpler and more practical methods.

> MORT identifies 222 "basic problems"—causal problems or preventive measures. These, in turn, underlie 98 generic problems composing successively broader areas in management and prevention. Yet the specified basic problems, if studied in

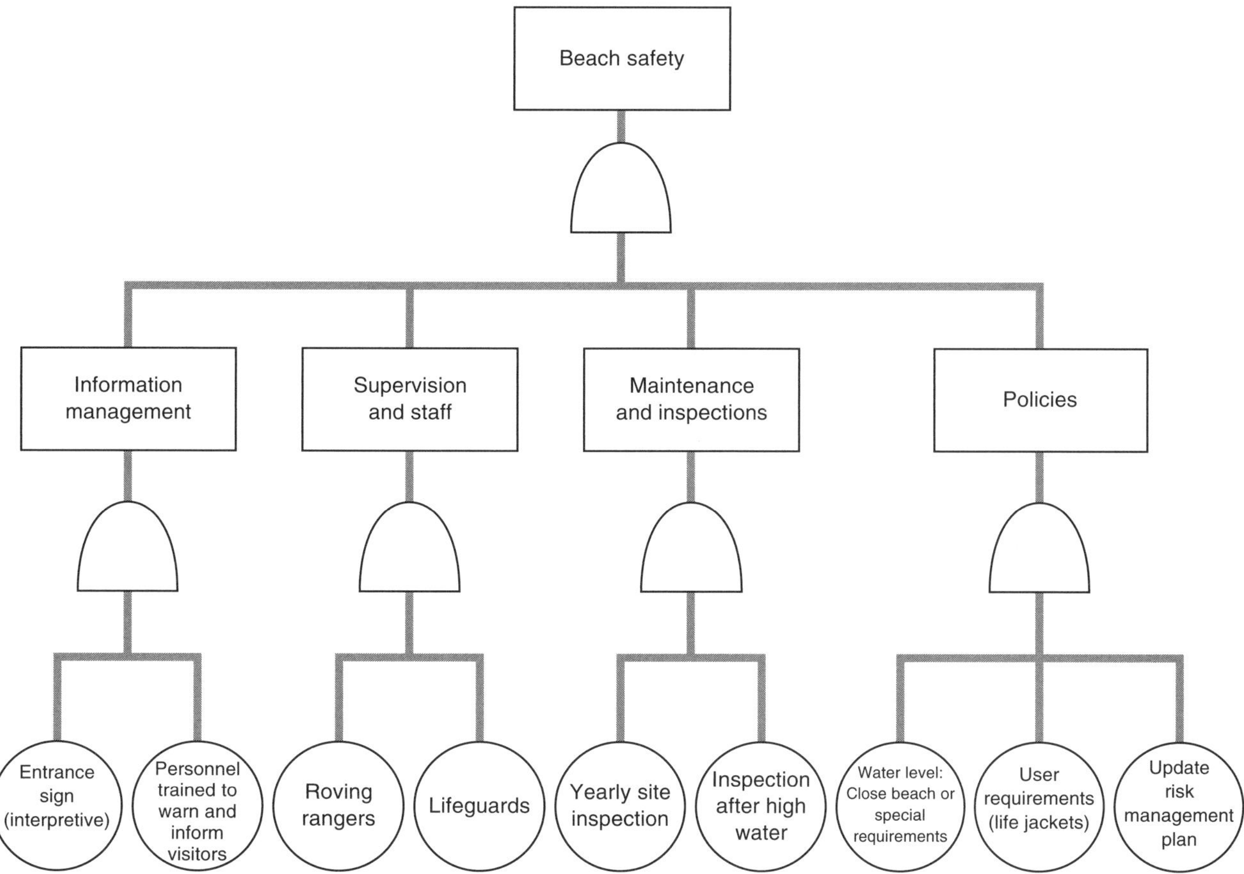


**Figure 5.15** Positive tree analysis is a proactive tool that management can use to analyze safety before an incident occurs. In this example, positive tree analysis analyzes the failure to prevent the drownings that occurred in the Meramec River incident into basic events so that management can address them using basic barrier analysis. The use of the *and* connector or gate symbol suggests that all of these basic events are necessary to facilitate beach safety.

> a continuously more analytic direction, may be only a good beginning in analysis. There may be other subproblems, and there certainly are thousands of criteria. Among the above concepts are about 70 "new ideas" and this is highly subjective, depending on a person's background. (Johnson, 1973, p. 133)

Although the totality of MORT is complex, it "is composed of relatively simple questions in a logical sequence" (Johnson, 1973, p. 137). Initially, the purpose of MORT was to analyze a single accident for failures that caused the accident. However, it became clear that the process was useful in appraising and assessing safety programs that controlled accidents in general.

Figure 5.7 lists four components of an accident: potential harmful energy transfer or environmental condition, barriers and controls, vulnerable people or objects, and events and energy transfers leading to an accident. In terms of MORT, all four components are necessary for an accident to occur. The *and* logical connector is used to define an accident. The following discussion is an extension of the MORT chart depicted in figure 5.7.

## Basic Approach

The MORT method consists of three steps. The first step is defining the events to be analyzed. Barrier analysis is discussed previously in this chapter. The difference in the use of barrier analysis within the MORT method is that barrier analysis is used as a prevention tool where previously it was used as an investigation tool. One can use the first three columns in figure 5.10 to analyze the energy transfer, the target, and the barrier. Barrier analysis is important in determining a complete set of events that could lead to the incident that occurred.

The second step is characterizing each event in terms of unwanted transfers of energy from the hazard or source of the energy to the target. This step builds on Haddon's (1973) 10 energy barriers. In this step the analyst seeks to understand how the injury, damage, or loss occurred.

The third step is to evaluate the hypothesis that the unwanted transfers of energy were the result of how risks were managed in the activity in which the accident occurred. This step focuses on the administration and management of the activity surrounding the incident. The MORT analysis pays considerable attention to the underlying management decisions, policies, and procedures because they often directly or indirectly facilitate the accident as much as the specific control factors do.

### MORT Tree

MORT is a tree analysis and has many of the same aspects of fault tree analysis. However, instead of creating a fault tree, the investigator uses the existing MORT tree analysis to analyze an incident or accident. The simplified tree presented in figure 5.16 can be subdivided into its major components. These components illustrate the main areas of investigation in the analysis.

The loss is identified and is subdivided into two branches: *oversights and omissions* and *assumed risks*. Oversights and omissions is manageable and is subdivided into two key branches: specific control factors and management system factors. *Specific control factors* are divided into the subsystems of accidents, which is defined by its four subcomponents: potentially harmful energy transfer or condition, vulnerable people or objects, controls and barriers, and events and energy transfers leading to an accident or incident. The *barriers and control* component is further subdivided into traditional operational components of the workplace. The second large branch of the MORT tree is *management system factors*.

Although the two trees (specific control factors and management system factors) may seem to be independent of each other, they are highly interactive. Policy and its implementation or lack thereof can directly affect the accident tree and its causal factors. A review of the MORT questioning process indicates that it captures the interaction between the specific control and the management system factors. In part, this interactive approach helps make the MORT process extremely complex. (Refer back to the large number of subproblems identified earlier in this section.) Regardless, even a cursory review of the MORT tree in figure 5.17 reveals that its basic systematic approach is useful in accident investigation and prevention.

Returning to the accident model in figure 5.6 and barrier analysis, the role of the analysis is to put barriers into one of three categories. The purpose of the investigation process is to determine all of the less than adequate (LTA) situations so that they can be rectified. Figure 5.17 uses a flow chart to depict the process of analysis and classification. If not enough information exists to analyze the element, it is colored blue and revisited later. If enough information exists to determine whether the element was a factor, and if it is determined that it was not a contributing element (i.e., LTA), it is colored green. If the element is determined to be LTA, it is colored red for additional barrier analysis. This process is used on each element in the MORT chart. One can use the basic approach in the other analytical tree approaches as well.

## THE FOUR TS: TERMINATE, TREAT, TRANSFER, AND TOLERATE

Once one determines the causal factors, the LTA, or the logical sequence of events, the question becomes what to do with the analysis from a management perspective. Stephenson (1991) introduced the concept of the four Ts: terminate, treat, transfer, and tolerate. People familiar with risk management will note that the four Ts are similar to the risk management alternatives of

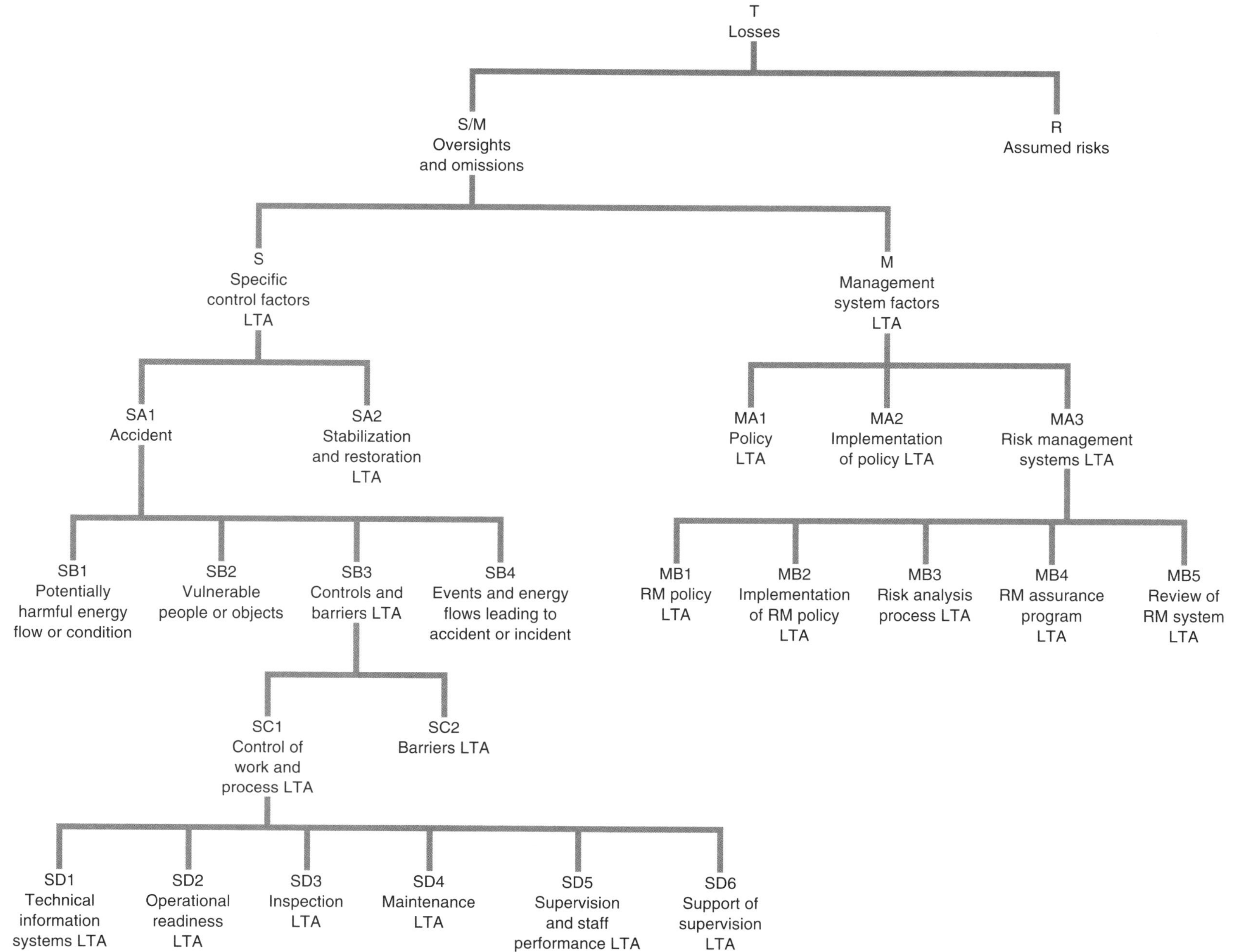


**Figure 5.16** The main tree branches of MORT are provided for informational purposes. The prevention of losses involves oversight and assumed risks as well as management system factors. If specific control factors are less than adequate, an accident can occur.

Reprinted, by permission, from J. Kingston et al., 2009, *NRI MORT user's manual—For use with the management oversight and risk tree analytical logic diagram* (AG Delft, Netherlands: The Noordwijk Risk Initiative Foundation), xvii.

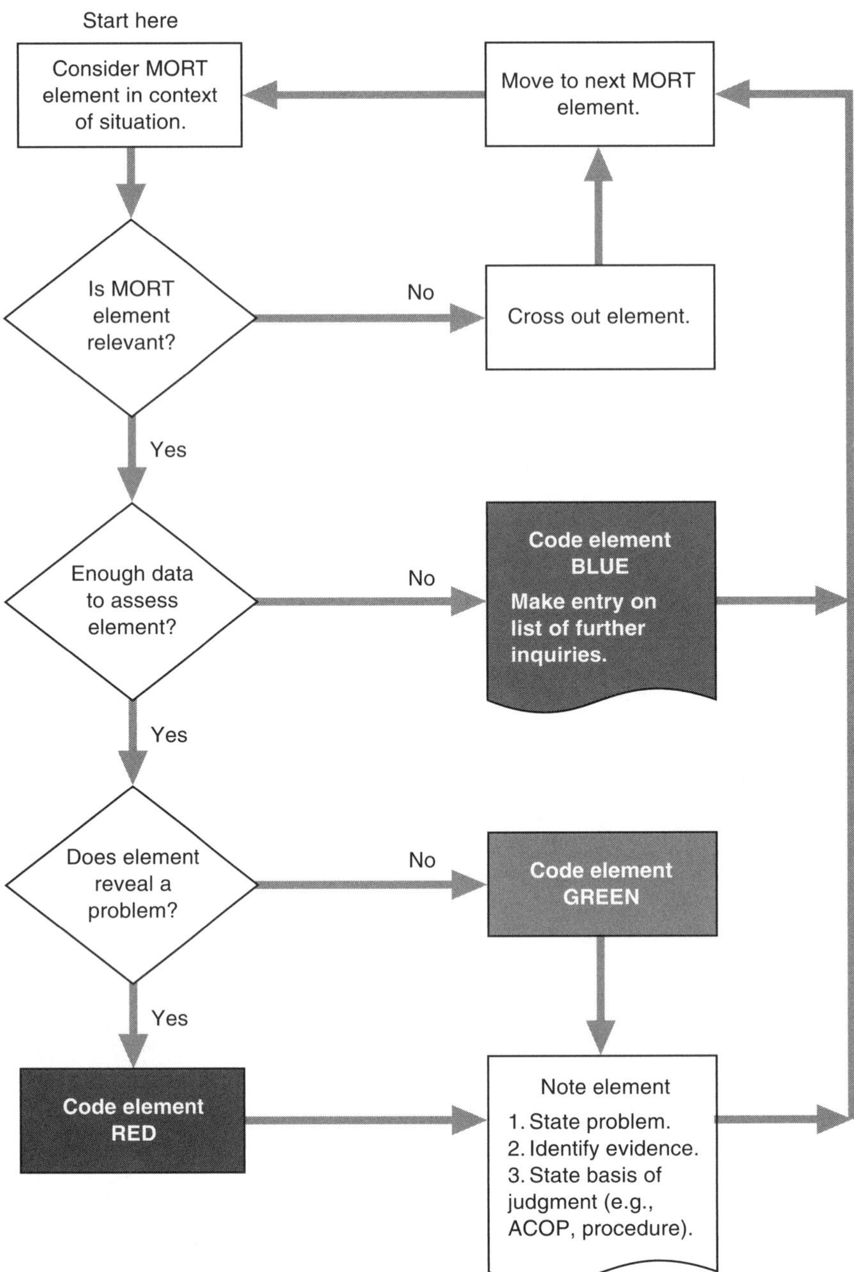


**Figure 5.17** The MORT charting process demonstrates the basic charting process involved in identifying and addressing a problem. The emphasis is on the process.

Reprinted, by permission, from J. Kingston et al., 2009, *NRI MORT user's manual—For use with the management oversight and risk tree analytical logic diagram* (AG Delft, Netherlands: The Noordwijk Risk Initiative Foundation), xxii.

reduction, avoidance, transfer, and retention (see chapter 8).

One can *terminate* risks in two ways. First, one can terminate or eliminate the activity. In the recreation and park discipline, which is activity based, this option is more viable than in industry, where production requires the process to occur. Second, one can often engineer major risks out of the system. For example, moving the public beach on the Meramec River could eliminate the drop-off hazard associated with the original site.

One can use administrative controls to *treat* and reduce the level of risk. Administrative controls usually include warning devices, safety devices, procedures, and training. In the Meramec River incident, adding an interpretive sign at the beach entrance that warns beach users of river hazards is an example of treating the situation.

Risks can be *transferred*. Stephenson (1991) indicates that insurance is the usual method of transferring the risk. Another typical method in the recreations and park field is waivers. These approaches do not diminish the risks; they only transfer the responsibility from one party to another.

If the risks cannot be terminated, treated, or transferred, they are *tolerated*. Inherent in toleration is the reality that one cannot eliminate all risks. If the risks are treated, a residual risk is often tolerated. If the state park system implemented all the recommendations regarding the beach site at Castlewood State Park, risks would still exist to be tolerated.

The underlying principle of the four Ts is that all risks should be eliminated or that any risk is a bad risk. Chapter 7 discusses a counterpoint to this approach in which risk is identified as an integral part of recreational activities.

## SUMMARY

This chapter discusses barrier analysis and the concept of energy transfer associated with it. In barrier analysis, one identifies hazards and the targets that those hazards can affect. One then identifies the LTA sources of energy transfers from those hazards and creates hard (physical) and soft (administrative) barriers to prevent or reduce the likelihood of the energy transfer. Barrier analysis is important because it can be used proactively to reduce the likelihood of injury, damage, or loss and thus assist in preventing accidents. Although directly related to analytical tree approach, barrier analysis is a technique that can stand alone and that can easily be integrated into other accident models. The concept is so fundamental that the conceptual framework of the traditional models discussed in chapter 4 have been modified to include energy transfer. The outdoor models presented in chapter 6 could easily incorporate the concept of energy transfer, even though many of these models do not actively do so.

This chapter also discusses the analytical tree approach. Most of the tree approaches have a conceptual or actual link to MORT. The chapter presents the fault tree and positive tree approaches and briefly discusses MORT. Both the fault tree and positive tree approaches are presented in the context of the charting techniques of event and causal factor analysis.

The techniques presented in this chapter can help change a person's thought processes regarding how he approaches leadership and programming. They can help him begin to look at all activities and how they can lead to potential accidents. They can also help him assess the likelihood of energy transfer sources that can harm his participants and then think of how he can protect, minimize, manage, or control these energy transfers with barriers.

# EXERCISES

## Exercise 1: Accident Sequence—Bouldering Rock

Figure 5.8*a* shows a bouldering rock at the Denver REI. The purpose of this exercise is to develop an accident sequence. Figure 5.8*b* shows some children playing on the bouldering rock in an inappropriate manner. Assume that one of the children falls and breaks his arm. Develop a sequence of events for the accident based on the information in the photo and the additional information provided here.

1. The parents arrived at REI at 11:00 a.m. and went shopping inside.
2. The children wanted to play in the minipark outside. The parents let the children play in the minipark unsupervised. The bouldering rock is one of several attractions in the minipark.
3. The children climbed the boulder at approximately 11:30 a.m.
4. The child broke his arm at approximately 11:45 a.m.
5. The parents were notified at 12:00 p.m.
6. The parents transported the child to the hospital at 12:20 p.m.

## Exercise 2: Fault Tree Analysis and *The Dirty Dozen*

The purpose of this exercise is to apply fault tree analysis to an incident. Use the brochure *The Dirty Dozen* (http://tinyurl.com/DirtyDozenBrochure) to help you determine your fault tree analysis. *Hint:* Use figure 5.14 as an example for developing your tree. It delineates the beginning of a fault tree.

Scenario: A group of children is playing on a swing set at the playground. They are playing a game in which they can see how high they can swing and then launch themselves off the swings. The winner is the person who lands the farthest from the swing. One of the children jumps, hits a nearby slide, and breaks his arm. Your investigation reveals the following information. *Note:* Not all the information is causal.

1. The mulch directly under the swings is eroded from the children dragging their feet. The mulch under the swings is 4 inches deep.
2. The mulch is 12 inches deep elsewhere.
3. The slide is located 5 feet away from the swing.

## Exercise 3: Positive Tree Analysis and *The Dirty Dozen*

The purpose of this exercise is to develop a positive tree analysis for playground safety using the brochure *The Dirty Dozen* (http://tinyurl.com/DirtyDozenBrochure). *The Dirty Dozen* was chosen because it is laid out in a logical way that facilitates this type of analysis. *Hint:* Use figure 5.15 as an example for developing your tree. It delineates the tree under the first topic heading of improper protective surfacing in the brochure. Simply list "playground safety" as the top event. Do not be surprised if your tree conforms to the basic organizational structure of the topics in the brochure. Consider limiting your analysis to the first three items in *The Dirty Dozen*.

### Exercise 4: Fault Tree Analysis and the Bouldering Rock

The purpose of this exercise is to develop a fault tree analysis for an incident. Figure 5.8*a* shows a bouldering rock at the Denver REI. Figure 5.8*b* shows some children playing on the bouldering rock in an inappropriate manner. Assume that one of the children falls and breaks his arm. Develop a fault tree analysis for the accident based on the information in the photo. Use the brochure *The Dirty Dozen* at http://tinyurl.com/DirtyDozenBrochure for assistance.

### Exercise 5: Haddon's Energy Transfer and the Meramec River Incident

The purpose of this exercise is to apply Haddon's (1973) principles of energy transfer to several recreational settings. Haddon (1973) articulated 10 ways of controlling harmful transfer of energy by developing barriers. In the Meramec River incident example, mandatory life jackets were listed as one way to potentially control the energy transfer. Several other alternatives were suggested:

1. Remove the drop-off or gradually taper the drop-off.
2. Install an interpretive sign at the beach entrance that explains river hazards, including the drop-off.
3. Close the beach to the public.

Discuss how these three alternatives would reduce the energy transfer in terms of controlling harmful transfers of energy or creating energy barriers.

### Exercise 6: Barrier Analysis—Bouldering Rock

The purpose of this exercise is to apply barrier analysis to a specific recreational example. Using the scenario in exercise 1, use the instrument in figure 5.10 to develop a barrier analysis for the bouldering rock.

Chapter 6

# Metaphorical and Outdoor Adventure Models

The outdoor adventure field, in which many outdoor leaders conduct their activities semi-independently from their agencies and organizations, has historically been interested in the accident process. Priest and Gass (2005) and Jillings (2005) report the traditional lineage of the accident process in the outdoor movement. The outdoor models incorporate many of the components found in traditional models, such as looking at unsafe acts and unsafe conditions or dividing the accident factors into human, environmental, and equipment factors. This chapter reviews this lineage of accident model in the context of metaphorical models.

Developmentally, the progression of outdoor accident models leads to the metaphorical models built on identifying the underlying factors that can contribute to an accident. This chapter presents several such models, including the Curtis model, the risk meter, and the domino model. A strength of these models is that they are very useful for people in a direct leadership role. They are leader focused ("what I do") rather than organization or system focused ("what someone else does"). This feature of these models makes them very attractive to people in a direct leadership role in the recreation and park field.

## WHAT ARE METAPHORICAL MODELS?

As discussed in chapter 4, the Heinrich accident model likens the accident process to a series of falling dominos. Most people can imagine a series of dominos, sitting upright on a table, being pushed over, and most people can intuitively relate the dominos to factors that lead to an accident. In contrast, it is not easy to visualize the concept of barrier analysis. One might envision figure 5.6, in which a rock wall protects the person behind it. Barrier analysis is logical and analytical, but it is not metaphorical. Lakoff and Johnson (1980) suggest that "human thought processes are largely metaphorical" (p. 5). Although barrier analysis and the tree analysis associated with it have many strengths, one weakness they share is that they are not always intuitive. They are logical and they are analytical, but in this sense, they lack the human dimension.

Metaphorical models are intuitive. They are easy for people to understand and to relate to. Accidents are like a series of falling dominoes, or safety management is like Swiss cheese. This advantage of metaphorical models is also its disadvantage. Metaphorical models usually make assumptions about accidents and the accident process that may not necessarily be empirically true. For example, some models assume that accidents result from unsafe acts outnumbering safe acts. This may not always be the case; one unsafe act can lead to an accident. The models also often assume that accident prevention results from offsetting unsafe acts with safety measures. Again, this may not always be the case. As discussed in chapter 4, Bird and Germain (1985) based their model on a fairly comprehensive industrial research study. In contrast, little research in the recreation and park field validates these models regarding balancing safe and unsafe acts or whether it takes a preponderance of many unsafe factors to cause an accident. Finally, metaphorical models often have unintentional implications on how people think about accidents. For example, if a model likens accidents to winning a slot machine, the model implies that accidents occur by chance. If accidents occur by chance, the implication is that a person can do little or nothing to prevent accidents. In terms of accident prevention and safety, this is not a good proposition to advocate because it negates the whole idea of accident prevention. This is an obvious unintentional implication; other models are often more subtle. Metaphorical models are valuable because they are intuitive and easily understood. However, it is important to understand that there may be methodological limitations with them also.

Accident prevention may be as much an art as it is a science. Although every metaphorical model is associated with assumptions and weaknesses, the models are still very useful. Most of the metaphorical models presented in this chapter incorporate components from the more analytical models within their models. For example, the domino model incorporates barrier analysis, energy transfer, and analyzing the underlying factors in terms of human, environmental, and equipment factors. Other models could easily incorporate these concepts (Curtis model). The result is that most of the models presented in this chapter are built on solid foundations.

For safety management to work, the professionals who work with participants and who

One strength of the metaphorical models is that they encourage recreation and park professionals to directly integrate accident prevention techniques into the activities and programs they deliver.

deliver recreation and park programs must fully integrate safe practices into their activities and programs. One strength of the metaphorical models is that they encourage recreation and park professionals to directly integrate accident prevention techniques into the activities and programs they deliver. This point is extremely important. Also, because the metaphorical models are intuitive, they affect the attitudes and thought processes of recreation and park leaders and programmers. The end result is safer programs.

## EARLY METAPHORICAL MODELS

The outdoor field has had a continuing interest in risk management and the accident process. Priest and Gass (2005) seem to provide the most comprehensive summary of these models; however, it is difficult to locate the original sources of many of these models. The early models discussed in this section provide the background for the development of the models presented later in this chapter.

### Dynamics of Accidents Formula

One of the first models reported in the outdoor literature is Hale's (1983) model (figure 6.1). Jillings (2005) reports that the model is from Hale's Outward Bound experience in Hawaii. Although it has a student emphasis, the model is easily adaptable to traditional leadership situations.

The model suggests that two types of hazards exist: environmental and human factor. Environmental factors include weather, terrain, plants, animals, and equipment. Human factors include anything that involves decision-making on the part of students, instructors, supervisors, and parents. The model suggests that the accident potential is equal to the intersection between the environmental hazards and human-factor hazards. The larger the overlap, the greater the chance for an accident. This definition of accident potential is a weakness of the model because it suggests that both hazards must be present and that the interaction of the two factors is what causes accidents. Although this is often the case, human factors alone are sufficient to cause accidents. Supporting this

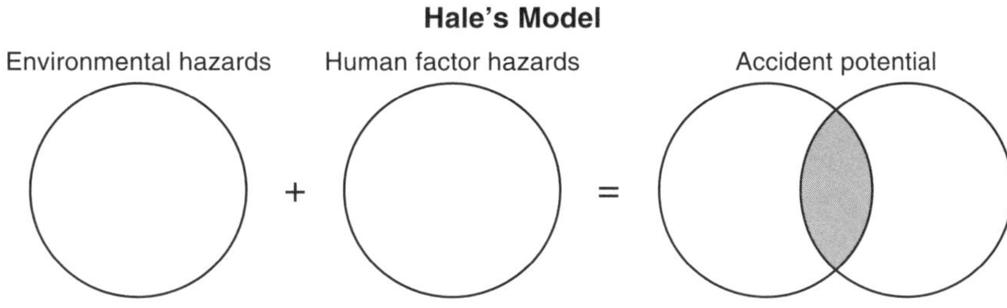


The larger the overlap, the greater the chance of an accident.

| Environmental hazards | Human factor hazards | |
|---|---|---|
| Rain forest | New boots | |
| Mountain terrain | Unaccustomed to wearing boots | |
| Hot sun | Need to prove oneself (macho) | Students |
| Bad weather | | |
| Cold temperature | "I told them. Now they have to pay the consequences." | |
| Faculty equipment | "I've tried everything." | Instructor |
| | Behavior not modeled to instructors | Supervisor |
| | Demand on student behavior | Parents |

**Figure 6.1** Hale's model overlaps environmental and human-factor hazards to determine the accident potential.

Adapted, by permission, from A. Jillings, 2005, *What's new in accident theory* (Tuscon, Arizona: AEE Conference); adapted, by permission, from A. Hale, 1983, *Safety management for outdoor program leaders.*

point, Dekker (2006) found that 70 percent of accidents are human related.

## Raffan's Slot Machine

Another early model is Raffan's (1984) slot machine (figure 6.2). It suggests that the potential for accidents is like a slot machine. The wheels in the machine spin, and occasionally three lemons line up, resulting in an accident. A significant weakness of this model is that it implies that accidents occur by chance and therefore lie outside of the control of the leader. This negates the purpose of studying the accident process to reduce accidents. However, this model captures the essence associated with using the term *accident* where accidents are viewed as unintentional and occurring by chance.

This model underscores the continuing discussion in the safety management literature between using the terms *incident* and *accident*. This was noted in the foreword. For the public, the term *accident* has the connotation of accidental, by chance, and therefore not under the control of the leader, programmer, or safety manager. For this reason, many in the field are favoring the use of the term *incident* in place of *accident*. However for the public, the term incident is more sterile and lacks the emotional impact of the term accident—the phrase *automobile incident* might not convey the same meaning as *automobile accident*. Again, this model underscores the continuing discussion regarding the use of these two terms.

**Figure 6.2** Raffan's (1984) slot machine model implies that accidents occur by chance. An accident occurs when three lemons appear.

Adapted, by permission, from A. Jillings, 2005, *What's new in accident theory* (Tuscon, Arizona: AEE Conference); Raffan 1984.

## Danger Analysis

Priest and Gass (2005) developed a 10-step analytic tree-type analysis of the accident process (figure 6.3). Their work is based on the previous work of Priest and Baillie (1987). Although Priest and Gass did not formally title their model, the section heading in their text is "Danger Analysis." Hence, the model is labeled the danger analysis model.

The model is a logical, analytical approach to assessing and reacting to danger or hazards. Using this model, a leader searches for potential dangers, develops a plan of action to deal with the identified danger, assesses the dangers associated with that plan, and determines whether the potential losses associated with that plan of action justify the continuation of the plan.

The steps in the model are as follows. First, a person plans ahead and analyzes accidents that potentially can happen (step 1). Next, she searches for dangerous conditions and situations (step 2). When she determines a potential danger, she identifies it to her coleaders, students, and participants (step 3). Once she identifies the danger or hazard, she can remove it (step 4), avoid it (step 5), or encounter it (step 6). Unless she can avoid the risk, she will encounter it or a variation of it. She will need to reassess the risk and danger (step 7). In typical risk management fashion, she estimates the probability of loss (step 8) and seeks to minimize it (step 9). In the last step, she makes the appropriate adjustments to manage the risks (step 10). She then identifies the next danger (step 2) and cycles through the model again.

For example, a backcountry group needs to cross a stream (step 2). Although the stream is

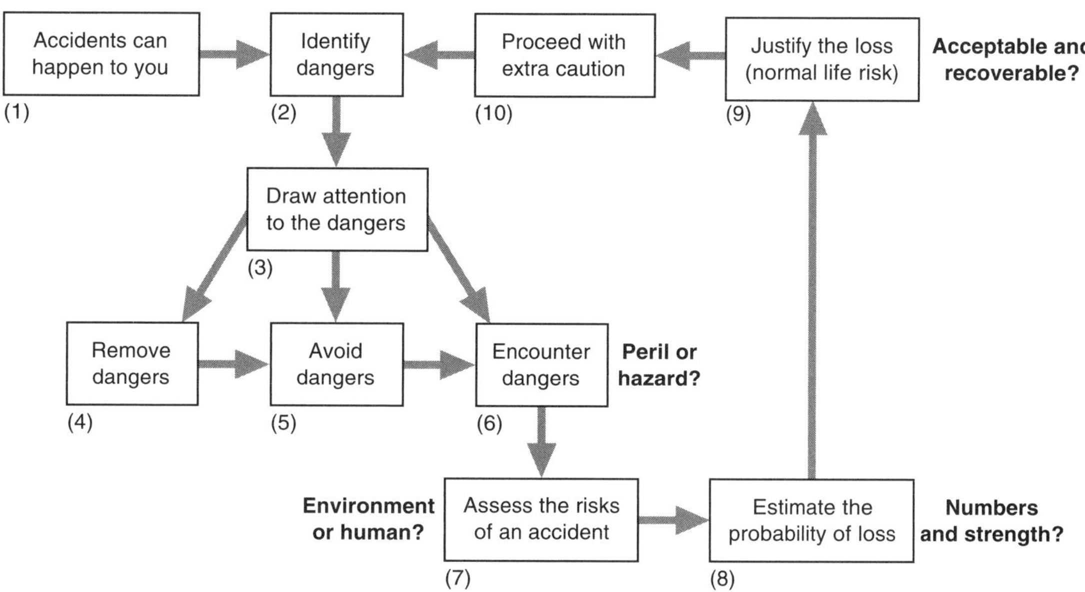


**Figure 6.3** The danger analysis model creates a flow chart of the decision process of addressing risks in an outdoor activity.

Reprinted, by permission, from S. Priest and R. Baillie, 1987, "Justifying the risk to others: The real razor's edge," *Journal of Experiential Education* 10(1): 16-22.

not at flood level, the flow of the stream is higher than normal (step 2). The leader discusses what to do with her coleaders and participants (step 3). She cannot remove the danger or wait until the water recedes (step 4). She could avoid the danger of crossing the river by hiking three miles out of the way to a bridge that crosses the river (step 5), or she could cross the stream using standard stream-crossing procedures. The leaders discuss each option—crossing the stream or doing a three-mile dogleg—in terms of the human and environmental factors present (step 7) and estimate the probability of loss (e.g., time to hike three miles, drowning, loss of gear; step 8). The leader chooses to perform a stream crossing and seeks ways to minimize potential loss (step 9). She discusses with the participants the dangers involved in crossing the stream, how to proceed, and what to do if they slip and fall in the water. She also sets up rescue. She proceeds cautiously with the crossing (step 10) and everyone crosses safely. She then looks up to the sky and sees storm clouds approaching. She has identified another potential danger and is back at step 2.

Priest and Gass note that their model is no guarantee that a person will eliminate severe accidents, and they even suggest that the preplanning phase may be the most important phase in eliminating accidents. Also, whether people really think in a logical 10-step progression is questionable. Priest and Gass (2005) recognize this and note that "outdoor leaders need not use all ten steps to reduce risk" (p. 97). Nevertheless, most leaders will systematically assess the program environment for potentially hazardous or dangerous situations. When they discover a potential situation, they weigh alternatives and seek ways to minimize or manage the risks. In addition, most leaders utilize a more heuristic method based on experience that mimics, to a degree, the more analytical method delineated in the danger analysis model. Lastly, the model assumes that the person knows a hazard exists. If a person cannot identify a known hazard (step 2), the model falls apart. For example, the backcountry leader may not think that a stream crossing is dangerous and venture forth across the stream.

## Accident Matrix

Dan Meyer, director of the North Carolina Outward Bound, published the original accident

## Potential Causes of Accidents in Outdoor Pursuits

**A matrix designed by Dan Meyer and edited by Jed Williamson (Meyer and Williamson, 2008)**

| Potentially unsafe conditions due to | Potentially unsafe acts due to | Potential errors in judgment due to |
|---|---|---|
| • falling objects (e.g., rocks),<br>• inadequate area security (physical, political, cultural),<br>• weather,<br>• equipment or clothing,<br>• swift or cold water,<br>• animals or plants, or<br>• physical or psychological profile of participants or staff. | • inadequate protection;<br>• inadequate instruction;<br>• unsafe speed (fast or slow);<br>• inadequate or improper food, drink, or medication;<br>• poor position; or<br>• unauthorized or improper procedures. | • desire to please others,<br>• trying to adhere to a schedule,<br>• misperception,<br>• new or unexpected situation (includes fear and panic),<br>• distraction,<br>• miscommunication, or<br>• disregarding instincts. |

**Figure 6.4** Used primarily to assess accidents, the accident matrix found wide use in analyzing mountaineering accidents.

Adapted, by permission, from D. Meyer and J. Williamson, 1979, *Potential causes of accidents in outdoor pursuits,* edited by J. Williamson 1989-2008©. Available: www.nols.edu/nolspro/pdf/accident_matrix.pdf.

matrix in 1979. Jed Williamson refined the original model, and both share authorship (Meyer and Williamson, 2008; figure 6.4). Williamson brought his involvement in mountaineering to the development of the model.

The accident matrix is divided into three sections: unsafe conditions, unsafe acts, and errors of judgment. Unsafe conditions include environmental conditions. Equipment, often considered a separate category in other models, is included as an environmental condition. Unsafe acts and errors of judgment make up the traditional category of human factors used in several of the other models described in this chapter (e.g., Curtis, domino model). Although the model is used primarily for accident investigation, it can also be used in accident prevention. The factors included in this model are similar to the underlying factors discussed in the next section.

# EXAMINING UNDERLYING FACTORS IN ACCIDENTS AND ACCIDENT MODELS

The list of underlying factors in this section was created by Kauffman (2004, 2005, 2006, 2007) using the basic factors (personal and job factors) in Bird and Germain's (1985, pp. 28-29) loss model as a starting point. The list of factors was developed in conjunction with the domino model (described later in this chapter), and changed over time. Generally, underlying factors are divided into three categories: human, environmental, and equipment. Much commonality exists between the list of underlying factors in this section and the different models. Although this list was developed for the domino model, it is equally applicable to the other models presented later in this chapter.

This list of underlying factors in an accident is fairly comprehensive, but it does not preclude additional factors. For example, the Meyer and Williamson (2008) matrix lists the factor *inadequate area security (physical, political, cultural).* In the list of underlying factors, the closest match is *cultural norms* under the category "leadership and group dynamics." Depending on the user's circumstances, it may be appropriate to create a new category that addresses this need. Also, although the list was created with outdoor activities in mind, it can easily be adapted to general recreation programs. For example, the factor *change in terrain conditions* can apply as well to a vehicle on an icy road as it does to an outdoor situation. The factor *inadequate or inappropriate equipment* is as applicable to sports such as football or soccer as it is to an outdoor activity.

This section examines these underlying factors in the context of the video *Cold, Wet, and Alive* (1989), which depicts the accident process as it occurs throughout a day-long canoe trip. Figure 6.5 is an abbreviated narrative of the

## *Cold, Wet, and Alive:* Abbreviated Narrative

*Cold, Wet, and Alive* (1989) is the story of an early-spring canoe trip taken by David, Dean, Michael, Becky, and Lisa. David gets hypothermia and loses his boat (injury, damage, or loss). The movie uses a series of computer graphics to describe what is happening to David physiologically as he gradually gets hypothermia. The following is a basic narrative of their trip.

When the movie begins, the group is crossing the bridge that will be the location of their lunch stop later in the day. They listen to the weather forecast on the radio: "Come on, all you late sleepers. The weather bureau is calling for a high of 70 degrees today. Sunday looks like it is back to normal with, you guessed it, cold and rainy. The normal high for today is 49 degrees." As they cross the bridge, the group members comment, "The water is really moving!"

**10:54 a.m.:** The group is at the put-in. The air temperature is 66 degrees Fahrenheit and the water temperature is 46 degrees Fahrenheit. The group members make their preparations for the trip. David comments that Dean and Becky are wearing wetsuits. David wears cotton and notes, "I dress for the moment." The group's attitude is enthusiastic and playful.

**11:25 a.m.:** The group is having fun. The air temperature is 71 degrees Fahrenheit and the water temperature is 46 degrees Fahrenheit. David demonstrates his roll by rolling his kayak. He exclaims, "My head hit that water!" The narrator notes that water removes energy at least 25 times faster than air does. David comments, "Even though that dunking was invigorating, I warmed up right away. I decided that it would be my last demonstration of the day!"

**2:30-4:00 p.m.:** The air temperature is 51 degrees Fahrenheit and the water temperature is 46 degrees Fahrenheit. While the others are snacking, David is charging up and down the river, expending energy. His fuel gage is nearing empty. David takes a couple of spills in the water and loses heat more quickly. It is late afternoon and the sun begins to drop behind the mountains. Wearing wet cotton, David loses more energy than those wearing wetsuits do. They are all becoming hypothermic; however, David is becoming hypothermic much more quickly.

**4:15 p.m.:** The air temperature is 51 degrees Fahrenheit and the water temperature is 46 degrees Fahrenheit. The group reaches the halfway point—the bridge they crossed earlier in the morning—and discusses what they should do. They are all cold and fatigued. They could take out at the bridge and hitchhike back to the car. They note that the river separates from the road at this location. David comments to himself, "What I wanted to do more was to finish the trip and get warm." David thinks to himself that their decision is a turning point. It was. They are cold and it is getting late, and they decide to continue their trip. It is a classic example of group think, where individually they know what they should do, yet they do what they think the group expects. Harvey (1974) calls this the Abilene paradox.

**5:15 p.m.:** The group is disintegrating. David is hypothermic and cannot maintain his core temperature. The weather front moves in early and it begins to rain. The water in the gorge is rising. The group decides to scout the rapids. David mistakenly thinks that Dean is waving him over to the shore and enters the rapids. He spills and comes out of his kayak. Fatigued and hypothermic, he clings to a rock in the middle of the rapids. Dean rescues David, but David loses his boat. They start a fire and warm David. They decide to end their trip there. They hike out to the road and hitchhike back to their car.

**Figure 6.5** Produced under a Coast Guard grant by the American Canoe Association, *Cold, Wet, and Alive* is the story of an early-spring canoe trip taken by David, Dean, Michael, Becky, and Lisa. The video has two complementing themes: hypothermia and the accident process.

Adapted from American Canoe Association 1989.

## *Cold, Wet, and Alive*: Underlying Factors

### Safe Acts and Conditions

#### Environmental Factors

Radio: "The high today is 70 degrees."
Dean: "The river runs next to the highway."

#### Equipment

Becky: "You've packed a ton of dry clothes."
David: "Dean and Becky decided to wear wetsuits."

#### Human Factors

Dean: "The day is late. If we take out here, we can hitch a ride back to the car."
David: "The water in the canyon is rising. Dean thought that maybe we should scout the rapids."
Dean: "It has been a long day. Maybe we should take out here."

### Unsafe Acts and Conditions

#### Potentially Unsafe Environmental Factors

David: "The water is really moving."
Lisa: "I didn't know that I was going to get my feet wet!"
Becky: "I felt the water and it was cold."
Dean: "This is the last we will see of the road. The canyon is just around the bend."
Dean: "The weather is changing."

#### Potentially Unsafe Equipment Factors

Narrator: "Cotton clothing offers little protection when wet."
David: "I tend to dress for the moment."

#### Potentially Unsafe Human Factors

David: "We were at the halfway point at 4:00 in the afternoon."
David: "We came to paddle."
David: "Chalk it up to my dull brain" (i.e., the effects of hypothermia).

**Figure 6.6** Quotes from *Cold, Wet, and Alive* (1989) that represent both safe and unsafe human, environmental, and equipment factors. Even though the members of the group commented on the factor, they may not understand the full impact of their comment. For example, Becky commented, "I felt the water and it is cold!" Her comment affected her decision to wear a wetsuit. In this sense, it was visible. However, she did not recognize its effect on David and his dress. In this sense, the effect of the cold water was invisible to David.

Adapted from American Canoe Association 1989.

video, and figure 6.6 includes quotes from the video that illustrate the underlying factors. These figures can help the reader complete exercise 2 without watching the video.

Most of the factors are written as deficiencies or as something done wrong. The operative words in the factors are *inadequate, inappropriate, lack of,* or *not using*. This is typical in the safety industry, which focuses on everything that is seemingly negative rather than on the positive or what people are doing correctly. Accident prevention is the reduction or mitigation of these negative factors. However, several of the models discussed later in this chapter (i.e., the Curtis model, risk meter, domino model) account for positive actions that tend to increase safety as well as the negative factors.

## Human Factors

Human factors are the underlying cause of most incidents. For example, approximately 80 percent of automobile accidents are related to human factors, 15 percent are related to environmental factors, and roughly 5 percent are related to equipment failures. Additionally, in a study that reviewed five years of boating accident statistics, human factors accounted for approximately 63 percent of all accidents related to recreational boating, environmental factors accounted for 33 percent of the accidents, and equipment failures accounted for 4 percent of the accidents (Kauffman, 1995). Given the effect of the outdoor environment, it is not unexpected that environmental factors account for a greater proportion of boating-related accidents. These findings are consistent with Dekker's (2006) statistic that 70 percent of accidents are human related.

Human factors include what is going on physiologically in the body; the mental state of the individual; the knowledge, skills, and motivation of the individual; the group and the dynamics of the group; and the amount and type of preparations made.

### Physical or Physiological Capabilities or Stress

Physical or physiological capability is the body's capacity to handle the stress placed on it. For example, as people grow older, they become less coordinated, their hearing and vision become impaired, and they become more susceptible to fatigue. Activity, such as completing a hike, and the environment can also place stress on an older person's capabilities. In general, an older person is more susceptible to this physical stress than a younger person. However, an older person who is in good shape and who has prepared herself is often better able to handle the stress than a younger counterpart who has more capabilities but less conditioning.

Prescription, over-the-counter, and recreational drugs can also place physical or physiological stress on the body. Participants taking any drug should check with a doctor regarding the effects of the drug in the activity environment. Also, particularly in the outdoor environment, long-term exposure to the sun can easily upset the body's systems through dehydration, sun glare, and sunburn.

Physical or physiological factors include the following.

- Conditioning
- Restricted range of motion
- Age-related issues
- Vision or hearing deficiencies
- Disabilities
- Allergies
- Coordination
- Previous injuries
- Illness
- Fatigue due to increased physical exertion
- Fatigue due to lack of rest
- Fatigue due to sensory overload
- Exposure to temperature extremes (hypothermia, hyperthermia)
- Oxygen deficiency
- Inadequate food intake
- Mental state (e.g., fear)
- Injury
- Drugs

In *Cold, Wet, and Alive* (1989; figure 6.5), at least three physical or physiological factors are present. First, there was exposure to temperature extremes. David became truly hypothermic late in the day (figure 6.5). Second, there was inadequate food intake. While the others in the group nibbled on food, David let his gas tank run low. Third, there was fatigue due to increased physical exertion. This became evident during the lunch stop (4:15 p.m.) when David commented, "What I wanted to do more was to finish the trip and get warm" (figure 6.5).

### Mental or Psychological Capabilities or Stress

Mental or psychological capabilities or stress deals with people's judgment, decision making, experience, and emotions. It is affected by age, culture, and physiological capabilities and stress. Children have different mental and decision-making capabilities than adults. Traditional western culture is goal oriented, which can easily affect decision making. Interactively, physiological considerations such as fatigue, diet, and medications affect decision making and judgment. These factors often work in conjunction with each other, and in some cases they escalate in their effects. For example, poor decisions resulting from poor judgment lead to emotional overload. Emotional overload, which results from having to make too many decisions and from inexperience, leads to confusion. The factors build on each other until an incident occurs that leads to injury, damage, or loss.

Mental or psychological factors include the following.

- Fears or phobias
- Poor judgment
- Poor decisions
- Inexperience
- Emotional overload
- Extreme judgment or decision demands
- Extreme concentration or perception demands
- Confusing directions
- Conflicting demands
- Preoccupation with problems
- Frustration

In the video *Cold, Wet, and Alive* (1989; figure 6.5), at least three mental or psychological factors are present. There were numerous instances of poor judgment and poor decisions, including not taking out at the lunch stop at 4:15 p.m., not leaving a car at the halfway point, David not eating, and David and Michael not wearing proper clothing. They were also inexperienced; David had practiced his Eskimo roll, but it was not reliable.

## Knowledge

Most activities require a knowledge set to perform the activity. Although some might define knowledge as book learning, it really includes all knowledge and is often experience based. Knowledge includes knowing the content or common practices and procedures of the activity being performed as well as the environmental effects on the activity. A touring cyclist needs to know how to repair a tire. This may include vulcanizing a patch on the tube. Knowledge can lead to obtaining the appropriate equipment and tools to include in the repair kit. Experience complements the knowledge. Actually repairing a tire reinforces whether everything the cyclist thought she needed was actually what she needed. Environmental factors include knowing how the weather, terrain, and animals and plants will influence the activity being performed. Do the leader and participant possess this knowledge set?

Because the primary focus of the movie is on how David got hypothermia, it is clear that he and others on the trip had little knowledge regarding how to prevent or minimize the onset of hypothermia. The primary purpose of the movie is to depict how a person gets hypothermia in a recreational setting and how insidious its onset can be.

An interesting sidebar and a problem in safety education is that the people for whom the safety education is targeted are often the least likely to realize that they have need for the knowledge. Numerous experienced paddlers would comment after the film that they had an experience similar to the one that was depicted in the movie. They would comment on how real to life it was and how it depicted in a step-by-step process how you get hypothermia. In contrast, many inexperienced paddlers to whom the film was targeted were often ho-hum. They did not have enough experience to know how insidious the onset of hypothermia really is in a recreational setting. In a sense, they did not know enough to know.

## Skill

Skill involves having the necessary skill set to adequately perform an activity. In contrast with knowledge, which tends to be more cognitive, skill is generally associated with a psychomotor skill. Knowledge is knowing; skill is doing. Paddling a canoe in a straight line, staying upright on a bicycle, or driving a vehicle including

ATVs are all skills. They require instruction, training, and actually doing the activity to become proficient in the activity.

Skill factors include the following.

- Inadequate initial instruction
- Inadequate practice
- Infrequent performance of activity
- Lack of coaching
- Inadequate skill level for the activity or setting

In *Cold, Wet, and Alive* (1989; figure 6.5), inadequate practice may have been an issue with David. He practiced his Eskimo roll over the winter, so he had some skill, but he was by no means an expert. At 11:25 a.m. (figure 6.5), David indicated that he was not going to come out of his boat again, yet he is seen swimming several times in the video. This demonstrates inadequate practice and inadequate skill level.

## Motivation

Cultural norms, which can easily be overlooked, can have a significant effect on facilitating accidents. American society tends to be achievement oriented, and this is reflected in people's activities. People want to be the best at what they do. If they start a project, they want to finish it. If they climb a mountain, they want to reach the top. For example, the title of the story about the Mt. Hood incident, "High Achievers' Climb to Their Deaths" (Reid and Phillips, 1986) suggests that the National Merit finalists were high achievers who transferred this motivation to their mountain climbing experience (see appendix A).

Motivation factors include the following.

- Improper attempt to save time or effort
- Improper attempt to avoid discomfort
- Peer pressure
- Aggressive behavior
- Passive behavior
- Cultural norms

In *Cold, Wet, and Alive* (1989; figure 6.5), at least one motivational factor, cultural norms, is in play. During the lunch stop, when asked by the group what they should do, David replied, "We came to paddle" (figure 6.6). His statement and their behavior imply their desire to complete what they started and run the river. They believed that to take out at the halfway point was the equivalent of failure (figure 6.5). Their belief reflects the cultural norm of completing whatever one starts.

## Leadership and Group Dynamics

Some groups have designated leaders. Other groups are an aggregate of individuals participating without a formal leader. Regardless, all groups have some type of group dynamics, interaction, or interplay between participants. In formal leadership settings, problems can easily result from an inappropriate leadership style, miscommunications, inappropriate goals, or differences with organizational protocols. In an aggregate group without a formal leader, many of the same issues can be present as well as those associated with not having someone in charge.

Leadership and group dynamic factors include the following.

- Miscommunications
- Inappropriate leadership style
- Cultural norms affecting group behavior
- Organizational norms
- Lack of group cohesion
- Lack of experience
- Lack of experience in similar setting
- Inappropriate goals
- Trying to adhere to a schedule

In *Cold, Wet, and Alive* (1989; figure 6.5), the group's leadership style was that of an aggregate group without a formal leader. At least three leadership and group dynamic factors are present in the movie. First, inappropriate leadership style is potentially present. Although Dean was the de facto leader, the group was really leaderless. Second, the group had inappropriate goals. Their goal of running the entire river turned out to be too much. Third, in the gorge, where the group was fatigued and hypothermic, miscommunication occurred when David mistakenly thought that Dean was waving him on through the rapids. Hypothermic, David's reflection of the scene was "Chalk it up to my dull brain" (figure 6.6).

## Preplanning

Preplanning includes those activities one does in preparation for the actual activity to be successful. In a program planning course, preplanning is a major focus of the course with the development of the program plan. Objectives scheduling, staff, facilities, risk management, marketing, and evaluation are some of the components found in a typical program plan. Preplanning includes the planning for any and all of the factors included under human, environmental, and equipment factors. From an accident prevention perspective, this makes using these factors so useful. They can be used as a checklist in the preplanning process. Also, the use of these factors can easily be integrated into traditional program planning as part of the risk management process.

Examples of problems in preplanning include not having an adequate risk management plan or inadequate planning for any of the human, environmental, and equipment factors. In *Cold, Wet, and Alive* (1989; figure 6.5), the group's entire trip reflects inadequate trip planning. Each one of the factors discussed so far, as well as the remaining factors to be discussed, can be discussed from the preplanning perspective. A lesson of the movie is that better preplanning would most likely have reduced the likelihood of the hypothermic accident from occurring in the first place. For example, not knowing how long the trip would take, they could have left a car at the lunch stop bridge. Also, this changes their goal from finishing the trip to one of having a good time. With a car at the lunch stop, they would most likely have ended their trip there. It suggests good preplanning. Review each of the factors from a preplanning perspective. Ask what they might have done differently in their preplanning.

Preplanning a rock climbing route is one aspect of the preparation needed for the activity to be successful.

### Unsafe Travel Speed

Unsafe travel speed generally includes traveling too fast or too slow. When people travel faster than they should, they make errors that can easily lead to an accident. Or, if they travel too slowly, they become bored, which can again lead to mishaps. For a more technical and in-depth explanation of this principle, see the inverted-U discussion in chapter 7 (figure 7.3). It is worth noting that *travel* includes other modes of travel such as hiking or walking, biking, or boating.

In *Cold, Wet, and Alive* (1989; figure 6.5), a case could be made that the group was not traveling fast enough to complete the trip. More likely, there was inadequate trip planning such that they did not plan for enough time to complete the trip, or they simply planned too long a trip.

## Environmental Factors

Generally, environmental factors include existing or changing weather conditions, terrain, and plants and animals. Many people think of environmental factors in terms of outdoor activities, but these factors can affect indoor activities as well. A broken air-conditioner or heating system or improper lighting can adversely affect an indoor program.

### Weather and Changes in Weather Conditions

Weather or changes in weather conditions can easily affect outdoor activities. In this case, weather is defined fairly broadly to include temperature, humidity, the type of weather conditions, and other factors affecting general environmental conditions. For example, a hot, sunny day in an open boat on open water can easily lead to dehydration. Winter camping can easily lead to frostbite.

Changes in the weather can have a significant impact also. A front moves in and turns a sunny day into a rainy day. The temperature drops 20 or 30 degrees while winter camping because of a front moving in or nighttime. The change can be more subtle also. In the northern hemisphere the sun is in the southern portion of the sky particularly during late fall, winter, and early spring. In mountainous areas, the sun and its heating effect can often be blocked by 3:00 or 4:00 p.m. by the mountains, effectively lowering the temperature by 10 degrees.

Conceptually, the definition of weather can easily be expanded to include indoor and manmade environments. For example, insufficient heating can lead to chronic hypothermia among the elderly. Or, the breakdown of the air conditioner or loss of electricity in a senior center can have a significant impact on the health and well-being of its participants.

In *Cold, Wet, and Alive* (1989; figure 6.5), both the weather and change in weather conditions had a major effect on the group. The radio report indicated that it was a 70-degree spring day. Interpreting the radio report is that the air was cold, the water was cold, and anything touched by the sun's rays seemed warmer than it really was. In addition, there was a change in the weather. The weather front moved in earlier than expected and it began to rain. This affected their preplanning for the trip and what they wore on the trip.

### Terrain and Changes in Terrain Conditions

The conditions of the terrain and surface of travel affect the activity and safety. Some types of terrain are inherently more dangerous than others. Needing to cross a stream at high spring flows is different than crossing the same stream during the low flows of summer. Steep mountainous terrain offers different challenges than hiking on level ground. The surface of travel affects the activity also. Bike touring on a primary road offers different challenges than biking on a secondary road, or a rails-to-trail trail.

Terrain conditions also apply to manmade environments and to situations not involving travel. For example, fatalities on the interstate highway system are 60 percent less than on other roads (primary and secondary roads) (Cox and Love, 1996). Exemplifying a non-travel situation, playground surfacing could be considered terrain. Playground standards discuss acceptable (e.g., pea gravel, mulch, rubberized materials) and unacceptable (e.g., grass, asphalt, ground) surfacing materials (National Playground Institute, 1994). Surfacing material affects the initial design of facilities. For example, designers must choose whether to use rugs, tile, wood, or nonslip surfaces for surfacing.

In park design, designers often indicate a changing situation such as an intersection, a stop sign, or a boundary by changing the paving material. Rumble strips along the side of the highway or a change in paving type are positive applications of changes in terrain. Figure 6.9 shows examples of terrain conditions.

In *Cold, Wet, and Alive* (1989; figure 6.5), the group entered a gorge where the river dropped more quickly. The increase in the drop of the river was a change in terrain. The group also noted that the river was rising, which was also a change in the terrain or the highway on which they were traveling.

### Animals and Plants

The last environmental factor is animals and plants. Animals can actively threaten the safety of participants. Grizzly bears, jellyfish, sharks, ticks, and poisonous spiders are examples of animals that can actively harm people through their bite, sting, or mauling. Animals can also be the host of the actual vector. Ticks carry Lyme disease and mosquitoes carry the malaria protists. Similarly, plants can create problems if ingested or if the body comes in contact with the plant. For example, the oil in poison ivy is an irritant that can cause blistering and discomfort. Animals and plants did not pose a problem for the participants in *Cold, Wet, and Alive.*

## Equipment Factors

The third category is equipment factors. It is included here as its own category. However, it should be noted that in some of the safety management literature, this category is merged into either the human or environmental factors, usually human factors. This is reflected in the terminology of *unsafe acts* (human factors) and *unsafe conditions* (environmental factors). For example, inadequate or inappropriate clothing can be considered an unsafe act when the person chose for whatever reason to have inadequate or inappropriate clothing. In this case, the emphasis is on why the person made the decision to commit an unsafe act. Or, inadequate or inappropriate clothing can simply be treated as inadequate or inappropriate clothing.

### Inadequate or Inappropriate Clothing

Next to the internal physiological process of sweating or increasing metabolism (e.g., exercise or shivering), clothing is the primary method people use to regulate and maintain their appropriate core temperature. The human body needs to maintain a core temperature on average of 98.6 degrees Fahrenheit. If the body begins to cool, it needs to increase heat production (e.g., exercise or shivering) or add thermal protection (clothing). Conversely, if the body's temperature increases, it needs to cool itself or add thermal protection (clothing). Cooling the body with evaporating sweat is the primary method of cooling the body. Also, clothing can provide thermal protection against the external source of the heat, usually the sun. In addition, clothing can provide a physical barrier from harmful animals (e.g., mosquitoes, ticks) and plants (e.g., poison ivy).

Inappropriate clothing can easily become problematic when there is a change in temperature resulting from a change in the weather. It is easy for a person not to pack enough clothing for protection when the weather turns colder. Conversely, people will expose themselves in the hot sun with little or no protection.

In *Cold, Wet, and Alive* (1989; figure 6.5), inadequate and inappropriate clothing were a primary contributing factor to David's hypothermia. David dressed for the temperature conditions of the moment whereas Dean and Becky wore wetsuits to protect against the temperature of the water. Although they all experienced some degree of hypothermia, David became hypothermic more quickly. In addition, David, Lisa, and Michael wore cotton (i.e., blue jeans), which wicks moisture and cools the body. In a hypothermic type of environment, cotton is inappropriate clothing. The inadequate and inappropriate clothing that he wore was a major contributing factor.

### Inadequate or Inappropriate Equipment

Equipment is the tools needed to perform the activity. One would not expect a carpenter to arrive at a construction site without a hammer and saw. Likewise, a recreation leader conducting an outdoor activity is expected to have the appropriate equipment to adequately perform the activity. In principle, a recreation leader should use equipment that adheres to the common practices in his activity or industry. If everyone else has a cutoff switch on the electric kiln in a ceramics class, he might want to have one also. If he is taking a backcountry trip three days out from the frontcountry and everyone else has a satellite phone, he might want to consider investing in one. If he is using an outdated version of a piece of equipment, he might want to upgrade to the modern version, particularly if the equipment has been substantially improved.

The recreation leader should also use equipment that is made specifically for his activity. Inappropriate use of equipment includes using equipment in ways for which it was not designed or using equipment designed for one type of activity in another activity. For example, using a whitewater helmet in a bicycling event is questionable because, normally, one should use a bike helmet with bicycles (see figure 12.1). In *Cold, Wet, and Alive* (1989; figure 6.5), inadequate and inappropriate equipment was not really a factor contributing to David's hypothermic accident.

### Inadequate Maintenance or Wear and Tear

This item complements the equipment item. If you have the appropriate equipment, it is also necessary to maintain that equipment. Many pieces of equipment have a normal life span and should be changed out when they reach the end of that time period. For example, climbing ropes may look fine but should be retired after extended use. This is where having periodic maintenance and review of all equipment and keeping maintenance records can be helpful in reducing equipment failure. In addition, if a lawsuit arises due to faulty equipment, periodic maintenance and record keeping can be helpful in mitigating this component in a lawsuit. In *Cold, Wet, and Alive* (1989; figure 6.5), inadequate maintenance was not really a factor contributing to David's hypothermic accident.

## METAPHORICAL ACCIDENT MODELS

Most metaphorical accident models incorporate in some configuration the underlying factors discussed in the previous section. This enables an approach in which one can easily adapt these factors to most of the models presented in this section. This allows a person to choose the overarching metaphor that suits his or her philosophical approach to the accident process and accident prevention. These models are built on a solid foundation of assessing and managing the underlying factors associated with accidents. Although these models are outdoor related, they can easily be adapted to the general recreation and park field.

### Curtis Model

Rick Curtis, director of Princeton University Outdoor Action, advanced his model in the 2005 edition of *The Backpacker's Field Manual* (Curtis, 2005). In the Curtis model, one side of the scale (safety measures) balances the weights on the other side of the scale (hazards present). If sufficient safety factors are not present, the scale becomes out of balance and the safety gauge enters the danger zone. The model presented in this chapter differs slightly from the model presented by Curtis (2005). The mechanism that transfers the movement from the hazard and safety pistons was modified into two levers that move the third piston in the center in a more mechanically correct way (figure 6.7).

The hazard portion of the scale is on the left side of the model. Hazards are divided into three categories: people, environment, and equipment. The hazards are represented by three containers that contain golf balls, which represent factors. The weight of the golf balls pushes the hazard piston down. The more golf balls, the more hazards and the further the hazard piston is pushed down. Curtis notes

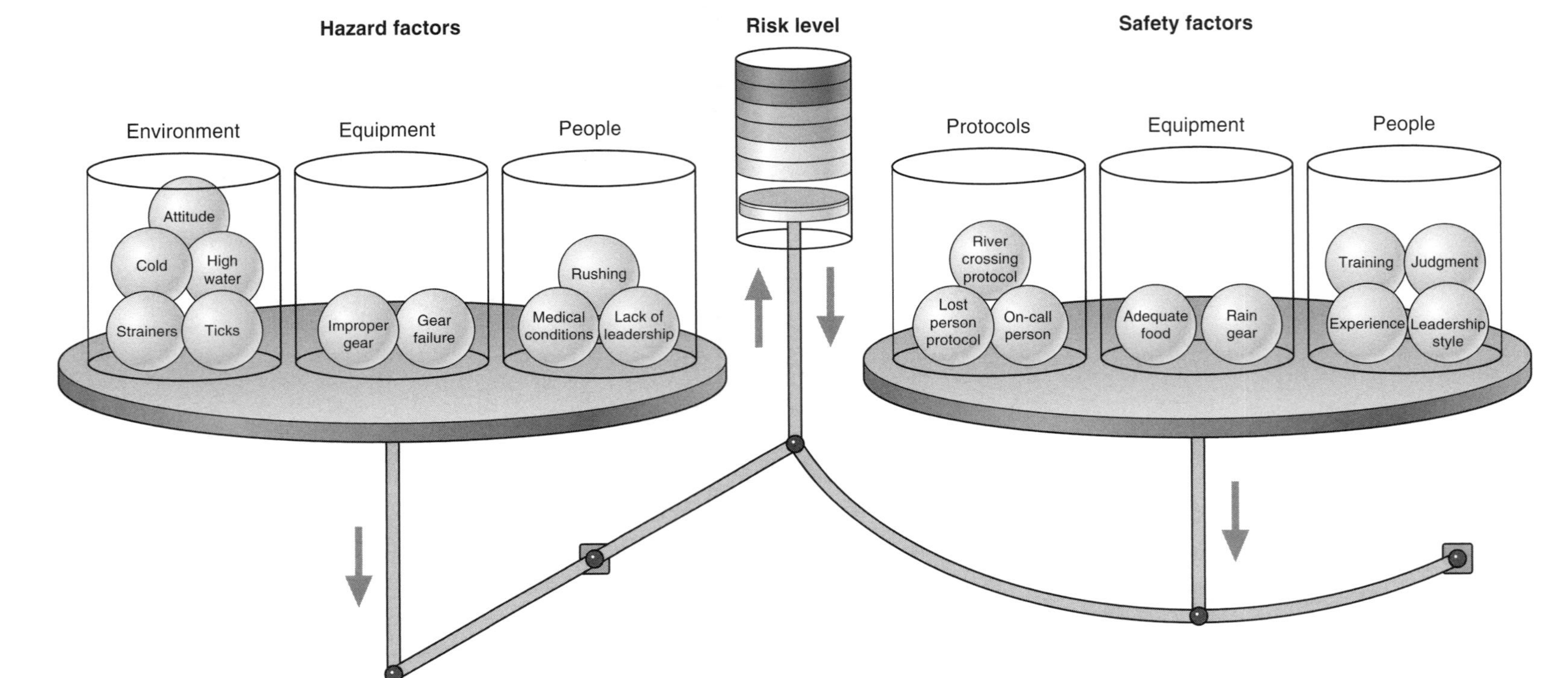


**Figure 6.7** In the Curtis model, hazard factors move the scale down, causing the risk piston to move up into the higher risk zone. In contrast, safety factors move the other side of the scale down and pull the risk piston down, indicating a decrease in the risk level. Good programming offsets hazard factors with safety factors.

that the size of the golf ball increases when the probability of its occurrence increases.

The safety factors portion of the scale is on the right side of the model. Safety factors are divided into three categories: people safety, safety protocols, and equipment safety. Like the hazard portion of the scale, the safety factors portion of the scale is represented by three containers. People safety involves the decisions people make and actions they take to counteract the hazards. For example, experience, judgment, training, and leadership style can help a person facilitate a safer experience. Equipment safety includes using proper equipment that is in good repair. Safety protocols are the rules and regulations, either written or unwritten, governing an activity (e.g., "everyone is always clipped in," "everyone is always belayed," or "always keep in sight the person in front of you and the person behind you"). Protocols allow for the inclusion of the rules, regulations, and policies of the organization or the industry.

In between the two trays on the scale is a third piston indicating the risk level. The risk-level piston is color coded from red at the top, indicating greater risk, to blue at the bottom, indicating less risk. As the hazard tray of the scale pushes down, it pushes the risk piston up into the red zone. In contrast, as the safety factor tray of the scale pushes down, it pushes the piston down into the blue zone. The degree of risk becomes the interplay between the hazard and safety factors. The objective is to offset the hazard factors with safety factors.

The Curtis model is intuitive and it captures the notion of offsetting hazards with safety factors. The model shows that if a person does X, then Y results. In addition, it suggests that the actions of the leader are instrumental in preventing accidents. Curtis notes that hazard and safety factors can change during the activity and that it is the responsibility of the leader to adjust safety measures accordingly.

Curtis adds that when accidents occur, one must close the loop and investigate the underlying causes. The model can provide the basic structure to examine incidents and to help prevent them in the future. Curtis lists common environmental, equipment, and human hazards. A person who prefers this model can easily increase its effectiveness by adapting and incorporating the underlying human, environmental, and equipment factors discussed earlier in this chapter.

If one expands this model into a general recreation model, it may be desirable to add a fourth cylinder for environment on the safety factor side of the scale. In an outdoor setting, a leader or organization does not normally have control over environmental factors. For this reason, the environment cylinder was most likely not included in the model. In an artificial or manmade environment, leaders can often

Brand X Pictures

By expanding the Curtis model into a general recreation model, the programmer should consider the environmental hazards and how to adjust safety measures.

modify and control the environmental safety factors. Choosing to walk in a mall because its environment is controlled with air conditioning and air filtration is an example of creating an environmental safety factor. Curtis' factors, as applied to an outdoor setting such as backpacking, are as follows.

**Common Environmental Hazards**

Poison ivy
Lightning
Bees and wasps
Overexposure to sun
Exposed ledges
Cold temperatures
Contaminated water

**Common Equipment Hazards**

Improper clothing
Faulty stove
Inoperative equipment
Missing equipment

**Common Human Hazards**

Previous experience
Physical condition
Previous medical conditions
No awareness of hazards
Trying to "prove" oneself
Fatigue
Anxiety or fear
Limited outdoor skills

**Hazards Among Participants**

Not interested in being on the trip
Poor communication skills
Not willing to follow instructions
Group lacks cooperative structure

**Hazards Among Trip Leaders**

Poor teaching ability
Inability to manage group
Poor judgment regarding safety
Inadequate skills to extricate self and others from hazards

## Risk Meter

The risk meter was developed by Steve Storck (2003; personal communication) as part of the instructional program in adventure sports at Garrett College (figure 6.8). The meter is intuitive and easily used by students or lay groups in discussing risk management, particularly in an instructional setting. Originally, the meter incorporated a general version of the underlying human, environmental, and equipment factors discussed earlier in this chapter. Formally integrating these factors in the model can significantly upgrade the model and increase its usability. As with the Curtis model, the meter conceptually creates safety by balancing the hazard factors with the safety factors.

Using the risk meter is fairly straightforward. One assesses the human, environmental, and equipment factors in terms of safety. Unsafe acts move the meter clockwise toward a potential disaster (red). Safe acts move the meter counterclockwise toward boredom (blue). The white area of the meter indicates the area in which the managed risks create a reasonably safe situation.

The ability of the leader to manage risks determines the location of the needle in the risk meter. The leader can discuss the underlying factors in terms of their risks and then discuss the safety measures taken to reduce these risks. The leader can tally up the risk factors and then tally up the safety measures that offset the risks

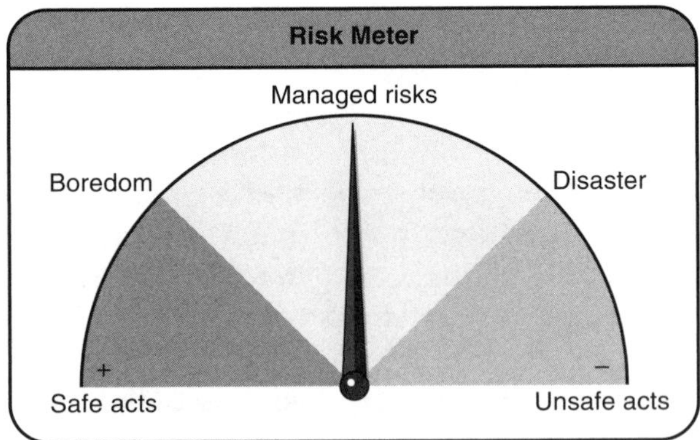


**Figure 6.8** In the risk meter model, unsafe acts move the risk meter needle clockwise; safe acts move it counterclockwise. If risks are managed appropriately, both challenge and safety can occur.

From Storck, 2003, Personal conversation.

to determine the location of the needle in the risk meter. If the group needs to bring the risk meter into a more acceptable range, the group members can discuss the safety measures that they should take.

Inherent in the risk meter is the assumption that adventure activities need a certain level of risk to make them challenging. The risk meter includes the concepts of the flow model and adventure experience paradigm discussed in chapter 7 (Csikszentmihalyi, 1975; Priest and Gass, 2005). Also, the meter assumes that removing the risks results in boredom. Although the literature provides considerable support for this proposition, this may not always be the case. In summary, the model is intuitive, uncomplicated, easy to use, and worthy of consideration.

## Domino Model

The domino model builds on Heinrich et al. (1980) and Bird and Germain's (1985) conceptualization of the accident process as a series of dominos and reflects the previous work of this author (Kauffman, 2004, 2006, 2007). Conceptually, it is closely linked with the models derived from the outdoor leadership field (chapter 5) and to Bird and Germain (1985). The model also incorporates barrier analysis and Haddon's (1973) concept of energy transfer (see chapter 5). The integration of these components helps provide the leader or programmer with a pragmatic model that can assist in the day-to-day operations of activities.

The domino model depicts the accident process as a series of dominos that, when pushed over, result in an accident (figure 6.9). It operates as follows. A leader or programmer conducts an activity or program. The protocols are rules, regulations, and policies affecting the organization's programs and activities. Any activity or program can be analyzed in terms of the underlying factors present. The underlying factors are represented by dominos. These factors may directly or indirectly contribute to an eventual incident. When an unsafe act occurs, a domino is metaphorically placed on the table. Acts of safety and prevention remove a domino. If a sufficient number of unsafe acts (dominos) are amassed, when an incident eventually occurs, the dominos fall and can lead to an accident and injury, damage, or loss.

If a leader or programmer inserts a large number of safety measures, he removes dominos from the chain. This is a metaphorical variation of barrier analysis. When an incident occurs, a couple of the dominos fall rather than all of them. This results in a near miss or an accident with less injury, damage, or loss than would otherwise occur. The following sections expand on the different components of the model shown in figure 6.9.

### Underlying Factors

The underlying factors of this model are listed figure 6.9 and described previously in this chapter. One will not and cannot know all of the underlying factors present in an activity or program. They are still there, and if they pose a hazard the hazard is still there. Generally, all of the invisible (unknown) underlying factors tend to become visible (known) in the postincident analysis. This is the benefit of hindsight. Regardless, the more dominos that one can identify, the more dominos one can manage and control with the four Ts (i.e., terminate, treat, transfer, and tolerate). The management of these factors is a form of barrier analysis in which one takes measures to prevent, reduce, or enhance these factors to create an appropriate experience for the participant.

A purpose of examining the underlying factors is to make them visible so that the leader or programmer can manage them and consciously reduce their effect on the activity. A leader's job is to analyze an activity or program in terms of the potential underlying factors present and to make invisible factors visible. This is the first step in making activities and programs safer.

### Protocols

In the domino model, protocols are defined by the environment in which one works or operates. The operative term is *environment*. Generally, protocols are the rules, regulations, and policies of the agency or the common practices of the activity or industry standards. They may be delineated as part of the risk

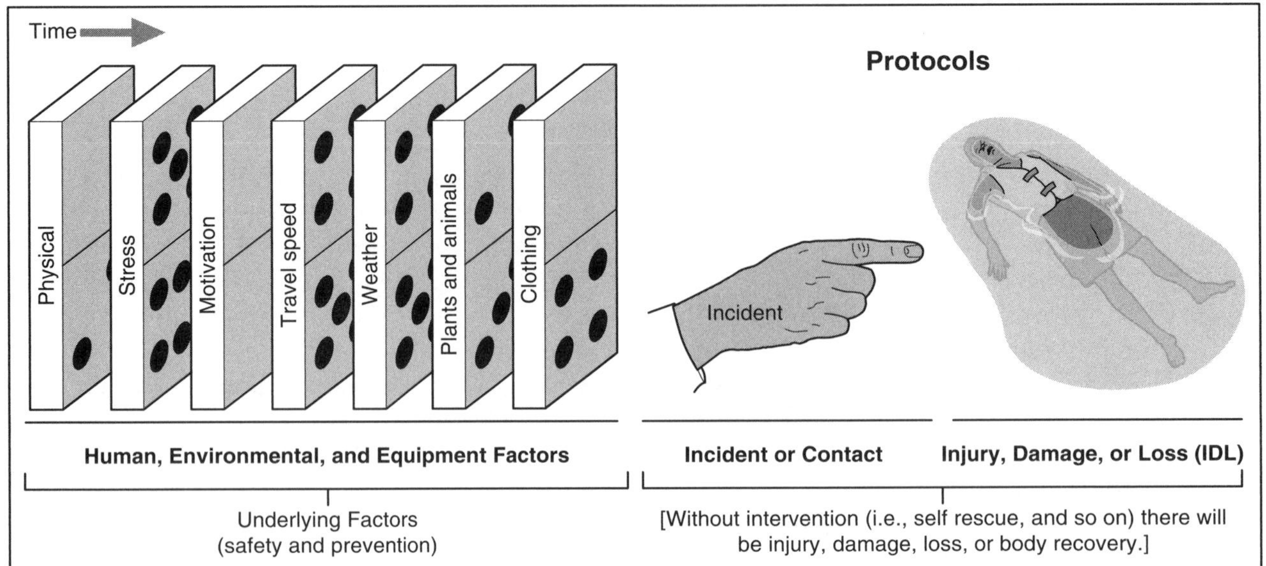


### Human Factors

**Physical or physiological capabilities or stress** (conditioning, restricted range of motion, age-related issues, vision or hearing deficiencies, disabilities, allergies, coordination, prior injuries, illness, fatigue due to sensory overload, exposure to temperature extremes [hypothermia/hyperthermia], oxygen deficiency, inadequate food intake, drugs, and so on)

**Mental or psychological capabilities or stress** (fears or phobias, poor judgment, poor decisions, inexperience, emotional overload, extreme judgment/decision demands, extreme concentration/perception demands, confusing directions, conflicting demands, preoccupation with problems, frustration, and so on)

**Knowledge** (lack of experience, inadequate orientation, inadequate training [initial and updates], not knowing the accident process, and so on)

**Skill** (inadequate initial instruction, inadequate practice, infrequent performance of activity, lack of coaching, and so on)

**Motivation** (improper attempt to save time or effort, improper attempt to avoid discomfort, peer pressure, aggressive behavior, passive behavior, cultural norms like high achievement, and so on)

**Leadership and group dynamics** (miscommunications, inappropriate leadership style, cultural norms, organizational norms, lack of experience, lack of experience in similar setting, inappropriate goals, trying to adhere to a schedule, and so on)

**Preplanning** (inadequate or no risk management plan; inadequate trip planning for any of the human, environmental, and equipment factors)

**Unsafe travel speed** (travel too fast, travel too slow, and so on)

### Environmental Factors

**Weather** (rain, snow, fog, sun, lightning, and so on)

**Change in weather conditions** (change in any of the above weather conditions [it begins to rain], change in intensity of the weather conditions [drizzle to pouring rain], and so on)

**Terrain conditions** (open water, restricted water passage, waves, whitecaps, hydraulics, eddies, strainers, tidal effects, current, desert, mountainous, hilly, avalanche prone, and so on)

**Change in terrain conditions** (change in any of the above terrain conditions, change in intensity of the terrain conditions [increase of the wave size], and so on)

**Animals or plants** (jellyfish, sharks, poison ivy, and so on)

### Equipment

**Inadequate or inappropriate clothing** (not using wetsuit/drysuit or other cold weather/water protection when needed, inadequate protection from elements, and so on)

**Inadequate or inappropriate equipment** (not using a sprayskirt when needed, use of canoe/kayak in an environment for which it was not designed, use of equipment in ways for which it was not designed, navigational equipment, and so on)

**Inadequate maintenance or wear and tear** (use of old or worn out equipment, material fatigue, and so on)

**Figure 6.9** The domino model likens the accident process to a series of dominos. Unsafe acts add dominos and safe acts remove them. When an incident occurs (i.e., when the dominos are pushed over), its severity and whether injury, damage, or loss occurs depend in part on the number of dominos present. Reducing unsafe acts reduces the likelihood of an accident.

Developed by Dr. Robert B. Kauffman, Professor Recreation and Parks Management, Frostburg State University, Frostburg, MD.

management plan of the organization or agency. They include local and state laws. If a professional organization services an industry, its accreditation standards or common practices affect protocols also. Protocols include the following.

- Rules
- Policies
- Regulations
- Laws
- Accreditation standards
- Risk management plans

## Incident

In the domino model, an incident is an event. Usually, it is characterized by an exchange of energy, such as a fall, electrical charge, or impact. This is an integration of Haddon's (1973) concept of energy flow and barrier analysis (see chapter 5). Without intervention, injury, damage, or loss will occur. If no injury, damage, or loss occurs, the incident is usually characterized as a near miss.

For example, while walking on the sidewalk, a woman slips on a banana peel. Her emotional stress and focus on work problems are underlying factors that lead to her inattentiveness and not seeing the banana peel. Once she slips on the banana peel, unless someone or something intervenes, she will fall and land awkwardly on the sidewalk. The transfer of energy changes from potential to kinetic. Intervention could happen in several ways. The woman can self-rescue. She might catch herself and prevent the fall or she might reach out and catch the railing. Or someone else could intervene on her behalf. They might extend a hand and prevent the fall or weaken the impact of the fall. If she breaks her arm during the fall, injury, damage, or loss occurs. If nothing is injured other than her pride and ego, a near miss occurs.

After she picks herself up, dusts herself off, and looks around to see if anyone saw her foolish act, she will most likely perform a quick analysis to determine why she slipped on the banana peel. Having reviewed the underlying factors in the domino model, she might approach this task with a little more sophistication. She might note that she was under considerable mental and psychological stress due to a series of recent life events and as a result was inattentive.

She might conclude that she needs to act more cautiously. Or perhaps she concludes that she needs to modify her behavior. Making recommendations and changes is an important part of the learning process and is the logical next step. To not apply what she has learned is to potentially repeat the same mistakes or repeat the same incident because the same underlying factors that resulted in her slipping on the banana peel are still there. The dominos are still there. Next time something else may take the place of the banana peel and become the cause of the incident.

## Injury, Damage, or Loss

Injury, damage, or loss includes bodily injury, property damages or loss, and any loss incurred because of an incident. A broken arm or broken leg is a loss. A fatality is a loss. Emotional duress can even be considered a loss. Also, a loss must be translated into monetary compensation. In the video *Cold, Wet, and Alive* (1989), David's loss of his boat on the trip is an example of a loss. In contrast, in the video *Decide to Return* (2007), Katie and Jack almost drowned and were rescued by a man who just happened to be passing by (see appendix B). In *Decide to Return*, no loss occurred. Had the captain of the lobster boat charged them for the rescue, a loss would have occurred.

The purpose of the domino accident model is to prevent incidents by removing or managing dominos that can lead to injury, damage, or loss. A strength of the model is that it emphasizes things one can do to reduce the likelihood that an accident will occur. It emphasizes safety. Many models tend to focus on the negative aspects or things that one did incorrectly. With the domino model, if a person assesses that he is traveling too fast or too slow, he can adjust his speed of travel and in doing so remove a domino. If he lacks knowledge or skill, he can gain it and remove a domino.

## NEGLIGENCE AND PROGRAM PLANNING IMPLICATIONS

The factors and concepts behind the models discussed in this chapter easily fit together with the typical considerations of leadership and program planning. The discussion of the human, environmental, and equipment factors includes several of the principles of negligence, including the standard of care of a reasonable and prudent professional. If a recreation and park leader integrates one of the models discussed in this chapter into the normal leadership and program planning structure, it will most likely help him act as a reasonable and prudent professional. In addition, he will most likely create a safe environment for the participants in his activity because he will be managing or eliminating many of the factors that can cause harm. There will always be factors that are invisible until an incident occurs, but by addressing as many factors that he can, he can reduce the impact of an incident. If an incident occurs, it will most likely result in a near miss rather than injury, damage, or loss. And if injury, damage, or loss occurs, the injury, damage, or loss will most likely be less than it would be otherwise. One should consider knowing the accident process and applying the principles of the domino model as part of the standard of care of a reasonable and prudent professional.

## SUMMARY

The outdoor and adventure field has a rich history of using accident models. These models are used by leaders in leadership situations. Their focus is on what *I* can do to act safely rather than what someone else (safety manager) should do to facilitate safety. One can easily adapt these models to a general recreation setting by modifying some of the outdoor-related factors. This makes these models particularly useful in a recreation and parks discipline dominated by activity leadership.

This chapter introduces the concept of underlying factors and includes a convenient list of factors that one can use to assess the potential safety of activities and programs. This chapter also presents several metaphorical models that help recreation leaders and programmers accomplish the objective of preventing accidents before they happen. The main strength of these models is that they approach accident prevention in an intuitive way by depicting the accident process as a series of dominos ready to fall, a risk meter, or a scale balancing out hazard factors and safety factors. When coupled with the underlying human, environmental, and equipment factors, these models become powerful tools for assessing potential accidents and facilitating safer programs.

## EXERCISES

### Exercise 1: Which Model Do You Like?

The purpose of this exercise is to help you determine which accident model you prefer. Use one of the recommended sources ("Mt. Hood"; *Cold, Wet, and Alive*; or *Decide to Return* in appendixes A to C) or an accident of your own with which you are familiar. If you use your own accident, you should briefly describe an accident that resulted in injury, damage, or loss, and you should be able to document the activities and events that preceded the incident. Analyze the accident in terms of one or more of the models discussed in this chapter. Which model fits the accident the best? Which model do you prefer, if any? (*Note:* Remember, this is a postincident analysis.)

1. Danger analysis
2. Accident matrix

3. Curtis model
4. Risk meter
5. Domino model

## Exercise 2: Mt. Hood Incident

The purpose of this exercise is to analyze an accident in terms of the underlying factors present. Review the newspaper account of the Mt. Hood incident in appendix A. First, identify as many underlying factors present in the event as you can based on the article. For example, the title of the article, "High Achievers' Climb to Death," suggests the effect of cultural norms (e.g., motivation) on the eventual accident. Second, discuss what you might have done differently, if anything, to prevent the incident if you were the leader on this trip. Although it is not necessary for this activity, people might find a time line of the tragedy helpful. If so, a time line is provided as part of exercise 4 in chapter 12.

## Exercise 3: *Cold, Wet, and Alive*

The purpose of this exercise is to apply one of the accident models to an accident situation. The video *Cold, Wet, and Alive* (1989) depicts the accident process and shows how the day's events on a canoe trip led to a hypothermic accident. After watching the video, discuss the following items in terms of the accident process. If you do not have access to the video, refer to figure 6.5 for a narrative of what happened on the trip.

1. Using the domino model, identify the human, environmental, and equipment factors that affected the trip and its eventual outcome. Identify both good and bad factors. Feel free to expand on the factors that are identified in this chapter. *Note:* You can use the Curtis model or one of the other models instead of the domino model.
2. Note the change in behavior of the participants as the day progressed. How would this change affect your decision making if you were the leader on this trip?
3. Discuss why the group made the decision they made at the lunch stop. If you are familiar with the concept of group think or the Abilene paradox, apply these concepts to their decision making (Harvey, 1974, 1988). Essentially, in the Abilene paradox, a group collectively makes a decision that is different from what each individual knows to be the correct decision.
4. What would have happened if the group had left a vehicle at the lunch stop? Discuss how it would have potentially changed the outcome. Next, not knowing the length of the trip, what would have happened if they had changed the goal of the trip so that their objective was to make it to the lunch stop rather than to the end?

## Exercise 4: *Decide to Return*

The purpose of this exercise is to apply one of the accident models to an accident situation. The sea kayaking video *Decide to Return* (2007) explores the accident process and how the little decisions you make can influence the outcome of your experience. After watching the video, discuss the following items in terms of the accident process.

1. Using the domino model, identify the human, environmental, and equipment factors that affected the trip and its eventual outcome. Identify both good and bad

factors. *Note:* You can use the Curtis model or one of the other models instead of the domino model.

2. Group dynamics is an important consideration in the decision-making process. Katie and Jack are good friends. Discuss the interplay between the two main characters and how it affected their decisions and the eventual incident. For example, why did Jack go along with Katie when she wanted to change plans and when he really knew better?

### Exercise 5: Postincident Analysis of a Personal Incident

The purpose of this exercise is to personalize the accident process and the application of one of the models. Think of an accident or near miss that you have had. First, analyze the incident in terms of the domino model and its factors. (*Note:* You may use the Curtis or risk meter models if you prefer.) How many factors, or dominos, were present? What was the final incident that caused the injury, damage, or loss (or, if it was a near miss, nearly caused it)? Second, which of these factors did you know about before the incident, and which of them became visible to you in the postincident analysis? Third, with what you know now, what, if anything, would you do differently? If this activity works well, you will personalize this model into the way you think and the way you approach the things you do.

### Exercise 6: Supplemental Resources

The purpose of this exercise is to expand the use of the accident models beyond the resources presented in this text. Numerous books and movies are built around an outdoor disaster or tragedy. The following three sources might be used to investigate the accident process. Review the movie or book of your choice that depicts an accident and analyze it in terms of one of the models presented in this chapter. Did the use of the accident model increase your understanding of how the accident occurred, and would you be better able to have prevented the accident from occurring?

1. In *Into Thin Air,* Jon Krakauer (1998) writes a personal account of the Mt. Everest disaster.
2. In *Lessons Learned II,* Deb Ajango (2005) documents two accidents in the outdoor field, the Diazlo incident used as an example in this text and the multifatality accident on Ptarmigan Peak in Alaska.
3. *Into the Wild* by Jon Krakauer (1997), also a motion picture, is the true story of Christopher McCandless and his odyssey into the backcountry of Alaska that eventually resulted in his death.

Chapter 7

# Programming for Risks

The risk management, accident causation, and safety management literature suggests that the role of the safety manager in an organization is to reduce and eliminate all risks. Risks are equated with hazards, and both are considered to be bad. It can be said that safety managers will leave no risk untouched in their effort to eliminate any and all risks. However, the recreation and park field, and the outdoor adventure area in particular, has embraced risks as an integral component of the activity or program. For a recreation leader or programmer, this situation can be confusing. Should activities include risks? If so, what level of risk is appropriate, and how much risk can one take without being sued? Equally important, what level of risk is appropriate for providing a meaningful experience for the participant? This chapter discusses how an outdoor adventure leader can manage risks in an activity to achieve the desired experience and at the same time avoid an accident and a potential lawsuit. This chapter presents two models for addressing risks in a recreational setting: the 2 × 2 risk matrix, developed by Kauffman (1991), and the adventure experience paradigm, developed by Priest and Gass (2005).

## 2 × 2 RISK MATRIX: PERCEIVED VERSUS ACTUAL RISKS

The 2 × 2 risk matrix expresses a relationship between perceived risks and actual risks for an activity (figure 7.1). The model evolved out of research conducted on the Potomac River for the Maryland Department of Natural Resources. The research consisted of a survey of Potomac River users that related users' perception of how dangerous their river experience was with their experience as measured by a specialization index (Kauffman, 1991; Kauffman et al., 1991).

The Potomac River study found that on the main stem of the Potomac River, most fatalities occur at moderate water levels, not at flood level or at the normal low flows during summer. These findings directly relate to three of the categories in the 2 × 2 risk matrix. These three water-level conditions (flood, moderate, and summer low flow) are used as examples of the 2 × 2 risk matrix categories in the following sections.

A recreation provider (i.e., resource manager, leader, or programmer) must assess the actual risks of the experience in terms of the participant's perception of the risks involved. This assessment helps the provider to determine which risk management approach to take. The model is applicable to outdoor experiences; it can easily apply to general recreation as well. This matrix complements the adventure experience paradigm, discussed later in this chapter.

### High Actual Risks and High Perceived Risks

In this category, the participant recognizes that a high-risk situation is high risk. Compared

| | | Perceived risk | |
|---|---|---|---|
| | | Low | High |
| Actual risk | High | **Drowning trap** The user perceives the risks to be low while they are actually high. This is a potentially dangerous situation. | **Upper Yough River** There are high actual risks present and the user perceives the risks as high. |
| | Low | **Lazy river** The actual risks involved are low and the user perceives these risks to be low also. | **Roller coaster** The user perceives the risk to be high while they are actually low. |

**Figure 7.1** From the perspective of the recreation provider (resource manager, leader, or programmer), the 2 × 2 risk matrix compares the participants' perceived risks with the actual risks present.

Based on Kauffman, Taylor, and Price 1991.

with a situation in which the actual risk is high and the perceived risk is low, in this category the participant tends to be more receptive to the needs of the situation because he recognizes the risks involved in the activity. In addition, for those seeking mastery, actual risk is an integral part of the activity. In this category, the task of the leader or programmer is to give the participant the knowledge, skills, and abilities to effectively participate in the activity. In addition, the leader or programmer needs to provide the usual support, including staff, equipment, preplanning, and activity selection.

In figure 7.1, the Upper Yough in Maryland exemplifies this category. It is a class IV and V whitewater river that drops 150 to 170 feet per mile. Its high gradient creates high actual risks. Most participants correctly perceive the risks as high. It is difficult for raft guides to reduce the actual risks on a natural river; they can only manage them at best. They need to provide the support services necessary for participants to perform in a high-risk environment. They run the river under known conditions and have designated routes through the rapids. They set up safety at the bottom of the major rapids and go through the rapids single file. The owner of the raft company, who also serves as safety, critiques the run of the rafts through the rapids. The guides are well trained. By managing the risks, they create a safer environment for participants.

On the Potomac River, people correctly perceived the actual dangers present and stayed off the river. The exception was kayakers, who sought the high-water challenge. Water flowing over the banks and into the trees, big waves, muddy water, and propane tanks floating down the river were characteristic of a situation of high actual risk and high perceived risk.

The situation did not present a problem for management. The general public perceived the dangers correctly and stayed off the river. The kayakers, who generally had the skill to paddle the river, perceived the risks for what they were and paddled the river without major mishaps. Management's task was to provide users with good information so that they could effectively decide whether to participate in a given activity. Usually, this was a gauge reading indicating the river level. This was reflected statistically in the lack of fatalities at high water levels.

## Low Actual Risks and Low Perceived Risks

During the normal low flow of summer, the Potomac River, like many rivers, pools and effectively loses its power to become a contributing factor in accidents. Dangers are still present, but the power of the river in terms of its depth and velocity no longer significantly contributes to fatalities. People are not drowning because the river is not deep enough and powerful enough to drown them. The public does not perceive the river as dangerous; based on fatality statistics, their perception is not unfounded. They go to the river to swim, wade, tube, kayak, and boat. From a management perspective, river flow is not a problem.

In figure 7.1, the "lazy river" ride at the water park exemplifies this category. On a lazy river, participants work on their suntans as they float slowly down the river on inflatable tubes. Many recreational activities, such as watching movies, driving for pleasure, taking a walk in the park, and attending a birthday party, fall into this category.

In this category, the task of the leader or programmer is to continually assess the activity to ensure that the low actual risks remain low and that the situation does not inadvertently creep into one of high actual risk and low perceived risk described in the next section.

## High Actual Risks and Low Perceived Risks

The Potomac River study found that most fatalities on the river occurred at moderate water levels when the river was well within its banks. The river looked normal to the people who visit once or twice a year. They did not perceive it as dangerous because they perceive a flooding river as dangerous and the river, at moderate water levels, was not characteristic of a flood. However, the river was in fact more dangerous, which was reflected in increased fatalities. Kauffman labeled this situation "the drowning trap" because it caught unsuspecting people (Kauffman, 1992, 2002; figure 7.2).

As a general rule, the leader or programmer should seek to avoid this category of actual and perceived risks. When a leader identifies such risks, she should compensate for the situation in two ways. First, she needs to manage and reduce the risks because the participants do not fully appreciate them. This strategy of overprotecting participants is found in most safety management programs today. Second, she can either educate or inform the participants of the dangers or risks. Both strategies are usually effective. However, because participants do not understand the actual risks involved, the leader or programmer may have to intervene significantly. Good leaders and programmers are constantly removing, reducing, or compensating for this situation to provide safer activities and programs.

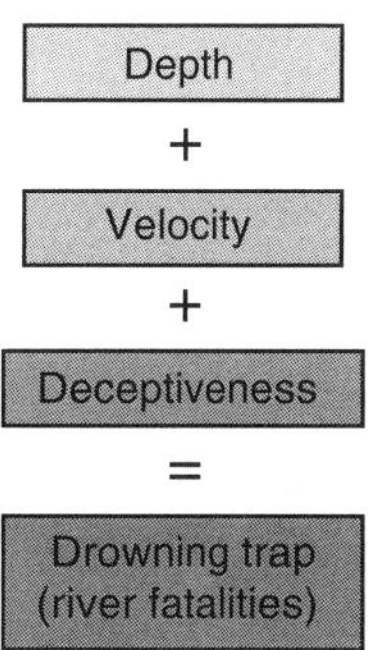


**Figure 7.2** In the 2 × 2 risk management paradigm, the category of high actual risks and low perceived risks is the most dangerous because people do not recognize and appreciate the dangers. In the Potomac River study, the drowning trap, where moderate river flows contribute to fatalities, exemplifies this category.

Based on Kauffman, Taylor, and Price 1991.

The "electric fence" on challenge courses exemplifies this category. The electric fence was discontinued after a long-term study indicated that, while being passed over the fence, many people fell and sprained or broke an ankle before someone could catch them. Depending on the height of the wire, participants did not perceive the danger associated with passing someone over the wire. The large number of injuries associated with this activity suggests a situation in which perceived risks are low and actual risks are high (Collard, 2001; Project Adventure, 1995).

One cannot overemphasize the importance of identifying the risks in this category. The following example shows why recreation professionals must be able to assess the potential dangers associated with this category. Many consider the modern playground to be low in actual and perceived risk. One criticism of the modern playground is that designers have taken out all of the risks, and hence the fun. In the following passage, Skenazy (2010) inadvertently advocates a potentially dangerous situation of high actual risk and low perceived risk on the seesaw.

> For the past 40 years or so, we have certainly been working to make our playgrounds safer than safe—maybe even safer than fun. Seen an old merry-go-round lately? Or a swinging gate? How about a seesaw—the kind without springs, where, when your so-called friend suddenly plopped you down, you felt it?

Skenazy makes the mistake of not understanding the danger involved. A thump on a seesaw is an example of a situation that is high in actual risk and low in perceived risk because a thump can lead to a back injury. Also, it is an unforeseen risk for the child because the child does not easily perceive that the springless seesaw is dangerous (i.e., it has low perceived risk). Playground designers must design acceptable levels of risks that children can perceive and appreciate. In this respect, Skenazy's point regarding taking the fun out of playgrounds is still valid. Risk is still an important ingredient. However, one must differentiate between risks that are foreseeable and those that are not and must identify situations of high actual risk and low perceived risk and modify the activity appropriately.

## Low Actual Risks and High Perceived Risks

Although this category was not actively utilized in the Potomac River study, this category may offer the most potential programming opportunities for recreation providers. The roller coaster exemplifies the category of high perceived risks and low actual risks (figure 7.1). Generally, this category is one of the safest of the four categories, and it may offer the most programming opportunities for recreation providers. Except for those whose activity involves seeking mastery (Ellis, 1973) or requires challenge as an integral part (e.g., adventure experience), many recreation providers should consider this category as the norm. In this category, the activity or program is full of challenge and thrills but low on real risks.

A roller coaster exemplifies this category. The ride maximizes perceived risk among riders while minimizing actual risk. The high

Blend Images/AP Photo

A roller coaster exemplifies the low actual risks and high perceived risks category; the ride maximizes perceived risk among riders while minimizing actual risk.

ropes course is another example. Because the participant is always belayed into the system and because the course is high enough that participants will be caught by the belay if they fall, participants have little chance of hitting the ground.

In describing the role of the facilitator on an initiatives course, Collard (2001) states, "In an ideal adventure program, an experienced facilitator will design a program/activity which aims to keep the 'perceived risk' as high as possible (to heighten the challenge, interaction and tension), while managing the actual risk to be as low as possible." In terms of the accident process and negligence, the leader's task is to reduce or manage the human, environmental, and equipment factors to reduce the likelihood that a severe incident or accident will occur. In essence, he is suggesting that the facilitator seeks to create activities in this quadrant of the matrix. His description is another way of suggesting a roller coaster experience.

## ADVENTURE EXPERIENCE PARADIGM

Priest and Gass (2005) developed the adventure experience paradigm. The paradigm builds on the previous works of Martin and Priest (1986), on Ellis' (1973) optimal arousal theory of play based on the inverted-U curve, and on the flow concept developed by Csikszentmihalyi (1975). The model is based on seeking optimal arousal or a flow experience and, from an outdoor leader's perspective, creating such an experience for participants.

Ellis (1973) suggests that people seek optimal arousal in their play as well as in their normal activities. He uses the example of typing to illustrate the inverted-U curve and the concept of seeking optimal arousal (figure 7.3). An optimum level of performance exists based on a person's skill level. If a person types faster than that level, his error rate goes up and his overall performance (i.e., words typed correctly less errors made) goes down. If he types slower than his optimal performance, his performance goes down because his is typing more slowly and he becomes bored and less attentive. The typist thus seeks to type at a rate that results in optimal performance.

The flow model developed by Csikszentmihalyi (1975) relates the skill level or competence of the participant to the challenges present. Csikszentmihalyi suggests that a flow experience can result when a person matches his skills (action capabilities) to the challenges (action opportunities). A flow experience is characterized by a merging of action and awareness, a loss of sense of time, and a total focus on or immersion into the activity. A person is experiencing a flow experience when he is not thinking about how he might be experiencing a flow experience. The flow model and the inverted-U model are very similar. The skill level or competence of the participant, which composes the X axis in the flow model, is implied in the inverted-U model. The relationship becomes apparent when the inverted-U graph is flipped on the X axis and rotated clockwise 45 degrees.

In developing the adventure experience paradigm, Priest and Gass (2005) superimposed on the flow model a participant topology based on

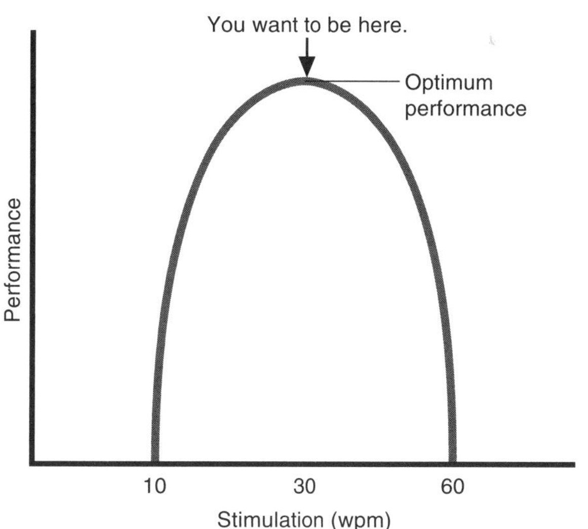


**Figure 7.3** If a person types slower than he is capable of typing, his performance is less than what it should be and he becomes bored. If he types faster than he is capable of typing, he makes errors and his performance goes down. Optimum performance occurs at a person's optimum capability.

From Ellis 1973.

risk and competence (figure 7.4); a description of the categories on the graph follows. In their model, competence and risk equal skills and challenges, respectively, in the flow model. If the risks far exceed the competence level of the participant, *devastation and disaster* will result. If the risks only slightly exceed the competence level of the participant, a *misadventure* results. Typical of a misadventure, some anxiety and mishap will occur. If the participant's competence far exceeds the risks, *exploration and experimentation* takes place on the part of the participant. If the participant's competence exceeds the risks, an *adventure* will occur. In this situation, the participant is not pushing herself in terms of optimal arousal because she is not performing at her optimum capability. A *peak adventure* results when the risks match the competence of the participants. This situation corresponds to the potential for creating a flow state as described by Csikszentmihalyi (1975).

Next, the adventure experience paradigm juxtaposes the participant's perceived risks and competence with the real risks and competence. The *expected outcome* is what the participant perceives or expects the outcome to be based on her *perception* of her skills and the risks involved. The *resultant outcome* is the result of the *real risks* (Y axis) and *competence* (X axis) that the participant experiences in the activity. The model analyzes the discrepancy between the expected outcome and the resultant outcome, called *adaptive dissonance*. The model can be viewed in terms of both the participant's and the leader's expectations.

For example, a participant with some previous rafting experience takes a rafting trip on a moderately difficult river. Her perception is that she should have a peak adventure because she perceives that her skill level and competence matches the challenges or risks that she perceives to be associated with the rafting trip (figure 7.5). However, the actual trip is different than what she expects. The water is high and the risks and challenges of the experience exceed her actual competence and skills. The actual experience is in the range of misadventure rather than peak adventure. A discrepancy occurs between what the participant expects on the raft trip and what she actually experiences. The experience may not be optimum. It may result in pushing the participant to develop new skills or to moderate

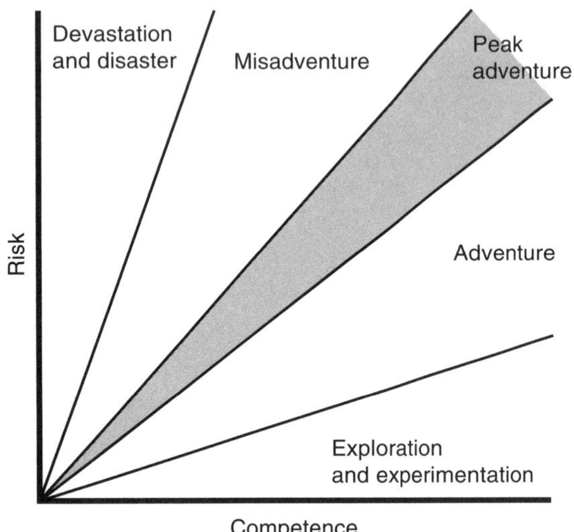


**Figure 7.4** The adventure experience paradigm integrates the inverted-U and flow models to create five adventure situations.

Reprinted, by permission, from S. Priest and M. Gass, 2005, *Effective leadership in adventure programming*, 2nd ed. (Champaign, IL: Human Kinetics), 50.

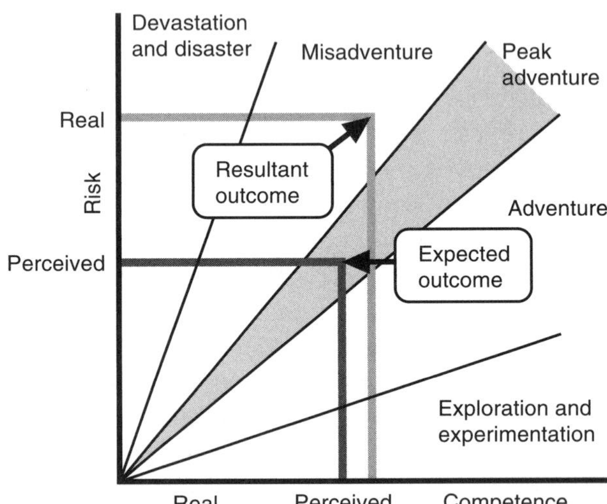


**Figure 7.5** In the adventure experience paradigm, perceived risks and competence lead to the expected outcome. This is compared with the actual risks encountered and the actual competence of the participant.

Reprinted, by permission, from S. Priest and M. Gass, 2005, *Effective leadership in adventure programming*, 2nd ed. (Champaign, IL: Human Kinetics), 51.

her challenges in the future. Or, if the guides on the trip do not handle the situation correctly, the participant may experience anxiety and not participate in the activity again.

An example of misadventure, or more likely devastation and disaster, is the raft trip from hell discussed in chapter 13. The novice participant did not expect to take a trip at flood level, nor did she expect the consequences that occurred because of the water level. In the segment of the deposition provided, the participant indicates her new fear of the water that resulted from the incident and summarizes her disastrous experience with the comment "I felt that I—could have drowned that day" (River Riders et al., 2007, p. 48, lines 10-11). In terms of the risks present, the resultant outcome far exceeded her expected outcome. In terms of the 2 × 2 matrix she expected more of a roller coaster ride rather than Upper Yough-type trip. From the perspective of the provider of this experience, is this really the experience you want your participants to have?

## PROGRAMMING IMPLICATIONS

The 2 × 2 risk matrix and the adventure experience paradigm complement each other. Both paradigms suggest situations to be avoided. In the 2 × 2 risk matrix, one avoids situations that are in the low perceived risk, high actual risk category. In the adventure experience matrix, one avoids the *misadventure* and *devastation and disaster* situations in which the risks present far exceed the competence of the participants. Both models also encourage leaders and programmers to design activities and programs that are congruent with what the participant seeks. This is consistent with the flow experience and the inverted-U curve. Wiggle room always exists where the actual experience is slightly above or below the perceived experience of the participant, resulting in either a slight stretch or an easy cruise for the participant. This is a sound practice. Also, congruence does not include dangerous situations. *Devastation and disaster* and even *misadventure* can be viewed as potentially dangerous situations.

Some question whether the adventure experience paradigm, developed for outdoor and adventure programs, is applicable to general recreation. Perhaps a good way to address this issue is to return to the underlying premises of the model. The model is framed in terms of challenges, capacities, and the flow model. Capacities tend to be skill related. Therefore, this model can apply to any activity that is challenging and requires participants to have specific capacities or skills. Because the model incorporates the flow model, one could apply this model to any of the activities or situations that Csikszentmihalyi (1975) suggests can lead to a flow experience. Hence, the adventure experience paradigm is applicable to general recreation experiences that fall outside of the outdoor and adventure programming fields, such as playing cards, music, or baseball. However, the adventure experience paradigm would not be applicable to activities and programs that are not challenging and do not require participants to have specific capacities or skills, such as watching movies, driving for pleasure, taking a walk in the park, or attending a birthday party. These activities do not embrace risks as an integral part of their experience.

## INTEGRATING UNDERLYING FACTORS AND ACCIDENT PROCESS

For a recreation leader or programmer, the question is how to transform either model into practice. One approach is to use the risk management process described in chapter 8. The easiest approach is to examine the activity or program in terms of potential effect of each of the human, environmental, and equipment factors (i.e., the underlying factors discussed in chapter 6) and determine which elements contribute to the overall experience and which do not. A leader should look for incongruence between the risks involved in the activity (underlying factors) and the experience he seeks to create in the activity or program. He should avoid creating a situation that would fall into the high actual risk and low perceived risk

Because the adventure experience paradigm incorporates the flow model, it can be applied to a general recreation experience that requires participants to have specific skills such as baseball.

category in the 2 × 2 risk matrix. For example, a heat alert is issued for the same time that an outdoor concert is scheduled. The heat alert affects the selection of a backup date in case of postponement (underlying factors: weather, preplanning). If heat alerts are problematic, the leader should consider taking compensatory measures such as providing shaded sites, free bottled water, or refunds (underlying factor: implied physical or physiological capabilities or stress). Or, although site selection is likely limited, the leader might consider reserving an indoor arena that is air conditioned (underlying factor: weather). These actions help reduce the actual risks present in the event. Also, these actions demonstrate how the accident process and the underlying factors can be used in the planning process.

In the adventure experience paradigm, a leader determines which elements contribute to the overall activity in terms of the level of challenge a participant seeks. The leader must manage these elements to ensure that they remain consistent with the skill level of the participants. For example, on a high ropes course, the element of height is used to create a sense of challenge. The belay system is used to provide an adequate level of safety on the course (underlying factor: adequate or appropriate equipment). On a rafting trip, the type and nature of the rapids are used to create a sense of challenge. Using a predetermined route through the rapids helps manage passage through the rapids to create a safer experience (underlying factor: preplanning and travel speed).

The leader must also determine which elements of the program do not contribute to the activity in terms of the level of challenge the participant seeks. In terms of the experience, these elements are not apparent to the participant. Using the underlying factors, the leader should manage, reduce, or eliminate the effect of these factors. For example, the wear and tear on the belay rope used on the high ropes course is not an element that contributes to the challenge the experience provides (underlying factor: inadequate maintenance or wear and tear). This element is managed to minimize unwanted risks. In the rafting example, the communication between raft guides, the order of rafts through the trip, and spacing between rafts do not directly contribute to the challenge but do contribute to safety (underlying factor: leadership and group dynamics). These elements are managed to minimize potential harmful effects.

Although not technically necessary, a simple next step is to integrate the accident models—the Curtis model, the risk meter, or the domino model—into the discussion. A leader or programmer can use these accident models to assess the program elements in terms of the underlying factors and to create a safe but challenging experience for the participants.

## LEGAL IMPLICATIONS

The chapter opens with two comments regarding negligence implications and programming for risks. The first is that outdoor and adventure industry has embraced risks as an integral and necessary part of the activity. The adventure experience paradigm is a reflection of this embrace. The second is that an examination of the legal liability, risk management, accident causation, and safety management literature suggests that the role of the safety manager in an organization is to leave no risk untouched

Photodisc/Getty Images

To transform the adventure experience paradigm into practice, the programmer should examine the activity in terms of potential effect of each of the underlying factors. The programmer then should determine which elements contribute or don't contribute to the overall activity in terms of the level of challenge a participant seeks and then manage those factors such as managing the spacing between rafts to contribute to safety.

in their effort to eliminate any and all risks. Because eliminating all risk is not possible and some activities in the leisure field involve risks, it is important to consider the legal implications.

A recreation leader must know his or her professional industry. As discussed in chapter 3, a recreation leader who is professionally active in her industry will better know the common *practices* and the *industry standards* to which she will be held. As is evident in Janice Cody's deposition in figure 1.8, Cody did not know much about the canoe livery industry and made no effort to know anything about it, even after the first fatality. She would most likely be unable to describe the common practices of other canoe liveries. She was acting in isolation of her professional industry.

Also, this may seem to be a subtlety, but a recreation leader should be sure that that her professional industry is the professional industry that can best help her. For example, Janice Cody may have joined the National Recreation and Park Association expecting the organization to serve her canoe livery needs. Although the National Recreation and Park Association would undoubtedly provide her some benefit, it does not focus on the nuances of being a canoe livery. She might have been better served by joining the Professional Paddlesport Association (Kauffman and Councill, 2005b). Regardless, being a member of either organization would be better than not being a member of any organization.

There is an issue regarding which industry really governs or defines your industry. A recreation leader should also be careful that the common practices and industry standards of her industry are not in conflict with those of the larger industry. For example, this author discussed with lawyers the issue of developing legal strategies regarding the rafting industry. Most people in the rafting industry do not have a problem with taking novices on a raft trip during flooding conditions. If asked whether this is a common practice, everyone associated with the industry would most likely answer yes. However, an argument could be made that there is not that much difference between a raft guide and a bus driver, pilot, or passenger boat captain. They are all responsible for safely transporting their passengers from one location to another. Would a bus driver be expected to continue driving in a major snowstorm, a pilot to take off during a severe thunderstorm, a boat captain to purposely steer his boat into a hurricane, or a raft guide to take passengers on a flooding river because it is fun and challenging? If rafting is viewed as part of the transportation industry, then the behavior of raft guides taking passengers on flooding rivers may be inconsistent with their counterparts in the larger transportation industry. You are beginning to see the issue regarding who really defines your industry. In addition, it emphasizes an underlying problem raised in this chapter in that the recreation and parks industry embraces risks while most other industries seek to eliminate them.

A recreation leader should understand that embracing risk as a necessary component of the activity does not mean that all risks in the activity are acceptable. It is not a license to do whatever one wants. For example, one cannot justify using a worn-out belay rope because it increases the challenge in a climbing activity. This point is addressed in this chapter as part of both the 2 × 2 risk matrix and the adventure experience paradigm.

Finally, in addition to these points, consider the points made in the first three chapters. Examine the underlying factors and reduce the likelihood of the accident occurring in the first place. Metaphorically, close one of the four negligence windows (duty; breach of duty; proximate cause; and injury, damage, or loss). In addition, review the strategies covered in chapter 3 to avoid being sued.

## SUMMARY

Contrary to most other industries, the recreation and parks industry and, in particular, the outdoor adventure industry tend to embrace risks as an integral component within their activities and programs. This chapter addresses the issue of programming for risk. This chapter presents two paradigms to assist in programming for risk. The models focus on actual and perceived risks and, in the case of seeking mastery, competence.

When risks are involved, the general recreation programmer will most likely want to consider the roller coaster ride (high perceived, low actual risks) or the lazy river (low perceived, low actual risks) and avoid the drowning trap situations (low perceived, high actual risks). Assess activities and programs in terms of the underlying factors associated with the accident process.

The adventure experience paradigm is applicable to any recreational experience involving mastery on the part of the participant. In terms of actual and perceived competency and risks, the model suggests an approach to provide a peak adventure for participants. Avoid creating recreational experiences that facilitate the *misadventure* and *devastation and disaster* categories. They can easily result in accidents and being sued.

In closing, it is worth noting again that while most industries seek to reduce any and all risks, recreation seeks to embrace them as an integral part of the activity. This chapter helps explain how to program for risks.

## EXERCISES

### Exercise 1: Inverted-U Curve

The purpose of this exercise is to apply the concept of the inverted-U curve to a recreational activity with which you are familiar. The inverted-U curve has two components: stimulation and performance. Choose a leadership situation with which you are familiar (e.g., playground leader, swimming instructor, outdoor leader, or special event leader).

1. Define stimulation for the activity that you chose.
2. Define performance for the activity.
3. Have you experienced optimum performance? Describe what you recall of your experience. *Hint:* Think of the flow experience.
4. Describe your experience if you exceed the optimum performance. Describe your experience if you drop below the optimal performance.

### Exercise 2: Flow Model

The purpose of this exercise is to apply the concept of flow to a familiar recreational activity. Choose a specific activity you are familiar with. Identify the challenges present for that activity. Next, identify the skills that you have for that activity. Are your skills matched to the challenges of that activity? How do you know whether they are? Have you had a flow experience? If yes, describe that experience or how you know that you experienced a flow experience.

### Exercise 3: Adventure Experience Paradigm

The purpose of this exercise is to apply the adventure experience paradigm to determine adaptive dissonance. Using the graph in figure 7.4, plot the expected and resultant outcomes for each of the following cases. Note the adaptive dissonance, or the difference between the expected and resultant outcomes.

**Scenario 1**

Expected outcome: peak adventure
Resultant outcome: devastation and disaster

**Scenario 2**

Expected outcome: misadventure
Resultant outcome: adventure

**Scenario 3**

Expected outcome: peak adventure
Resultant outcome: exploration and experimentation

**Scenario 4**

Expected outcome: exploration and experimentation
Resultant outcome: devastation and disaster

## Exercise 4: High Actual and Low Perceived Risks

The purpose of this exercise is to explore the effect of high actual and low perceived risks. For the recreation programmer, situations in which the actual risks are high and the perceived risks are low are often the most troubling because participants often do not fully appreciate the risks of the activity. Select an activity of your choice that is high in actual risks and low in perceived risks. If you are a resource manager, select a setting that meets these criteria.

1. Explain why you chose this program or setting and why it meets the criteria of high actual and low perceived risks.
2. Do you believe that you have a greater responsibility to provide a safer activity for the participants? Why or why not? Explain what you would do to increase safety.

## Exercise 5: Roller Coaster Ride

The purpose of this exercise is to explore how activities low in actual risks and high in perceived risks affect how you program your activities. Select an activity that is low in actual risks and high in perceived risks.

1. Are risks still involved in the activity or setting? Should you reduce these risks? What can you do to reduce these risks?
2. Defend or argue against the following statement: "Recreation programmers or resource managers should design all recreational activities and settings as if they were designing a roller coaster."

## Exercise 6: High Actual and High Perceived Risks

The purpose of this exercise is to explore how activities high in actual risks and high in perceived risks affect how you program your activities. Select an activity that is high in actual risks and high in perceived risks.

1. Describe how you would manage the actual risks in the activity to provide a safe environment for your participants.

2. Assume that the participants perceive the risk involved in the activity. Describe the role or the amount of responsibility that the participant has in the experience.
3. In any circumstances should the actual risk exceed the perceived risk? Should it exceed the capabilities of the participants?

## Exercise 7: Risks Versus Capabilities

The purpose of this exercise is to explore your attitude toward the relationship between risks and the capabilities of participants. Answer the following questions.

1. As a recreation programmer or resource manager, in any situation should the actual risks far exceed the capabilities of the participants? If yes, what are the situations? If no, explain why not.
2. If you facilitate or allow this situation, do you increase your liability? Why or why not?
3. If you facilitate or allow this situation, do you increase the likelihood of an accident occurring? Why or why not?

# PART III

# Risk Management

The third leg in the integrated risk management model focuses on the development of risk management plans. The risk management approach presented in this section is applicable at both the organizational and leader and programmer levels. At the organizational level, the Commission for Accreditation of Park and Recreation Agencies and other sources indicates the need for a risk management plan. Conceptually, the risk management process described in chapter 8 is foundational. As an approach to reducing injury, damage, or loss, it complements the approaches discussed in previous chapters. Organizationally, having a risk management plan is considered a common practice or industry standard in the field.

The risk management model depicted in figure III.1 is representative of the typical four-part process of developing a risk management plan. First, one identifies the risks facing the agency or organization. Generally, this identification is much broader than the accident process or even the legal liability discussions. Second, one identifies how the risks affect the organization in terms of probability or frequency of occurrence. Third, using one or more of four strategies, one seeks to reduce, avoid, transfer, or retain the risks. Fourth, one evaluates and monitors the risk reduction. Chapter 8 discusses these steps in depth.

It is important to frame part III in terms of the other parts of this text. First, the underlying proposition of the risk management plan is that the process is implemented at the institutional level. This is consistent with many of the previously mentioned approaches to safety management. Second, the process of creating a risk management plan is much broader in scope than simply focusing on accidents and accident prevention. This is an important point to continually emphasize. Third, the risk management plan seeks to reduce injury, damage, or loss that results in accidents, being sued, or other legal actions against an individual or an organization. Fourth, a sexual harassment suit or a discrimination case can easily lead to many of the postincident strategies discussed in part IV.

It is also important to frame this section in terms of the leader and programmer. The risk management process affects a leader's behavior and attitude toward providing safe recreation and park experiences. Think of the risk management process as a way to sort through risks in terms of their frequency of occurrence and their effect on the organization. The process prompts a leader to ask the question "What is the likelihood of this occurring and, if it does occur, what is its effect on me, the participants, and the organization?" If a leader or programmer asks these two questions, the process of risk management planning was successful.

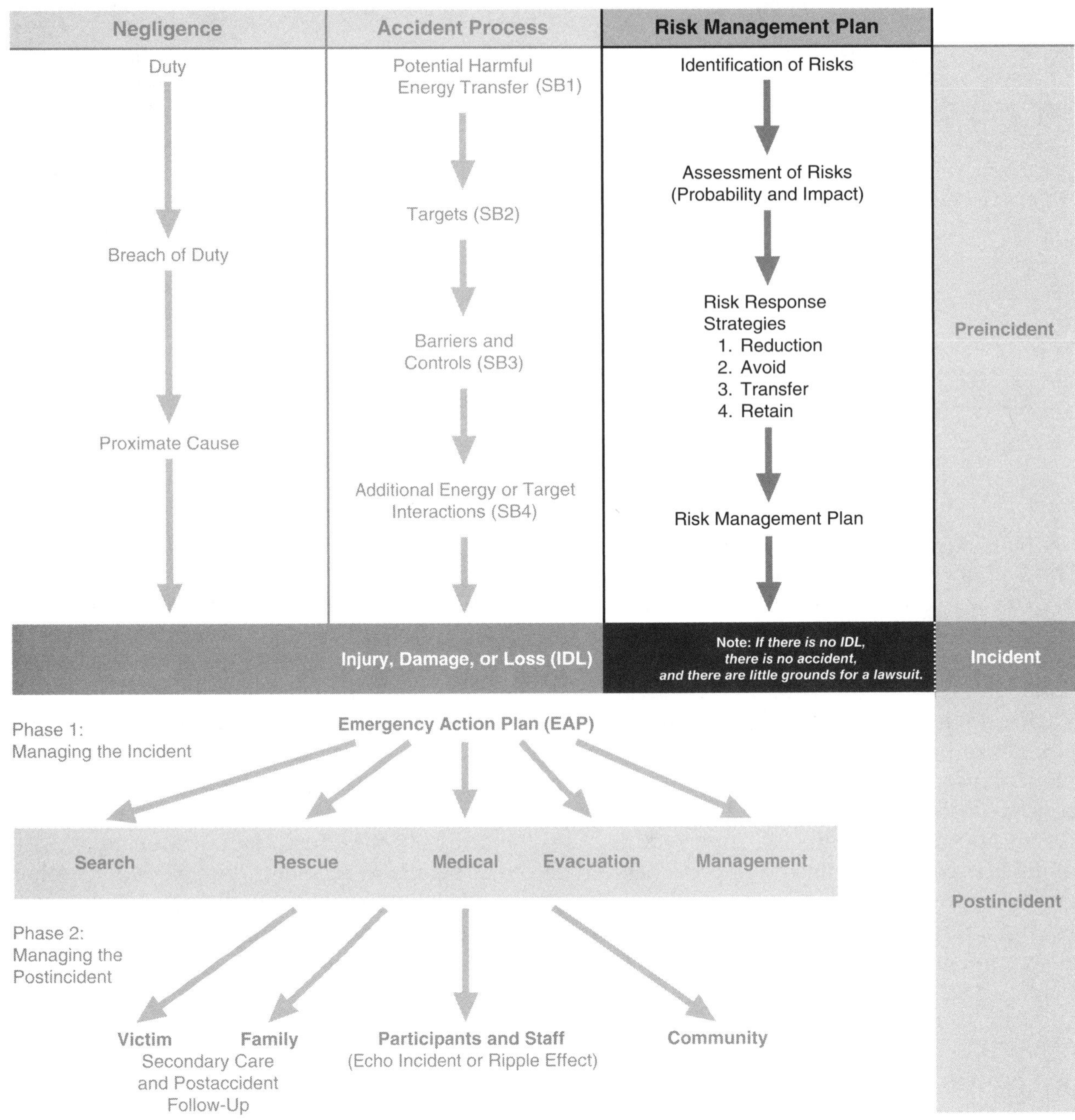


**Figure III.1** Developing a risk management plan as part of the risk management model.

Chapter 8

# Risk Management Plans

The purpose of a risk management plan is to reduce injury, damage, or loss to an organization. A risk management plan is broader in concept than the accident process (discussed in in part II) because injury, damage, or loss to the organization can result from things other than accidents or incidents.

In the recreation and park field, having a risk management plan is considered a common practice or industry standard. Standard 9.1 of the Commission for Accreditation of Park and Recreation Agencies (CAPRA) states "There shall be a risk management plan reviewed on a regular basis which encompasses analysis of risk exposure, control approaches, and financial impact for the agency" (CAPRA, 2009; see figure 8.1). The standard also suggests that an organization can provide evidence that it is in compliance with the standard by "provid[ing] the current risk management plan with the most recent review date and approval by the proper authority." The opening statement in the risk management plan for Howard County Recreation and Parks (2006) captures the essence of a risk management plan:

> A risk is any unintentional event or situation that leads to injury or damage. Risk has an element of chance to it, but risk management is foresight and control. Foresight is essential to risk management because being proactive has a greater influence on risk than being reactive. Control means action, for only through thoughtful action can any organization reduce the probability of a risk event or its consequences. (p. 4)

Risk is any event or situation that can lead to injury, damage, or loss to the agency or organization. These risks are much broader in scope than those involved with accidents. The risks described in this chapter include property loss due to natural and manmade forces; human rights issues, including discrimination, sexual harassment, and disabilities; and contractual losses from vendors and subcontractors. One must have the foresight to identify these risks and be proactive in controlling or reducing them. This chapter presents a systematic plan for identifying, prioritizing, and reducing or controlling these risks.

## WINDING RIVER CANOE RENTALS CASE STUDY

Winding River Canoe Rentals was a small livery operation on the Clinton River outside of Detroit, Michigan. The operation was run by Janice Cody and her daughter. Shelby Township subcontracted the privilege to operate on the Clinton River to Winding River Canoe Rentals.

Two boating fatalities occurred on the river on the same day. On July 4, 2000, Melanie Carlson and her boyfriend rented a kayak from Winding River Canoe Rentals. Due to recent

## Risk Management Plan

*Standard:* There shall be a risk management plan reviewed on a regular basis that encompasses analysis of risk exposure, control approaches, and financial impact for the agency.

*Commentary:* A comprehensive risk management plan is essential to minimize legal liabilities and personal injuries. A risk management plan analyzes the programs/services offered and facilities/areas managed for personal injury and financial loss potential and identifies approaches to handle such losses. It sets forth basic policies and procedures to manage the identified risks. The agency shall implement approaches for identification and control of risks based on the specific needs of the agency. There is no prescriptive method for identification of all risks suitable for all entities; the method and tools used will vary. Risk management is an on-going process and its effectiveness must be systematically evaluated and adjustments made as appropriate. Responsibilities must be assigned and structure set in place to implement an effective plan. The analysis shall include the direct costs (staffing, insurance, prevention) and indirect costs (time lost from work by injured employees, damage to equipment and facilities, failure to provide services, and loss of income) of the agency's risk management. In some cases, the risk management plan and function may occur outside the park and recreation agency by a higher government authority.

*Suggested Evidence of Compliance:* Provide the current risk management plan with the most recent review date and approval by the proper authority.

**Figure 8.1** The CAPRA standards suggest the need for a risk management plan in any public agency.

Reprinted, by permission, from CAPRA 2009, *National accreditation standards* (Ashburn, Virginia: Commission for Accreditation of Park and Recreation Agencies, National Recreation and Park Association).

rainfall, the Clinton River was running at more than 900 cubic feet per second. The normal flow during summer was 250 cubic feet per second. When Carlson came to a bend in the river, the current forced her toward the outside of the bend and into a strainer (i.e., an obstacle in the river such as a fallen tree). When she tried to avoid the strainer, she fell off her kayak and was swept into the strainer, where she was pinned and drowned. The second fatality was a drowning in the hydraulic behind Yates Dam. Other than both fatalities occurring at moderate water levels, there was no direct connection between the two fatalities.

The strainer pictured in figure 8.2 is the strainer in which Carlson drowned. The kayaker in the photo was involved in a near drowning that occurred later that same day at exactly the same site. The news media went to the river to film the site of the fatality for the evening news. As soon as the crew arrived on site, they saw that the person in the photo was in distress and rendered help.

In her deposition, Cody testified that she had taken no remedial actions (e.g., risk management study or accident analysis) since the death of Joe Miranda the year before, when he got trapped in the hydraulic behind Yates Dam and drowned. Figure 8.3 shows Yates Dam at high water. Although the photo was taken on the day of the Carlson fatality, it illustrates the water level the day Joe Miranda

Fox News

**Figure 8.2** Melanie Carlson died in this strainer earlier in the day. When the news media arrived to film the site for the evening news, they captured this near fatality of another kayaker. Note the compression wave made by the force of the current on the rear deck of the kayak.

Fox News

**Figure 8.3** This photo was taken on the day of the Melanie Carlson incident. At high water, the dam is runnable and the hydraulic below the dam is a potential hazard. It killed Joe Miranda the previous year and it killed a kayaker on the same day the Carlson incident occurred. (*Note:* The kayaker fatality was not related to Winding River Canoe Rentals.)

drowned. For comparison, figure 8.4 shows Yates Dam at the normal low flows during summer. During low flows, the dangerous hydraulic is absent and boaters need to portage around the dam.

Numerous strainers were present on the stretch of river involved. On some stretches of the river, strainers were present every 50 yards. At the normal summer flow of 250 cubic feet per second, these strainers pose little or no problem because the river current at this level is relatively benign. However, at 900 cubic feet per second, noticeable current pressed against these strainers. Figure 8.5 shows one of many strainers on the river that can become hazardous at higher water levels.

In addition, Cody testified that the gauge for determining water level had been removed several years before the incident occurred. Such a gauge is important for making decisions regarding boating operations. Winding River Canoe Rentals approximated the water level in the river based on the height of the water on the flood wall. They had no accurate way to determine water levels. Based on this imprecise method of measurement, they did limit the use of canoes, but water levels did not enter into management decisions. They did not cease operations when water levels became dangerously high.

## RISK MANAGEMENT PROCESS

Although differences exist between various risk management processes, the steps in the risk management process are essentially the same for most models. These steps are included in the basic risk management model in the integrated

© 2012 - Janet M. Hug

**Figure 8.4** At normal summer flows, boaters have to portage this dam because water flow over the dam is insufficient. Close inspection of the dam breast reveals that very little water is going over the dam.

Photo courtesy of Robert B. Kauffman.

**Figure 8.5** The river is littered with obstructions like the one pictured here. During normal summer flow, pictured here, the flow is relatively benign and paddlers simply step over the obstruction. At higher water levels, this obstruction can become a dangerous strainer.

risk management model used in this chapter (figure 8.6). This model is consistent with most other models of risk management (Campfire Girls, 1993; Herman, 2009, p. 27; Kaiser and Robinson, 2005, p. 594; Oliver, 2004, p. 7; Patterson and Oliver, 2004, p. 8). The basic steps are as follows.

Step 1: Identify the risks.

Step 2: Assess the risks (i.e., probability, impact, and severity).

Step 3: Develop risk strategies (i.e., reduction, avoidance, transfer, retain).

Step 4: Evaluate and continually assess the risks.

The risk management process described in this chapter utilizes the working table (table 8.1) to determine the risks to the organization, prioritize them, and address them in terms of the risk management strategy. This working table is the key to the risk management process and the completion of the first and second steps (identify and assess the risks) in the risk management process. The value of the working table is a key element in the risk management process. First the working table enables the assessment and systematic ranking of the

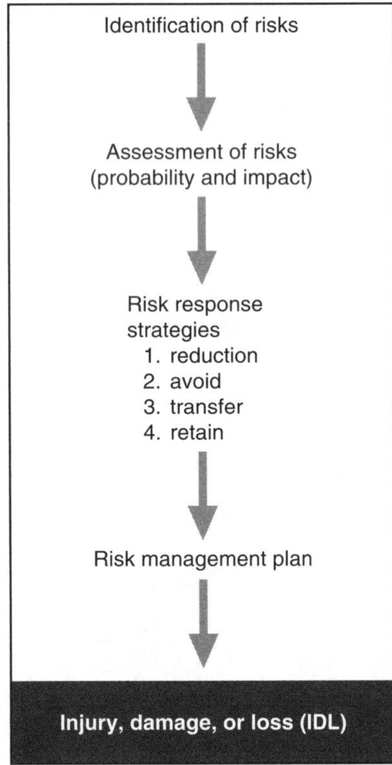


**Figure 8.6** The risk management model discussed in this chapter is part of the integrated risk management model used in this book and it follows four basic steps, which is consistent with most other models of risk management.

**Table 8.1** Risk Management Working Table

| Risks (1) | Consequences (2) | Probability (3) | Effective probability (4) | Impact (5) | Effective impact (6) | Severity (7) | Effective severity (8) |
|---|---|---|---|---|---|---|---|
| | | | | | | | |
| | | | | | | | |
| | | | | | | | |
| | | | | | | | |

Adapted from Kene et al. 2010.

risks present. Second, the ranking suggests a systematic approach for the recreation and parks professional to reduce the risks. Third, after modifications have been made, the working table enables the reassessment of the risks, and fourth, it allows for the calculation of the effective risk reduction due to the modifications made.

Procedurally, the first step in the risk management process is identifying the risks the organization faces. These risks and their consequences are entered in columns 1 and 2 of the working table. The second step in the risk management process is assessing the likelihood, or probability, that an incident will occur (column 3) and, if an incident occurs, the potential impact of the risk on the organization (column 5). Probability and impact are combined to determine severity (column 7). Once severity is determined, risks can be ranked in terms of severity on the organization.

The third step in the risk management process is developing risk management strategies for mitigating potential losses. Two of these strategies—reduction and avoidance—focus on reducing or eliminating the risks. Changes the organization makes to mitigate risks are reflected in the effective probability (column 4), effective impact (column 6), and effective severity (column 8). In addition, the measures the organization takes can be used to determine the effectiveness of the risk management measures.

The fourth step in the risk management process is to continually evaluate and assess the risks. The organization can modify and update the risk management plan based on previous incidents and on additional risk management actions taken.

## Step 1: Identification of Risks

The first step in developing a risk management plan is identifying the risks that could harm the organization and examining both internal and external sources to determine the likelihood that an incident will occur. When filling in the working table (table 8.1), a recreation professional lists the identified risks in column 1. The following section lists several types of risks that are specific to organizations in the recreation and park field. Normally, the risk management process described in this chapter can be done at the organizational, program, or activity level. This enhances the usability of the process as a program planning tool.

### Determining Hazards and Risks

A person developing a risk management plan should think of the risks as events, occurrences, hazards, or incidents that can happen to an individual or an organization. Kaiser and Robinson (2005) suggest that six types of hazards are common to the recreation and park field.

- *Environmental hazards* are physical and environmental hazards found in one's environment, such as slippery surfaces, dangerous plants or animals, weather conditions, or water. These hazards are similar to the environmental factors listed in the underlying factors in chapter 6. Yates Dam and the strainers on the Clinton River are examples of environmental hazards.
- *Infrastructure hazards* are hazards associated with facilities, buildings, roads, recreation areas, and trails. They include design, layout, and maintenance issues.

- *Program hazards* are hazards associated with conducting programs, such as supervision, instruction, proper use of equipment, and the failure to warn.
- *Emergency care hazards* are hazards involved in search and rescue operations, medical care, and evacuation of the victim. Many of the issues revolve around the factors discussed in chapter 10.
- *Crisis management* hazards involve large-scale disasters such as hurricanes, forest fires, terrorist attacks, building fires, or major chemical spills (Kaiser and Robinson, 2005).
- *Transportation hazards* include hazards involved in maintenance, driver training and licensing, and selecting the correct vehicle for the task.

### Sources of Information

A recreation professional can use several different sources to determine the likelihood that an event will occur and the impact that the event will have on the organization. These sources can be both internal and external to the organization:

- Heuristics
- Historical records
- Similar organizations and programs
- State or national professional organizations
- Accreditation bodies
- National statistics

*Heuristics* is the process of learning, discovering, understanding, and solving problems by using experimentation and trial-and-error methods. One must often rely on past experience and judgment when determining how frequently a risk will occur and what the impact will be.

A recreation professional can examine *historical records*, including past incident reports. Although incident reports will provide some insights, they should be used with care. If the incident report is a form, the categories on the form shape the outcome and findings. Also, if an organization sought to smooth things over after an incident occurred, vital information may be omitted from or de-emphasized in the incident report in order for the organization to put the incident behind them. For example, when doing the Potomac River Study, this author had access to all of the accident reports for the fatalities that occurred on the Potomac River in Maryland. It quickly became evident that much of the information was unreliable. In private and in confidence, several Department of Natural Resource officers associated with one incident or another indicated that certain incidents really involved alcohol or some other factor, but for insurance reasons that information was not included in the incident report. The historical information provided some useful insights, but it was not accurate. When using historical data, look beyond the immediacy of the information to how it was collected and to why the information could be inaccurate.

A recreation professional can also ask people in *similar organizations and programs* what problems and incidents they have encountered. *State and national organizations* often compile this information, as do *accreditation bodies*. In some cases, organizations such as the National Safety Council (2009) compile *national statistics* on accidents and incidents that can provide insights. However, the information compiled is often not specific enough for the recreation and park setting.

## Step 2: Assessment of Risks

The second step in the risk management process is performing a risk assessment to determine the severity of a harmful event. *Severity* is a composite index of the *probability* that an event will occur and the *impact* the occurrence will have on the organization. When assessing risks, a recreation professional rates probability, impact, and severity as high, medium, or low. If the information is available, one can use actual probabilities rather than assessing risks as high, medium, or low. However, in most cases, available data are insufficient to accurately determine actual probabilities.

## Determining Probability

Using the criteria in table 8.2, the recreation professional assesses all of the identified risks in terms of probability or frequency of occurrence. The professional rates the probability of each risk as high, medium, or low and enters the assessment for each event in column 3 in table 8.1. For example, at a swimming pool, cuts and bruises occur with some frequency and would be rated as medium or high. In contrast, drownings should occur infrequently and would be rated as low. The order of the risks in the table is not a concern during this step.

*To be determined* (TBD) includes items about which more information is needed in order to make a determination. The recreation professional rates these items as high because it is better to err on the side of caution. Treating a high risk as a low risk is more likely to result in an accident, whereas treating a low risk as a high risk in the assessment process leads to being overly safe.

As a sidebar, the classification scheme is often color coded in red, yellow, and green. People often associate this color scheme with traffic lights. Red is associated with danger and with high risk. Yellow is generally associated with caution and with medium risk. Green is generally associated with safety. People mistakenly assume that everything is okay as they proceed through an intersection on a green light; however, risks still exist. A green situation is one with low risks, not one that is risk free.

## Determining Impact

Impact relates to how catastrophic the event is to the organization or how the harmful event affects the organization. For example, although drownings occur infrequently at swimming pools (i.e., low probability), a drowning has a significant impact on the organization. Reporters will arrive at the pool to take photos, and the drowning will be reported on the evening news. The organization's program and the normal routine of the pool are disrupted. The public might even lose confidence in the organization's ability to deliver safe programs to the public. In contrast, cuts and bruises that occur at a swimming pool have a low impact. They will not be reported on the evening news, and public confidence in the organization will be relatively unaffected.

Table 8.3 lists the impact criteria that are used to assess the impact of all of the identified risks. The recreation professional rates the impact of each risk as high, medium, or low and enters the assessment for each event in column 5 in table 8.1. The order of the items in the table is not a concern during this step. Again, the TBD category is for items about which more information is needed in order to make a determination. The recreation professional should take a conservative approach and rate TBD items as high in order to avoid underrating the impact of the risk.

## Determining Severity

Severity is a composite index of the probability that an event will occur and the impact the event will have on the organization. The recreation professional uses table 8.4 to calculate severity

**Table 8.2** Determining Probability that the Event Will Occur (Column 3 in Table 8.1)

| Abbreviation | Risk | Description |
|---|---|---|
| H | High | The event or item has a high probability of occurring. It is a common or semiroutine occurrence. |
| M | Medium | The event or item occurs occasionally. |
| L | Low | The event or item has a low probability of occurring. It occurs infrequently. People are often surprised when it occurs. |
| NA | Not applicable | This event or factor is not relevant. |
| TBD | To be determined | Additional study or information is needed to determine probability. Until determination is made, it is treated as a high probability of occurrence. |

Adapted from Kene et al. 2010.

**Table 8.3** Impact of the Event on the Organization (Column 5 in Table 8.1)

| Abbreviation | Risk | Description |
|---|---|---|
| H | High | The incident will have a major impact on the organization. It might lead to loss of programs, community support, or even the organization itself. |
| M | Medium | The incident will have some impact on the organization. There will be some media attention. There may be a drop-off in participation, and community support may wane. |
| L | Low | Little or no service or program interruption will occur. There will be little or no internal or external impact or visibility of the incident. |
| NA | Not applicable | This event or factor is not relevant. |
| TBD | To be determined | Additional study and investigation is required to determine the impact. Additional information is needed. It is treated as a high impact until determined otherwise. |

Adapted from Kene et al. 2010.

**Table 8.4** Determining Severity (Columns 7 and 8 in Table 8.1)[1]

| Impact | Probability | | | | | |
|---|---|---|---|---|---|---|
| | | L | M | H | TBD | NA |
| | TBD | M | H | H | H | NA |
| | H | M | H | H | H | NA |
| | M | L | M | M | H | NA |
| | L | L | L | L | M | NA |
| | NA | NA | NA | NA | NA | NA |

[1]The "to be determined" category is treated as a high probability or high impact until obtained information classifies it otherwise.

Adapted from Kene et al. 2010.

for each item in the working table and enters it in column 7 of table 8.1.

Table 8.5 shows all the possible combinations presented in table 8.4 except the TBD category. In general, items with high impact tend to have high severity and items with high probability and low impact tend to have lower relative severity. A recreation professional can modify the categories in table 8.4 to suit a specific organization, activity, or philosophy. For example, one might rate an item with high probability and low impact as having medium severity rather than low severity. If a recreation professional chooses to change the severity ratings, he must use it consistently throughout the entire process. Although the cross-tabulation of the factors can be changed to meet the specific needs of special situations, most people will find table 8.4 more than satisfactory in determining severity.

After rating each item in terms of severity, the recreation professional ranks the items from high severity (listed first) to low severity (listed last). If items have the same severity scores, items with higher impact scores are listed before those with high probability scores. Table 8.5 illustrates this ordering.

If the recreation professional does not determine *mitigating* and *contingencies*, the analysis ends here. In this case, he prioritizes the risks by their severity scores. Most likely, he will develop mitigating and contingency plans covered in the next section. In this case, he ranks the risk factors later in the process.

## Step 3: Risk Management Strategies

Once the recreation professional has identified the risks, he needs to mitigate or manage them. Traditionally, one uses four approaches when managing risks: reduction, avoidance, transfer, and retention. Reduction and avoidance tend

**Table 8.5** Risk Management Working Table

| Risks (1) | Consequences (2) | Probability (3) | Effective probability (4) | Impact (5) | Effective impact (6) | Severity[1] (7) | Effective severity (8) |
|---|---|---|---|---|---|---|---|
| Risk 1 | Consequence | H | | H | | H | |
| Risk 2 | Consequence | M | | H | | H | |
| Risk 3 | Consequence | L | | H | | M | |
| Risk 4 | Consequence | H | | M | | M | |
| Risk 5 | Consequence | M | | M | | M | |
| Risk 6 | Consequence | L | | M | | L | |
| Risk 7 | Consequence | H | | L | | L | |
| Risk 8 | Consequence | M | | L | | L | |
| Risk 9 | Consequence | L | | L | | L | |

[1]This table presents all the risk combinations of probabilities and impacts that lead to severity. This structure can be used when prioritizing severity.

Adapted from Kene et al. 2010.

to relate to reducing the likelihood that the incident will occur. Transfer and retention tend to relate to transferring the cost of the risks to someone else (e.g., the victim, the insurance company, or another agency). One can use more than one risk reduction approach. For example, in the Melanie Carlson incident, one can both remove strainers from the river (reduction) and have insurance protection (transfer).

Although the risk management strategies will vary somewhat with different disciplines and industries, there is general agreement regarding the use of these four strategies with other fields and disciplines. The nonprofits recommend the four strategies of avoidance, modification, sharing, and retention (Herman, 2009; Oliver, 2004; Patterson and Oliver, 2004). Avoidance and retention remain the same as above. Modification is essentially another synonym for reduction. Sharing is a slight modification of the transfer concept in that the term reflects that the organization will still bear some of the costs even if they seek to transfer the losses.

The four Ts (terminate, treat, transfer, and tolerate) were introduced in chapter 5 as the risk management approach used in the safety management literature (Stephenson, 1991). Terminate is similar to avoidance or the elimination of the activity. Treating is similar to reduction, transfer is transfer, and tolerate is a cross between reduction and retention. The traditional risk management strategies of reduction, avoidance, transfer, and retention used in the recreation and parks field are consistent with those used in other fields and disciplines. Also, it is important to understand that there may be some slight variations from field to field.

## Reduction

Reduction includes measures that one takes to reduce the likelihood that an incident will occur. Administrative policies (e.g., training in van driving or sexual harassment prevention) and program practices (e.g., scheduling, staff, alternative facilities, postponement dates, and emergency care) that affect the management of risks are examples of reduction.

One can also reduce the likelihood that an event will occur by applying principles discussed in this text. For example, in barrier analysis (see chapter 5), one reduces risks by placing physical and administrative barriers between the hazard and the potential victim. In the accident models presented in chapters 6 and 7, one analyzes activities in terms of the human, environmental, and equipment factors present and manages or eliminates the factors to reduce their impact. Accident models are a form of reduction because they reduce the probability that an incident or accident will occur. Even the principles of negligence reduce risk. Supervising, warning participants, developing appreciation, and acting like a prudent and reasonable professional help a recreation and park professional address risks and reduce the likelihood that an incident will occur.

## Avoidance

Avoidance is the elimination of a risk or the activity that results in the risk. Avoidance is generally the most effective risk management approach. The following questions and statements, adapted from a list developed for the Campfire Girls (1993), are helpful in determining whether to avoid or eliminate an activity or program. (One must remember, however, that if all activities are eliminated, a program would not exist. A program will always include some degree of risk.)

- Does the activity really relate to the mission of the organization?
- Is the risk justified?
- If the activity has little or no value, would it be better to terminate the activity?
- Is someone else already doing the activity? Could someone else do it just as easily? Could someone else do it better?
- If the risk is great compared with the benefit or value of the activity, perhaps the activity should be eliminated.
- If the risks are still high after taking all the reduction measures, perhaps the activity should be eliminated.

Most people think of avoidance as the elimination of the entire activity. However, completely eliminating the activity may not be necessary. One can eliminate a portion or component of an activity and essentially achieve the same end. For example, one could eliminate the third leg of a triathlon because of the risks involved and convert the activity to a biathlon. In addition, chapter 7 discusses programming for risks and the use of the $2 \times 2$ risk matrix and the adventure experience paradigm to modify and eliminate components of programs.

## Transfer

As discussed in chapter 3, an individual or organization uses transfer strategies to transfer to someone else any or all of the four components of negligence or the cost of the injury, damage, or loss. There are three transfer approaches. One can transfer monetary losses to someone else through the use of insurance. One can transfer the loss to the participant through the use of waivers and hold harmless agreements. Or, one can transfer the loss to another organization or company through subcontracting, leases, and contracts.

In the Winding River Canoe incident, all three approaches were used. Shelby Township subcontracted the livery service to Winding River. When the lawsuit ensued the judge removed them as a defendant. They successfully transferred the potential settlement costs to Winding River. Second, Winding River had participants sign waivers and they had insurance that transferred the cost of settlement to the insurance company.

It is important to remember that unlike the strategies of reduction and avoidance, transfer does not eliminate or reduce the original hazard or risk—it merely transfers the cost of the accident to someone else. In the Winding River incident, signing waivers, having insurance, and subcontracting did little or nothing toward making the canoe livery safer. Removing the strainers (reduction) or ceasing operation during high water (avoidance) would have made the canoe livery operations safer. Although the transfer strategies are extremely important to include as a risk management strategy, it is also important to remember that the transfer strategy merely transfers who pays or accepts responsibility once injury, damage, or loss occurs. It does not make programs safer.

## Retention

In retention, a person assumes part or all of the losses. Most people purchase insurance that has a deductible, which is the portion that one pays if a loss occurs. The deductible portion of the insurance is a form of retention because one pays out of pocket any expenses up to the deductible amount. Generally, the higher the deductible portion, the lower the premium.

If a person determines that risks are infrequent or the payout amount usually falls within the deductible range, paying for the expenses out of pocket may be less expensive than paying insurance on what amounts to incidental costs. In negligence cases, the amount for which the defense is insured is not supposed to enter into the case. However, it is known, and often the amount in the lawsuit mysteriously hovers around the total amount of the insurance. If a person pays costs out of pocket, the plaintiff may no longer consider him the deepest pocket to go after.

A person can also self-insure. Usually, self-insurance involves the creation of a separate fund. For example, if a person wants $1 million to cover lawsuits, he can put $100,000 into a fund each year for 10 years. If no lawsuits or losses occur, he still owns the $1 million. In contrast, if insurance costs him $100,000 per year, after 10 years he has spent the same $1 except the funds went to someone else.

## Mitigation and Contingencies

Using these risk management strategies, the recreation professional develops strategies to reduce the potential severity (probability and impact) of the risks identified. One can reduce the risk level using mitigation and contingencies. Using *mitigation*, one reduces the probability that the risks will occur. Using *contingencies*, one reduces the impact on the organization. Generally, reducing the impact on the organization is difficult to achieve, but long-term public education and public awareness campaigns can be effective in reducing the impact of an incident on the organization. Most agencies focus on reducing risks through the mitigation approach.

Implementing one or more risk management strategies can potentially reduce the risk level for each risk item. When completing the working table (table 8.6), the recreation professional enters a change in the probability (effective probability) in column 4 and a change in impact (effective impact) in column 6. After reassessing the effective probability and the effective impact, the professional can calculate effective severity using table 8.6 and enter the new rating in column 8.

After determining effective severity, the recreation professional can prioritize the risks from high to low using the structure in table 8.5. For example, an item with high probability and high impact is ranked highest. An item with high impact and medium probability is ranked next. This is followed by an item with high impact and low probability. Examination of the ranking system suggests that it tends to favor the impact on the organization over the probability that the incident will occur.

## Including Financial Losses

As discussed earlier in the chapter, severity is a composite index of the probability that an

**Table 8.6** Determining Effective Severity

| Risks (1) | Consequences (2) | Probability (3) | Effective probability (4) | Impact (5) | Effective impact (6) | Severity (7) | Effective severity (8) |
|---|---|---|---|---|---|---|---|
| Risk 1 | Consequence | H | M | H | M | H | M |
| Risk 2 | Consequence | M | M | H | M | H | M |
| Risk 3 | Consequence | L | L | H | M | M | L |
| Risk 4 | Consequence | H | M | M | M | M | M |
| Risk 5 | Consequence | M | M | M | M | M | M |
| Risk 6 | Consequence | L | L | M | M | L | L |
| Risk 7 | Consequence | H | M | L | L | L | L |
| Risk 8 | Consequence | M | M | L | L | L | L |
| Risk 9 | Consequence | L | L | L | L | L | L |

Adapted from Kene et al. 2010.

event will occur and the impact that the event will have on the organization (e.g., the effect on public relations and on the organization's ability to carry out its programs). Impact also includes financial losses. Using an adaptation of Kaiser's (1986) model, severity can be related to the organization's potential financial losses (figure 8.7). The figure is helpful in assisting the recreation professional in choosing the primary risk management strategy to use. As the severity and financial losses increase, the model suggests that an organization tends to move from a strategy of reduction and retaining to a strategy of transfer and then to a strategy of avoidance (i.e., eliminating the activity).

If one primarily considers financial impacts, the model and strategy makes sense. However, if one considers other impacts on the organization, little difference exists between transfer and avoidance because transfer does not change the underlying factors that led to the incident or accident. It affects only the financial impact of the loss. The Winding River Canoe Rentals case illustrates this point. By her own testimony, Janice Cody did nothing to improve operations in the period of time between the death of Joe Miranda and the death of Melanie Carlson the following year (figure 1.8). However, she successfully transferred the impact of the loss from the fatality to her insurance company. Unfortunately, because she took no steps to mitigate the underlying causes present, her company suffered other impacts and went out of business. In the end, avoidance and transfer became essentially equivalent.

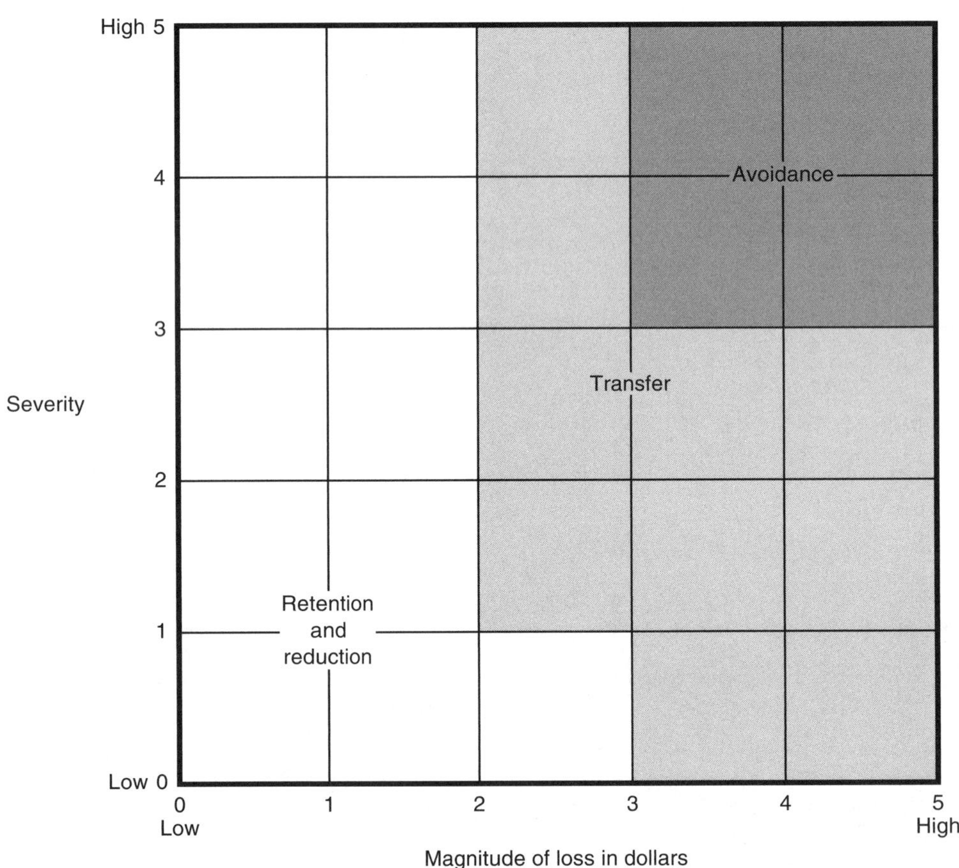


**Figure 8.7** The model suggests avoiding risks with high severity and high financial losses, transferring risks with moderate severity and moderate financial losses, and reducing or retaining risks with low severity and low financial losses.

## Step 4: Evaluation and Continued Assessment

The risk management plan is a working document. Organizations can keep the plan up to date by reassessing policies and practices, updating procedures and forms, and updating the risk assessment.

### Reassessment of Policies and Practices

As discussed earlier in this chapter, an organization can use several sources—past experience, historical records, similar organizations, state or national professional organizations, accreditation bodies, and national statistics—to assess its risks. Organizations should periodically monitor or reexamine the risks using these sources. For example, CAPRA standard 9.1 (figure 8.1) states that organizations need a risk management plan and suggests that risk management plans are a common practice or industry standard in the recreation and park field. This standard is fairly generic, and the standard may change over time. Organizations should review the standard periodically to determine whether to update their policies and procedures in accordance with the standard.

After the Joe Miranda fatality occurred, Janice Cody of Winding River Canoe Rentals could have taken several steps to identify potential hazards on the Clinton River and reassess her policies and practices. First, she could have contacted the Professional Paddlesport Association (PPA), which services the professional paddlesport industry (Kauffman and Councill, 2005b). She could have attended a PPA conference or reviewed PPA publications in an effort to determine the common practices of her industry. With the help of PPA, she could have identified another owner of a canoe livery such as hers and discussed with this person the common practices of liveries.

She also could have invited a local canoe club to paddle the river and tell her about the hazards present. The first thing that they would have noted is the large number of strainers and their potential danger at higher flows (figure 8.3). Cody then could have developed a plan to systematically remove and monitor the strainers in the river.

By researching her industry, Cody would have discovered that most liveries rely on accurate gauges to determine what types of craft to permit and when to no longer permit rental boats on the river. Operating a livery without using a gauge is like trying to maintain the speed limit in a car that lacks a working speedometer. A livery operator must know the river level and how it relates to flows. Cody could have easily reinstalled a gauge to accurately measure the water level. At minimum, or in conjunction with the river gauge, she could have used the U.S. Geological Service gauge on the Clinton River, which provides real-time data on the Internet.

At the very least, she could have developed a rudimentary risk management plan that follows the outline presented in this chapter. A simple reassessment of her policies and practices could have profoundly reduced the probability that an incident would occur and the impact of the risks associated with her operation.

### Updating Procedures and Forms

Policies and practices outline what to do. Procedures and forms, including waivers, health forms, and participant forms, outline how to implement the policies and practices. An organization must develop good forms because the categories in the forms are often important in reassessing risk levels. When an organization develops forms, it should consider how the data collected from the form can be used in analyzing risk levels.

Janice Cody of Winding River Canoe Rentals could have developed procedures regarding when to cut off use of canoes and kayaks based on water levels. She also could have developed a risk management form similar to the working table in table 8.1 that identified strainers on the river, prioritized their impact to boaters, and tracked their removal, if necessary. The systematic and periodic review of the strainers would suggest that Cody had a responsible maintenance program.

### Reassessment of Risks

Using the methodology presented in this chapter, an organization can reassess risks and quantify improvements in risk management in order to monitor the effectiveness of its risk management actions taken over time. A recreation professional fills in the effective probability (column 4), effective impact (column 6), and effective severity (column 8) columns in table 8.6 after reassessing the risks. Usually, reassessment occurs during the course of a year, and the results reflect the improvements made throughout the year.

Table 8.7 converts risk level to an equivalent probability. In table 8.8, each item is converted to its equivalent probability using the data in table 8.7. One can easily calculate the percentage change using the differences between the effective severity and the severity. To calculate the percentage change, one sums the severity and effective severity probabilities, then divides the effective severity by the severity, and then subtracts 1. In table 8.8, reducing three high-level risks to moderate risk level resulted in a 23 percent reduction in risks. One can easily construct an additional table (not shown) that lists the severity risk level for each risk along with the total risk and the percentage change from one year to the next or over time.

**Table 8.7** Conversion Table

| Risk level | Probability equivalence |
|---|---|
| High | 0.8 |
| Medium | 0.5 |
| Low | 0.2 |
| Not applicable | 0.0 |
| To be determined | 0.9 |

Adapted from Kene et al. 2010.

## STRUCTURE OF THE RISK MANAGEMENT PLAN

A risk management manual (figure 8.8) outlines an organization's risk management and public safety practices. The manual includes the risk management plan. The contents of a risk management plan can vary greatly. Organizations can use the outline presented in this section as a guideline and modify or reorder the content and structure of the plan to meet their specific needs. Organizations should, however, check that the format and content of their risk management plan is consistent with that of others in the same field.

Section 1 includes the purpose, stakeholders, and any guiding principles of the risk manual. The purpose is usually to identify risks, concerns, or problems that the organization

**Table 8.8** Calculating Effectiveness of Risk Management Measures

| Severity from table 8.6 (7) | Severity converted to probability using table 8.7 | Effective severity from table 8.6 (8) | Effective severity converted to probability using table 8.7 |
|---|---|---|---|
| H | 0.8 | M | 0.5 |
| H | 0.8 | M | 0.5 |
| M | 0.5 | L | 0.2 |
| M | 0.5 | M | 0.5 |
| M | 0.5 | M | 0.5 |
| L | 0.2 | L | 0.2 |
| L | 0.2 | L | 0.2 |
| L | 0.2 | L | 0.2 |
| L | 0.2 | L | 0.2 |
| Total | 3.9 | | 3.0 |

Effective severity/severity – 1 = percentage change
3.0/3.9 = 0.796 – 1 = –0.23, or a 23 percent decrease in severity of risk.

Adapted from Kene et al. 2010.

## Risk Management Plan Outline

**Section 1: Purpose, Stakeholders, and Guiding Principles**

**Section 2: Risk Management Policies and Procedures**

- Guiding principles and operational policies
- Scope of the program
- Responsibilities of managers, staff, and department directors
- Employee responsibility
- Responsibilities of participants
- Risk manager

**Section 3: Human Resources**

- Hiring procedures and policies
- Termination procedures and policies
- Review and evaluation of personnel
- Volunteer policies and procedures
- OSHA and occupational safety standards
- Workers' compensation (e.g., coverage, incident reporting, medical providers, benefits)
- Violence in the workplace
- Sexual harassment

**Section 4: Program**

- Americans with Disabilities Act
- Leases and contracts
- Waivers
- Warning
- Health forms

**Section 5: Facilities and Developed Areas**

- Americans with Disabilities Act (ADA)
- Security
- Sanitation
- Lighting
- Roads, walkways, and trails
- Signage

*(continued)*

**Figure 8.8** A suggested outline for a risk management manual.

Adapted from Howard County Department of Recreation and Parks, 2006, Howard County Department of Recreation and Parks risk management plan (Howard County, Maryland: Howard County Department of Recreation and Parks); R. Kaiser and K. Robinson, 2005, Risk management. In Management of park and recreation agencies, edited by B. van der Smissen, M. Moiseichik, and V. Hartenburg (Ashburn, VA: NRPA), 593-616.

**Section 6: Equipment**

- Special equipment (e.g., high ropes courses, challenge courses, playgrounds, sports)
- Maintenance and repair
- Purchase, lease, rental

**Section 7: Crisis Management and Emergency Care**

- Major disasters (e.g., hurricanes, tornados, forest fires, chemical spills)
- Civil disturbances
- First aid
- Chain of notification
- Accident reports
- Emergency action plans
- Supervisory responsibilities

**Section 8: Transportation and Vehicles**

- Coverage
- Safety courses
- Rules and procedures for use
- Accident reporting
- Insurance
- Injuries

**Figure 8.8** *(continued)*

faces and to develop a course of action for addressing them. The stakeholders are people and agencies (i.e., contractors, employees, volunteers, concessionaires, and the public) who are affected by the plan. The guiding principles include the general principles used in assembling the plan, such as understanding the factors that contribute to accidents, using a risk assessment to analyze the types of events that result in incidents, or working with other agencies, organizations, and the public to achieve safety.

Section 2 includes general principles that affect risk management. An organization should note in this section whether it uses the standards or guidelines of a national accrediting organization. It should also note any general policies generated by an overseeing board or central organization that affect its operations. This section also includes the policies and procedures that are specific to the organization and defines the scope of the risk management program (i.e., whether the program affects everything or whether it is limited to specific areas of the organization). It includes the general responsibilities of players in the organization, including the managers, staff, department directors, employees, and participants. The risk manager is the person in the organization who is responsible for carrying out the risk management plan. The plan should delineate the risk manager's role and responsibilities.

Section 3 focuses on human resources. It deals with the rules and practices of hiring and terminating personnel, including volunteers. It also focuses on the rules and practices regarding employee behavior, including evaluation, violence, sexual harassment, and compliance with Occupational Safety and Health Administration standards. This section also describes workers' compensation procedures, including coverage, incident reporting, medical providers, and benefits.

Section 4 focuses on program-related functions, including leases and contracts, waivers, warnings, and required health forms. It also includes requirements of the Americans with Disabilities Act that affect the program.

Section 5 addresses risk management practices and procedures for facilities and developed areas, including design, management, repair, and maintenance. It includes standards of federal laws, such as the Americans with Disabilities Act, that the organization must address. It also includes sanitation, lighting and signage needs. It addresses the security of buildings and areas, such as who is using the facilities, and monitoring areas for attractive nuisances. It also includes evacuation and security plans in case of emergencies. This section addresses maintenance and design of roads, walkways, and trails and the separation of incompatible transportation types into separate roadways or trails (e.g., bikers versus automobile, bikers versus hikers, and equestrians versus hikers).

Section 6 focuses on equipment needs, including the purchase, lease, rental, maintenance, and repair of equipment. It also addresses the use of specialized equipment (e.g., equipment for high ropes courses, challenge courses, playgrounds, or sport).

Section 7 covers crisis management and emergency care. If desired, an organization can include the emergency action plan (see chapter 9) in this section or as a subsection of this section. This section also addresses how to handle major disasters (e.g., hurricanes, tornados, forest fires, or chemical spills) and civil disturbances. In addition, it covers the chain of notification and the completion of accident reports.

Section 8 focuses on transportation and vehicles, including coverage, required safety courses, rules and procedures, insurance, and reporting accidents and injuries. An organization needs to monitor traffic violations because they have an impact on driving company vehicles.

The risk management plan should be reviewed by legal counsel. If a lawsuit or other legal action occurs, the plaintiff's lawyer will review the policies and practices delineated in the risk management plan. If an organization includes something in its risk management plan, it must do it. Failing to do so may be an act of omission, and doing it different than stated may be an act of commission. Terms such as *normally* or *should* are good hedge words to use in the plan and are preferable to terms such as *will* or *must*. (See "Writing EAP Statements" in chapter 9 for more detail.)

## RISK MANAGEMENT PROCESS APPLIED TO WINDING RIVER CANOE RENTALS

This section applies the risk management process to the Winding River Canoe Rentals case to show how Janice Cody could have lowered the risks associated with her operations. Shortly after the death of Melanie Carlson, Winding River Canoe Rentals went out of business. It is clear from Cody's testimony (figure 1.8) that she took no action after the fatality of Joe Miranda. This section describes what might have happened if she had implemented some of the risk reduction measures discussed in this chapter.

### Risks and Consequences

Cody identified three risks: strainers, Yates Dam, and the lack of a river gauge. (Although other risks exist and could have been included, this example is limited to these three risks.) In a working table (table 8.9), Cody listed these three items and the potential consequence of each item.

At low flow, or the average flow of 250 cubic feet per second (see figure 8.4), strainers are fairly benign. However, at a flow of 500 or 750 cubic feet per second, they become dangerous and have the potential to kill because the river has the depth, velocity, and power to pin a submerged person helplessly against the branches (see figure 8.2). Because a lot of strainers are present on the river and because the river fluctuates a good deal during the summer, Cody rated the probability of strainers as medium. Because they are killers, Cody rated their impact as high.

**Table 8.9** Winding River Canoe Rentals Risk Management Working Table: Determining Probability, Impact, and Severity

| Risks (1) | Consequences (2) | Probability (3) | Effective probability (4) | Impact (5) | Effective impact (6) | Severity (7) | Effective severity (8) |
|---|---|---|---|---|---|---|---|
| Strainers | Potential fatalities at higher water | M | | H | | H | |
| Yates Dam | Potential fatalities at high water in hydraulic | M | | M | | M | |
| Gauge | Relates to water level and administrative-use practices | M | | L | | L | |

Adapted from Kene et al. 2010.

At low water, or a flow of 250 cubic feet per second, Yates Dam (see figure 8.4) is impassable because not enough water goes over it. Boaters have to portage it or physically slide their boats over the breast of the dam. At low water, the risk of drowning is relatively low. At high water, however, the hydraulic behind the dam can become a potential killer. Because the drop-off is vertical, any boaters going over the dam with some speed will most likely not get caught in the hydraulic. However, if a boater goes over the dam sideways or without sufficient speed, he can easily become trapped in the hydraulic and drown. Because most people run the dam and avoid becoming trapped in the hydraulic behind it, Cody rated the probability of risk as medium. She rated the impact as medium because a portage trail is provided and anyone who runs the dam does so voluntarily and against the advice of the company.

The third risk Cody identified was the lack of an appropriate river gauge to indicate water levels. A gauge is important because it affects Winding River's decision to rent boats and provides valuable information regarding water levels to river users. Because the lack of a river gauge does not affect every day of boating, Cody rated the probability as medium. Cody rated the impact as low because the lack of a gauge has little direct impact on the organization.

## Applying Mitigating Strategies

This section describes what might have happened if Cody had conducted an informal investigation on the river after the death of Joe Miranda. She checked with other livery owners who were members of the PPA and she invited a local canoe club to paddle the river and identify hazards for her. The strainers quickly moved to the top of her risk list, and she developed a risk reduction strategy to mitigate the risks. She identified the strainers that were the most dangerous and then took measures to systematically remove the hazards (reduction). She monitored the river for new hazards, particularly after periods of high water that moved debris into and down the river (reduction). She also created a report form that listed the location of major strainers and the steps taken to reduce their impact on paddlers (reduction). Finally, she installed a new river gauge so that she could monitor flows and accurately determine the cut-off points for rentals (reduction).

Yates Dam was problematic. She improved the portage trail around the dam (reduction) and placed warning signs on the river upstream of the dam (reduction and transfer). She also placed a warning in her brochure (transfer) and on a poster on the bulletin board next to the put-in (transfer). She added an item to her waiver in which the participant assumed the risks of going over Yates Dam (transfer) and, when conversing with customers at the beginning of a trip, she suggested the need to portage Yates Dam (reduction). After implementing these and other measures, Cody determined the effective probability, impact, and severity and entered the new risk levels in column 8 of table 8.10.

**Table 8.10** Winding River Canoe Rentals Risk Management Working Table: Determining Effective Probability, Impact, and Severity

| Risks (1) | Consequences (2) | Probability (3) | Effective probability (4) | Impact (5) | Effective impact (6) | Severity (7) | Effective severity (8) |
|---|---|---|---|---|---|---|---|
| Strainers | Potential fatalities at higher water | M | M | H | M | H | M |
| Yates Dam | Potential fatalities at high water in hydraulic | M | L | M | M | M | L |
| Gauge | Relates to water level and administrative-use practices | M | L | L | L | L | L |

Adapted from Kene et al. 2010.

In her interactions with other professionals, Cody learned about the drowning trap and the impact of moderate flows. As a result, she temporarily ceased operations during moderately high and high flows using her new gauge to determine water levels (avoidance). If during her investigation she concluded that the strainers and Yates Dam were insurmountable problems, she might decide that it was time to voluntarily go out of business and seek other employment (avoidance).

## SUMMARY

CAPRA standard 9.1 states that organizations need a risk management plan and suggests that risk management plans are a common practice or industry standard in the recreation and park field. The risk management process is fairly simple and straightforward. The first step is to identify all of the risks affecting the organization. The second step is to determine the severity of the risks in terms of the probability that they will occur and the impact they will have on the organization. During this stage, one can rank the risks in terms of severity in order to address the higher or more important risks first. The third step is to develop a mix of risk management strategies (i.e., reduction, avoidance, transfer, and retention) to address the risks identified. Reduction and avoidance address managing or reducing the actual risks. In contrast, transfer and retention address the costs of the loss rather than reduce the likelihood that an incident will occur. The fourth step is to evaluate and continually assess the risks. This chapter also includes a sample outline for a risk management manual.

Risk management plans are usually written from the perspective of the organization, and a risk manager is responsible for implementing and monitoring the plan. However, an organization can personalize the process by applying the methods discussed in this chapter to assess the probability, impact, and severity of risks in its activities and programs and to mitigating the risks using one or more of the risk management strategies.

# EXERCISES

## Exercise 1: Risk Management Steps

The purpose of this exercise is to explore the effectiveness of the risk management steps that Winding River Canoe Rentals could have taken to reduce its level of risks. Review the "Evaluation and Continued Assessment" section of this chapter, which discusses measures that Winding River Canoe Rentals could have taken to reduce the risks. Do you agree with these measures? Can you recommend any other measures that Winding River could have taken to reduce the risks?

## Exercise 2: Maintaining Program Quality While Subcontracting Services

The purpose of this exercise is to explore some of the problems an organization may face when subcontracting services in an effort to transfer risks. In the Janice Cody case, Shelby Township successfully transferred the loss from the fatalities to Winding River Canoe Rentals. This exercise explores the responsibility and ethics of Shelby Township in transferring the responsibility to Winding River Canoe Rentals.

**1.** Winding River Canoe Rentals and Janice Cody took no risk management steps after the Joe Miranda incident. The objective of Shelby Township is to provide the residents of the Detroit area with an enjoyable and safe outing on the Clinton River on hot summer days. In subcontracting to Winding River Canoe Rentals, should Shelby Township have required Winding River to take steps to improve operations? If yes, make a list of items that Shelby Township might contractually require Winding River to do to help ensure that they provide a safe and enjoyable experience.

**2.** The case study demonstrates how Shelby Township successfully transferred their potential losses to Winding River Canoe Rentals. The judge in the case excluded Shelby Township from the suit. Ethically, does Shelby Township have a responsibility to require Winding River to take the steps you outlined in the first part of this question? Discuss your position.

## Exercise 3: Integrating Barrier Analysis into Risk Management at Castlewood State Park

The purpose of this exercise is to integrate the risk-reducing techniques discussed in other chapters into the risk management plan discussed in this chapter. Refer to the Castlewood State Park incident in chapter 5. This exercise focuses on the drop-off and on reducing the risks associated with it.

Using the barrier analysis techniques discussed in chapter 5, assess the drop-off risk in terms of the measures recommended in the chapter. Using the risk management techniques in this chapter (i.e., probability and impact), can you effectively lower the severity level?

1. Assess the initial risk level of the drop-off before you apply any reduction strategies. *Note:* You can consider it a potential drowning site based on what eventually happened.

2. Using barrier analysis, list the barriers that you would put in place to reduce the eventual fatality that occurred. You can use suggestions mentioned in the chapter, such as mandatory life jackets or interpretive signs, as part of your analysis.
3. Assume that you implemented your recommendations. Did you effectively lower the risk level associated with this site? Reassess the site in terms of your recommendations and the risk level (i.e., effective severity). What is your reassessment?

## Exercise 4: Assessing the Risk Level of the Drop-Off

The purpose of this exercise is to work through the assessment process of the risk management process. This exercise focuses on the drop-off in the Castlewood State Park incident (see chapter 5). It incorporates your analysis from exercise 3. Using table 8.1, follow the steps to determine the effective severity for the drop-off.

1. Column 2: What are the consequences of the drop-off?
2. Column 3: Use table 8.2 to assess the probability or likelihood that an incident will occur.
3. Column 5: Use table 8.3 to assess the potential impact of the drop-off on Castlewood State Park (e.g., drowning).
4. Column 7: Use table 8.4 to determine severity.
5. Columns 4, 6, and 8: Using the information from exercise 3 to mitigate probabilities or reduce the impact of the drop-off on the park, reassess your effective probability, impact, and severity. List the measures that you would take.
6. Columns 7 and 8: Use table 8.7 to convert the risk level (H, M, L) to probabilities (0-1.0), and use table 8.8 to reassess the effectiveness of your risk management measures. (*Note:* Use the process described in table 8.8 and the formula at the bottom of table 8.8 to calculate the reduction in severity or effectiveness.)
7. Did you have any problems assessing the risk level of the drop-off and the effective severity? Explain.

## Exercise 5: Examining a Risk Management Plan

The purpose of this exercise is to determine the effectiveness of an actual risk management plan. Obtain a risk management plan for a recreation agency or organization of your choice.

1. Compare and contrast the sections of the risk management plan with the sections outlined in figure 8.7. Are any items missing from the risk management plan, or should any sections of the risk management plan be added to the plan in figure 8.7? Review the plan's method regarding how they collect and analyze their data to determine probabilities and impacts. This may be part of the interview.
2. Who is responsible for the risk management plan (e.g., risk manager)? If possible, interview this person and ask the following questions. This can be done as part of this exercise or as its own exercise.
    - Why does the organization have a risk management plan? Is it because of the CAPRA standard? Is it because similar organizations have one? Or is it because the administration indicated that the organization should have one?

- How often does the organization update the risk management plan?
- What component of the risk management plan has been most effective in reducing risks, and which has been most problematic? Explain why.
- If the risk manager could change one thing in his or her job, what would it be?
- What is the biggest problem the risk manager faces in trying to create safety? What would he or she like to do to effect change?
- Do employees buy into the organization's risk management efforts, or do they tend to view these efforts as what someone else does to facilitate safety? Explain why this occurs and what the risk manager would do to rectify the attitude, if it exists.

# PART IV

# The Postincident Response

The first three parts of this text focus on preventing an accident before it happens. If no injury, damage, or loss occurs, there should be no lawsuit because there is no negligence. Perhaps the risk management plan did its job. Perhaps a leader understood the accident process and applied it to his leadership and programming skills to reduce the likelihood of an accident occurring. Perhaps the leader understood negligence and took the steps to help prevent it.

Unfortunately, however, one cannot eliminate all accidents all of the time. Sooner or later an accident will occur. The actions taken after the accident occurs are as important as the actions taken before it occurred. Part IV focuses on the behavior of a leader or organization after the occurrence of an accident or major incident. How an organization handles the situation can easily determine its survivability and that of its programs. It can also make the difference of whether the organization is sued.

The postincident response is divided into two phases: the incident and the postincident (figure IV.1). The incident involves managing the victim or the environmental emergency (e.g., hurricane, storm, tornado, wildfire, or rogue animal) in terms of search, rescue, medical, and evacuation functions. Usually, the incident ends when the victim is evacuated to an area of safety or when the environmental emergency ends.

The postincident involves what a leader or organization does with the victim and the victim's family to prevent a lawsuit and poor publicity after the incident occurs. The actions taken after the incident can significantly affect the future survivability of the organization.

Chapter 9 provides the basic framework of an emergency action plan, which provides a blueprint for safely negotiating the postincident landscape. The emergency action plan document can be expanded or modified to meet an organization's specific needs. Chapter 10 discusses managing incidents, which involves finding the potential victims, removing them from the source of potential harm, providing medical care if needed, and evacuating them to a place of safety or a place where they can receive help.

Chapter 11 focuses on crisis management and managing communications. This chapter focuses specifically on the role of the public information officer (PIO) both during the incident and when dealing with the media after the incident. Most people reading this text will not become a PIO. However, many may be called on to perform the functions of a PIO.

Chapter 12 focuses on addressing the needs of the victim and the victim's family. By virtue of the incident, a relationship exists between the organization and the victim and their family. It is important to develop this relationship and to establish rapport with the victim and the family without admitting guilt or wrongdoing.

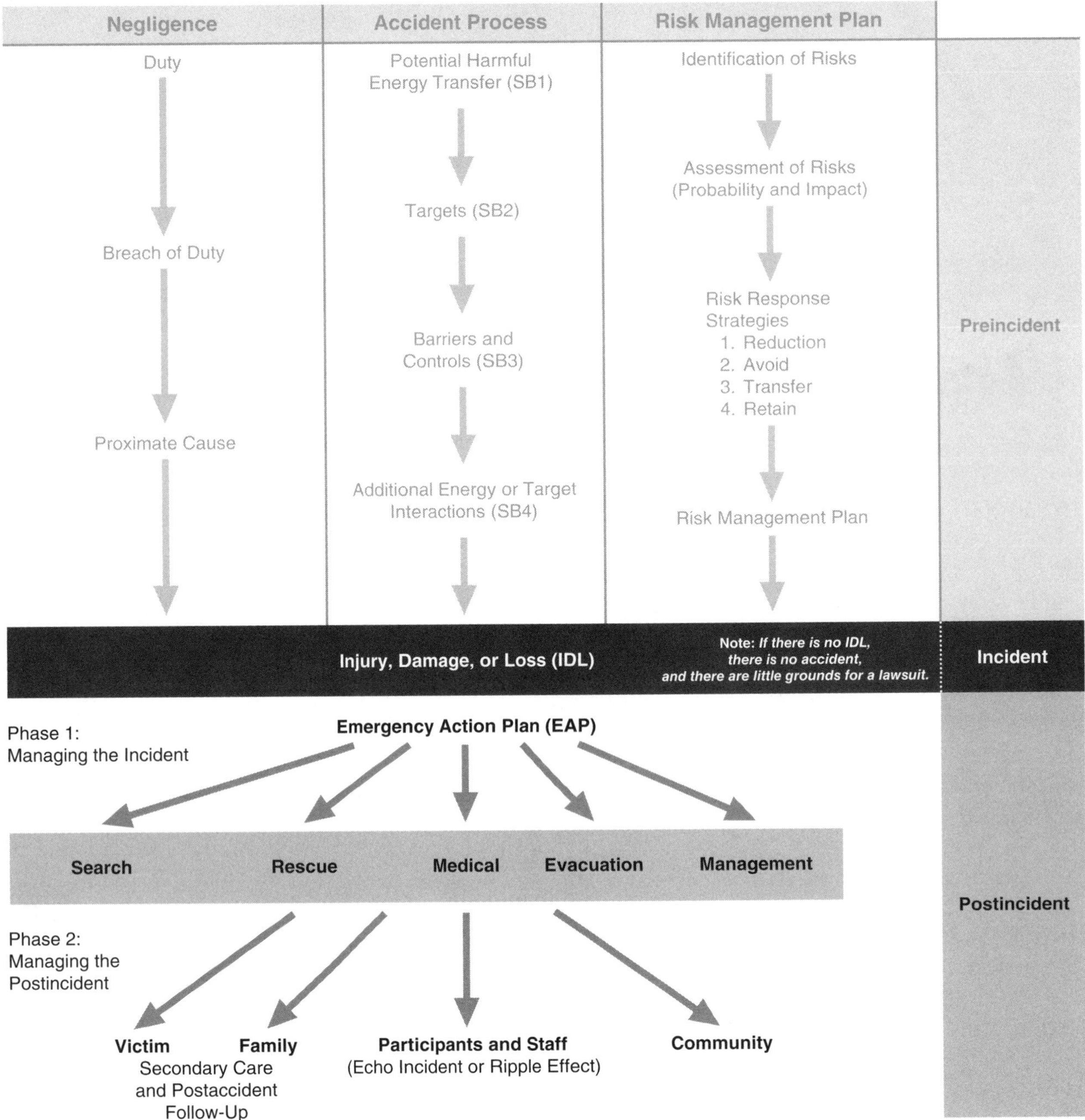


**Figure IV.1** The postincident response as part of the integrated risk management model.

Chapter 13 addresses the ripple effect. Normally, people do not think of the nonvictims as victims. However, the ripple effect explains how other participants, employees, and the community can become secondary victims of the original incident. If the incident is not addressed, participants may never again participate in the activity or may even sue. Employees who are ancillary to the original incident may leave their profession. Professional staff may become depleted. The organization may even go out of business.

Chapter 14 provides feedback, in the form of review and analysis, to help an organization improve operations and avoid future mishaps. This chapter addresses how to conduct an investigation. Most people think that an investigation fuels a potential lawsuit; however, the purpose of an investigation is that it helps prevent accidents in the future and it reduces the likelihood of being sued. An investigation is part of an organization's continual process of learning from the past in order to improve future operations.

Chapter 9

# Emergency Action Plans

Once an incident, accident, or emergency occurs, a recreation leader or organization needs to assist the victims and minimize potential negative impacts. An emergency action plan (EAP) is a plan of action that an organization enacts once an incident occurs. In an EAP, the time period after an incident occurs is divided into the incident and postincident phases. The postincident phase begins when the victims or patrons are removed from the site of the incident. An EAP includes the functions of managing the incident (i.e., rescue, emergency medical plan, and communications) and long-term functions involved with the postincident (i.e., dealing with the victim, family, participants, employees, and community). This chapter discusses the basic components of an EAP and how to develop one.

## COMPONENTS OF AN EAP

This section delineates the basic components of an EAP (see figure 9.1). The structure of this section is adapted from an EAP developed for the adventure sports program at Garrett College (Garrett College, 2009). Because the programs, facilities, and settings in the recreation and park field are extremely diverse, an organization will need to tailor the basic structure to meet its unique needs. For example, a large national park probably needs to have an extensive search plan for lost users. The EAP should include consideration for a base camp and guidelines for supporting extensive search functions and personnel. In contrast, an EAP for a child lost in a recreation center will focus on notifying the police, preventing kidnapping by parents and deviants, and finding the lost youth in the center.

### Title

The title should convey the basic elements of what the reader will find in the document. At bare minimum, the title includes the term *emergency action plan* and the name of the facility or event for which it was written. If the plan will be pulled from a larger document or viewed separately from the larger document on a regular basis, the EAP title should include the name of the organization and the address of the agency, facility, or setting.

### Purpose of the EAP

The purpose of the EAP defines the content of the document. From an organizational perspective, most EAPs focus on caring for the victims, protecting the organization, and returning the organization to normalcy. Every item included in an EAP should facilitate one or more of these three objectives. If an item does not, an organization may reconsider including it in the EAP.

First, an EAP delineates how to take care of the victim. It includes medical care at the site of the incident as well as long-term care after the initial incident. Ajango (2005, p. 111) notes that one out of five lawsuits occur after the incident because the victim wants information

## Emergency Action Plan Components

1.0 *Title*

1.1 ***The Purpose of the Emergency Action Plan:*** The purpose of the emergency action plan (EAP) is to outline the actions to be taken in case of serious accidents, incidents, or other related emergencies involving [organization name] employees, students, participants, visitors, or property.

The single most important response to emergencies is prompt action to ensure that the problem is not compounded and to maintain compassion in dealing with people under trying circumstances. The EAP is a guide to be used in conjunction with common sense, compassion, and the wisdom of those responsible.

1.2 ***Definition of an Emergency:*** An emergency is defined as any serious incident or situation that significantly threatens or injures a [organization name] employee, student, participant, or guest or results in significant property damage.

Examples of emergency plans include the following.

- A serious accident, incident, or fatality
- A situation that has the potential of endangering the organization
- An illness or injury leading to the removal of an employee, participant, student, or guest from a facility, park, or area under the jurisdiction of the organization
- A serious personal or behavioral problem caused by a participant in which they leave a program offered by the organization
- A situation that could result in adverse public-relations problems
- An unscheduled loss of contact with a participant in the field if it extends beyond [specify time] hours
- Any situation where the employee thinks the situation could adversely affect the organization
- Any situation that negatively affects a facility or endangers life

1.3 ***Appropriate Emergency Response Requirements:*** Adequate response to emergencies requires the following considerations.

- Emergency respondents will act to contain the extent of injury or damage.
- Emergency respondents will act to notify appropriate people.
- Emergency respondents will act to prevent a recurrence of the injury or damage.
- The staff will act to conduct effective public relations and release appropriate information to the media through the prescribed offices of the organization, as defined in this document.

1.4 ***Managing the Incident:*** At least one staff member on site will have, at minimum, Red Cross first aid or CPR or equivalent training. Other staff may have lesser, equal, or greater training in emergency first aid. All staff qualified to perform first aid are permitted to perform emergency first aid actions to the level of their training. The staff member with the highest level of emergency first aid training shall lead and direct other qualified field staff in the emergency medical treatment of the victim. (An organization's EAP will identify who the person is; everyone should know this information.)

1. Qualified staff will conduct a search in accordance with the search plan for the victim(s) if needed.

*(continued)*

**Figure 9.1** An example EAP from Garrett College that can be tailored to meet the needs of any activity, facility, and setting.

Adapted, by permission, from Garrett College, 2009, *Emergency action plan (EAP)* (McHenry, MD: Adventure Sports Institute).

2. Qualified staff will survey the scene of the incident to minimize the possibility of rescuers becoming victims.
3. Qualified staff will stabilize the victim.
4. Qualified staff will initiate a process to obtain appropriate rescue personnel or emergency medical services (EMS) if necessary.
5. Qualified staff will provide EMS to the victim(s) if needed.
6. Qualified staff will attend to the well-being of the injured person(s).
7. A qualified staff member shall keep a fact sheet (included as part of the incident or accident report form) outlining the details of the event, including the date, time, subject, action, responsibility, a list of any witnesses, and phone number of each communication.

**1.5** ***Managing Communications:*** The following is the normal sequence of events in the chain of notification.

1. The lead staff member at the incident or other qualified staff will notify the appropriate supervisor in a timely manner that an incident has occurred. (Refer to the laminated "emergency numbers and calling sequence" card.)
2. In the case of a nonfatal incident, the executive director will notify the next of kin.
3. In the case of a fatal incident, the executive director will notify appropriate agencies and individuals—normally the sheriff for the area in which the incident occurred.
4. The executive director, or designee, will act to coordinate any local emergency response and to gather documentation regarding the incident.
5. With the prior approval of the public information officer (PIO), the executive director will serve in the capacity of the PIO until the arrival of the PIO. Unless indicated otherwise, a gag order is in effect on all employees.
6. The executive director will coordinate through the public information office of the organization or their representative public relations and the preparation of information to be released to the general public.
7. The executive director will notify the insurance carrier and involve legal counsel as appropriate.
8. The executive director will coordinate, as necessary, any internal or external critical incident investigation(s).

**1.6** ***Care of Nonvictims*** (*Note:* These items are not ordered.)

- When needed, the executive director is responsible for providing an area for the demobilizing needs of EMS and for coordinating with EMS personnel to provide demobilization debriefing during the incident.
- When needed, the executive director is responsible for having a crisis management briefing or similar function in place to handle the debriefing needs of large groups of non-operational personnel during or just after the incident.
- When needed, the executive director is responsible for providing defusing sessions to handle the debriefing needs of small groups of 3 to 20 people 6 to 12 hours after the incident.
- When needed, the executive director is responsible for providing critical incident stress debriefing sessions to handle the debriefing needs of small groups of 3 to 20 people 1 to 10 days after the incident.

**1.7** ***Special Requirements***

**1.8** The executive director is responsible for periodically reviewing and updating the EAP.

---

**Figure 9.1** *(continued)*

about what really happened. Long-term care of the victim and the victim's family protects the organization by reducing the likelihood of a lawsuit. (See chapter 12 for more information on supporting the victim and the family.)

Second, an EAP helps protect the organization, including the organization's brand, employees, assets, and interests. The trick is to satisfy all of these interests. An accident can easily result in the loss of key personnel, which can set the organization back significantly in terms of its ability to deliver its program. It can also negatively affect the community's perception of the organization. (See chapter 13 for more information on how an incident affects nonvictims, the organization, and the community.)

Finally, an EAP helps an organization return to normalcy, or to the condition it was in before the incident occurred. Lawsuits, a large turnover in personnel, and the potential of losing a program are distractions from the normalcy of delivering programs. If the organization handles the crisis well, growth of personnel and an improved public image of the brand can result.

The following is an example of a purpose for an EAP. It is fairly broad in scope and covers most circumstances. The second paragraph is merely a helpful reminder to the person reading the EAP and helps set the tone for use of the EAP. Technically, it is not necessary. An organization can modify the purpose to meet its needs.

1.1 *The Purpose of the EAP:* The purpose of the emergency action plan (EAP) is to outline the actions to be taken in case of serious accidents, incidents, or other related emergencies involving [organization name] employees, students, participants, visitors, or property.

The single most important response to emergencies is prompt action to ensure that the problem is not compounded and to maintain compassion in dealing with people under trying circumstances. The EAP is a guide to be used in conjunction with common sense, compassion, and the wisdom of those responsible.

## Definition of an Emergency

The definition of an emergency defines the circumstances or situations that will activate the EAP. The definition in this EAP is broad. The examples listed after the definition are typical situations that would activate the EAP. An organization should tailor the examples in the EAP to meet its specific situation.

1.2 *Definition of an Emergency:* An emergency is defined as any serious incident or situation that significantly threatens or injures a [organization name] employee, student, participant, or guest or results in significant property damage.

Examples of an emergency include the following.

- A serious accident, incident, or fatality
- A situation that has the potential of endangering the organization
- An illness or injury leading to the removal of an employee, participant, student, or guest from a facility, park, or area under the jurisdiction of the organization
- A serious personal or behavioral problem caused by a participant in which they leave a program offered by the organization
- A situation that could result in adverse public-relations problems
- An unscheduled loss of contact with a participant in the field if it extends beyond [specify time] hours
- Any situation where the employee thinks the situation could adversely affect the organization
- Any situation that negatively affects a facility or endangers life

## Appropriate Emergency Response Requirements

The previous section indicates what activates the EAP. This section focuses on what the emergency respondents will do in response to the emergency. An organization should tailor this section to meet its needs.

1.3 *Appropriate Emergency Response Requirements:* Adequate response to emergencies requires the following considerations.

- Emergency respondents will act to contain the extent of injury or damage.
- Emergency respondents will act to notify appropriate people.
- Emergency respondents will act to prevent a recurrence of the injury or damage.
- The staff will act to conduct effective public relations and release appropriate information to the media through the prescribed offices of the organization, as defined in this document.

## Managing the Incident

Managing a recreation and park incident involves four phases: locating the victim, removing the victim from the source of harm, administering first aid and medical treatment, and moving the victim to a location from where he can be transported to a hospital or appropriate facility. Each of these phases is discussed in more depth in chapter 10.

Depending on the setting, clientele, and circumstances, an organization may find that one or more of these phases may be minimal. For example, a large national park will most likely require an extensive search and rescue plan as well as an evacuation plan. In contrast, if a youth falls off a piece of playground equipment, the search function may be minimal because the location of the youth is known. Also, rescue may be minimal because the youth is sitting on the ground and waiting for the ambulance. First aid may consist of simply stabilizing the arm with a splint and waiting for transport. Because the ambulance can back up to the site, load the victim, and transport her to the hospital, evacuation is minimal. Although the phases may be minimized in some circumstances, they are still present. For this reason, an organization should develop the appropriate mix of these phases to meet the needs of its setting and situation.

### Search

The search function involves locating the victim or victims. If a child falls and breaks her arm during a basketball game at a recreation center, the search function is fairly straightforward because the location of the victim is already known. In contrast, the search function in a large park can be a significant task. Planning for search is discussed in more depth in chapter 10.

### Rescue

During rescue, the victim is removed from the source of the injury or harm to a site where he can be stabilized. Different settings can pose different challenges during rescue. In a large park, the rescue function is often integrated into the search function. In swiftwater rescue, the search function is usually less important because the location of the victim is usually known; however, the rescue function involving extraction of the victim is major. In the recreation center example, rescue is a nonissue because the child is sitting on the floor with a broken arm, waiting for emergency medical care. Rescue is discussed in more depth in chapter 10.

### Medical

If the incident occurs within three hours of a hospital, the normal medical protocol is to stabilize and transport the victim to the hospital. Stabilizing involves rendering first aid, and transport involves transporting the victim to the hospital in an ambulance. A similar injury can require different protocols based on the situation. In a recreation center, a broken arm may require the first aid practice of "splint it where it lies." If the ambulance arrives quickly, paramedics may even do the splinting. A broken arm in the remote wilderness presents a very different medical situation because backcountry situations may have more extensive protocols. Medical planning and developing an emergency medical plan are discussed in more depth in chapter 10.

Depending on the setting, the rescue function is often integrated into the search function. In swiftwater rescue, the search function is usually less important because the location of the victim is usually known; however, the rescue function involving extraction of the victim is major.

The example text at the end of this section defines the minimum medical qualification of at least one person on site. If an EAP indicates that a higher qualification is required, the organization will be held to that standard. In medical situations, the person with the highest level of medical training is responsible for providing medical services. As written, the medical protocol is not a chain-of-command function. (See the discussion of highly reliable organizations in chapter 4.)

## Evacuation

Evacuation is defined as transporting the victim from the incident site to a site from where he can be taken to the hospital or other suitable facility. Depending on an organization's needs, it might need to have an evacuation plan. If a youth breaks her arm at a recreation center, a staff member may splint the arm and remove the youth to the nearby director's office, where they wait for the ambulance to arrive. In a large park, a litter or helicopter evacuation can be a major task of the operations. Evacuation plans are discussed in more depth in chapter 10.

## Management

Management involves managing the incident and the functions of search, rescue, medical care, and evacuation. Often it is associated with an incident command structure. Depending on circumstances, management can become extensive and organizations can implement an incident command structure. This would be typical in a search and rescue operation at a large park. In contrast, the incident in which a youth breaks her arm at the recreation center would require a low level of management as the victim and a staff member wait in the director's office for the ambulance to arrive. Management is discussed in more depth in chapter 10.

## Specialized Training Requirements

An organization should note in the EAP any specialized training requirements of staff or people needed for management of the incident. Searches require specialized training, as do the rescue, medical, and evacuation functions. Swimming pools require lifeguard training. Most recreation personnel have some level of first aid and CPR training.

### Specialized Setting Requirements

An organization should note in the EAP any specialized setting or facility requirements that are necessary for the management of the incident. For example, search and rescue operations in a large park might require a staging area that includes a helicopter landing area, electricity, food service, sanitation, sleeping area, and other services.

### Subcontractors

A subcontractor is anyone involved in the incident or postincident who is not an employee of the agency. This may include volunteers and Good Samaritans at the scene of the incident. It also includes emergency and rescue personnel, whether they are volunteers or professionals. An EAP should clarify the roles of subcontractors and should note whether they need specialized training or certification.

### Example Text

The following sample text includes most of the items discussed in this section. An organization can expand or modify the text as needed to meet its specific search and rescue needs.

1.4 *Managing the Incident:* At least one staff member on site will have, at minimum, a Red Cross first aid and CPR or equivalent training. Other staff may have lesser, equal, or greater training in emergency first aid. All staff qualified to perform first aid are permitted to perform emergency first aid actions to the level of their training. The staff member with the highest level of emergency first aid training shall lead and direct other qualified field staff in the emergency medical treatment of the victim.

1. Qualified staff will conduct a search in accordance with the search plan for the victims if needed.
2. Qualified staff will survey the scene of the incident to minimize the possibility of rescuers becoming victims.
3. Qualified staff will stabilize the victim.
4. Qualified staff will initiate a process to obtain appropriate rescue personnel or emergency medical services (EMS) if necessary.
5. Qualified staff will provide EMS to the victims if needed.
6. Qualified staff will attend to the well-being of the injured persons.
7. A qualified staff member shall keep a fact sheet (included as part of the incident or accident report form) outlining the details of the event, including the date, time, subject, action, responsibility, a list of any witnesses, and phone number of each communication.

## Managing Communications

During a crisis, an organization must manage communications effectively. Communications include the chain of notification, or who needs to notify whom (e.g., the family) when. It also includes documenting and investigating the incident and working with the media. Several of these topics are discussed in more depth in chapter 11.

### Chain of Notification

The chain of notification outlines who notifies whom and when to do it. Often, one or more people in an organization are designated to handle crisis situations. As with medical personnel, the chain of notification may follow a path that is different from the chain of command on the traditional organizational chart. For example, the person designated to work with the media is usually notified early in the process but after the initial emergency is under control.

In the following chain of notification, the sequence of notification is delineated by the order of the list. A staff member makes the initial notification to the executive director. (This notification is item 1 in the list.) In this example, the executive director is responsible for all of the notifications. However, an organization may adjust this based on its needs. The larger the organization, the greater the tendency to delegate this function down in the chain of command. The greater the significance of the incident, the greater the tendency to delegate this function up in the chain of command.

1.5 *Managing Communications:* The following is the normal sequence of events in the chain of notification.

1. The lead staff member at the incident or other qualified staff will notify the appropriate supervisor in a timely manner that an incident has occurred. (Refer to the laminated "emergency numbers and calling sequence" card.)
2. In the case of a nonfatal incident, the executive director will notify the next of kin.
3. In the case of a fatal incident, the executive director will notify appropriate agencies and individuals—normally the sheriff for the area in which the incident occurred.
4. The executive director, or designee, will act to coordinate any local emergency response and to gather documentation regarding the incident.
5. With the prior approval of the public information officer (PIO), the executive director will serve in the capacity of the PIO until the arrival of the PIO. Unless otherwise indicated, a gag order is in effect on all employees.
6. The executive director will coordinate through the public information office of the organization or their representative public relations and the preparation of information to be released to the general public.
7. The executive director will notify the insurance carrier and involve legal counsel as appropriate.
8. The executive director will coordinate, as necessary, any internal or external critical incident investigations.

## Notification of Next of Kin

Depending on circumstances, the family will be either on site or off site during the incident. If they are off site, they will need to be notified in a timely manner. The EAP should indicate who should notify the next of kin and when they should do so. Notification of next of kin is reflected in items 2 and 3 in the "Managing Communications" example text.

There should be some flexibility in when the next of kin are notified. Normally, they should be notified as early in the process as feasible. Waiting too long can make the family feel left out of the process. Often, they feel as if they should have done something even if they can't because of time and distance constraints. In the flight home incident (see figure 12.3), a student on a backcountry trip to the Everglades cut her thumb to the bone with a knife. It was three or four hours later before the family was notified. A thousand miles away, there was little the family could do. Although nothing happened in this case, in retrospect, they might have been notified a little earlier.

## Fact Sheet

A fact sheet or communication log lists the events that occurred during an incident and when they happened. A fact is something that a person has observed or done. If appropriate, people involved in the incident or who witnessed the incident can write statements that include the facts of what they saw or what they did. They should avoid any speculation. (Initial statements written shortly after an incident are given a lot of weight if litigation occurs because they are written before lawyers can counsel the witness.) Because the fact sheet should be started as soon as possible after the incident begins, it is included as item 7 in the "Managing the Incident" example text.

Photographic documentation of the incident can also be important. Given the plethora of cell phone cameras and video cameras in today's society, an organization should assume that photographic documentation of the incident will exist. Making a list of people who have photographic documentation of the incident can be helpful, especially if litigation occurs. An organization should consider a policy on whether to include photographic documentation of the incident as part of normal reporting.

Some photo documentation techniques are discussed in chapter 14.

### Working With the Media

The chain of notification should include who is responsible for working with the media and under what circumstances they should work with the media. Normally, this is the role of the public information office (see chapter 11). Considerations should include when and under what conditions the public information officer (PIO) should be notified and who handles the PIO's responsibilities before the PIO arrives or in lieu of their involvement. Also, if a gag order is in place, it should be noted in this section of the EAP. Working with the media and the notification of the PIO are reflected in items 5 and 6 in the "Managing Communications" example text.

### Other Notifications

In this section an organization should list any other people or services that need to be notified in case of an incident. One item to include might be who is responsible for contacting the insurance carrier. Notification of the insurance carrier is reflected in item 7 in the "Managing Communications" example text.

### Incident or Accident Investigation

If the situation warrants, an investigation may be necessary. Some of the issues associated with completing an investigation are whether it is an internal or external investigation, who is responsible for initiating the process, and under what circumstances should they conduct it. Conducting an investigation is discussed in chapter 14. At this time an organization might implement a gag order. Normally, a gag order has two components: "No comment" and "See the PIO for further information." Gag orders are effective as a temporary measure in managing how employees communicate with those external to the organization, including the media, until the PIO can sort things out. An organization should take care when implementing extended gag orders. After a major incident occurs, people need to talk and are going to talk regardless of the gag order. The organization must deal with the ripple effect (see chapter 13) and understand that a universal gag order can actually be counterproductive.

## Care of Nonvictims

An incident affects not only the victim and the victim's family. It can affect everyone involved, including incident personnel and people who are ancillary to the incident (i.e., participants, employees, and the community). An organization must take care of the needs of nonvictims as well as those of the victim and the victim's family. Chapter 13 discusses how an incident affects the nonvictims.

### Management of Incident Personnel

When incidents require extensive emergency medical services (EMS), search, rescue, medical, or evacuation operations, it is often necessary to establish demobilization debriefings during the first several work shifts. These services help the responding personnel work through the trauma with which they are dealing. An organization should consult with the incident commander or the directors of the services to determine the need for such services. Chapters 10 through 14 focus on dealing with the incident and postincident situations in term of EMS and rescue personnel.

1.6 *Care of Nonvictims*

1. When needed, the executive director is responsible for providing an area for the demobilizing needs of EMS and for coordinating with EMS personnel to provide demobilization debriefing during the incident.
2. When needed, the executive director is responsible for having a crisis management briefing or similar function in place to handle the debriefing needs of large groups of non-operational personnel during or just after the incident.
3. When needed, the executive director is responsible for providing defusing sessions to handle the debriefing needs of small groups of 3 to 20 people 6 to 12 hours after the incident.

4. When needed, the executive director is responsible for providing critical incident stress debriefing sessions to handle the debriefing needs of small groups of 3 to 20 people 1 to 10 days after the incident.

### Management of People Ancillary to the Incident

An EAP should include plans for addressing the needs of people who are ancillary to the incident, including participants, employees, and the community. These people are considered to be the second group of victims. An organization can address their needs using crisis management briefing, defusing, and critical incident stress debriefing. Crisis management briefing is used for large groups of non-operational personnel during or just after the incident. Defusing is used with small groups of 3 to 20 people 6 to 12 hours after the incident occurs. Critical incident stress debriefing focuses on the debriefing needs of 3 to 20 people 1 to 10 days after the incident occurs. The ripple effect and how it impacts secondary victims are discussed in more depth in chapter 13.

## Special Requirements

This section provides an organization with the opportunity to outline special needs and procedures that are specific to the program. It may include the procedure for dealing with a fatality, initiating a search for a lost person, backcountry situations, or travel situations. For example, a recreation center might develop specific policies and procedures for how and when to initiate a search for runaway participants. Programs that include extensive travel might develop specialized procedures for addressing accidents that occur while on the road.

1.7 *Special Requirements*

## Legal Requirements

An organization should identify any legal requirements that it may have in case of accident or fatality. These requirements can be included as part of the chain of notification or can be included in this section. In the sample EAP, notification of the authorities is included in the chain of notification.

## Review and Revision

An organization must keep the EAP updated and current. Phone numbers and other information that is constantly changing should be updated yearly or as personnel change. The organization should review the EAP when new programs are developed or when the organizational structure changes, and management should familiarize new hires with the plan. Staff should review and practice it often so that they know exactly what to do when an accident occurs. When an accident occurs, one does not normally have time to update the EAP or even to read it. One implements it.

1.8 The executive director is responsible for periodically reviewing and updating the EAP.

# WRITING EAP STATEMENTS

When writing an EAP, it is easy to write too much. An EAP can quickly become outdated, and updating a long EAP can be a major undertaking. An EAP should be mean and lean. An EAP documents who does what immediately after an incident. Coordinating the critical incident or accident investigation is fairly extensive; an organization can delineate elsewhere the procedures for actually conducting the investigation. It is only necessary to note in the EAP who is responsible for the investigation. The sample EAP statement states only that the executive director is responsible for conducting an accident investigation.

The person writing the EAP should consider using equivocal language. If a lawsuit occurs, the plaintiff often begins with the organization's EAP. If an organization writes that it *shall* do something, then it had better do it in accordance with what is written. If it does not, it is potentially providing the plaintiff with ammunition for his case. In contrast, if the organization writes the EAP with more equivocal language, it may not be giving the plaintiff the bullet to shoot it with.

The person writing the EAP should use the following example as a model and consider including the following elements in the statement: who will do the action, the conditions under which EAP will be implemented, what the people involved will do, and when they will do it.

*when*
[8.]

*who*
[The executive director]

*conditions*
[will]

*what*
[coordinate, as necessary, any internal or external critical incident investigation(s).]

The subject of the sentence is who is responsible for performing the task or the directive. This sentence states that the executive director is responsible for coordinating the investigation. Although he can delegate the actual coordination of the investigation, he cannot delegate the responsibility. If someone else can or may do the task, the EAP should include additional verbiage such as "the executive director or his designee."

The verb in the sentence usually denotes the conditions under which the task or directive is performed. Verbs such as *shall, will, should, can, may,* or *is encouraged to* each have special legal meaning. Legally, *shall* and *will* have different meanings. *Shall* indicates that the organization must do the task or directive and that to not do it is potentially an act of omission. The meaning of *will* is slightly less strong, particularly if the document uses both terms (*shall* and *will*). However, many will interpret the use of *will* as essentially the same as the use of *shall,* particularly if *will* is the only term used in the document. *Should* has even more wiggle room because it implies that the directive may not occur under some circumstances. In contrast, *may, can,* and *is encouraged to* suggest that the directive is optional.

The predicate of the sentence usually indicates the task or directive to be performed. In the example, the executive director will coordinate an investigation. The operative term is *coordinate*. The sentence also describes how this activity is coordinated.

Often, a clause in the sentence describes when an activity is performed. In this example, the item is the eighth activity to be performed. The EAP uses both bulleted and numbered items. Bulleted items suggest that the order of the items is less important. Numbered items suggest that the order is important. Because this is a numbered item, it implies that the order of the list is important. This may seem to be a fine distinction. If the order of the items is important, the organization may wish to specifically note this.

Normally, the EAP is a subplan of a larger plan. Numbering the items uses the systems approach. The first level (i.e., the title) is indicated by the code 1.0. The second level is denoted by 1.1, 1.2, 1.3, and so on. The third level is denoted by 1.1.1, 1.1.2, 1.1.3, and so on. In the example, the item is listed as item 8. This could also be written as "1.5.8" or "item 8 under the item 'Managing Communications' (1.5)."

## LEGAL REVIEW

An organization's legal counsel should review the EAP, especially from the perspective that the plaintiff's lawyer will use this document to show that the organization was negligent. If an incident results in a lawsuit, the EAP often provides the plaintiff's lawyer with a good starting point regarding what the organization did and when. The plaintiff must demonstrate the presence of the four components of negligence. Item 1.4.1 of the sample EAP states, "The staff member with the highest level of emergency first aid training shall lead and direct other qualified field staff in the emergency medical treatment of the victim." If the staff member with the highest level of emergency first aid training does not perform emergency first aid, does this constitute a potential breach of duty? The plaintiff's attorney will be quick to note that the EAP states one thing and the employees did something else that was in direct violation of the EAP. This is where the use of *will* instead of *shall* or *should* instead of *will* may be prudent.

## ALTERNATIVE EAP FORMAT

So far, this chapter presents a highly formalized structure for the EAP. At one end of the spectrum it defines everything that can be included in an EAP. It is important to remember that the purpose of the EAP is to provide directions regarding what to do if an incident occurs. The issue becomes how directive and how specific the EAP needs to be. This is for the organization to determine. The alternative EAP format presented in this section shows how an organization can have a streamlined EAP that essentially accomplishes the same purpose. The important thing for the organization is that it has an EAP.

Figure 9.2 provides an alternative format for the EAP. The EAP is divided into four sections: general, managing an incident, crisis com-

### Effective Elements of Emergency Action Plans

**General**

An effective emergency action plan (EAP) is grounded in what risk management consultant Deb Ajango calls an organization's "core values."

- The organization's primary goal with an EAP is understood.
  - Protect organization at all costs
  - Care for victim(s) regardless of cost
  - Care for staff regardless of cost
- Employees at all levels are united around this goal.
- Employees can speak to the organization's mission in explaining its programming.
- The philosophy for communication during an emergency is clear.
  - Open communication or "no comment"
  - Compassionate responses without admissions of guilt
- Legal counsel for an organization accepts the EAP before an incident and follows it.
- Trained employees handle the public relations surrounding an incident.

**Managing an Incident**

- Initiate rescue procedures and remove the victim from a dangerous setting.
- Provide immediate aid to injured party.
- Clarify leadership roles in the team, especially when using third-party contractors.
- Initiate care for remainder of group and designate roles.
- Clarify roles of outside contributors (i.e., volunteers and Good Samaritans at the scene).
- Seek external rescue assistance if necessary.
- Know state legal requirements in the event of a fatality.
- Ask for additional help from the organization to provide support in the field.

*(continued)*

**Figure 9.2** These guidelines for a simplified, alternative EAP were developed by Gullion (2007) for a session at the Association for Experiential Education Conference.

Reprinted, by permission, from L. Gullion, 2007, Effective elements of emergency action plans (EAP). In *So you've just been sued: The Deerfield Case Study*, by R. Kauffman and L. Gullion (St. Paul, Minnesota: Association of Experiential Educators Conference).

**Crisis Communication**

- Communicate from the field to the designated agency contact.
- Agency contact knows how to implement an internal communication plan.
- Agency contact knows which upper-level employee contacts family, next of kin, the media, and other parties.
- A schedule for communication between the field and agency is established.
- A schedule for communication between the agency and other external parties is clear.
- A system for documenting the details of phone calls is established in an effort to enhance the accuracy of details.
- When incident details have been corroborated from a variety of sources, release the information publicly in a systematic way (e.g., press conference, fact sheets, press releases).
- Assign one or several key individuals to be spokespersons for the agency.
- Maintain communication between all employees in the organization, even those who were not involved in the response.
- Begin to collect documentation within the organization that will be useful in an internal review.

**Postaccident Considerations**

- Establish a proactive process for maintaining communication with internal and external parties in the days and weeks following the incident.
- Provide ongoing support to the injured person(s) and family members.
- Provide ongoing support to the employees directly involved in the incident.
- Consider a critical incident stress debriefing led by a qualified facilitator.
- Conduct an internal review of the incident.
- Share the results of the internal review within the agency and with external parties.
- Revise the EAP if necessary with a variety of employees.
- Develop a training program that tests the EAP.

**Figure 9.2** *(continued)*

munication, and postaccident considerations (Ajango, 2005; Gullion, 2007). The general section includes the purpose, philosophy, and legal concerns. Managing the incident focuses on clarifying roles, relationships, and responsibilities. Crisis communication focuses on working with the media and internal communications. Postaccident considerations focus on debriefings and the ripple effect. The structure of the alternative format offers flexibility, compactness, and helpful suggestions. In this sense, it is a good working document because it provides direction but is not cumbersome in length and complexity.

The EAP in figure 9.2 was prepared by Laurie Gullion as part of a workshop on the lessons learned from the Dzialo incident. This EAP places a lot of emphasis on working with the victim and the victim's family, which is one of the lessons learned.

## SUMMARY

An EAP is a plan of action that an organization enacts once an incident occurs. The EAP focuses on caring for the victim, protecting the organization, and returning the organization to normalcy. A properly executed EAP can help prevent a lawsuit and can help an organization return to normal operations more quickly.

As a general rule, the EAP should be practical and usable. It should indicate who does what when in managing an incident and the postincident phase. An EAP should be reasonably short. Not everything needs to be delineated in the EAP; many directives can be delineated in other documents. This chapter provides a sample structure for an EAP. Chapters 10 through 14 explore in greater depth some of the key themes mentioned in the EAP.

## EXERCISES

### Exercise 1: Tailoring the EAP to Your Needs

The purpose of this exercise is to apply the components of an EAP to a specific setting with which you are familiar. Choose a recreation and park setting. (*Hint:* Consider using a specific facility.) Identify the setting, and then select a specific emergency. Using this chapter and figure 9.1, tailor the EAP to the needs of your facility and the emergency. If you would not make any changes, indicate why.

### Exercise 2: Writing EAP Directives for Managing the Incident

The purpose of this exercise is to gain experience in writing EAP items. Review the section in this chapter on writing EAP criteria and apply the principles to the following scenario.

You are the director of an urban recreation center that deals with a large number of youths in a day care-type setting. Some of the youths do not want to be at the center and run away. When you are first notified that a youth is missing, you do not know whether the youth is a runaway, an abduction, or a temporarily misplaced person. You want to write a series of directives to address the problem. Write a series of directives similar to the items in section 1.4, "Managing the Incident," of figure 9.1 to delineate what you should do when notified that a youth at your urban recreation center is missing.

### Exercise 3: Writing EAP Directives for the Mt. Hood Incident

The purpose of this exercise is to gain experience in writing EAP items. Review the section in this chapter on writing EAP criteria and review the newspaper article in appendix A that describes the Mt. Hood incident. Write a series of directives similar to the items in section 1.4, "Managing the Incident," of figure 9.1 to delineate what the school should do when the group has not returned by a specific time.

### Exercise 4: Managing Communications

The purpose of this exercise is to focus on managing communications. This exercise focuses on section 1.5, "Managing Communications," in figure 9.1 and the chain of notification.

1. Apply the chain of notification listed in section 1.5 to the scenario identified in exercise 2. Are any of the items not applicable? Do any items need to be added? Do any items need to be changed? If so, how?
2. Apply the chain of notification listed in section 1.5 to the scenario identified in exercise 3. Are any of the items not applicable? Do any items need to be added? Do any items need to be changed? If so, how?

## Exercise 5: Managing Communications—Castlewood State Park Incident

The purpose of this exercise is to focus on managing communications. Refer to chapter 5 and review the incident that occurred at Castlewood State Park near St. Louis, Missouri. Imagine that you are the manager of the park. Your task is to determine whether there are any omissions, additions, or changes in the directives listed in section 1.4 of figure 9.1. Apply the chain of notification listed in section 1.5, "Managing Communications," of figure 9.1 to the incident that occurred at the park. Are any of the items not applicable? Do any items need to be added? Do any items need to be changed? If so, how?

## Exercise 6: Managing the Incident—Castlewood State Park

The purpose of this exercise is to focus on managing the incident. Refer to chapter 5 and review the incident that occurred at Castlewood State Park near St. Louis, Missouri. Imagine that you are the manager of the park. Your task is to determine whether there are any omissions, additions, or changes in the directives listed in section 1.4 of figure 9.1.

Section 1.4, "Managing the Incident," in figure 9.1 lists several directives for managing an incident. These are generic steps. In terms of the incident that occurred at the park, are any of these items not applicable? You might want to note items that might be applicable in other situations but not in this incident. Do any items need to be added? Do any items need to be changed? If so, how?

Chapter 10

# Managing the Incident

Managing an incident consists of four ongoing tasks: search, rescue, medical care, and evacuation. The respective purposes of these functions are to locate the victim, remove the victim from the source of harm, stabilize the victim and prepare the victim for transport, and transport the victim to the hospital or appropriate facility.

Managing the incident involves orchestrating these basic elements in the appropriate mix to achieve the desired goals. The appropriate mix of these functions depends on the recreation site and setting. For example, a national park will most likely have an extensive search and rescue plan that includes provisions for a base camp area and an incident command structure. In contrast, the search plan for a missing youth at a recreation center will be much more limited in nature and scope. Regardless, a recreation professional needs to recognize the four functions, even if one or more plays a minor role in a particular recreation setting. An organization can have a separate plan for each of these functions or can combine several of the functions into one plan. For example, a national park would most likely combine the search and rescue functions into a single plan.

Generally, these functions occur chronologically. The rescuer needs to find the victim before she can rescue him and apply first aid. The rescuer then needs to move the victim from the mechanism of injury to a safe location so that she can render first aid or medical treatment. After the victim is stabilized, the rescuer can evacuate and move the victim to a site from where he can be transported to a hospital. The phases often overlap considerably. For example, first aid is often rendered during the rescue phase and continues during the evacuation phase.

The clientele, situation, and setting determine the amount of emphasis an organization places on each function. For example, if a youth playing basketball in a recreation center falls and breaks his arm, the search and rescue functions are quickly accomplished and are generally minimal: The person helping the victim renders first aid and splints the arm. Evacuation may be relatively simple: The victim and the person helping him walk to the office and wait for the ambulance to arrive. In contrast, a camp or recreation center dealing with a runaway youth tends to emphasize the search function. Once the youth is found, the other functions (i.e., rescue, medical care, and evacuation) may be minimal. This chapter discusses in chronological order each of the four functions of managing an incident, as well as the fifth component, management.

## SEARCH PHASE

The search is the first phase in managing the incident. The purpose of the search phase is to locate the victim. The search function can be relatively easy (e.g., locating a youth who falls and breaks his arm while playing basketball in a recreation center) or can be a major activity (e.g., large numbers of trained personnel searching over several days for a lost person in a national park). The search can be a major function in cases of abduction or runaways.

Searches can occur in any recreation and park setting. The following list of search sites and specialty groups is adapted from a list developed by Stoffel (2001, p. 134) and Koester (2008). Each setting and type of search has unique requirements. For example, an abducted child or lost person wants to be found. A runaway or a youth who is autistic normally behaves as if he does not want to be found. A person with Alzheimer's or dementia is ambivalent about being found.

**Search Types by Setting**

- Forest, park, or wilderness area
- Lake
- River
- Disaster area
- Urban environment
- Attractive nuisance
- Single-story building
- Multistory building

**Search Types Affecting Specialty Groups**

- Alzheimer's
- Despondent
- Dementia
- Autistic
- Mentally challenged
- Psychotic
- Outdoor recreationist (hiker, climber, skier, fisherman, hunter, mountain biker, ATV driver, snowmobiler, and so on)
- Crime victim
- Runaway
- Child lost in urban environment
- Abducted child
- Child homicide

In general, searches for missing persons are divided into the following phases: preplanning, first notice, callout, and disengagement. The preplanning phase includes everything that one does before the first notice occurs to prepare for an incident. The first notice phase occurs when one identifies that a person is missing. The actual search process begins at this time. During the callout phase the search process escalates in terms of personnel and resources. Depending on the type of search, this phase can be subdivided into rescue, medical, and evacuation phases. The final phase, disengagement, involves demobilizing, ending, and critiquing the search.

A recreation professional should ask the following questions in terms of search efforts for his activity, facility, or area. These questions relate to the four phases of the search.

1. Do I have a plan for missing persons?
2. Have I identified the missing person as potentially missing?
3. Do I need to expand the search to include outside resources and authorities?
4. Have I found the missing person? Or, have I concluded that I likely will not find the missing person? Or, have I concluded that I have expended my available resources?

The story in figure 10.1, "The Runaway Camper," depicts these four stages. The preplanning phase consisted of activities that preceded the first notice, such as performing head counts at meals and bedtime and covering the general protocols during staff training. Usually, the first-notice phase occurred after staff performed a head count. This phase included a quick search of the camp, and could also include the notification of the missing camper's parents. Commitment of resources (e.g., personnel or funds) was still fairly minimal during this stage. The callout phase began when camp personnel searched the two main roads out of camp. Rarely, this phase included the formal involvement of the police and other rescue personnel. (Usually, the camper returned home or was returned to camp.) The search was over at the disengagement phase.

## Preplanning

The preplan is a written document that may be included as part of the emergency action plan

## The Runaway Camper

Camp Conrad Weiser is located in Wernersville, Pennsylvania. The resident camp is located in a rural area on top of South Mountain approximately 15 miles from Reading, Pennsylvania. It is a typical camp located on the outskirts of a medium-sized city. With its relatively close proximity to the city, the camp had a problem with runaway campers. This example demonstrates that the formal search principles are applicable in general recreation and park settings and in seemingly simple search situations like the runaway camper.

Most runaway campers were fairly predictable. Generally, they ran away within the first two days after arriving at the new session. Usually, the camper was homesick or simply did not want to be there in the first place. In most cases, it was easy to identify potential runaways from their behavior. For this reason, it was important to keep tabs on the campers during the first two days of the new session. A head count was conducted at each of the three meals during the day and at bedtime.

There were two roads into camp. Most runaways took the back route out of camp because it was the quicker route off the property. They simply took the path to the riding stable and continued down the mountain, where they picked up the road that took them into Sinking Springs, which was about eight miles from the camp. Once the runaways reached Sinking Springs, finding them became problematic because they could take many different roads. An adolescent can easily move three to four miles per hour, meaning that one could easily reach Sinking Springs in two hours. The rule of thumb was that there was a two-hour window of opportunity to track down the camper.

If a camper was identified as missing, a semiformal search plan was mobilized. Initially, the matter was treated as an internal matter. The appropriate staff members were notified that the camper was missing and staff were given the camper's name as well as a general description of the camper's appearance and what he or she was wearing. The counselor in charge of the camper was interviewed to assess whether the camper had the symptoms of a runaway. A "hasty search" was conducted to determine whether the camper was still on camp property but simply in the wrong place. Many campers were found asleep in their tents and had missed lunch simply because they were tired. Next, a preliminary search was conducted because it would be quite embarrassing to go to the callout phase and notify the police and other enforcement agencies only to find the camper asleep in his or her tent.

Given the two-hour window of opportunity, depending on when the camper was last seen and when the camper's absence was first noticed, key staff would use the camp vehicle and search the main roads. They had to look carefully because the youth would normally hide from the camp vehicle (the camp's logo was plastered on the side of the vehicle). Unless the situation warranted, the search was strictly in house up to this point. Normally, the camp did not contact the parents, police, or other agencies at this time.

If the "hasty search" suggested that the camper was likely not at the camp and if the key staff did not find the camper along the main roads, it was time to notify the parents. One of the more embarrassing situations was to receive a call from a parent notifying the camp that their child was at home and not at camp. From an emotional perspective, it was important to contact the parents before the youth arrived home because it implied that camp staff were ahead of the curve rather than playing catch-up. Also, once notified, the parents could aid in the search. The camp also contacted any friends or relatives that the camper might go to.

Finally, at a preselected time, authorities were officially notified. Usually, the time was calculated to allow sufficient time for the youth to get home. Normally, at this point the staff responsible for the search gave the authorities a heads-up for their planning purposes. If the youth arrived home, as he or she usually did, the authorities were notified that the runaway camper was found.

**Figure 10.1** This story illustrates most of the general principles of a normal search for a missing person.

(EAP) or may be a separate document. According to Stoffel (2001), the preplan accomplishes two things. First, it provides a framework with which to solve problems. Second, it defines authorities, jurisdictions, and legal ramifications so that people do not have to question in the middle of a major search operation who is in charge or whether the organization has the authority to conduct the search. Figure 10.2 lists items an organization may include in the preplan.

Stoffel (2001) advises keeping the preplan simple and flexible, avoiding duplication of documents, and keeping explanations short. The preplan should address only what is necessary. When creating the preplan, an organization should consider the following.

1. Develop written memorandums of understanding with the agencies with which the organization may become involved, and keep the memorandums updated. A memorandum of understanding is a letter stating a working relationship between two organizations. In this case, the memorandum of understanding would state that if a search and rescue operation were to occur, the rescuers would use the services or the organization with specialized knowledge, skills, and abilities, how they would utilize them, and whether there were any limitations on their use. These documents do not need to be complicated.
2. Check with local, state, and federal agencies regarding laws or regulations that affect the organization's operations.
3. Address the chain of command.
4. Determine who is in charge of what.
5. Assess the area and the potential problems that the organization could face or has faced in the past.
6. Have legal staff review all documents.

When determining what issues it might face, an organization can start by reviewing and analyzing previous incidents and incident reports. Past incidents can often foreshadow potential future occurrences. One should remember, however, that incident reports may not include all available information because organizational culture tends to hide facts in order to avoid recognizing and analyzing incidents.

Clientele will, in part, determine the organization's preplan needs. An organization that deals with children in an urban environment may need to consider runaway and abduction incidents. In a wilderness park, searches will likely consist of finding lost hikers and campers.

An organization should also consider facility conditions. Does the facility have a central entrance and security point? Does it have security cameras? Are other potential entrances and exits secured? Is the area surrounding the facility fenced, patrolled, and secured? If the facility is a large outdoor area, where do people frequently go (e.g., the visitor's center, campground, interpretive trail, beachfront, or other major attraction)? The features that surround a facility can also influence the search needs. For example, abandoned or rundown buildings can be attractive nuisances for youths. The landscape surrounding a large park can affect search requirements.

Finally, in the preplan phase, an organization should examine its administrative procedures. Health forms, medical releases, and parental and guardian information become important documentation if an emergency occurs. Policies and procedures should be examined in terms of how they can affect a crisis situation. Sometimes simple administrative policies can have significant impact. For example, in the story in figure 10.1, the camp performed a head count during meals. Because campers were assigned to a table at mealtime, it was a simple matter to determine if someone was missing and to take appropriate action. Contrast this with a camp where meals are served cafeteria style and campers can sit wherever they want. In addition, there was a head count at bedtime, and they emphasized unit programs during the first two days of a new session. Unit programming where everyone in the unit participated together in activities made it easier to keep track of campers.

## Preplanning Plan Outline

1. *Plan objective or purpose:* To save lives in the most efficient and safe manner
2. *Priority of resource allocation:* State what is needed, and secure agency agreement that search is life threatening and has agency priority over activity.
3. *Specific agency guidelines:* Acceptable landing zones for helicopters during emergencies, public relations, and so on
4. *Preparedness:* Training, standards, minimum staffing, equipment caches
5. *Organizational tasking:* Who does what during an event (e.g., command, transport, reserve personnel versus regular staff)
6. *First notice*: Mobilization plan, telephone trees, authorities that must be notified
7. *Initial responsibility:* Who is in charge on notification, and when does the responsibility change hands?
8. *Investigation:* Performed by whom, according to type of incident? What is the role of the search and rescue team? What special equipment is required?
9. *Priorities and decisions:* What does the crew need to know in order to make decisions? Is it possible to preplan decisions (i.e., if such and such is true, we will do this and this)?
10. *Strategy:* Consider when the incident command needs to be implemented. What are the situations for escalation or demobilization? When are additional resources called on? What logistical support is needed?
11. *Preference for resources:* In what situations are certain resources mandatory (e.g., anyone entering water above the knees must have a personal flotation device and a wetsuit)?
12. *Callout:* Procedures for mobilization, resources and logistics needed, and personnel (paid and volunteer)
13. *Tactics:* Whatever is necessary to carry out the strategy
14. *Clues:* Emphasize clue awareness.
15. *Base camp:* Logistics of support, preplan phases for small missions and large, extended missions
16. *Communications:* Internal and external (e.g., news media, telephones)
17. *Medical considerations:* For both the subject and the searchers
18. *Rescue and evacuation:* The rescue is on. What is to be done by whom? Different resources may be essential.
19. *Fatalities:* Agency procedures, contacting and cooperating with proper authorities
20. *Mission suspension or de-escalation:* How and when does one decide this?
21. *Demobilization:* How will it occur? What is the priority of release? Who is responsible?
22. *Documentation and reporting:* What is required?
23. *Critique procedure:* Detailed, recorded, and implemented results widely available
24. *Prevention:* Public safety and search and rescue training programs to act on new ideas

**Figure 10.2** Setnicka's (1980) outline provides an extensive list of considerations to include in the preplanning process.

Reprinted, by permission, from T. Setnicka, 1980, *Wilderness search and rescue* (Boston, MA: Appalachian Mountain Club), 53-54.

## First Notice and Urgency

The first-notice phase begins when the recreation professional receives notice that a person is potentially missing. The professional should first test the reliability of the information and determine whether a problem really exists. Is the allegedly missing person really missing, and is a search mission necessary? He could simply be temporarily misplaced. He might be in the bathroom for an extended period of time or with the wrong group. A recreation leader should first check the facility for the missing person. In the story in figure 10.1, the staff did a quick search to ensure that the camper was indeed missing and not sleeping in his or her bunk.

Next, the leader should begin collecting information about the missing person in order to shape a search plan. Figure 10.3 lists information that is typically collected on a missing person report form. Who is missing? Where and when were they last seen? What are they

---

### Items on a Missing Person Report Form

The following is a list of information that can be used to develop a missing person report form. Depending on circumstances, some of the information may be of less importance and conversely, some information may become more important. For groups, modify this form accordingly or use more than one form.

- Name, address, and phone number(s) of missing person
- Nickname
- Number of persons missing
- Age
- Race
- Gender
- Height
- Weight
- Physical description
- Physical condition
- Primary language
- Medical and mental history
- Experience and ability
- Point last seen or last known position
- Time last seen
- Activity last seen participating in
- Clothing (descriptions of all layers of clothing)
- Equipment (the immediate resources available to victim for survival)
- Vehicle (description, model, color, license number)
- Has this person(s) been the subject of a search before? If so, when, where, why, and what was the outcome?

---

**Figure 10.3** The basic items on a missing person report form. Depending on circumstances, some of the information may be less important and some more important. For a missing group, the recreation leader can modify this form accordingly or use more than one form.

Adapted, by permission, from R. Stoffel, 2001, *The handbook for managing land search operations* (Cashmere, WA: Emergency Response International, Inc.), 59.

wearing? How tall are they? What is their race? Do they have a medical condition? This information helps staff identify the missing person when he or she is found. Also, these factors may influence the urgency of the search. Urgency may increase if a missing person has a known medical condition, if a major storm is advancing, or if some other environmental emergency is present. Information regarding the missing person's skill level, experience, and equipment helps the recreation leader determine the survivability of the missing person, which also may affect the urgency of the search.

## Callout

The actual search operations begin during the callout phase. This phase is often characterized by a major escalation in operations and the application of additional resources, such as personnel, food service, lodging, medical care, communications, helicopters, technical specialists, or an incident command structure. Figure 10.4 illustrates a hypothetical staging area that an organization might use during a major callout.

As figure 10.4 suggests, a callout can become fairly extensive. The callout phase can involve the other functions, including rescue, medical care, and evacuation. It can also include highly specialized functions that are specific to the environment in which the callout takes place. For example, an entire science examines the behavior of persons missing in the outdoors. Rescuers can use the point last seen to determine where to search for a missing person (figure 10.5).

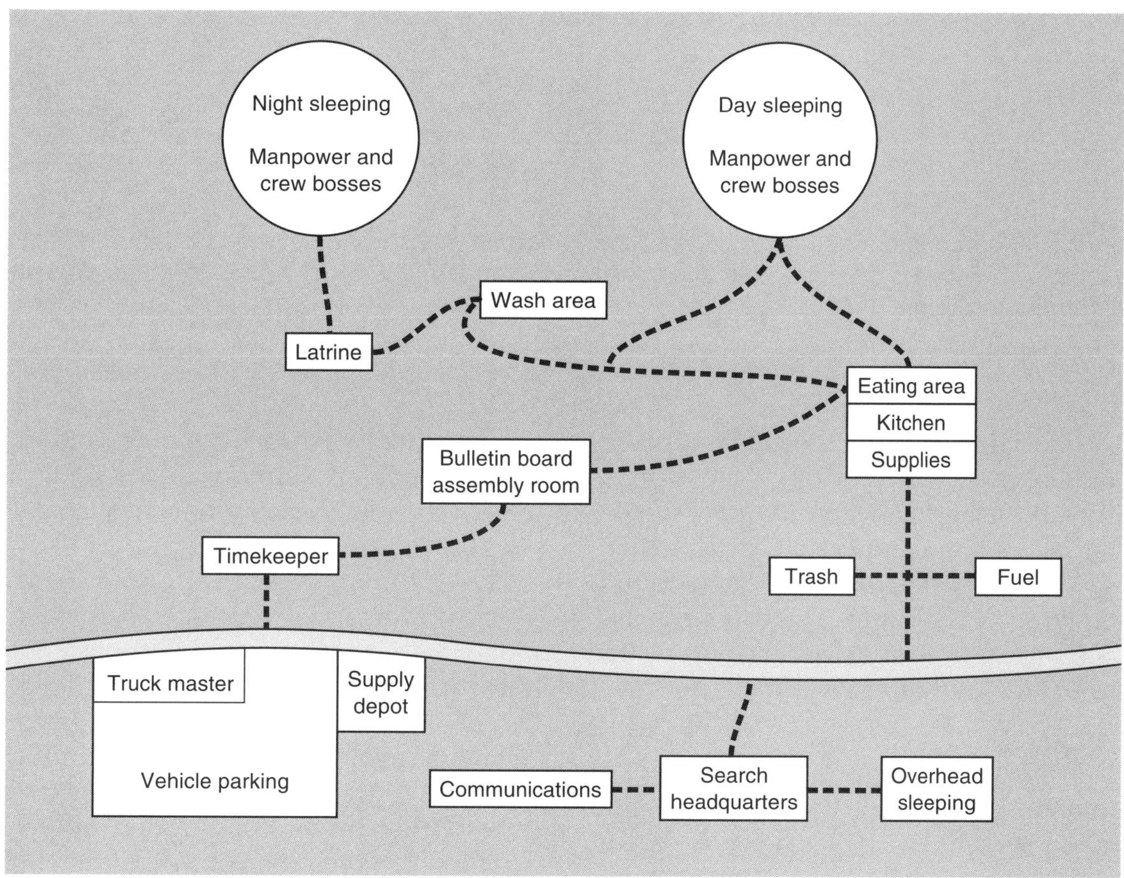


**Figure 10.4** This layout of a search and rescue staging area indicates the extent to which a full-scale search and rescue operation can easily grow. The operation includes night and day sleeping areas, food service, latrines, wash areas, communications, parking, and headquarters to service a full-scale operation.

Reprinted, by permission, from T. Setnicka, 1980, *Wilderness search and rescue* (Boston: Appalachian Mountain Club), 140.

**Determine the Search Area**

- Determine point last seen (PLS)

- **Theoretical method**
Time versus distance which a person can cover

- **Statistical method**
Example of lost children (6-12) on flat land
  - 38% found less than 1.6 km from PLS
  - 38% found 1.6 km from PLS
  - 18% found 3.2 km from PLS

- **Subjective method**
  - River acts as barrier.
  - People walk downhill rather than up a hill (40%).
  - The search area could be cut in half.
  - A hasty search along the river would probably reveal good results.

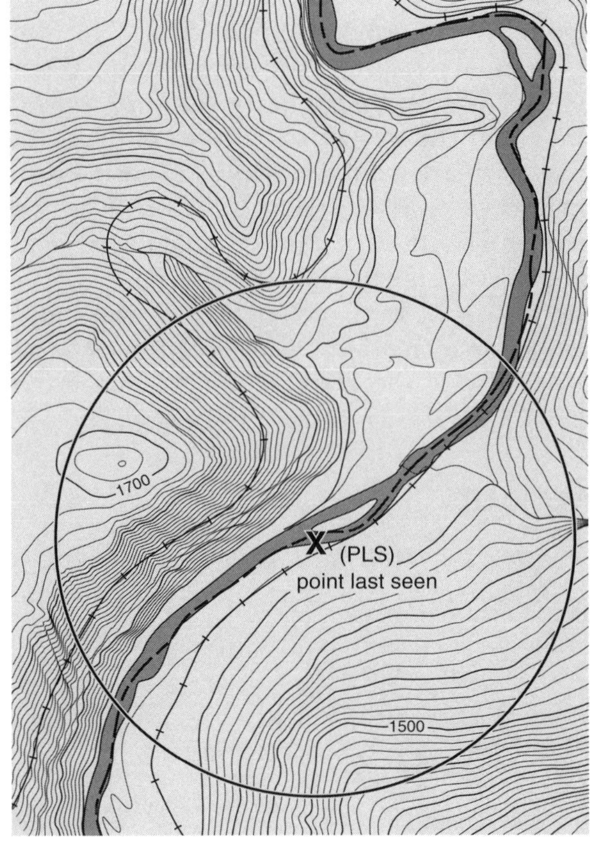


**Figure 10.5** Search and rescue can become a sophisticated, scientific operation. After determining the point last seen, rescuers can use theoretical, statistical, and subjective methods to determine where to best search for the victim.

Adapted from Stoffel 2001.

In the story in figure 10.1, the callout phase began when staff began checking the two main roads to Sinking Springs for a runaway camper. In most cases, the campers either returned home in a short period of time or were found and returned to the camp. The callout phase rarely escalated to include notification of the police or other local officials.

## Disengagement

Disengagement involves demobilizing and ending the search. Disengagement can occur when the missing person or victim is found and evacuated and the extensive operations associated with the search are no longer needed. Disengagement can also occur when the missing person or victim is not found and the likelihood of finding him decreases. An organization should have protocols in place to help define the circumstances under which demobilization occurs when the victim cannot be found.

When the search reaches disengagement, the organization should critique and evaluate the operations in order to improve them for the next time an incident occurs. Chapter 13 discusses in detail the process of demobilizing personnel who are involved in the incident. In the story in figure 10.1, the disengagement phase began when either the youth was found and returned to camp, or when the youth returned home.

# RESCUE PHASE

The purpose of the rescue phase is to remove the victim from the source of harm. This section uses the rescue curve, which describes rescue in terms of who does what when. In the rescue curve, rescue begins with the safety and prevention measures that a participant takes and expands to include individuals in, and external to, the organization. This section also discusses the management implications of the rescue curve.

Each activity area, particularly outdoor activities, usually has its own highly specialized rescue techniques. A recreation leader should consult specialty resources for information on rescues in his specific activity or area. The purpose of this section is to explain rescue as it relates to the bigger picture of the organization. In terms of rescue efforts, a recreation leader should do the following.

- *Identify the typical types of rescues for an activity, facility, or area.* Typically, rescues will be determined by the type of activities conducted. These rescue activities are influenced by the business of the organization, setting or terrain, and informal activities. For example, at an aquatics center, lifeguards may have to rescue a swimmer who is drowning. On a ropes or challenge course, a person may become trapped in the middle of the zip line, stuck on the ladder, or fall off the commando crawl (figure 10.6). The setting or terrain may determine the type of rescue that will be performed. In a park with a rock face or caves, eventually someone will become stuck on the rock face or lost in a cave and will need to be rescued (figure 10.7). Informal activities are activities that people do on site but that may not be formally sanctioned by the organization. For example, if people are found to be ice fishing on a frozen lake during winter, the organization may want to consider that there will eventually be a need for an ice rescue (figure 10.8). Or, if people are swimming at the beach on the Meramec River in Castlewood State Park (see chapter 5), and there is a known drop-off in the river, the park might want to develop a rescue plan for this informal activity because someone will eventually step off the drop-off again. In an interesting update, two youths nearly drowned at the same site on June 26, 2012 (KTVI Fox News, 2012).

Photo courtesy of Robert B. Kauffman.

**Figure 10.6** If a person freezes or becomes trapped on one of the elements, can the recreation leader rescue them?

The recreation leader should also become familiar with the types of rescues performed in his industry by becoming involved with the professional organization for his industry and attending conferences, training sessions, and workshops. In the examples above, if there is an organization that deals specifically with the activity area (ice rescues, cave rescues, or high angle rescues), it is usually prudent to use them to determine the common practices of rescue for that activity area.

- *Ensure that personnel have the training necessary for the types of rescues identified or that the appropriate personnel are on call to assist in the types of rescues identified.* In determining the necessary training for personnel, there are two issues to address: First, does everyone need the training, or just one person on duty? Second, what is the minimum level of rescue skills required of everyone?

For example, on a high ropes course, participants occasionally become trapped and need to be extricated and lowered back to the ground. Because this occurs infrequently, at least one person on site should have this rescue training. Although it would be good for everyone to have this training, it may not be necessary. Also, *on site* can be defined as the overall course and not just the specific element being performed at the time. In contrast, when participants belay other participants, instructors may need to transfer the belay to themselves and lower the climber. In this case, all leaders should be able to perform this type of rescue. At an aquatics center, all lifeguards must have expertise in rescuing drowning victims.

Some rescues require specialized knowledge and abilities that staff may not have. In this case, the recreation manager must identify external personnel who possess this knowledge and ability, develop formal relationships with them, train with them, and conduct rescue operations with them. These people may

Photo courtesy of Robert B. Kauffman.

**Figure 10.7** Many rescues require specialized knowledge and training to be effective. A recreation professional should identify environments in which these rescues might be necessary and train for the rescue before he actually needs to perform one.

Photo courtesy of Robert B. Kauffman.

**Figure 10.8** Assess what your users are actually doing, and sooner or later you will need to perform a rescue for that activity. If they are ice fishing on a park lake, an ice rescue will eventually need to be performed.

be on call. For example, the park may work with the local grotto regarding cave rescue rather than providing their personnel with the high level of training necessary.

• *Perform the rescue in a timely manner.* The victim's situation determines what constitutes a timely rescue. In general, the more life threatening the potential threat, the more the personnel in close proximity need to be able to perform the rescue. For example, a lifeguard needs to be able to perform a rescue immediately and correctly because time is of the essence for a drowning victim. Swiftwater rescue illustrates this principle. A victim is either "heads up" (the victim's head is above water and breathing) or "heads down" (the victim's head is below the surface of the water and in a drowning situation). In a heads-down rescue, time is of the essence. In contrast, a heads-up rescue allows rescuers more time to perform the rescue. In a heads-up rescue, the rescue squad could be called and potentially rescue the victim alive. In contrast, by the time the rescue squad arrived in a heads-down rescue, the rescue will most likely have become a body recovery. Because of the likelihood of a heads-down rescue, *timely* in this case suggests personnel who are trained in swiftwater rescue techniques in close proximity to participants.

• *Practice rescues on a regular basis.* Practice helps to hone rescue skills and to keep personnel current, up to date, and practiced. Also, when possible, practice rescue scenarios at the actual sites being used. A lifeguard should practice rescuing drowning victims. A ropes course operator should practice extricating victims from the zip line or the commando crawl. Where there are site-specific situations, practicing scenarios at these sites can save considerable time and increase the efficiency of a rescue. On a rock face, the staff will already have belay points in place. They will already have practiced scenarios similar to those that have occurred and are likely to occur on site, and they have preplanned what is needed to perform rescues. In the Dzialo incident (see chapter 1) where there was near drowning during a swimming exercise on the Deerfield River, the staff as part of their training might have simulated a foot entrapment scenario on site. The scenario would have quickly revealed that two throw bags were necessary to reach across the river. Site-specific practice would have helped the staff to save time and frustration by having already addressed these issues.

## Rescue Curve

The rescue curve describes rescue in terms of who does what when and what will happen if those attempts fail. The rescue curve states that once an incident occurs, the probability of survival or avoiding injury, damage, or loss decreases as time without intervention increases. The rescue curve has been refined several times since it was first developed by Kauffman and Carlson (1992; see figure 10.9). Although the model was originally developed in the context of outdoor activities, it has been generalized to nonoutdoor activities (Kauffman, 2003).

According to the rescue curve, the first line of defense is safety and prevention. These include the active and passive measures that the participant should take to avoid a rescue situation or, if a rescue situation occurs, to better help survive the situation. *Active measures* are measures a participant takes to help prevent an incident from occurring. The participant uses knowledge, skills, and abilities to avoid a situation in which a rescue is necessary. A climber's

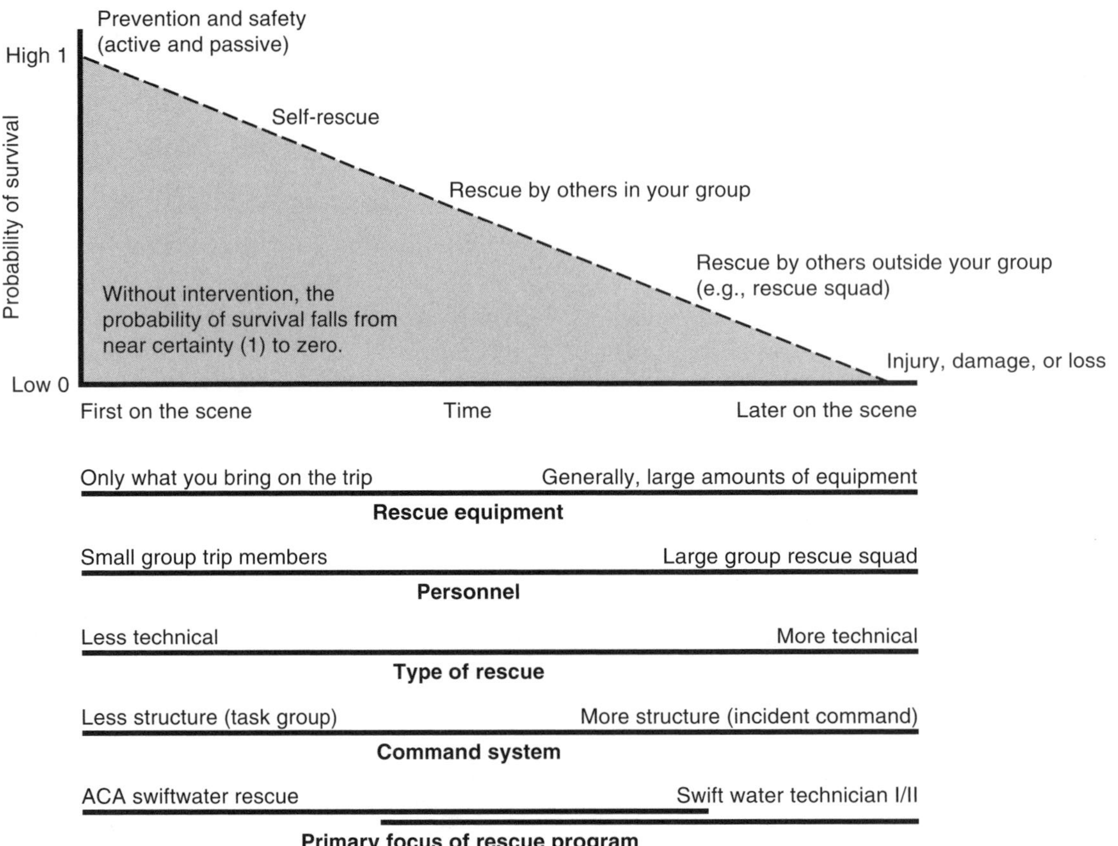


**Figure 10.9** The rescue curve suggests that once an incident occurs, without intervention the probability of survival decreases as time increases. The four stages of the rescue curve are prevention and safety, self-rescue, rescue by others in the group, and rescue by others outside the group. The differences in rescue equipment, personnel, type of rescue, and command structure are addressed with the curve.

From Kauffman and Carlson 1992; Kauffman 2003.

climbing ability, a paddler's paddling ability, or a driver's driving ability are examples of active safety measures. *Passive measures* are measures that normally do not help prevent the initial incident from occurring but that do help during the rescue phase. For example, a climber uses climbing ropes and protective gear as protection against a fall, but ropes and protection do not aid in the actual climb. A paddler's life jacket aids the paddler only if she comes out of her boat. A spare tire has little value to a driver unless the car has a flat tire. On a playground, surfacing, fall zones, and equipment design are examples of passive measures.

Once an incident occurs, injury, damage, or loss normally occurs unless there is intervention. Intervention is defined as self-rescue, rescue by others in your group, or rescue by others outside your group. Occasionally, intervention will occur naturally. A person falls from the rock face and lands in a tree; the branches cushion the fall, and the person lands relatively unharmed on the ground. A child falls off a climbing apparatus on the playground and hits the pea gravel surfacing underneath the apparatus. The pea gravel breaks the fall (intervenes) and the child continues to play, uninjured.

The first level of defense after an incident occurs is self-rescue, or what the victim can do to rescue himself. For example, a climber who falls several feet as a rope suspends his weight can grab hold of the rock face and continue climbing. The paddler can Eskimo roll or swim with her boat to the shore. The driver can remove the flat tire and put on the spare tire. On a playground, a child slips on a climbing apparatus, catches herself, and continues climbing. The child self-rescued.

Rescue by others in the victim's group is the next line of defense. If the climber is belayed, the belayer may lower the climber to a safe area. If the paddler comes out of her boat, a member of her group may paddle over, extend the stern and grab loop to her, and paddle her to shore. The passenger in the car may help change the tire or assist by directing traffic. On the playground, the child climbs to the top of the climbing apparatus, looks around, gets scared, freezes, and starts crying. Her mother rushes over and with outstretched arms lifts her daughter off the climbing apparatus. The daughter is rescued by others in her group. Anyone participating in the activity alone bypasses this phase and directly enters the next phase.

The next line of defense, rescue by others outside the victim's group, includes the rescue efforts of people passing by or the rescue squad. If the climber is injured in a fall or the rescue escalates beyond the capabilities of the other climbers, a rescue squad with specialized training is summoned. The same is true for the paddler. On the playground, the child is crying atop the climbing apparatus, and the mother is standing there not knowing what to do. A passerby rushes over and lifts the child off the apparatus. The passerby performs a rescue by someone outside of the group. Or, in the same situation, the passerby calls 911, and the park sends the fire department and the fireman lifts the child off the apparatus. Again, it is a rescue by someone outside of the group, in this case the rescue squad.

If no one rescues the victim, additional injury, damage, or loss usually occurs. Even if the climber is not injured by the initial fall, he will experience additional injury or even death without intervention. The paddler who is not rescued may eventually flush through the rapids and naturally wash up on the shore. If no one rescues the driver, he may be stranded in a desolate area. On the playground, it is difficult to envision someone not eventually coming to the rescue. Most likely the child will eventually stop crying and attempt to climb down the apparatus (self-rescue). Or the child will fall and injure herself and need treatment. Or the mother will come to her senses and help the child off the apparatus (rescue by others in the group). This example illustrates the principle that the previous stages can be re-entered again.

## Available Resources and the Rescue Curve

The rescue curve is useful in helping to explain the resources available to or influencing the rescuers. The rescue squad is in the business of performing rescues. As a general rule, the rescue squad has lots of personnel and equipment at their disposal to perform a rescue. In addition, they have trained extensively in rescue procedures. In contrast, people participating in the recreational activity are interested in performing the activity. Rescue is what happens when something goes wrong performing the activity. It is not that participants are not interested in rescue—they are. However, they are more interested in performing the activity. Often they think in terms of how they can adapt the equipment used in performing the activity to a rescue situation, or they will bring along with them simple devices as long as these items don't interfere with the performance of their activity. In terms of personnel, they are limited by who is in their group unless, of course, they are doing the activity alone. In that case, they bypass this phase for the next phase. The following examples illustrate the difference in resources between participants interested in rescue and the rescue squad. In terms of personnel, a group of climbers might consist of 2 instructors and 10 youths. Although the group comprises 12 people, only 2 are well trained (1 if the victim is an instructor). In a paddling group of 5 people, 4 people must conduct the rescue assuming that 1 person in the group is the victim; this is a small group for a whitewater rescue. In contrast, a rescue squad could have 20 to 30 trained rescuers available to them for a rescue.

Regarding equipment, climbers usually do not bring rescue pulleys and a Stokes litter with them; the rescue squad does. The paddler group might have two carabiners per person and several rescue bags. This makes any rescue involving a lot of carabiners or several hundred feet of rope difficult. In contrast, the rescue squad usually arrives with large amounts of specialized rescue equipment.

The difference between equipment and personnel in terms of the rescue curve is illustrated by the child stuck atop the climbing apparatus. If the children become stuck on a bouldering rock (climbing apparatus) similar to the one depicted in figure 5.8, it is not expected that the mother supervising the children will have brought a ladder along with her in case she needed to rescue the children. However, if the fire department is called, they would bring a ladder. In this case, the rescue squad (rescue by others outside your group) would have the equipment and personnel necessary to perform the rescue in contrast to the children (self-rescue) or the mother (rescue by others in your group), who would not.

### 911 Syndrome

The 911 syndrome focuses on the difference between inexperienced and experienced participants. More experienced, specialized participants tend to begin their rescue efforts with safety and prevention. They focus on their equipment and on developing their skills and rescue techniques. They know that if a potential incident occurs, their first line of defense is self-rescue, and that if they do not self-rescue, they can move very quickly through the stages of the rescue curve and run out of options. Experienced participants tend to front-load their activity with safety and prevention because they know their survival depends on it.

In contrast, inexperienced or "activity for a day" participants usually do not have the necessary skill, knowledge, or training to perform a rescue, and they most likely do not possess or know how to use rescue equipment. They tend to quickly skip over the first three phases of rescue (i.e., safety and prevention, self-rescue, and rescue by others in the group) and immediately go to the fourth phase—rescue by others outside the group. They call 911 and hope that someone comes to rescue them. Usually, they believe that it is the responsibility of someone else to rescue them (Kauffman and Carlson, 1992; Kauffman et al., 1991), and rely almost completely on the resource manager or the rescue squad for their survival.

## Resource Management Implications

In terms of rescue needs, a less obvious management consideration is differentiating between specialized participants who have less need for management control and nonspecialized participants who need extra management supervision and control (Kauffman,

1991; Kauffman et al., 1991; Ewert and Hughes, 2005). This principle is illustrated with the 911 syndrome. For example, in a study of Potomac River users, tubers were nonspecialized users who visited the river once or twice per year (Kauffman, 1991). They needed and expected increased management, including rescue by others. Often they were illustrative of the 911 syndrome because they began their rescue efforts by calling for someone else to rescue them. In contrast, canoeists were more specialized boaters and expected rescue to begin with their efforts (i.e., safety and prevention). They needed and sought less management of their experience. It is often difficult for management to differentiate between the needs and expectations of different types of users. Often, the specialized users get lumped in with everyone else or they simply go somewhere else where management interferes less.

Second, in an effort to reduce rescue, resource managers can provide users with the appropriate information to perform the activity safely. In part, the rescue curve can be used to frame the message. The resource manager can utilize a plethora of venues to deliver their safety message and help prepare users for their experience while reducing the need for rescue. Addressing the pre-experience, the manager can create websites, brochures, guidebooks, and other sources to properly prepare users in terms of safety and prevention. Also, self-rescue can be addressed in this phase. When users arrive on site, visitor centers, kiosks, and interpretive safety signage are helpful in addressing the same needs. Also, rangers, police, maintenance, and visitor center personnel can help deliver the safety message to users.

For example, each year thousands of people climb Mount Washington in New Hampshire. Their experience is managed more than they realize to reduce rescues and, of course, to provide the climbers with a good experience. Most people begin their climb at the AMC (Appalachian Mountain Club) visitor's center at Pinkham Notch (figure 10.10). It is a one-day climb to the summit and back to the visitor's center using the Tuckerman Ravine Trail. Consider the climb from a management perspective. Websites, brochures, and even word-of-mouth advertise this route as the climb. These information sources tend to funnel users into Pinkham Notch and Tuckerman's Ravine Trail. Before climbing, climbers stop at the visitor's center, where personnel provide an informal screening. Simple conversation reveals their knowledge, skills, and experience, and a simple scan of their clothes and equipment reveals if they are prepared for the climb. Suggestions are made if needed. These suggestions are reinforced with displays, posters, and other information. The messages received by the climber are all congruent. The trail is well marked. If someone gets lost or injured, it is relatively easy to find and evacuate them. U.S. Forest Service rangers and AMC personnel have done all this before. In addition, they are found at key points on the route to the summit. They serve to informally monitor the progress of climbers. From a management perspective, the entire operation is geared to manage the experience in a seemingly informal and unobtrusive manner while at the same time reducing the need for rescues.

## Rescue and Changing the Experience

Rescue considerations can often affect the experience the resource manager is seeking to create. A resource manager must often weigh participant safety against the experience provided. This management dilemma is exemplified in figure 10.10. During summer when the stream is at low flow, the rocks on this popular trail are simply stepping stones across the stream for backcountry users (figure 10.11). The crossing is perfectly safe. However, during spring or early summer, the rocks are usually covered with water, and a stream crossing here could easily be life threatening. During spring, this crossing represents a potential hazard. Management assessment of users on this trail indicates a large number of users with 911 syndrome. Empirically, management knows this because the rescues performed at this site are more than would normally be expected. The users do not know the dangers of a river crossing let alone how to self-rescue if someone

## The Dilemma of Two Bridges

Two bridges in the White Mountains of New Hampshire have a profound impact in terms of user safety and the experience provided. Figure 10.11 depicts a series of stepping stones across a stream. Figure 10.12 depicts a bridge built over the stream by the Forest Service for $50,000. Both photos were taken from locations in close proximity during the low flows of summer. When the water level is low, anyone can easily walk across the stream. In contrast, when the river swells during spring, traversing this same spot can be potentially dangerous, particularly for users who are not trained in crossing rivers.

Consider the wilderness experience that each bridge provides and which is more appropriate. The stepping stones are natural and consistent with providing a wilderness- or backcountry-type experience. The bridge is typical of the frontcountry. From a design perspective, the bridge lacks a rustic nature and real charm and is urban in appearance.

Then juxtapose the experience with safety and rescue concerns. During spring, many hikers and backpackers would need to traverse the swollen stream. If they do not recognize the potential hazard and if they are not trained in how to traverse swollen rivers, they are at risk. This increases mishaps, rescues, and management costs. Without the bridge, numerous rescues and potential fatalities would occur at this site each year.

Hence the dilemma. Should management build the bridge and, in doing so, change or lose the experience provided? At what point do simple management decisions change the experience provided so that the desired experience is lost? Once management begins to manage the experience to reduce search and rescue costs, where do they end? Even marginal returns in terms of safety can be justified.

Photo courtesy of Robert B. Kauffman.

**Figure 10.11** In spring, these rocks are covered with water and this stream can create a dangerous crossing situation for hikers and backpackers.

*(continued)*

**Figure 10.10** The dilemma of two bridges exemplifies the management dilemma of weighing the safety of the participants against the experience provided.

Photo courtesy of Robert B. Kauffman.

**Figure 10.12** The U.S. Forest Service built a $50,000 bridge so that hikers would no longer use stepping stones to cross the stream. The bridge alters the wilderness experience provided but reduces incidents and fatalities and search and rescue expenditures.

---

**Figure 10.10** *(continued)*

in their party is swept away. The same is true for others in their party. Very quickly, rescue passes to the resource manager and the rescue squad. They now have a problem with people being injured or killed at this spot on this popular trail. (*Note:* Management can easily use barrier analysis, and they face a variation of the safety discussion of the beach area on the Meramec River in chapter 5). On one hand, the manager desires to create a wilderness experience. On the other hand, rescue and safety concerns suggest implementing practices that potentially change and diminish that experience. If management performs several rescues a season at this site (figure 10.11), the obvious management conclusion is to build a bridge and eliminate the hazard (figure 10.12). However, in building the bridge, management significantly changes the wilderness experience. In this case, they built the bridge even though it significantly changed the experience.

## Interpretive Signs

In terms of the rescue curve, interpretive signs give users information about their safety and accident prevention, self-rescue, and rescue by others in their group. Interpretive signs present the common practices of the activity in a way that is not condescending and that makes people want to use the information. They follow many of the principles presented by Tilden (1957) and, more recently, Beck and Cable (2002). In a legal sense, the information presented on a sign potentially represents the common practices of the activity. When developing this sign, a recreation professional should consult books, publications, experts, and legal counsel about which information to include.

Figure 10.13, *a* through *c*, shows a typical interpretive sign. The sign is located at the put-in on the Middle Youghiogheny River in Pennsylvania. Figure 10.13*a* shows the general

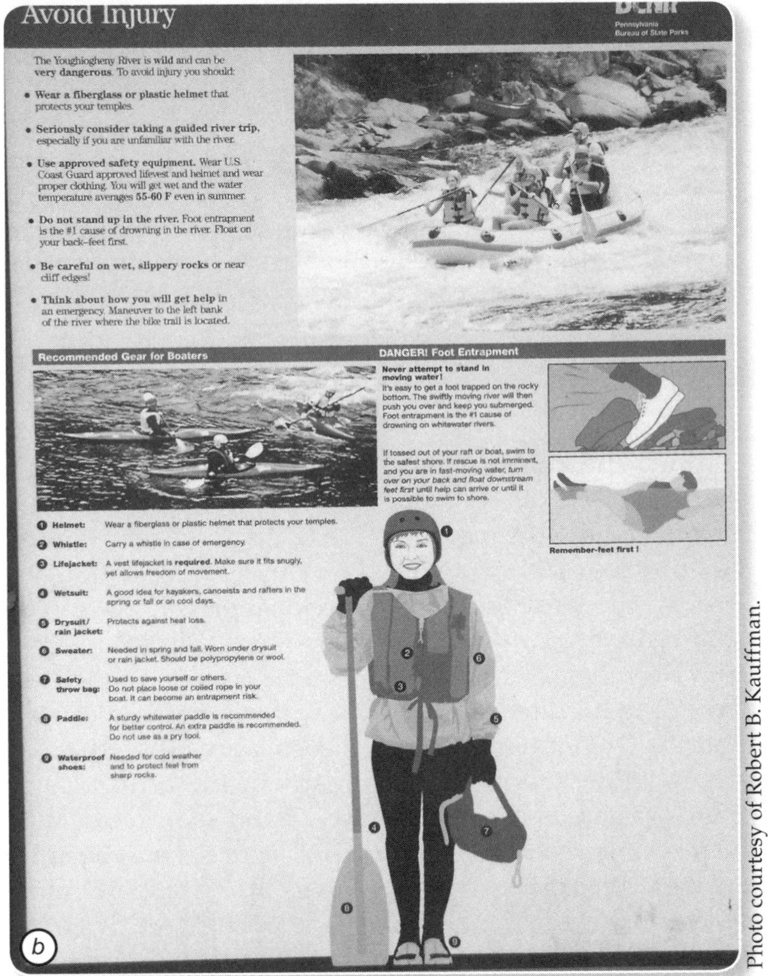


**Figure 10.13** *(a)* The location of the interpretive sign. The location includes a bulletin board and another sign warning users of rapids at the put-in. *(b)* The actual interpretive sign. *(c)* The paddler on the interpretive sign. The picture and accompanying text recommends what paddlers should take with them on their trip.

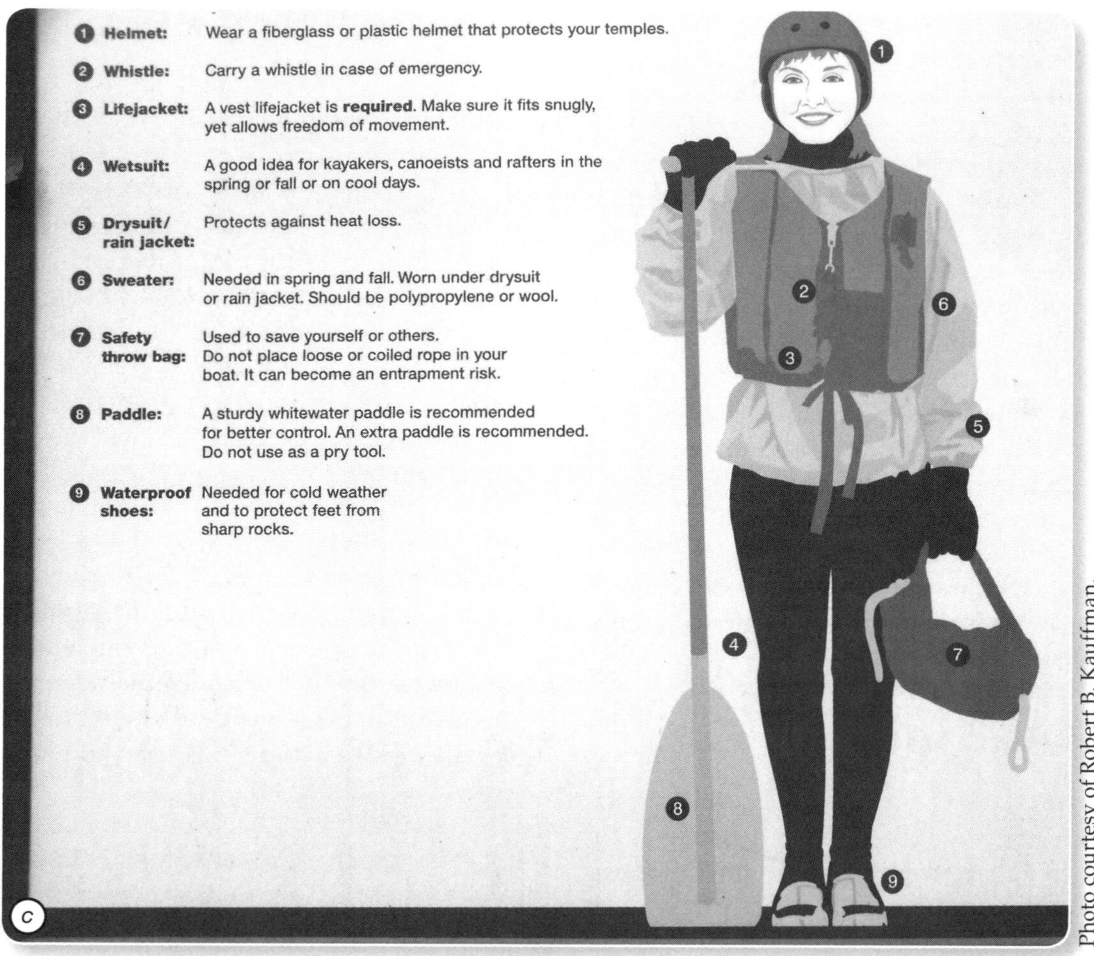


**Figure 10.13** *(continued)*

view of the area, which contains a warning sign regarding a rapid just downstream of the put-in, an interpretive sign, and a bulletin board with administrative notices. Figure 10.13*b* is a close-up of the interpretive sign, and figure 10.13*c* is a close-up of the paddler on the sign. The sign suggests common safety practices and equipment (helmet, whistle, life jacket, wetsuit, drysuit or rain jacket, sweater, throw bag, paddles, and waterproof shoes) that paddlers should consider using on their trip. This information helps paddlers avoid incidents and tells them what to do if a mishap occurs. The sign also explains the potential hazard associated with foot entrapments and the self-rescue technique of swimming with the feet up in the water.

Chapter 5 discusses improving river safety at Castlewood State Park near St. Louis, Missouri. One suggested way to improve safety is to provide an interpretive sign. The sign should include information about common river hazards, including drop-offs, strainers, foot entrapments, and how the current moves a person downstream. It could include safety and prevention information about wearing a life jacket and self-rescue information about swimming diagonally to the shore if a person is in a current over his head. Such a sign is a much better option than simply posting a sign that says "swim at your own risk," where recreation visitors know as much after reading the sign as they did before reading it—nothing.

Interpretive safety signs are located at the point of contact. This means that the user contacts and interacts with the sign just before doing the activity. The paddlers on the Middle Youghiogheny River encounter the sign just before beginning their trip on the river. After reading the sign, if they don't have the proper equipment, are they going to terminate their trip on the river because they don't have the equipment depicted on the sign? Probably not. When entering the beach area on the Meramec River, is a family not going to go swimming if the interpretive safety sign suggests wearing a life jacket and the family didn't bring life jackets with them? Probably not. This is a significant disadvantage with interpretive safety signage. Also, it reinforces the need to deliver the interpretive message as early as possible in the user's decision making process regarding their experience. Regardless, interpretive safety signage provides a powerful educational tool because it describes the common practices of the activity and most people generally want to conform with these common practices, even if it is on their next trip.

## MEDICAL PHASE

The purpose of the medical phase is to stabilize the victim and prepare the victim for transport. Normally, medical treatment deals with treating cuts and bruises. In more serious medical situations, first aid is characterized by stabilizing the victim's medical condition and transporting the victim to the hospital. Recreational situations vary greatly, and organizations should tailor protocols to meet the needs of the activity or industry. In terms of first aid and medical protocols, a recreation leader should address the following concerns.

1. How far am I from the hospital?
2. Have I identified the typical medical situations for my activity, facility, or area?
3. Do my personnel have the appropriate first aid training necessary for the types of activities that I have identified? In terms of first aid and medical assistance, what standard of care do I need to offer?
4. Did I manage the scene and perform appropriate medical care?
5. Have I protected myself from bodily substances and other contaminants?
6. Do I practice for these first aid situations on a regular basis?

### Distance From the Hospital

The distance of the incident from the hospital determines whether it is a frontcountry–backcountry issue and determines the standard of care protocols that an organization should consider. In trauma cases, the term *golden hour* refers to the finding that if the victim is stabilized and transported to the hospital within the first hour of the incident, the victim has a high probability of survival. This is the normal situation in the urban environment. The appropriate response is rapid notification (call 911), rapid response (emergency medical services [EMS] arrives), and rapid evacuation (transport to the hospital). For example, at a swimming pool, a lifeguard is generally required to perform CPR on a drowning victim until the EMS personnel arrive on scene and can assume CPR and transport the victim to the hospital. Most medical situations on a challenge course consist of cuts, bruises, and sprained and broken feet and arms from falls.

In contrast, in a backcountry situation, the *golden hour* can easily transform into the *golden day*, where the hospital is one or more days away from the scene of the incident. Backcountry medical situations change the traditional protocols in two ways. First, the recreation leader needs to take care of the victim—keep him warm, take care of his urination and defecation needs, and, depending on the injury, feed him. Second, some first aid treatments may change. For example, if victim suffers a dislocated shoulder in the frontcountry, the rescuer splints the shoulder where it lies and lets the hospital personnel reset it. In the backcountry, when the nearest hospital is a day or more away, the appropriate treatment may be to reset the dislocation because permanent damage can result if the dislocation is not reset.

### Typical Medical Situations

The recreation leader should become familiar with what type of medical situations to expect for his activity, facility, or area and with typical incidents that other facilities and areas in his industry face. This can be determined from the past history of the parent organization, communication with others in the discipline at conferences and workshops, books and publications, and analysis of the activity to determine potential mechanisms of injury. For example, programs involving water environments may face drowning and hypothermia medical emergencies. Programs with extensive hiking may need to deal with blisters, sprains, and broken bones. A playground with climbing apparatuses may need to deal with falls and contusions. Each sports activity has a set of medical emergencies associated with it.

## First Aid and Medical Training

An organization must identify the minimum level of staff medical training that is appropriate for the activities being conducted. The minimum level of medical training may differ significantly among different types of recreation activities and industries. An organization should review the recommendations of the accrediting agency or the professional organization governing the activity and consider following the recommendations even if it has not gone through the accreditation process. If an accrediting agency or professional agency recommends a minimum standard of care, it is incumbent on the organization to provide it. A standard first aid and CPR course is often considered a minimum standard for most situations. However, in backcountry situations, Wilderness First Responder may be considered more appropriate. If an organization has a sport facility or organized sport teams, it may need to have an athletic trainer on duty at the facility or during activities. The question to ask is what are the common practices of the industry in this regard, and what are the typical medical situations faced by others doing similar activities? Then the decision becomes either conforming to these common practices or having a good reason why you do not.

## Managing the Scene and First Aid

The recreation professional must manage the scene of the incident, particularly if she is the first person on the scene. The professional first surveys and secures the scene in order to prevent more people from becoming victims. Then, for both her protection and the victim's, the professional identifies the mechanism of injury. She then manages the scene in terms of spectators and noninvolved personnel. It may be necessary to usher spectators away from the scene or provide the victim privacy by shielding him from spectators. Figure 10.14 provides the typical patient assessment process. Although it is for a backcountry situation, with minor adaptions it is equally adaptable to frontcountry situations. The entire first step is to manage the scene.

These protocols are applied to the following example. (This example is a primer and is not a complete discourse on the topic.) A youth sits beneath a tree on a playground holding his arm protectively. The rescuer, Mary, approaches. Mary should first survey the scene and identify the mechanism of the injury. What caused the injury? Did the youth simply fall out of the tree, or did something, such as a dead tree branch, fall on the youth? A falling branch could injure Mary also. Mary looks up into the tree and, seeing nothing of concern, chooses to use available people to help her. Mary most likely will not need to keep everyone warm and dry because it is not raining. (Keeping the victim warm and dry is a long-term concern in the outdoors or during late fall or winter.) It is well within the golden hour, and the ambulance should arrive soon.

The victim sits on the ground, holding his arm. Mary assesses the patient for any immediate threats to life. She asks him his name, and he responds. Mary quickly conducts a primary survey. The victim's airway, breathing, and circulation (ABCs) are okay. The victim is conscious, awake, verbal, responsive, and in pain.

Mary begins the secondary survey. The victim's arm is obviously deformed. He tells Mary that he fell out of the tree. Mary asks him whether she can check the rest of his body, and he consents. Mary checks for other deformities or pain. The arm seems to be the only injury, and no blood is present. Mary takes his pulse and records it using a SOAP (subjective assessment, objective assessment, assessment or problem list, and plan) note. When the ambulance arrives, Mary gives the EMS personnel the information she

## Typical Patient Assessment

1. STOP! Size up the scene.
   A. Establish control.
   B. Survey the scene for hazards.
   C. Determine the mechanism of injury.
   D. Isolate body substances.
   E. Count the number of patients.
   F. What is your general impression?
   G. Establish a relationship.
2. STOP! Assess the patient for immediate threats to life.
   A. Perform an initial assessment.
   B. Establish responsiveness or control the cervical spine.
   C. A is for airway.
   D. B is for breathing.
   E. C is for circulation (and bleeding).
   F. D is for disability or decision.
   G. E is for expose or environment.
3. STOP! Complete a focused exam and patient history.
   A. Perform a physical examination—What hurts?
   B. Check vital signs.
   C. Take the patient's medical history.
   D. SAMPLE—Symptoms, allergies, medications, pertinent medical history, last intake or output.
   E. OPQRST—Onset, provokes or palliates, quality, radiates or refers—region, severity, time.
4. STOP! Make a problem list and a plan.
   A. Write a SOAP note (subjective, objective, assessment, plan).
5. STOP! Monitor the patient's condition.

**Figure 10.14** Although these general protocols are tailored for a wilderness first aid setting, they are applicable to most settings and can be tailored to meet an organization's specific needs.

Based on Tilton 2010.

recorded. The EMS personnel splint the youth's arm and transport him to the hospital.

## Body Fluids and Contamination

The rule of thumb is to avoid creating additional victims. A first aid provider's natural instinct is to help the victim. However, the rescuer must protect herself first. When a rescuer first arrives at the scene of the incident, she should check the site for the mechanism, or cause, of the victim's injury and should isolate body substances.

When working on the victim, the rescuer needs to protect herself from body fluids and other contaminants (Hubbell, 2005) and prevent transmitting her body fluids to the victim. The rescuer should put on gloves before working on the victim to prevent making direct contact with body fluids. The rescuer should also consider washing her hands both before and after working with the victim in order to reduce hand-to-mouth transfer of pathogens. Depending on the clientele, the rescuer may want to wear a mask or gown. Resuscitation equipment should contain appropriate barriers and valves to prevent direct mouth-to-mouth resuscitation.

Contamination can result from environmental elements, including items that are directly related to the mechanism of injury or that are incidental to the actual injury. For example, a flash flood transports everything downstream, including overflowing septic systems, animal wastes and bodies, propane tanks, and chemicals. Contamination can also result from the products used in treating the victim. For example, gauze used to clean a wound is a contaminated material and needs to be disposed of in an appropriate container.

### Practicing First Aid Situations

The retention of first aid training often has a half life of six months, meaning that without review or training a person can easily lose half of what he learned after six months and half again after another six months. A person who is certified needs to practice in order to maintain the ability to perform. In addition, certification demonstrates only that a person was exposed to the correct procedures on the day he took the course (van der Smissen, 1975, 2005). Merely being certified to perform first aid training is not enough to protect a person from being negligent; it is what the person actually does that counts.

Spengler et al. (2006) note that in several legal cases the decision turned on the fact that a facility did not have a written plan or medical EAP. Whether an organization has a separate medical EAP or includes general medical procedures as part of its EAP (see chapter 9), it must document the general first aid process. Once is has established basic procedures, it should develop scenarios that allow staff to practice and refine them.

### Reporting Medical Situations

For some injuries, an organization may be required to report the incident to the appropriate agency or authorities (Hubbell, 2005). Examples of these injuries include animal bites, apparent suicide or homicide, injury sustained during a crime, and abuse (child, spouse, or elderly).

## EVACUATION PHASE

The purpose of the evacuation phase is to transport the victim to the hospital or appropriate facility. Evacuation of the victim can be as simple as sliding the gurney into the back of the ambulance and transporting the victim to the hospital. Or, in a remote location like a large park, it could include a two-mile trek over rough terrain while carrying a Stokes litter to the nearest road or location where the victim can be helicoptered to the hospital. In terms of evacuating the victim, a recreation leader should address the following questions.

1. Where are the access points for ambulance and helicopter, if applicable? (This includes facilities as well as parks. A leader should consider multiple access points in large parks.)
2. Have arrangements been made to provide EMS personnel with easy access? For example, do EMS personnel have a key to unlock a gate or bollard to gain access to trails or roads, or do they need staff to unlock the gates?

The evacuation portion can require considerable expertise and can consume considerable personnel resources. For example, if 6 people carry a 200-pound person in a Stokes litter, each person is carrying 50 pounds one-handed. Also, uneven terrain and other factors will distribute the weight unevenly among the carriers, and rough terrain and sloped inclines might require belaying the litter. For this reason, people are constantly rotated in and out of a carry. A backcountry carry can easily involve 12 to 18 people. Figure 10.15 shows the transport of a Stokes litter by a team of carriers in a caving rescue.

Once the victim has been evacuated and transported to the hospital or appropriate facility, operations are suspended and the staging area is closed down. Operations enter the post-mission phase. Disengagement and debriefing are discussed in chapters 13 and 14.

Photo courtesy of Robert B. Kauffman.

**Figure 10.15** A litter team is carrying the Stokes litter in a simulation of a cave rescue. The carriers at the end of litter just outside the photo will cycle into the carry and the two people at the front will cycle out of the carry.

## MANAGEMENT FUNCTION

In the integrated risk management model, the fifth component involves management. It is a catch-all category that reflects what goes on behind the scenes to make the operations occur. The incident command structure is used to discuss this function. It has become the widely accepted management structure for managing the incident.

The incident command structure grew out of efforts to fight wildland fires in the early 1970s. At the time, problems existed with communications and intra- and interagency coordination. With federal funding, the incident command structure evolved, and today it is widely used in most search and rescue situations. Hudson (1992) is the source of the following discussion.

The incident command structure consists of five basic functions: command, operation, logistics, planning, and finance (figure 10.16). The command function and the incident commander are at the top of the organizational chart; the other functions work under the incident commander. Figure 10.16 shows the public information officer of an agency interfacing with the incident commander.

Hudson (1992) notes several advantages of the incident command structure. First, the system is based on the functions needed in a rescue operation. Second, it features a modular system in which the functions can vary with the size of the operations. For example, in small operations, one or more functions can be combined. As the operation expands and becomes more complex, combined functions can be separated into individual functions to meet the changing needs of the situation. In theory, the system and its organizational structure can be expanded to meet the needs of the incident being handled.

The incident command structure can be expanded or contracted as needed. The expanded structure of the incident command structure can include the incident commander, chief, director, supervisor, and leader (table 10.1). When conceptualizing the potential size and structure of a large operation, a recreation leader can review the meeting, sleeping, and eating areas of the hypothetical staging area in figure 10.4.

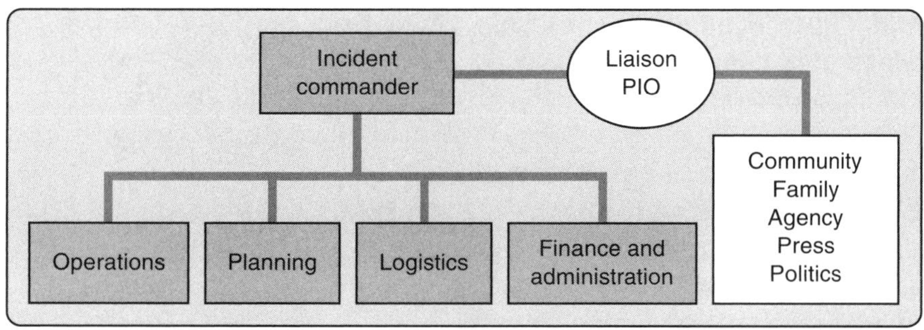


**Figure 10.16** The incident command structure consists of five components: command, operation, logistics, planning, and finance. This structure has been expanded to include a liaison with the host organization.

**Table 10.1** Functional Levels in the Incident Command Structure

| Functional level | Title of responsible person(s) |
|---|---|
| Incident command | Incident commander |
| Section | Chief |
| Branch | Director |
| Unit | Supervisor |
| Team | Leader |

*Command section.* The incident commander is responsible for all of the incident activities, including assessing the situation, preparing objectives, determining the overall strategy, conducting briefings, and working with section chiefs. Additional functions may include the safety officer, who is responsible for recognizing and identifying any hazardous and unsafe situations; the liaison officer, who handles interagency coordination; the site security manager, who is responsible for protecting personnel and property from loss and damage; and the information officer, who is responsible for releasing information about the incident to the news media.

*Operations section.* The operations section is responsible for transforming search and rescue objectives and strategies into the actual plan of action. Stoffel (2001, p. 106) notes that the operations section coordinates tactical activities, determines and orders the resources to carry out the tactical activities, and determines the plan of action to accomplish the mission of the operation. If the primary mission is a search, operations is responsible for conducting the search. If it is a rescue, operations is responsible for conducting the rescue. If it is an evacuation, operations is responsible for coordinating transport. If there is a formal incident action plan (IAP), operations is responsible for implementing it.

*Logistics section.* The logistics section is responsible for providing support services for the operation, including communications, facilities setup (e.g., sleeping, sanitation, and shower facilities), food service, and ordering, receiving, and distributing supplies and equipment. If there is a formal incident action plan (IAP), logistics is responsible for providing the necessary resources to implement it.

*Planning section.* The planning section is responsible for providing the planning functions of the operation. According to Stoffel (2001, p. 107) this includes collecting, compiling, evaluating, and disseminating information regarding what has happened, what is currently happening, and what is likely to happen in the future. For example, if operations is actively searching for the victim, the planning section is compiling information on possible evacuation routes. They are monitoring the weather and making recommendations to operations regarding changing weather conditions. If there is a formal incident action plan (IAP), planning is responsible for developing the plan.

*Finance section.* The finance section is responsible for all financial matters and analysis of the costs of the incident. This includes recording participants' time and contracting with specialist personnel. The cost of a rescue varies with the terrain and the length of the search. For example, one ski resort in California charges the victim $1,000 per hour if the victim is lost on ungroomed slopes (Eck, 2002). In most states the burden of rescue is on the taxpayers, but whenever a rescue occurs in which the victim has done something he should not have done, the discussion of who should pay for the rescue reignites.

Although the incident command structure can be expanded and contracted to meet the needs of the situation, it is generally less applicable to small-group situations, which tend to function more like a task group. Regardless, the incident command structure still represents functions or tasks of the operations.

For example, an incident command structure is often an inconvenient structure for a group of five or six paddlers or climbers involved in a rescue. A family of four who temporarily loses their child in the park or at the playground and needs to find the missing person are not thinking in terms of structuring their search using the incident command structure. They are thinking in terms of its functions. Normally, one person may take charge (incident commander), and the incident functions (operations, plans, logistics) may be assumed by this person or delegated to other members of the team as needed. The family may discuss where the child was last seen (planning), and then they plan a systematic search of the area (planning). One person will check the bathrooms, another will check the playground, and another will check the ball field. They conduct the search as planned (operations). If operations expand and more personnel are used, operations will at some point gravitate to an incident command structure. If the family does not find the child, they will call the police, and when the park personnel and police arrive on site, the search will quickly escalate into a formal incident command structure.

## SUMMARY

This chapter provides an overview of the four functions involved in managing an incident in which injury, damage, or loss occurs: the search, or finding the victim; the rescue, or removing the victim from the source of harm; medical treatment, or stabilizing the victim; and evacuation, or transporting the victim to the hospital or appropriate facility. The fifth component, management, is represented by the incident command structure. The recreation professional must remember that although one or more functions may play a minor role in some incidents, they are still present to some degree when managing any incident. Also, recreation professionals should use the information presented in this chapter as a starting point in preparing to meet the specific search, rescue, medical, and evacuation needs identified for their facility or area and should seek out more specialized sources as appropriate.

Managing the incident begins when an incident occurs, and it ends when the victim is finally transported to the hospital or appropriate institution or goes home because they are uninjured. It is important not to view the end of the incident phase as the end of the organization's involvement in the incident. It is the beginning of the postincident phase and focusing on the victim, their family, participants and staff, and the community.

# EXERCISES

## Exercise 1: Missing Persons

The purpose of this exercise is to develop a simple preplan for a missing person at your recreation facility. Imagine that you are preparing the preplan for a recreation center of your choice in an urban area. Review the text in this chapter as well as figure 10.2, which presents a preplan outline. Use the abbreviated outline listed here to create your preplan.

1. Objective or purpose
2. List of collaborative agencies
3. First notice
4. Callout
5. Medical considerations
6. Rescue and evacuations
7. Demobilization

## Exercise 2: Rescue Identification

The purpose of this exercise is to identify typical rescues that those working in a recreation facility or area might face. Choose a recreation facility or area of your choice and complete the following steps.

1. Identify the typical types of rescues for your activity, facility, or area.
2. Identify any specialized training that personnel need to have to perform the rescue.
3. Can the rescue be performed by the personnel at the facility or area, or do you need external resources? Explain why.

## Exercise 3: Mt. Hood Incident—Assessing Survivability

The purpose of the exercise is to focus on the concept of urgency as it relates to the search process. Imagine that you are the person who is in charge of assessing the survivability of the missing group in the Mt. Hood incident. Using the newspaper description in appendix A, assess the survivability of the group in terms of the following items: food and equipment, training and knowledge, and weather. Write a brief synopsis of the three categories. Based on your analysis, do you think the group has the resources needed to survive from when they started the hike to the time of rescue? This includes Monday the day of the trek, Tuesday, Wednesday, and Thursday, the day of their eventual rescue and recovery.

## Exercise 4: The Dilemma of Two Bridges

The purpose of this exercise is to address the dilemma posed by the two bridges described in figure 10.10. Assume that you are working for the resource manager of a wilderness area. Someone has proposed building a bridge in the area in order to reduce the two fatalities and five rescues that normally occur at this site during the high flows of spring. Write a brief position paper that supports either building the bridge or leaving the stream crossing as part of the experience. If you consider leaving the stream crossing, you may want to consider updating the interpretive safety sign at the entrance to warn users of the potential hazard (see chapter 5).

### Exercise 5: Interpretive Signs

The purpose of this exercise is to develop the text for an interpretive warning sign. First, review the signs in figures 10.13 *a* through *c*; use these examples as models. Next, review the entrance to the beach shown in figure 5.1. The sign you develop will most likely be placed to the side of the entrance. Third, review the discussion in this chapter regarding the items that might be included on an interpretive sign at the entrance to the swimming beach at Castlewood State Park near St. Louis, Missouri.

Write the text for the sign. Items that you might want to include are listed here. You may also create artwork and the general design of the sign.

1. Common river hazards
    - Drop-offs
    - Strainers
    - The current, which constantly moves a person downstream
    - Foot entrapments
2. Wearing a life jacket
3. Swimming diagonally to the shore if you are in current that is over your head

### Exercise 6: Managing the Scene

Think of a recreation and parks site with which you are familiar. Think of an accident that could occur there or that has already occurred. Imagine that you have just arrived at the scene. Using figure 10.14, answer the following questions.

1. Are there any other hazards present?
2. What was the mechanism of injury?
3. Did you take measures to isolate body substances? Why or why not?
4. Did you determine the total number of patients or simply focus on the primary victim?
5. Did you establish a relationship with the patient? What did you say to the victim?

Chapter 11

# Crisis Management

Crisis management is defined as the management of an incident, accident, or crisis in an effort to better inform the public, manage the response of the media, and reduce or manage the impact on the organization (Bittenbring and Paczan, 2000). The public information officer (PIO) is responsible for managing the incident for the organization by working with the media, the people in the organization involved in the incident, and the victims of the incident. This chapter reviews the basic responsibilities of a PIO in a crisis situation.

A recreation and park professional should understand the role of the PIO because he or she can be called on to assume the role of the PIO in several situations. A professional might be called on to perform the PIO's role until the PIO arrives on site and takes charge of the situation. In this case, it is particularly important to understand the principles of crisis management because the situation can easily escalate out of control during the beginning stages of a crisis. A professional may also perform the role of the PIO if the incident is too small for the organization's PIO to handle. In a small organization, the owner or the principal supervisor may serve as the PIO. By understanding the principles of crisis management, a recreation professional can better work with an organization's PIO or serve as the PIO should the need arise.

## THE NEED FOR GOOD CRISIS MANAGEMENT

The PIO is responsible for managing the incident for the organization. The PIO works with the media, the people in the organization that is involved in the incident, and the victims and the people who are actually involved in the incident. If an incident command structure is in place, the PIO works closely with the incident commander or their public-relations officer. In managing the incident for the organization, the PIO monitors and evaluates events as they unfold and evaluates and follows up on the success of their organization's efforts after the crisis.

Poorly managing the incident results in severe repercussions for the organization, such as

- poor community image,
- increased chances of litigation,
- loss of public confidence in the organization's services,
- loss of visitation and business,
- loss of political confidence and support, and
- mistrust of the organization by the media.

Normally, an organization wants to maintain its image, continue its level of service to its customers, and avoid or reduce its liability.

The public information officer (PIO) is responsible for managing the incident for the organization by working with the media, the people in the organization involved in the incident, and the victims of the incident.

Properly managing a crisis can help ensure that the organization meets these objectives.

Generally, three players are involved in crisis management: the PIO, the organization, and the media. The media may have a different agenda than the PIO and the organization. The job of the media is to report on a conflict. A good story sells newspapers and gains television viewers. The more sensational the story, the more the media sells, so they have an incentive to sensationalize an organization's crisis. The bottom line is that the media may seem like an organization's friend, but it is not.

The collection of news and its dissemination have changed significantly, and this has affected how to handle crisis management situations. It has transformed from the local television station and newspapers disseminating news once or twice a day to a 24-hour continuous news cycle on cable TV and the Internet, including bloggers. There used to be a morning newspaper that reported the overnight and previous day's news, and there was an evening newspaper that reported on the previous day's news and then the news of the day until the paper went to press. The evening news on television captured and reported the news of the day. There was a 12-hour news cycle during which the news was collected and disseminated in half-day increments. The PIO had time to interview witnesses, prepare statements, and issue a press release in time for the evening news.

In contrast, today there is a continuous news cycle. News is posted virtually as it happens on the Internet. Bloggers comment on the news two or three times within what was the old 12-hour news cycle associated with newspapers. Today, cable television will often have continuous coverage of major events. Also, those who disseminate the news have changed. In the past, it was newspapers and television stations. Today it is anyone who has a computer and access to the Internet. These changes impact how the PIO approaches the management of a crisis over traditional approaches.

## GENERAL RULES AND PRINCIPLES FOR THE PIO

The following are some general rules or principles that the PIO (or the person who is performing this role) should follow. A recreation professional will find these principles useful when working with a PIO or the media or when he has to assume the role of the PIO.

*State the facts and only the facts.* A fact is something that someone personally did or saw (e.g., "I did this" or "I saw that"). A secondary source is something that someone learned about from another person (e.g., "John told me that…" or "John said that he heard that this is what happened"). Secondary sources are not factual because they do not come from someone who personally saw or did something. They can become factual if the PIO interviews the secondary sources. The role of the PIO or the person acting in this capacity is to document the facts involved in the incident. This process will be discussed in more depth later in this chapter.

Stating the facts applies to people who are not the PIO and who are not acting in that capacity. It is useful to distinguish between events that are directly related to the incident and those that are not. In figure 11.1, the cashier states when she came to work (fact) and that she did not see the accident (fact). These facts are not directly related to the incident; they involve when she came to work. However, if what the cashier saw or did relates to the incident, one thing can lead to another and the cashier can inadvertently say too much. For this reason, some people correctly argue that the best thing to do is transfer the questioner to the PIO. In figure 11.1, the cashier smoothly and efficiently transfers the reporter to Mr. Smith, the PIO. She was polite and conversant. If the media is persistent with their questions, the person should simply repeat the transfer. The questioner will eventually get the message.

*Enforce a temporary gag order.* During an incident, an organization usually enforces a temporary gag order. Under a gag order, those involved in the incident are not allowed to talk to the media and are to transfer the questioner to the PIO. If the PIO has not yet arrived on site, a person being questioned should simply note that the PIO will handle the questions when she arrives on site. It is important to differentiate the temporary gag order from a long-term gag order. A temporary gag order is in place for the duration of the actual incident. The short duration minimizes the potential harmful effects of the gag order in terms of the ripple effect. Also, the purpose of a temporary gag order is to direct questions from the media to the PIO. If the temporary gag order transforms to a general gag order after the incident is over, problems can occur. (See chapter 13 for a discussion of the ripple effect.)

*Have only one spokesperson.* One and only one spokesperson should communicate with the media regarding the crisis. Normally, this spokesperson is the PIO; however, it can be anyone in the organization. In some situations, the PIO will wear a badge that indicates her

**Figure 11.1** The cashier states only that facts that she knows to be true. The cashier was in the cashier's office and did not see the accident occur.

position. Anyone who is questioned about the incident should transfer the questioner to the PIO, who will handle the situation.

*The incident is an unfolding event.* At the beginning of the crisis, not everything is known or it might not be appropriate to release certain information. For example, a PIO does not usually release the name of the victim until the victim's family has been notified, even though the PIO might know who the victim is. No one wants to find out from a news source that a family member was the victim of an accident.

The PIO should not be afraid to say that the information is not yet known. One is not expected to know everything in the early stages of an unfolding event. The PIO should indicate that she will make information available to the media as it becomes known, and should follow through by keeping the media up to date.

*Be proactive, not reactive.* The PIO should, if appropriate, release information as it becomes available. As a general rule, an organization cannot hide anything from the media because it will find out everything there is to know. It is better to get the information out sooner than to allow it to fester and cause problems later.

*Think sound bites.* A person being filmed for television or recorded for radio broadcast might want to consider developing some sound bites. A television sound bite is normally 10 to 15 seconds long. If a PIO can speak 20 words in 10 seconds, she is doing well. Normally, good sound bites relate directly to the PIO's talking points. Developing talking points are covered later in the chapter. Examples of good sound bites are "Our pools have a tremendous safety record. This is the first accident to occur at our pools in the past 10 years." and "Each year, park and planning spends more than $200,000 on training its personnel to be safer."

*Never go off the record.* It is easy to be lulled into thinking that something that is said off the record will not be repeated. As a rule, a PIO should assume that anything she says is on the record, even if she thinks otherwise. If the PIO does not want something to be repeated, she should not say it. Figure 11.2 depicts this temptation. In addition, the statement of the person going off the record in figure 11.2 undermines their credibility and message. If the PIO wasn't forthcoming when discussing this item publicly, should the news reporter expect the PIO to be forthcoming and honest on other items? Second, it undermines the message, because no matter what anyone says, the reporter will believe that horseplay occurred. They will believe it because it was said off the record. For this reason, it is important to have a consistent message and not go off the record.

*"No comment" is a bad comment.* "No comment" may in essence be a good policy, but it is a bad public response because it tends to imply that one is guilty or hiding something. It is not what the public wants to hear. A better response is "We do not have the information available to us at this time."

*To break a story or not to break it?* If the organization breaks the story, it is out. If the organization does not break the story and the story gets out, the organization may lose credibility with the media because it held back information. The general rule is not to break the story because if the story doesn't break, no crisis occurs. An important exception to this general rule is that an organization needs to release the story if the public may be harmed if the story is not released. For example, if an environmental spill occurs in a park, the public needs to be warned about the potential dangers in order to protect itself. To not do so will make an organization look like it is working against the public interest. The public backlash against the organization can be very harsh.

The organization should be ready to move on the story when it breaks and be prepared to release information to the media. If an organization does nothing to prepare and hopes that the media does not find out about the incident, it will most likely be in a reactive situation. When the media does find out, the organization will be digging itself out of a hole.

## MANAGING THE CRISIS

On arriving at the scene, the PIO or the person acting as the PIO must begin taking control of and managing the events surrounding the crisis. As part of this process, the PIO will

**Figure 11.2** A PIO must not fall into the trap of speaking off the record.

interview the key people, create a fact sheet, develop key objectives and talking points, and craft an official statement. As events unfold, the PIO should interview additional people as necessary, continually update the fact sheet, modify the key objectives and talking points as needed, and update the official statements or news releases.

## Interviewing Key People

Although interviewing can be a fairly sophisticated process, the PIO should consider keeping her interviewing techniques simple. The PIO should let the interviewee tell his or her story regarding what happened. Most people will tell their story chronologically, which is helpful in determining a time line. The PIO should not argue with the interviewee; the interview is not a cross-examination. However, the PIO may clarify a fact or refocus the discussion to get it back on track. The PIO should focus on who, what, where, and when, but not on why. The first four items are factual; the fifth tends to be more speculative. If the interviewee says something speculative, the PIO should make a note of it and verify it with the actual person who saw it or said it. Something is not a fact unless someone witnessed it. Finally, the PIO should note the source of the information provided. On the fact sheet in figure 11.3, the PIO notes that the source of the victim's name was from the driver's license. In addition, the PIO documented the notification source by phone.

## Fact Sheet

A PIO's task is to work with the media in order to better inform the public, manage the response of the media, and reduce or manage the impact of the incident on the organization. The fact sheet helps the PIO meet each of these three objectives of crisis management. It is a chronological listing of information as it is obtained by the PIO. Although it can include other sources of information, its primary source of information is from interviews and the information they provide. It is one of the principal sources of the information that the PIO gives to the media.

The PIO should consider recording data in a spiral notebook rather than in a three-ring binder, where pages can be added or removed. The PIO should list events chronologically as she interviews people and uncovers new information. The information can be reorganized later on. The information gained will aid in the investigation and will help the PIO determine the objectives and talking points for working with the media. The information has other uses as well. If the incident results in a legal case, the fact sheet can be obtained by counsel as part of discovery. The information can also be used as part of a systematic accident investigation (see chapter 14) or in determining the accident sequence (see chapter 5).

Figure 11.3, a fact sheet for an incident at Anytown Swimming Pool, is a chronology of events from the perspective of the interviewer. It includes the time the interviewer arrived on site and the time that the interviewer interviewed Perky Alice. It includes Alice's account of what happened and what she did. Perky claimed that she rescued the victim within one minute. The interviewer labeled it as a claim.

The media wants to know what happened and the sequence in which the events occurred. Even when a volatile or contentious environment surrounds an incident, the media needs to communicate the basic facts to its audience. Normally, the fact sheet is the foundation to separate fact from supposition, and it is sufficient to answer most of the media's questions.

## Initial Statement and Key Objectives

The fact sheet is useful in developing the initial statement and key objectives that the PIO will use as talking points. The initial statement is the first statement released to the press shortly after the incident occurs. Typically, the initial statement indicates the who, what, where, and

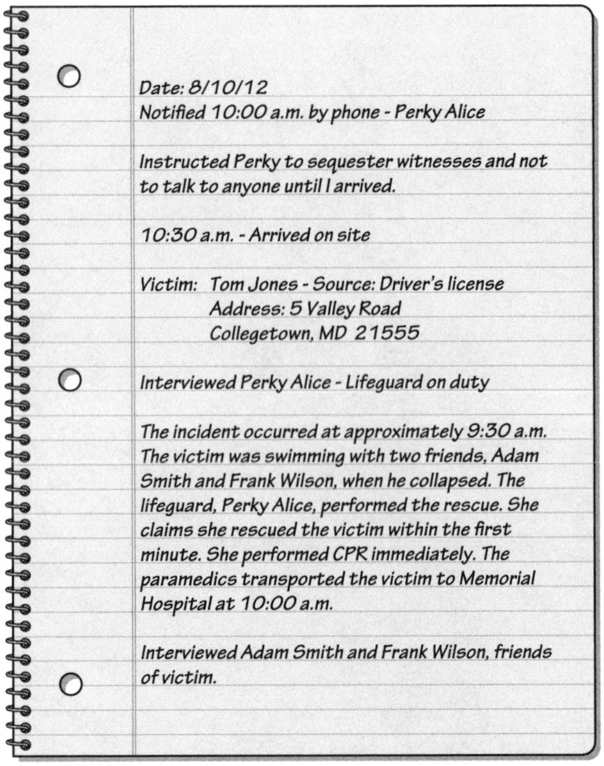

*Date: 8/10/12*
*Notified 10:00 a.m. by phone - Perky Alice*

*Instructed Perky to sequester witnesses and not to talk to anyone until I arrived.*

*10:30 a.m. - Arrived on site*

*Victim: Tom Jones - Source: Driver's license*
*Address: 5 Valley Road*
*Collegetown, MD 21555*

*Interviewed Perky Alice - Lifeguard on duty*

*The incident occurred at approximately 9:30 a.m. The victim was swimming with two friends, Adam Smith and Frank Wilson, when he collapsed. The lifeguard, Perky Alice, performed the rescue. She claims she rescued the victim within the first minute. She performed CPR immediately. The paramedics transported the victim to Memorial Hospital at 10:00 a.m.*

*Interviewed Adam Smith and Frank Wilson, friends of victim.*

**Figure 11.3** Developing a fact sheet helps a PIO determine the objectives and talking points for working with the media.

when (but not the why) of the incident (figure 11.4). In the statement in figure 11.4, the PIO does not reveal the victim's name because the family had not yet been notified. If asked to identify the victim, the PIO would normally respond that the name of the victim will be released when the family has been contacted. The PIO should then be sure to follow up and reveal the name of the victim to the media once the family has been notified.

Reviewing the fact sheets provides insights that will help the PIO develop the key objectives. In figure 11.5, the objectives are to show that the lifeguards followed procedures, that they maintained a safe environment, and that they did everything possible to rescue the victim. Another objective is to note the organization's previous safety record in an effort to reduce the impact of the accident.

Why were these objectives selected? The first objective relates to following procedure, which is always an important concern when an accident occurs. Following procedure suggests

**Figure 11.4** The initial response should include the who, what, where, and when (but not the why) of the incident.

competency on the part of the lifeguards and the organization. The PIO correctly anticipates that she might be questioned about horseplay or situations in which the lifeguards are socializing rather than lifeguarding. The second objective relates to the issue of creating a safe environment. The third and fourth objectives present the organization in a positive light. Noting the amount of training that the lifeguards receive or the overall safety record of the swimming pool addresses the safety record of the organization and gives the organization the opportunity to use the incident to sell itself to the public.

## Talking Points

Objectives can easily serve as talking points. Talking points are the points that the PIO wants to convey to the media. The PIO should try to limit objectives and talking points to no more than four or five total. The more one has, the easier it is to become confused.

Based on previous experience or from information gleaned from interviews, a PIO might be able to anticipate the questions the media will ask (figure 11.6). A review of the fact sheet will provide insights and suggestions about the types of questions the PIO might field. Most of the questions will normally address the who, what, where, and when. (The PIO should avoid responding to the questions of why.)

Metaphorically, talking points are the destination. The challenge is to get from any starting point (question asked) to one or more of the destinations (objectives and talking points). It is not as difficult a process as it might seem. The first technique is to simply restate the talking point or a variation of it. The first point (lifeguards followed procedure) lends itself to this technique. The PIO can either start or end with simply restating the point. In figure 11.7, the PIO starts with essentially restating the talking point and then explains what Perky Alice did.

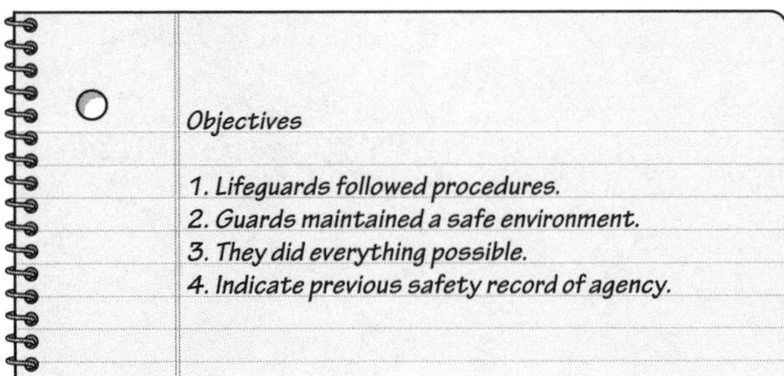


**Figure 11.5** The PIO listed four objectives that she wants to communicate to the media. These objectives easily morph into talking points.

*Anticipated Questions*

*1. Who performed the rescue?*
*2. What first aid and rescue procedures were utilized?*
*3. To which hospital was the victim transported?*
*4. Was there horseplay or other distractions?*

*1. Perky Alice*
*2. She did:*
*a.*
*b.*
*3. Victim was transported to Memorial Hospital.*

**Figure 11.6** Using the interviews, fact sheet, and personal experience, a PIO may be able to anticipate the questions the media will ask.

A second technique is to make an association between the topic being discussed or the question asked and the talking point. In the previous example the PIO is discussing what Perky Alice did and why she followed correct procedures. The PIO could easily make the jump to the fourth talking point (indicate previous safety record). Alice followed the correct procedure, in part due to the excellent training and safety program of the organization. The association or connection is made. The PIO could simply include another statement such as "Over $50,000 a year is spent on safety training. The payoff of that training is exemplified by Perky Alice's excellent rescue today."

## Official Statement

As soon as the PIO collects sufficient information, she will develop an official statement to release to the media. An official statement includes hard data regarding who, what, where, and when. In the example in figure 11.8, the incident occurred at Anytown Swimming Pool (where) at 9:30 a.m. (when). The title and text indicate that it was a near drowning (what) and involved the lifeguard, Perky Alice (who). It does not specify the victim (who) because the family has not been notified. Official statements form the foundation for what the media reports.

A press release (figure 11.9) should be printed on an organization's letterhead and should include the following components (California State Association of Counties, 1999; Colorado Nonprofit Association, 2010). Near the top, the PIO should indicate whether the release should be released right away ("FOR IMMEDIATE RELEASE") or should provide the date on which it should be released. In a crisis management situation, most releases are immediately releases. The PIO should include all relevant contact information, including multiple phone numbers and an e-mail, and even social media contact information (e.g., Twitter). Often, the media will have additional questions or may want to follow up for a feature story.

The PIO should choose a catchy title for the news release. In a crisis management situation, however, the title will usually be more utilitarian. In the news release, the title is centered between the margins. A newspaper reporter may write his own title for the article rather than use the title provided.

The press release should be brief. The first paragraph should summarize the who, what, where, and when. This can usually be accomplished in one or two sentences. The body of the release contains an expansion upon the information presented in the first paragraph.

The PIO should write the release in third-person voice (i.e., *he, she, they*); writing the release in first-person voice (i.e., *I, we*) makes the press release seem like a promotion rather than news. The primary purpose of the release is to get the information out to the media, so the PIO should keep it factual. The release should be no more than 1.5 pages of double-spaced

**Figure 11.7** The PIO avoids the quagmire associated with directly answering the question and quickly moves to addressing his first objective. By implication, he addresses the reporter's question.

## Anytown Park and Recreation Department

Anytown, Anystate

FOR IMMEDIATE RELEASE

month/day/year

Mr. Joe Smith, Public Information Officer

Office: (301) 555-1212

Cell: (301) 555-2424

E-mail: jsmith@anytown.gov.md

## Near Drowning at Anytown Swimming Pool

ANYTOWN—At 9:30 a.m., a near drowning occurred at Anytown Swimming Pool. The victim was rescued by Perky Alice, the lifeguard on duty. Alice performed CPR until the paramedics arrived. At 10:00 a.m., the paramedics from Anytown Ambulance Service transported the victim to Memorial Hospital. Further details are forthcoming as they become available.

###

**Figure 11.8** A typical news release to the media released shortly after the near-drowning incident at Anytown Swimming Pool.

**Organizational Letterhead**

FOR IMMEDIATE RELEASE (Sample News Release)

(Date) (Contact)

(Phone) (E-mail)

FOR IMMEDIATE RELEASE

**(Offer a headline suggestion)**

**News Is Whatever Is Important to the Reader, Viewer, or Listener**

(Dateline) (Lead or first sentence)
ANYTOWN—News can be defined as any issue that is important to the residents of a particular area. (See the discussion of newsworthiness.) The who, what, where, when, why, and how of a particular issue or topic are best summarized in the first or second paragraphs of a news release.

(Body copy)

News releases should be relatively short and deal with a single topic or idea. They should rarely exceed 1.5 pages in length and should always be double spaced and typed in Microsoft Word or a similar format that has been deemed acceptable. When e-mailing the news release, one should include the text of the news release in the body of the message as well as attach the release. Many people do not like opening attached files.

News releases should present the facts and background of a particular issue in descending order of importance so that the most important information is on the first page and as close to the beginning as possible.

(Summary)

Depending on the issue, quotations from relevant officials or spokespeople can be included. All news releases announcing or detailing events, meeting, or other public gatherings should include complete information about time, date, place, and people to contact. Directions and location information for events, as well as alternative phone numbers for contacts, are also useful.

### [### indicates the end]

**Figure 11.9** A structural outline and typical components of a news release.

Adapted from CSAC 1999.

text, and all abbreviations should be spelled out.

In the news business, the standard way to end a news release is with a centered ### at the bottom of the page. An alternative is to simply write *end* or ### *end* ###. If the news release is longer than a single page, the word *more* should be centered at the bottom of the first page so that the media knows that the news release continues on another page.

If it seems appropriate, a PIO can follow up with specific reporters to make sure that they have received the news release and to see whether they have any additional questions. This is particularly true in an unfolding event. In the near drowning at the Anytown Swimming Pool, the identity of the victim was not released. The PIO could release another press release or call the news reporters and update them on the victim's identity.

## Newsworthiness

In the news business, newsworthiness determines how long the crisis remains on the front page of the newspaper. The following are criteria for newsworthiness. Normally, when an organization is attempting to promote itself, it looks to these elements to make its events more newsworthy (California State Association of Counties, 1999; National Mental Health Association, 2010). Conversely, in a crisis management situation, an organization normally seeks to remove these elements to make the event less newsworthy in the hope that the crisis will go away more quickly.

*Importance.* Importance is whatever is significant to a large group or segment of the population. Importance varies by geographical area. What is important to a local community may not be important to a national audience, and what is important to a national audience may not be important to the local community. The incident with Perky Alice is most likely extremely important to the local community but of little significance nationally.

*Timeliness.* Old news is no longer news. The Perky Alice incident is timely because it just happened. In two months, the incident will no longer be timely and will be old news, unless something else occurs and makes it timely once again. An exception is the Meramec River incident discussed in chapter 5. The local newspaper ran a big spread on the deaths of the five youths on the one-year anniversary of the accident. Even though the incident was old news, the one-year anniversary made the event timely again.

*Magnitude.* Magnitude is defined in terms of amount. It could include something that affects a large number of people, or it could include a large area. A flood of the Mississippi River has greater magnitude than a flash flood on a local stream. Stealing a million dollars has greater magnitude than stealing a candy bar. The Perky Alice incident had considerable magnitude in the local community. Nationally, it was insignificant.

*Conflict.* As the title suggests, conflict results anytime two people have opposing opinions. The media commonly uses conflict to create interest among readers. No conflict occurred in the Perky Alice incident. However, if someone accused Perky Alice of horseplay, conflict would exist over the issue of whether she condoned horseplay.

*Proximity.* Proximity refers to something that hits close to home. The Perky Alice incident occurred at the local community pool, so it has proximity to the local community. The Meramec River incident discussed in chapter 5 had proximity to the St Louis, Missouri, media market because it occurred in that area. However, few people outside of that media market heard about the incident.

*Oddity.* Oddity refers to something that does not normally happen and that has a bizarre twist. The near drowning in the Perky Alice incident does not normally happen, but it does not have the element of oddity because it does not have a bizarre twist. If the victim was rescued by a nearby dog rather than by Perky Alice, the story would have the element of oddity.

*Prominence.* Prominence is similar to importance. Well-known people receive more attention than less-known people. This is why movie stars receive so much news coverage. Perky Alice does not have much prominence in the community. However, if the victim was the mayor of the community or if Perky Alice was the daughter of a prominent community member, the story would suddenly have prominence.

*Human interest.* Human-interest stories tend to have a touch of sentimentality. Often, they pull at the heart strings by focusing on what makes the person in the news story special. If Perky Alice is a local college student studying to become medical specialist, this story now has a human interest element to it because saving a person's life is what medical specialists do. There is a connection.

## MEDIA

The traditional media includes newspapers, television, and radio. Today it also includes the new media found on the Internet. This section provides some tips for effectively dealing with the media. In addition to these tips, the PIO should keep several things in mind (figure 11.10): the media should never roam anywhere unescorted, the PIO should make the reporter look good, and the PIO will need to make the reporter an expert on the subject in the brief time he is on the scene.

## Working With the Reporter: A Case Study

The second river rescue symposium was held at Great Falls on the Potomac River outside of Washington, D.C. The event attracted the Washington news media. One of the local television stations sent a crew and one of their reporters to cover the event.

As one of the organizers, one of my jobs became escorting the news reporter around the site. Normally, it is protocol to not leave reporters unescorted. If they are unescorted, no one is there to interpret what they see and they could easily misinterpret what they are viewing. Also, when reporters are escorted, the escort has an opportunity to direct their experience and to educate them about what is happening.

I quickly learned that my main job was to educate the reporter about what we were doing, both on site and nationally in boating safety. I also needed to frame the big picture for the reporter. A reporter's job is to go to events they know very little, if anything, about and become instant experts. In this respect, my role was to provide the reporter with the knowledge to make him look like an expert in the field.

I also discovered that it was my job to make the reporter look good. We decked him out in a life jacket but removed the knife. On the river, one needs to have a knife handy around ropes. Unfortunately, the knife would raise additional questions among viewers that the reporter did not have time to answer. Eliminating the knife eliminated the need to answer additional questions and it did not divert the focus of the story.

That evening on the news, the reporter presented his 30-second report decked out in his life jacket with the river in the background. He looked good and so did our event.

**Figure 11.10** A case study of working with a reporter. Had this been an actual drowning rather than a training exercise, we would have developed the same rapport with the reporter and made him look good on television.

## Hints for Dealing With the Media

Numerous dos and don'ts exist when dealing with the media during an interview or press conference. A PIO is formally trained in these techniques. In contrast, a recreation and park professional who is asked to perform the duty of a PIO will be focusing on survival rather than nuance. A person in this situation should stick to the facts and consider the following pointers.

*Repeat the question.* The PIO or person acting as PIO can ask the reporter to repeat or rephrase a question if it is unclear. This also buys the PIO time to phrase a response.

*Avoid simple yes and no responses.* When one answers a question with a simple *yes* or *no* response, the response is viewed as being abrupt or even curt. For example, a reporter asks, "I heard that Perky Alice was socializing with a male friend, which resulted in her being distracted when performing the rescue. Is this true?" The PIO's response is a simple *no* followed by a long pause. Murmurs ripple across the group of reporters. It is not what the PIO said, it is what the PIO did not say. Even though one can respond with a simple *yes* or *no*, a better response is *no* followed by the talking point that Perky Alice followed procedure and that she initiated the rescue in a timely manner.

*Answer one question at a time.* Reporters often ask multifaceted questions that comprise several subquestions. By asking a confusing question, the reporter loses control of the question and the PIO can respond in several ways. She can answer the last subquestion first, answer the most important question, reframe the question to suit her response, or answer the question that best relates to her talking points. After giving a response, the PIO can simply move on to the next question or can ask the reporter whether the question had another part. Regardless, the PIO should answer one question at a time to maintain focus and should be courteous and polite to the reporter.

*Turn negatives into positives.* When responding to questions, the PIO should take the high road rather than the low road and should think positively. Rather than providing a response such as "No, we would never do that," which is reactive and defensive, the PIO can provide a response such as "We have initiated a new policy" or "Our current procedure is…." These responses may not be truly proactive, but they move the conversation in a positive direction.

*Say what you mean.* A PIO should be careful of leading questions (e.g., "Would you say…"). A person skilled in this questioning technique can often lead a PIO down a path where, in the end, the questioner has the PIO agreeing with something she does not really agree with. The PIO may agree with three fourths of the question, but the problem lies in the part that she does not agree with. A PIO in this situation should take control of the question and say what she means. Figure 11.7 illustrates the PIO taking control of the question and directing the response to one or more of the talking points.

*Avoid hypothetical questions.* A PIO faced with a hypothetical (i.e., "What if…") question should stick to the facts. Explaining what will unfold in the future is not necessarily making a hypothesis; it is merely explaining what will happen. Although it is easier said than done, the PIO can simply respond that the question is hypothetical and that she cannot answer it. Or she can indicate that a policy or procedure in place should address the hypothetical question.

*Correct inaccuracies.* The PIO should correct inaccuracies when they become known. Inaccuracies normally occur because a news story is unfolding and new and more accurate information is discovered. Sometimes inaccuracies can arise because the media chooses to editorialize on the facts. At the beginning of a press conference, the PIO should state the pertinent facts and avoid any political editorializing.

*Do not let your guard down.* The PIO should never go off the record and should avoid hypothetical questions and speculation. The PIO must stick to the facts and objectives or talking points.

*Do not linger.* A crisis is an unfolding event, and information becomes available as the event unfolds. When meeting with the press, the PIO can announce the new information and indicate that the event is unfolding and that she will present more information as it becomes available. Normally, she will announce at the beginning of the press conference that she won't be taking questions. After presenting the new information, she can then leave. If appropriate, the PIO can take a question or two, but she should not linger—it will only invite more questions that she cannot answer. Usually taking one or two questions during an unfolding event suggests to anyone watching on TV that the PIO is being responsive to the media. Close inspection of the questions usually reveals that the question being asked has already been addressed or the question can't be addressed because the event is unfolding, the answer is not yet known, and it can't be answered because it would be speculative.

## Press Conference

As the crisis unfolds, the PIO may need to hold a press conference. In a crisis management situation, an organization may not have the luxury of preplanning the press conference. For example, the Perky Alice incident unfolded quickly and the PIO first met with the press at the swimming pool. The Colorado Nonprofit Association (2010) suggests the following regarding the setting and the format of a press conference.

### Setting

The press conference should be held in a room that is not too large. Empty seats imply lack of interest. If the press conference takes place at the site of the incident, the PIO should select a site that is away from incident command center. The PIO and the press both have needs. The following items are useful when holding a press conference:

- Podium
- Speaker system (if needed)
- Microphone stand on podium

- Backdrop (blue, if possible)
- Chairs for media (theater style with large center aisle)
- Easels (if needed)
- Electric outlets
- Table for media sign-up
- Water

If the conference is being held in a noncontrolled setting (i.e., not against a blue background), the PIO should examine the background for anything that is potentially inappropriate. The media and the camera can easily focus on background activity. For example, if some lifeguards or even patrons are playing around in the background of the press conference for the Perky Alice incident, the camera will capture the scene and set the organization up for criticism for permitting horseplay at the pool. If the PIO chooses to stand in front of a bulletin board, she should inspect what is on the bulletin board and temporarily remove anything that might be viewed as inappropriate. A no horseplay poster suggests horseplay and should be removed.

### Format

If appropriate, the PIO can open the press conference with a brief statement that provides an update of events, corrects errors, or clarifies misunderstandings. Because events are unfolding, not all information may be known at the time of the conference. Depending on circumstances, the PIO may end the conference at the end of the statement. If the PIO plans to end the conference in this manner, it is normally appropriate to indicate at the beginning of the statement that questions will not be taken.

If the PIO does take questions from the media, the questions will follow the opening statement. The PIO should review the section of this chapter on what to say and what to avoid and should refer to the fact sheet and integrate facts into the talking points when possible. A PIO must also think of the needs of the media. Radio and television need sound bites, and newspapers need more information. News releases are helpful to the media.

The end of the press conference is often determined by the information presented and the questions asked. Normally, if the media starts asking similar questions or questions seeking similar information, it is a signal to begin moving quickly to the end the conference. Ending a conference is sometimes as much an art as it is a science.

## Radio

Radio is known as a hot medium. A person speaking on the radio creates word pictures in the minds of the listeners. A person's voice is the key to keeping the interest and attention of a radio audience.

When speaking on the radio, a person can use notes. He should lay the notes out in front of him and take care to not rustle pages. Also, he must be careful to not sound monotone when reading from notes. If the radio station is simultaneously broadcasting a video image, the speaker might approach the situation as if he were on television and forego using notes.

Bittenbring and Paczan (2000) provide the following suggestions for delivering a message on the radio.

- Keep the message direct and to the point.
- Listen to the question and respond with short answers. Listeners have short attention spans. Use short sentences, simple vocabulary, and a variety of voice modulation.
- If possible, get interview questions before interviews.
- Notes can be used on radio, but avoid rattling papers or reading.
- Speak slowly. Short answers do not require talking fast.

## Television

Television is image oriented. It is considered a cool medium, meaning that a person speaking in normal tones may sound dull, boring, and monotone. On television, a person needs to be animated but not too animated.

Bittenbring and Paczan (2000) and Stewart (2004) suggest the following guidelines on dressing for a television appearance. A PIO who is in doubt about what to wear can emulate what other professionals on television do or seek advice from people who have experience in the medium.

- Consider using makeup, particularly if you are under the lights for some time.
- Men: Do not fold your hands on your lap.
- Women: Cross your legs or hold them together.
- Dress conservatively; a uniform is best.
- Men: Wear a dark suit, solid shirt, and conservative tie.
- Women: Wear a simple suit or dress.
- Avoid patterns, horizontal lines, busy prints, and lots of jewelry.
- Avoid facial piercings.
- Wear classic colors such as grays, blues, and lighter shades (but not white).
- Check your appearance before the interview.
- Wear nonglare glasses. Photo-sensitive glass darkens under camera lights and hides the eyes.
- Wear a good watch. A small, tasteful amount of jewelry is okay.
- Have groomed nails that look natural.

Walker and Todtfeld (2007) provide the following list of dos and don'ts for looking more natural on camera.

- Do lean forward in your seat. It makes you look leaner than you really are.
- Do not lean back and relax in your seat. You will look 20 to 30 pounds heavier.
- Smile for the camera.
- Move your head. All actors do.
- Keep your tongue in your mouth.
- Do not lick your lips.
- If you gesture naturally when you talk, gesture.
- Avoid butterfly arms (i.e., excessive gesturing and movement with the arms).

## Blogs, Facebook, and Other Internet Media

Blogs, social media, smart phones, and the Internet are often called the new media. The Internet offers instant access to news and is updated 24 hours a day. Often, by the time an incident hits the 6:00 evening news, it is old news on the new media.

Internet media is increasingly becoming a source of information. Usually, the news media has access to the same information that everyone else does. A PIO can prepare for managing a crisis by reviewing the Facebook or blogs of people involved in the incident. For example, a PIO knows that alcohol was allegedly involved in the incident. The PIO visits the Facebook page of the victim involved in the incident and finds numerous photos of the victim holding alcoholic beverages. The victim also has red eyes that are not from the camera flash. The PIO should not be surprised if the press has also reviewed this site and asks about the victim's drinking behavior.

Social media sites, blogs, and personal websites are also becoming purveyors of news. People write blog posts or Facebook status updates shortly after receiving information. Recreation and park departments use Facebook to disseminate their messages. A PIO needs to follow the story online as well as in the newspaper.

Organizations are increasingly expected to disseminate stories online. PIOs may be expected to write a blog post regarding what the organization is doing in response to the crisis. In the future, the formal news release may give way to an organization's website as the source of information for the traditional media.

## SUMMARY

The PIO for an agency is responsible for, among other things, managing a crisis. PIO is a specialized role that requires professional training. All recreation professionals should understand the role of the PIO because anyone may be asked to perform the tasks of the PIO at any time. This chapter provides some helpful tips on working with the media in a crisis management situation.

# EXERCISES

## Exercise 1: The Evening News

The purpose of this exercise is to assess how people present themselves on television. Watch a television personality (e.g., newscaster) of your choice and answer the following questions.

1. Overall, how effective is the person's presentation?
2. Does the person lean forward in the chair? Or does he or she slouch and lean back in the chair?
3. Does the person move his or her head?
4. Does the person make arm gestures?
5. Does the person smile? Does he or she smile even when a smile might not be warranted?
6. Close your eyes and focus on what the person is saying. Listen to the person's tone, inflection, and volume. What conclusions can you make about how they say what they say?

## Exercise 2: Talk Radio

The purpose of this exercise is to determine the effectiveness of presenting information on the radio. Choose a talk radio host. Listen to the host's presentation and respond to the questions below. If the host's presentation is also available on video, listen to the radio presentation and then watch the video and compare the two.

1. How animated is the voice of the talk radio host? Compare it with the voice of a television celebrity on the evening news in the previous exercise.
2. Is the host's message direct and to the point, or does he or she ramble?
3. Does the host use notes?
4. Does the host tend to speak more slowly than people in a normal conversation or the television celebrity in the previous exercises?
5. If you watched the video, did the host's gestures and movement seem more animated than normal? Which presentation was more appropriate: radio or video?

## Exercise 3: The Press Conference

The purpose of this exercise is to analyze how a PIO or press officer interacts with the press. Choose a press conference that is being broadcast on television. Using the information in this chapter, analyze the press conference in terms of the following factors.

1. Was the dress of the press officer appropriate?
2. What were the talking points, if any, of the press officer?
3. Did the press office lead with a statement? Was it effective? Did he or she follow with questions from the press? Did the press officer cut off the questions at what seemed like an appropriate time? Explain why.
4. Was the press officer effective in delivering the message? Why or why not?

## Exercise 4: Mt. Hood Incident—Crisis Management

The purpose of this exercise is to gain some experience as a PIO by addressing changing circumstances of an evolving situation. The article titled "High Achievers' Climb to Death" (appendix A) provides a good chronicle of an evolving crisis. Write a news release and develop three talking points to use in each of the press conferences. If you wish, you can use another incident in place of the Mt. Hood incident.

### Monday

It is 7:00 p.m. on Monday. The group split up and five members of the group have returned. The remaining 10 climbers have not returned by the designated time. You have a potential problem, and you know very little about what has transpired. You are at the school. Write a news release that states what you know at this time, and write three talking points. *Note:* The article provides details about what was happening on the trip that you would not know at this time. You can use the details to hypothesize what the hikers might be doing in an emergency. For example, you can hypothesize that the hikers might build a snow cave.

### Tuesday

It is 5:00 p.m. on Tuesday. The climbers have not been found or rescued. You are now on site at the U.S. Forest Service headquarters and in close proximity to the ongoing rescue operations. Summers and a student (Molly Schula) have stumbled back into Timberline. You are going to update the press. Develop a news release that states what you know at this time. List three talking points that you would emphasize in your press conference.

### Wednesday

It is 12:00 p.m. on Wednesday. Three students have been found in the snow and their deaths confirmed. In addition, five students returned Monday evening and Summers and Schula returned on Tuesday morning. This leaves eight people unaccounted for. You are updating the press regarding the recent developments. Develop a news release that states what you know at this time. List three talking points that you would emphasize in your press conference.

### Friday

It is 7:00 a.m. on Friday. Eight victims have been transported to the hospital. Six of them are pronounced dead and two are revived. You are still at the U.S. Forest Service headquarters. The search and rescue operations are winding down and events will focus on the recovery of the survivors in the hospital. Write a news release that is appropriate for this time. List at least three talking points that you would emphasize during your press conference.

# Chapter 12

# Supporting the Victim and the Family

Once an incident occurs, a relationship exists between a recreation leader or organization and both the victim and the victim's family. The leader or organization must address this relationship and develop a connection with the victim and the family regardless of whether such a relationship is desired. If the leader or organization fails to recognize this connection and to help people through their grieving process, they will inevitably have problems, including getting sued.

Most of the discussion in the literature involving the victim and the victim's family seems to involve lawsuits. Most people tend to sue for reasons other than monetary compensation. Often, individuals or organizations are sued because they did not provide ongoing support to the victim and the victim's family. Preventing a lawsuit is always important. However, addressing the needs of the victim and the family is also a matter of good ethics.

The primary case study in this chapter is the Dzialo case (see chapter 1). While participating in a summer camp-type experience (Team Adventure) provided by Greenfield Community College, Adam Dzialo had a near-drowning experience that left him permanently impaired. After the incident, the lawyer for the college placed a gag order on everyone, so no one could talk about the incident with anyone else. In part, the gag order and the barrier it created between the victim's family and the college eventually resulted in the lawsuit against the college.

## IMPORTANCE OF PROVIDING SUPPORT TO VICTIMS AND THEIR FAMILIES

The victim and the victim's family are the injured party. If a fatality has occurred, the family bears the brunt of the loss. Recovering from the injury is important for the victim, but how he is treated is important too. If the victim or family perceives that an organization does not care about them, they get angry and they are apt to sue.

This conclusion is supported by the literature. In the health field, Vincent et al. (1994) surveyed 227 patients and relatives who were taking legal action. They found that more than 70 percent of respondents indicated that the incident for which they were suing had long-term effects on their work, social life, and family relationships. Although the original injury was significant in their decision to sue, insensitive handling of the situation and poor communications after the original incident also affected their decision to sue. Of those surveyed, 39 percent reported that they would not have sued had they received an explanation and an apology. Another 18 percent indicated that a correction of the mistake would have prevented litigation, and 15 percent indicated that an admission of negligence would have prevented litigation. Only 18 percent of the respondents sought monetary compensation.

Ajango (2005), referencing a Porter–Novelli public opinion poll quoted in Henry (2000), notes that people sued 75 percent of the time when an organization refused to accept responsibility for its role in an accident and 71 percent of the time when they felt that the organization had given them incomplete or inaccurate information. Hickson et al. (1992) found similar results. Nine out of ten people surveyed about why they sued agreed with the statements "So that it would not happen to anyone else" (91 percent), "I wanted an explanation" (91 percent), and "I wanted the doctors to realize what they had done" (90 percent). Approximately two thirds of the people agreed with the statements "Because I was angry" (65 percent) and "So that the doctor would know how I felt" (68 percent).

Moss (2008) echoes this theme when he discusses the disconnect between the plaintiff and defendants in lawsuits. In discussing the Dzialo case, he notes that the only thing the court can provide is money. Unfortunately, the plaintiff wants more than money. According to Vincent et al. (1994), 81 percent of the respondents seeking litigation wanted an explanation, admission, or correction of the problem. In contrast, 18 percent sought monetary compensation. Moss notes that plaintiffs rarely ask for money in their statements. They want answers.

The Dzialo case and the case outlined in figure 12.1 provide an interesting juxtaposition regarding addressing the concerns of the victim and the victim's family. In the Garrett College case (formerly Garrett Community College), the college avoided a suit by addressing the emotional needs of the victim and his family. The faculty and administrators made a connection and developed a relationship. By providing the family with information and keeping them in the loop, they avoided a lawsuit that very easily could have happened. In contrast, in the Dzialo case, Greenfield Community College had an emergency action plan in place to handle such situations. Unfortunately, their lawyer ignored the emergency action plan and placed a gag order on everyone. In discussing the Dzialo case, Moss (2008) notes several of the objections that the Dzialo family had regarding the lack of communications with Greenfield Community College. These statements are representative of why people often sue. Compare the statements with the findings of Vincent et al. (1994) regarding the health care industry, discussed earlier.

1. "They wanted to know why they were not notified first by college officials but nearly two hours later by the hospital where their son was taken for treatment."
2. "The Dzialos say they have gotten little response from officials at the Massachusetts college."
3. "...And to help educate the community about camp safety."
4. "But they say what they really want is an apology from the institution."
5. "'Instead of dealing with all these issues of honesty, they would rather protect their mortar and bricks,' says Adam's father, Philip A. Dzialo."
6. "'I'm hoping that there is enough community response that the college will say, Because these are our consumers, we should sit down with these people and hear what they have to say,' he says."

It does not matter whether a leader or organization makes the connection because it is the right thing to do, because they are empathetic, or because they want to reduce the likelihood of a lawsuit. The end result is the same. A connection must be made.

## DEALING WITH THE ANGER OF THE VICTIM AND THE VICTIM'S FAMILY

In *On Death and Dying*, Kübler-Ross (2005) describes the five well-known stages of griev-

## The Other GCC

A student participated in a triathlon event sponsored by Garrett College (formerly Garrett Community College, or the other GCC). While wearing a whitewater helmet during a mountain biking leg of the triathlon, the student ran off the trail and went over the handlebars. He suffered a severe concussion and was in a coma for several days. He was hospitalized for several weeks, but he eventually made a full recovery.

The question is, why did he not sue? On the surface, he had a potentially winnable case in which the organizers allowed a rider to use improper equipment. Whitewater helmets are not normally designed for bicycle use. Also, proximate cause existed between the extensive head injuries and the use of the whitewater helmet. Initial analysis suggested potential negligence, yet the student did not sue. In fact, suing was never really a consideration.

Immediately after the accident, the faculty in the adventure sports program implemented their emergency action plan. They met with and consoled the student's family. They traveled to Ohio several times to visit the student and his family in the hospital. They maintained communications with the family and with the victim as he regained consciousness and as he eventually improved. They were sorry for what happened, but they acted without admitting guilt.

**Figure 12.1** In this case, the college made a connection and developed a relationship with the victim and his family. It may have helped prevent a lawsuit against the college.

ing: denial, anger, bargaining, depression, and acceptance. When injury, damage, or loss occurs, the victim's family members are swimming in emotions, and anger is one of the main emotions in which they immerse themselves. The anger can manifest in many ways. The family members may be angry at themselves because they believe they should have done something differently. Or they may become angry with the organization that provided the experience because they perceive that it caused the harm.

Hickson et al. (1992) indicate that 67 percent of the people in their study agreed with the statement that they sued because they were angry. Left unchecked, the anger phase in the grieving process motivates people to direct their anger outward. Their grief festers. A lawsuit can easily become the manifestation of the family's grief and their directed anger.

A recreation professional can often mitigate the anger of the victim and the victim's family by addressing their questions, empathizing with them, and grieving with them. By merely being there for them, a recreation professional can help reduce the amount of anger addressed at him or his organization and help the family transition through the anger phase of the grieving process.

Compare the Dzialo case with the case described in figure 12.1. By becoming involved with the victim and the family and being part of their grieving process, the faculty of Garrett College helped mitigate the family's anger. In contrast, in the Dzialo case, their lawyer decided after the incident to institute a gag order. The Dzialo family became angry and they sued.

## EMERGENCY ACTION PLAN

An emergency action plan includes steps a recreation or organization should take before, during, and after an incident. The organization must tailor the plan to meet its specific circumstances and needs. The recreation and park environment varies greatly and includes recreation centers and playgrounds that are located in close proximity to hospitals as well as large outdoor areas that are located far from emergency and rescue personnel. Or a recreation program may include travel. In this case, the emergency action plan should be flexible and based on the various locations of the program.

## Preincident

Preincident preparation sets the tone for how a recreation professional reacts during an actual incident, when events tend to unfold quickly. The first line of defense is to develop and implement policies that delineate the responsibilities of the organization and the participants in an emergency. For example, in the situation described in figure 12.2, the school could have included a disclaimer in their literature that if a student is required to return home for any reason (e.g., arrest, medical incident, disciplinary action, family emergency), the family bears the cost. The policy is clear, easily understood, and leaves little doubt about who is responsible.

Sometimes it is important to see the bigger picture rather than the small picture of the costs involved. It is easy to determine in the preincident planning process that participants cover all costs and to include such a disclaimer in the literature. A lawyer would even agree that such action is prudent. However, when setting policies, a recreation professional must consider what is fair and appropriate. One should ask "If I were in a similar situation, what would I want the organization to do?" For example, in the situation in figure 12.1, the college could have made the student and her family pay for the flight home. It would have been appropriate for them to do so. However, by absorbing the cost of the flight, they were looking at the bigger picture and the long-term benefits. The student stayed in the program and went on the trip the following year. The school made more revenue than they would have otherwise. However, of equal importance is the goodwill that the school maintained.

Discussion groups or class sessions with staff are often quite useful during the preplanning process. Topics might include what to say and what not to say, developing rapport with the family, selecting the setting where the interaction occurs, how to express sympathy without admitting guilt, and who should and should not meet with the family. An organization might develop general protocols as part of these discussions. For example, an organization might decide that it is okay for the person involved in the incident to meet with the family, but only when accompanied by one or two other staff who can help keep the person involved from becoming overwhelmed and cornered with questions.

Role-playing exercises complement discussion groups and class sessions. Most search and rescue exercises include dealing with family members. Role-playing exercises could include the Stokes litter exercise in the next section, which focuses on dealing with the victim as part or the incident, or it could include role playing meeting with the victim and the victim's family in the hospital after the incident. These exercises can help recreation professionals hone skills regarding what to say and what not to say to family members. For example, in a role-playing exercise, the victim is dying and the family senses that he is dying. He looks up at his rescuer and asks, "Am I dying?" The rescuer knows from role-play training that one does not lie to the victim. On the other hand, one does not tell the victim that he is dying and the rescuer is most likely not qualified or in the position to make the diagnosis. Rather than responding "yes," which would be inappropriate, the rescuer responds based on his training with "The emergency people will arrive shortly and we will transport you to the hospital." The rescuer's reply helps the victim focus on the future rather than what is happening to him at the moment.

One cannot preplan for all contingencies. A recreation professional needs to determine or estimate the probability of the event occurring. For example, in the situation in figure 12.2, we discussed whether to take a computer on future trips in case we need to make flight reservations again. We decided against it because the probability of needing the computer was low. It was useful for only two days on a fourteen-day trip, and it was another item to carry in a crowded van. However, the same benefits could be obtained with a smart phone.

## Incident

The first concern immediately after an incident occurs is dealing with the victim, the family, or both on site. Developing a rapport with the victim or the family at the scene of the inci-

## The Flight Home

On the 2009 canoe trip to the Everglades over the winter intersession, a major incident reinforced the concept of establishing a basic plan of what to do in case of emergency.

After a long drive, the group left Florida City for Flamingo in the Everglades. They were ahead of schedule, so they played tourist and stopped at several visitor sites along the main road. One of the students, Alison, was playing with a knife. She was warned against it, but she continued and sliced her thumb to the bone. We did an about-face and headed back to Florida City, and Alison had her thumb stitched up.

The question was what to do. Essentially, the instructors had three choices. First, they could take Alison with them. However, they quickly eliminated that option because she could not paddle a canoe and she was not supposed to get the wound wet. Taking her on a trip to the wet and bacteria-rich environment of the Everglades was out of the question. Second, they could end the trip, turn around, and head home. Had this incident happened a day or two out in the Everglades, this would have been the most likely option. Third, they could send Alison home. They quickly concluded that the best option was to fly her home.

An instructor called director of the program at the college to coordinate our activities. After discussing the logistics involved in making reservations, getting her to the airport, and having someone pick her up at the airport, the topic quickly turned to who would pay for the $400 flight home. The director made the case that Alison should bear the costs because the accident was her fault. The instructor suggested that it might be in his best interest to absorb the costs. The $400 was an incidental cost compared with the cost of getting sued by angry parents. Also, if Alison or her parents became disgruntled, Alison might transfer to another school and the school would lose the revenue of her tuition. Last, by assuming the costs, the program would gain considerable goodwill from the parents. It was not a question of right or wrong; it was a question of what was prudent.

The group went to a coffee shop in Florida City, borrowed a computer from a patron, and made flight reservations. The instructor drove Alison to the airport in Miami the next day. Meanwhile, during the layover day in Florida City, the group practiced paddling strokes and prepared for their trip. Alison arrived home safely, and they left Florida City on schedule the next day for a 10-day trip in the Everglades.

Alison stayed in school. She went on the Everglades trip with them the next year. The program needed to reconsider its policy regarding who would pay for a student returning home for reasons other than disciplinary issues.

**Figure 12.2** Preincident planning is important. Having a policy that requires a student to pay for the return flight home because of medical reasons is a prudent policy. However, when looking at the bigger picture, if the college pays for the flight home, they may develop goodwill that more than offsets the cost of the flight home.

dent is essential because it sets the tone for the relationship. Good rapport can easily continue into the postincident phase at the hospital or when meeting with the family at their home or another facility.

At some point, one needs to notify the victim's next of kin that an incident has occurred. Those involved in the incident must decide who will notify the family, when in the process is it appropriate to notify them, and what information to communicate to them. For example, in the situation in figure 12.2, we did not contact the family immediately because they could not assist in rendering emergency care and their involvement at that point would have slowed down what needed to be done. In contrast, in the Dzialo case, the family complained because the college waited two hours to notify them of the incident.

Developing rapport with the victim begins at the incident. Depending on the situation, a recreation professional may be asked to work with the victim. The victim knows she is injured and may be in pain. Taking care of the victim's emotional and psychological needs is important because it gives the victim comfort, aid, information, and reassurance. In the Stokes litter story (figure 12.3), for a brief period of time the friend was the victim's primary connection to the outside world. If the friend is from the organization involved in the incident, the friend begins establishing the relationship and postincident rapport with the victim and the family.

## A Stokes Litter Experience

If you want to know what it is like to be a victim, volunteer to be the victim in a mock rescue exercise. The following is Dr. Kauffman's reflection on such an experience.

I had a compound fracture of my leg and other internal injuries. Hearing is the last sense to go. I could hear the whispers of the rescuers as they discussed my injuries. I had fallen off a ledge in a climbing accident. They had me in a Stokes litter (see photo), so I knew that I was in bad shape. A Stokes litter immobilizes the patient and helps move him to a location from where he can be transported to a hospital.

I was the center of attention for a small group of rescuers who seemed to work methodically on me. They covered me on the top and bottom with blankets, yet I still had a chill. They placed a

Photo courtesy of Robert B. Kauffman.

In a Stokes litter, the victim is immobile, helpless, and at the mercy of the rescuers.

(continued)

**Figure 12.3** Experiencing the role of a victim will help a recreation professional be more sympathetic and understanding when interacting with a victim.

collar around my neck and bandaged my head to immobilize it. All I could do was strain my eyes to see what was going on. I could see a small group talking a couple yards away from the Stokes litter. They must have been talking about me because I was the only victim. Even though it was a mock exercise, not knowing what was going on sent another chill up my back and made me even more scared.

No one needed to tell me that my injuries were severe. I could feel the pain. Some people were feeling my feet and asking me questions, and others were touching all parts of my body and asking me if I was in pain. Of course I was in pain. I had just fallen from a ledge. They removed some of the blankets and rotated the Stokes onto its side so that I could pee. Although I was in pain, I felt as though people were watching as I relieved myself.

I was helpless. The rescuers were in total control. If I had an itch on my forehead, someone had to scratch it for me. If they bumped me into a tree, I felt it. If someone made a mistake, I heard the expletive and tried to guess what it referred to. I was scared and confused, and I took in just enough information to fuel my imagination about what might be wrong. I was helpless and alone as I stared up at the sky and the tree branches above me.

This is what it was like until Joe arrived. Joe's purpose was to be my friend and to tend to my emotional and welfare needs. He talked to me and asked me how I felt. I could tell that he was monitoring my alertness to determine whether my state of consciousness changed. He asked me my name, where I lived, if I had any medical conditions, and a lot of other background information that I do not remember.

He kept me informed. He told me what they were doing. If they took my vitals, he let me know that they were taking my vitals. He would even ask me if he could touch me before he actually touched me. He was considerate and respectful. He could touch me whenever he wanted because I was completely helpless to do anything about it, but he respected me in my helpless state. Although he kept me informed, he did not tell me everything. He did not tell me about my medical situation.

His voice was calming and he spoke in a soothing tone. He did not get excited. He made eye contact with me as often as he could and he smiled. Although we joked about my situation, he always avoided telling me how bad my injuries were. He spoke of and attempted to focus my thoughts on the future. He informed me of what others were doing to me or doing to care for me. If I asked him about my injuries, he focused the discussion on how we were getting out of there. He was my link to the world around me.

They transported me out of the woods and the exercise was over. This role reversal taught me to think about the plight of the victim. The victim knows that he is injured and that he is in bad shape. In this respect, they kept me informed but they did not tell me everything. The friend who accompanied me on the rescue and transport made it more bearable. The presence of the friend probably did not change the medical outcome of the situation, but his presence helped me to survive emotionally, even in this mock rescue situation.

**Figure 12.3** *(continued)*

According to the literature (Hardee, 2003; Henry, 2000; Keller and Carroll, 1994; Platt, 1992; Small, 2008; Weissmann et al., 2006), an important doctor–patient issue in developing patient rapport is *empathetic communication*. Although differences and limitations exist between the behavior of a doctor and of rescue personnel, some of the principles are directly applicable to the recreation and park setting. Traditionally, the doctor diagnoses the patient and prescribes treatments. The doctor must explain the diagnoses and treatments empathetically. In contrast, in an emergency situation in the recreation and parks field, a rescuer's role is to collect important information from the victim (e.g., name, address, next of kin, and medical history) in an empathetic manner. The rescuer can also divert the victim's attention to things other than the immediate emergency. When tending to a victim during an incident, a rescuer often has a lot of time to occupy. The conversation can easily end because, after discussing the situation, there is nothing new to discuss. Discussing hobbies or personal interests can develop immediacy and take the focus off the victim's injury. It also helps develop rapport with the victim during and after the incident.

When dealing with a one-on-one situation with the victim or the victim's family, a recreation professional should consider the following points, which integrate many of Small's (2008) principles for improving one's bedside manner (figure 12.4).

- Learn empathetic communications, including warmth, immediacy, genuineness, and empathy.
- Respect the person's body and their personal space.
- Keep communications focused and to the point.
- Spend as much time with the victim or the family as necessary.
- Do not admit guilt.
- Do not lie to the victim or the family. Simply redirect the conversation.

*Learn empathetic communications.* Empathetic communications include Small's (2008) traits of warmth, immediacy, genuineness, and empathy (figure 12.4). Warmth includes speaking empathetically and in soft tones and focusing on voice inflection. It is not always what one says that makes the difference, but rather how one says it. Warmth also includes nonverbal communications, such as making eye contact with the victim. A rescuer should avoid looking down at the victim. For example, a youth with a broken arm is sitting on a chair. Rather than standing over the youth in a superior position when speaking to her, the rescuer should physically lower himself to her level by sitting on a chair or kneeling down. Genuineness is acting sincerely and in an authentic manner rather than acting phony or defensive. Genuineness is conveyed largely through nonverbal communications and mannerisms. Normally, one's interest in and willingness to assist the victim conveys the trait of genuineness to the victim. Empathy normally relates to one's ability to relate to or feel for the victim's plight. In the Stokes litter example, the friend may briefly mention that he had been strapped into the Stokes litter during a mock exercise. This implies that he understands the discomfort and plight of the victim because he has been there.

*Respect the person's body and their personal space.* Before touching the victim, the rescuer should ask permission or tell the victim that he is about to touch her. For example, if a youth has a broken arm, rather than just reaching out to inspect the arm, the rescuer should ask the victim for permission (e.g., "I need to look at your arm, alright?" or "May I look at your arm?").

*Keep communications focused and to the point.* Small (2008) calls this *concreteness,* or the act of getting to the specific details of relevant concerns. A rescuer should always be personable but to the point. For example, the youth with the broken arm is in pain and does not want the rescuer to splint his arm. A concrete response is "I need to splint your arm to stabilize it. I need to do it now. Please don't fight me. You will feel better after I splint it." The message is "You will feel better after I splint it." In keeping communications focused and to the point, occasionally a rescuer may need to be confrontational and make the victim take responsibility or address the situation at hand. In the previous example, the rescuer is confronting the youth and telling her that he has to splint her arm and that he has to do it now.

*Spend as much time with the victim and the family as necessary.* In the literature (Hardee, 2003; Henry, 2000; Keller and Carroll, 1994; Platt, 1992; Weissmann et al., 2006), spending time with the victim and the family is normally a doctor–patient concern because doctors often deal with a backlog of patients and a hurried schedule. They simply do not have large amounts of time to spend with each patient. This is less of a problem in most recreation and park settings. Regardless, if a recreation professional is going to spend limited time with the victim or the family, he should announce it at

## Improving Bedside Manner

*Warmth:* Being warm and open-hearted in one's reception of another. In conversation, one often demonstrates warmth through eye contact, tone of voice, and smile.
*Immediacy:* Direct awareness in the present moment. Involves taking the emphasis off of the content of the problem and focusing on the process of what is going on between one's self and the victim.
*Genuineness:* Sincere authenticity and willingness to be one's self. Acting in ways that are not phony or defensive. No discrepancy exists between one's outer behavior, including what one says, and inner feelings.
*Empathy:* The capacity for participating in or vicariously experiencing another's feelings, volitions, or ideas in both content and context. In conversation, the ability to perceive or feel another's experience and to then communicate that perception back to the individual so that he feels understood.
*Respect:* Noticing with considerate attention the views and feelings of another, and displaying high regard for every person, even those whose culture, lifestyle, or habits differ greatly from one's own.
*Concreteness:* The act of getting to the specific details of relevant concerns, keeping communications focused and to the point, and focusing on the immediacies at hand. One should always be personable but to the point.
*Confrontation:* The act of compelling another to face, and take responsibility for, some dangerous, disturbing, or untruthful communication or situation.
*Potency:* The therapeutic variable in one's personality that wields the force of passion or authority and that has the capacity to influence thought or feeling.
*Self-disclosure:* The act of exposing one's own feeling, attitudes, beliefs, and experiences to another. One should be careful not to disclose too much information initially or personalize the victim's situation because self-disclosure can diminish one's credibility as an expert.
*Self-actualization:* The act of enjoying relative independence and self-sufficiency, being one's self, and having a broad-minded attitude toward others. Self-actualization is the result of advanced personal, emotional, mental, and philosophical or spiritual development. It can be defined as an individualized personality.

**Figure 12.4** The following is gleaned from Small's (2008) *Improving Your Bedside Manner.* Although differences exist between the doctor–patient relationship and the rescuer–victim relationship, one can easily adapt the principles to the recreation and park field.

Adapted, by permission, from J. Small, 2008, *Improving your bedside manner: A handbook for physicians to develop therapeutic conversations with their patients* (Austin, TX: Morgan Printing). To order contact www.eupsychia.com.

the beginning of the meeting if possible so that his departure is not unexpected.

*Do not admit guilt.* One can and should feel sorry for the victim. However, one should be empathetic without admitting doing wrong. If asked what they did, a recreation professional might respond "We did this because it was the best choice at the time" or "This is what we normally do in this situation." Better yet, the professional can focus the conversation on what is happening now and what will happen in the future.

*Do not lie to the victim or the family.* One should not lie to the victim or the family, but one does not need to tell them everything (i.e., omission rather than commission). The rescuer can simply redirect the conversation by focusing on what he is doing to remedy the situation or what will happen in the future. For example, if the victim asks the rescuer if she going to die, the rescuer might respond with "We are doing everything that we can." If the victim asks whether she broke her arm, the rescuer might respond with "I don't know for sure, but trained medical personnel who can answer your question will arrive shortly." Although the response begs the question, the rescuer is likely not qualified to tell the victim about the medical situation and should not do so at this time.

## Postincident

The recreation professional or organization involved in the incident must begin interacting with and developing a relationship with the victim and the family as early as possible. Generally, the longer one waits, the more difficult and awkward it becomes to make the initial contact. Lowry (2007) notes that the critical period to avoid lawsuits in a hospital setting is the period immediately after the incident. The recreation professional must maintain that connection with the victim during the recovery or convalescence period. In the case of a fatality, the professional should help the family through the healing process. One can share the grief of the victim and the family without admitting guilt or doing wrong.

Postincident communications and activities can include the following:

- Sending condolence letters or flowers.
- Providing immediate access to key people (e.g., cell phone number, e-mail address).
- Recommending pastoral assistance, counseling, or psychological assistance as needed.
- Visiting the hospital.
- Visiting with the family at their home or a neutral site.
- Paying for medical equipment or procedures that are not covered by insurance.
- Attending memorial services, if appropriate.

If one has developed the appropriate relationship and rapport with the victim or the family, most of these activities should be fairly easy to perform. If one has not, these gestures will most likely seem out of place or inappropriate. Even a simple gesture of sending flowers or a condolence letter might be met by a sneer or snicker. To prevent this from happening, an organization must build relationships, integrate building relationships into the emergency action plan, and ensure that everyone in the organization is on board.

# SUMMARY

A recreation professional or organization should begin developing a relationship with the victim or the family as soon as possible after an incident occurs and should provide ongoing support to help them work through the grieving process. If this does not happen, the victim or family might direct their anger toward the professional and the organization. Their anger can easily turn into wrath and into a lawsuit. Maintaining a relationship can reduce the likelihood of being sued; however, more importantly, it is the humanitarian thing to do.

## EXERCISES

### Exercise 1: Developing Good Patient Bedside Manner

The purpose of this exercise is to help develop good bedside manners. Review figures 12.3 and 12.4 for suggestions on managing the victim. Imagine that you are a staff member at a recreation center. While playing basketball in the gym, one of the youths trips, falls on the floor, and breaks her arm. Other staff members splint the youth's arm. Your task is to sit with the youth in the office for half an hour while waiting for emergency medical services to arrive.

1. Describe your conversation with the youth.
2. If you have a friend, role play the situation.
3. Change the situation to one of your choice if you would like.

### Exercise 2: The Hospital Visit

The purpose of this exercise is to help develop good bedside manners. From exercise 1, assume there were some complications with the broken arm and the victim is hospitalized for three days. The parents notify you of the hospital stay. On the phone, the parents did not seem contentious. Should you visit the youth in the hospital? Should the parents be there during the visit? Describe or write a script of the visit. If the parents were contentious, would you change anything?

Chapter 13

# The Ripple Effect

An incident affects more than the victim and the victim's immediate family. Participants and staff who have an ancillary role but not a direct relationship to the incident can be secondary victims. They think, "It could have been me," "I've done that also," or "I was next." Because of this association, they become involved in the incident. Ajango (2005) calls this the ripple effect.

The ripple effect is a form of post-traumatic stress syndrome that affects participants, staff, and ancillary people involved in an accident. It is called the ripple effect because, like ripples spreading outward when a pebble is dropped in water, the ripples of an incident spread out and affect everyone involved. For this reason, an organization must provide ongoing support to participants, employees, emergency personnel, and the community. This chapter discusses the impact of the ripple effect and presents critical incident stress management processes and strategies.

## IMPACT OF THE RIPPLE EFFECT

The ripple effect can be profound. It can affect other participants, employees, and the organization itself. An organization must address the ripple effect in its emergency action plan (EAP) and in its postincident involvement because the costs of not addressing the incident and the associated ripple effect can be significant. It can lead to loss of public support for the agency or service, loss of key personnel, or even the loss of the program or organization.

### Impacts on Other Participants

The most apparent effect on the other participants is that they had a bad experience. Depending on the experience, it may be a lost patron of your services, or they may never again participate in the activity. If the experience is bad enough, the participants will sue for damages. In the story in figure 13.1, the participants did sue but did not win. However, even when participants do not win the case, the cost to an organization in terms of time, money, and goodwill can be enormous.

In terms of the ripple effect, this group is most likely to slip through the cracks. It is usually a group that disperses and goes home after the incident. In terms of the total pool of customers, this group is most likely small, and if they never participate in the activity again, they won't be missed. For this reason, servicing this group in terms of the ripple effect is difficult at best and requires a concerted effort on the part of the recreation professional and agency. Regardless, the techniques described in this chapter can be equally applied to the participants also. Perhaps the departing words of advice as they disperse are to seek additional professional help at home.

### Impacts on Employees

The ripple effect can have a significant impact on not only those employees directly involved in the incident but also other employees. Other employees can easily be affected several ways. They do the same activities that led to the

## The Raft Trip from Hell

On September 30, 2004, a group of employees from a major company in the Washington metropolitan region participated in a team-building exercise on the Shenandoah River near Harpers Ferry, West Virginia. The raft trip down the Shenandoah River was one of the major components of the program. The river was at flood level. Several of the rafts flipped and one of the passengers drowned.

Two lawsuits were filed. One involved the fatality of Roger Freeman, and the second involved the trauma the participants on the trip experienced. The court merged the two cases into one, and the case went to trial. Regarding the fatality, the parties reached a settlement during the trial. Regarding the harmful experience, the trial went to the jury and the jury decided in favor of the defense. The participants did not collect damages.

As usually happens in these cases, everyone lost. Is this the experience that a raft company wants its passengers to have? Is this the experience that a recreation leader wants his participants to have? Although the company won the second case when it went to trial, the damages permeated their entire operation, including their personnel and their ability to conduct business. Most of the participants will not go rafting again.

The following passages are from the deposition of a woman who participated in the team-building experience. Although the following passages are from a single person, 18 other people gave similar depositions with similar comments. The first passage from her deposition describes her experience when the raft flipped in the flood waters. The second passage describes the long-term ripple effects that this experience, including the fatality, had on her.

Q: Plaintiff's lawyer

A: Jane Doe

Excerpts from deposition of [xxxx xxxxxxx]

Page 33

A I remember feeling the boat shift. I
remember the boat flipping over, myself being thrown
into the water. I remember the water was very rough,
waves, a lot of waves, being pushed down deep into the
water. I remember gulping in a lot of water right
away and then came up (crying)—excuse me. I

Page 34

remember coming back up underneath the raft, panicking
because I felt like I wasn't getting enough air. It
was very difficult to get—to get some air and to
go—I was pushed back down again several times, so
I was taking in a lot of water.
And I remember came—coming up under
the raft, trying to get some air and I couldn't. And
I remember thinking if I'm going to get out of this, I
have to get from underneath the boat. So I remember
trying to—when I got pushed down again, trying to

*(continued)*

**Figure 13.1** This excerpt from a deposition highlights how a participant in an activity can be affected by a bad experience.

River Riders v. Cathy Freeman et al. (October 18, 2007). Deposition of [xxxx xxxxxxx]. Circuit Court of Jefferson County, West Virginia.

force myself to swim—swim backwards to try and get from underneath the boat.

Page 47

Q In your interrogatory answers, you note that you have nightmares and flashbacks and difficulty going into the ocean and, you know, general mental and emotional suffering and anguish. Why don't you explain to me that claim or those claims?

A Right, well, I have a severe fear of deep water now. I—

Q Let me ask you something: What do you consider "deep water"?

A Anything taller than myself.

Q Okay.

A It was—right away, it was very difficult to deal with water at all, feeling of having water splashed in my face reminded me of the—of the

Page 48

event. I've been in situations where I've been on vacation since where I've had panic attacks when having to, you know, go in—in the ocean, near the ocean or dealing with any kind of boats. I no longer want to—no longer like being on a boat or being any—near any rivers such as the river we were in. I had a lot of anxiety about the event that happened, feelings that I could have died. I was supposed to sit in the seat that Roger sat in at the front of the boat. That could have been myself. I felt that I—could have drowned that day.

Statement of participant 2

1 On September 30, 2004, I participated in a team-building exercise for my employer….

2 As part of the team-building activities, I was to go rafting with other employees on the Shenandoah River by Harper's Ferry, West Virginia.

3 I cannot swim and was terrified of going rafting. My co-worker Roger Freeman shared my fear because he also could not swim. Everyone on the trip, including our guide and co-chairs, knew that he could not swim. We both felt that we were compelled to go rafting and there were no other options presented to us.

4 When one of the guides asked if anyone had a medical problem, I told him that I had…. He told me to let my guide Tim know and I did.

5 I do not remember falling out of the raft. I do remember being stuck under the raft and feeling like I was in a nightmare. I remember thinking that I had to get from under the raft, otherwise I would die under there. I then remember a hand coming toward me. The next thing I remember is crawling out of the river.

**Figure 13.1** *(continued)*

mishap. It could have been them instead of the person involved. It is a variation of the participant in the raft stating at the end of the excerpt from her deposition (figure 13.1), "I was supposed to sit in the seat that Roger sat in front of the raft. That could have been me." Employees drive the same routes, they do the same types of programs, and they do similar activities. It could have just as easily been them.

Second, because there was an accident, the organization and its employees must have done something wrong. That includes employees not directly involved in the incident. It is a form of guilt by association. Because you work for the same organization, it is assumed that you do the same things or behave the same way as the person who had the mishap. Although it is not necessarily logical or rational, it is often a connotation that becomes associated with those in the organization.

The ripple effect can lead to the loss of key personnel. In any organization, turnover in personnel occurs frequently because people retire or seek new jobs. However, the turnover resulting from the ripple effect can seem like a mild epidemic. Many of the people involved in the incident will find another job in another field and leave their profession forever. If they leave the field, all of their education, training, and experience in the field are lost.

Employees not directly involved in the incident may be part of this migration to new positions. Often, they are parallel moves. When asked why they are seeking new positions, they will give every reason but the real reason. They may cite that it is time for a change, a better opportunity, or better working conditions. They may not admit that it was really the ripple effect after the incident. Or, they may not cite the ripple effect because they are unfamiliar with the concept. However, a broad view of the organization will reveal that there is more employee movement than normal.

Most times, people tend to focus on the negative aspects of the ripple effect. These impacts are significant and covered in a subsequent section on the symptoms of stress and the ripple effect. However, the ripple effect can also result in growth, a positive benefit. Adapting their work on burnout, Pines and Aronson (1981) suggest that incidents provide the opportunity to learn, refocus, and grow. It can give employees a chance to refocus what they are doing and give them additional purpose. In a sense, the Unadilla incident described in figure 13.2 enabled Dr. Kauffman to grow and make more of a contribution to boating safety than he would have otherwise.

## Impacts on the Organization

The impacts on employees and loss of key personnel to other fields can have devastating effects on the organization and its culture for many years after the incident occurs. As noted, this affects not only the employees directly involved in the incident but also those who are ancillary or have no relationship to the incident other than that they work for the same organization.

The ripple effect can permeate the organization and its employees and threaten public confidence in the organization. The constant media attention can erode public confidence in the organization. Employees can begin to have self-doubt regarding their abilities as well as those of the organization. For this reason, it is important for the administration to keep employees informed and address the morale of the organization. The role of crisis management in chapter 11 is important in this respect. An investigation of the incident discussed in the next chapter (chapter 14) can be cathartic for those in the organization as well as the public.

Unchecked, the ripple effect coupled with a loss of employee morale and a diminished sense of public confidence can collectively lead to the loss of the program, and in severe cases the loss of the organization. If the key personnel involved in the program where the incident occurred leave the organization, it becomes easy for the administration to phase out the program.

In a contentious case like the Dzialo incident, it became difficult for Greenfield College to maintain the Team Adventure program affiliated with the college. The staff members involved in the incident left for other jobs. Key administrative personnel at the college affiliated with the program eventually left. It would

## The Unadilla Incident: A Case Study of Hypervigilance and Growth

It was 1972. I (Dr. Kauffman) was on the whitewater slalom racing circuit at the time. The whitewater course was a fairly nondescript course located directly below the dam on the East Sidney Lake in New York. The course began in the pool of water where the dam flushed into the creek. The course was a quick but easy class II whitewater stretch that ran for a quarter of a mile. It had one significant but relatively easy drop next to the bridge. The race attracted most of the experts in whitewater at the time.

The race course was the same as it was every year. They turned the water on and the course assumed the exact configuration that it had the previous year. This year, some of the experts noted that the major drop looked slightly different, but not much was made of it. However, it was different. A rock had shifted and slid downstream slightly, becoming an undercut rock and a foot entrapment.

It was not if but when the accident would happen. One of the racers came out of his boat, stood up in the river, and became trapped on the undercut rock. It was a heads-down entrapment and the victim subsequently drowned. It could have been anyone.

Like a lot of other people on the course, I was completing a practice run. Other than being there, I had no connection with the victim. I got out of my boat and, like everyone else, tried to rescue the victim. I was one of two people who finally pulled the victim off the foot entrapment. I got the job of talking to the sister of the victim in the back of a van about what happened. Much expertise was assembled at this mediocre rapids, but we were helpless to perform a rescue.

The fatality had an effect on me. For the next year and a half, I had a classic case of hypervigilance. Every time someone stood up in a rapids, I feared a potential foot entrapment. I finally got over it one day while watching people come down through Bull Falls on the Shenandoah River. Most people dumped going through Bull Falls. There should have been 100 foot entrapments in an hour, but there were none.

The other issue is how this event affected my long-term boating career. I could have easily dropped out of boating and taken up another outdoor activity and no one would have ever suspected that the event was the cause. However, this event helped to solidify my involvement in boating safety and education. Along with other things, I went on to create the first River Safety Symposium, where experts from across the country assembled to address the issue of whitewater rescue and safety.

The ripple or echo effect is real. If not addressed, it can easily destroy a person, even if he or she was not directly involved in the incident. If addressed and handled well, it can lead to a growth experience.

**Figure 13.2** A personal case study that demonstrates how the ripple effect can lead to personal and professional growth.

have been easy for the president of the college to phase out the program.

## SYMPTOMS OF STRESS AND THE RIPPLE EFFECT

In the ripple effect, the stress of the original incident ripples outward from the immediate victim and the family to secondary victims, including fellow employees, the agency, and community. This section covers some of the symptoms of stress people may experience after an incident occurs. The general symptoms of stress can be caused by normal life events and do not necessarily indicate that a person is experiencing the ripple effect. In contrast, three specific symptoms indicate that a person is experiencing the ripple effect: the need to talk, hypervigilance, and shame and guilt.

## Symptoms of Severe Stress

Figure 13.3 lists the cognitive, emotional, and behavioral symptoms and physical ailments associated with severe stress. These general symptoms are applicable to many normal stresses that one encounters during day-to-day living. However, they are still potential indicators of the ripple effect after an incident occurs.

## Need to Talk

After a major incident occurs, the secondary victims have a need to talk, and they will talk. Ajango (2005) notes that people have a compulsion to tell their story—not just once, but over and over again to whoever will listen. If a lawyer puts a gag order on everyone, it will not work; people will still talk because they have a need to. The most prudent strategy is to direct their talking through appropriate channels so that they can work through the ripple effects caused by the incident.

Debriefings and counseling are useful in helping people work through the situation. People who have technical ability, such as psychologists or licensed counselors, tend to provide the best assistance to the secondary victims. People who have experienced similar types of trauma and are involved in the activity or industry can also possess technical ability.

Pines and Aronson (1981) identify several types of support roles for secondary victims. *Social support* is defined as information that leads subjects to believe that they are cared for and loved, esteemed, and valued and that they belong to a network of communication and mutual obligation. *Technical appreciation* is provided by someone who can appreciate what the subject is doing because they have expertise in the field. *Emotional support* is provided by someone who is willing to listen without being judgmental. One does not need to possess technical appreciation in order to provide emotional support. *Shared social reality* comes from people who share the same type of experiences. When one needs sound advice in times of stress or confusion, a person with similar priorities, values, and views can be very helpful. Knowing these support roles can help a recreation professional relate to the needs of secondary victims. For example, if a professional is providing emotional support and suspects that the subject needs someone with technical appreciation, the professional

### Symptoms of Excessive Stress

**Cognitive**

- Confusion in thinking
- Difficulty making decisions
- Lowered concentration
- Memory dysfunction
- Lowering of higher cognitive functions

**Emotional**

- Emotional shock
- Anger
- Grief
- Depression
- Feeling overwhelmed

**Physical Ailments**

- Excessive sweating
- Dizzy spells
- Increased heart rate
- Increased blood pressure
- Rapid breathing

**Behavioral**

- Changes in normal routine
- Changes in eating
- Decreased personal hygiene
- Withdrawal from others
- Prolonged silences

**Figure 13.3** These symptoms of excessive stress can be indicators of the ripple effect.

Reprinted from Mitchell and Everly 2001.

can direct the subject to someone who might be able to provide better assistance.

## Hypervigilance

*Hyper* denotes arousal or heightened activity. *Vigilance* means to keep watch or stay awake. *Hypervigilance* is a state of heightened awareness (hyper) to keep watch or provide protection (vigilance). People in this state tend to become overprotective, and they tend to feel that a potential accident exists behind everything. They become extremely cautious and take every step possible to prevent an incident. Because of the extreme caution displayed, hypervigilant behavior is usually easy to identify.

The Unadilla incident in figure 13.2 presents a classic example of hypervigilance involving this author (Dr. Kauffman). He was indirectly involved in a fatality. For 18 months after the incident, there was a sense of being overly protective and overly cautious on the river. Eventually, the hypervigilance passed and normalcy ensued. It became a growth experience; however, the experience could have easily pushed him out of the boating field. Although this author was interested in boating safety prior to the incident, the incident helped focus his professional interest in boating safety.

## Shame and Guilt

People experiencing the ripple effect will often feel shame or guilt. Ajango (2005, p. 164) notes that guilt is feeling bad about what one has done and shame is feeling bad about who one is. People in an organization who are removed from the actual incident often feel shame and guilt over what happened because they think they should have done something differently or simply because they are associated with the same organization in which the incident occurred. Compared with hypervigilance, shame and guilt are a little more difficult to detect. People experiencing the ripple effect will often make the following statements or variations of these statements:

"It could have been me."

"I've done the same thing."

"I've done similar things."

"Had we done . . . it might not have occurred."

People making these statements have internalized what happened to someone else (e.g., "It could have been me..." or "I've done similar things...") and believe that only luck or chance prevented the same thing from happening to them. In this way, they become secondary victims. For example, in the Unadilla incident, the victim could easily have been anyone on the race course. Everyone stood up in the river, so anyone could have died, but they did not. Was it because of luck or chance, or was it simply not their time? Subconsciously, people felt as if it could or should have been them.

The description of the raft trip from hell (figure 13.1) illustrates these points. The last paragraph in Jane Doe's deposition includes most of the elements listed previously: "I had a lot of anxiety about the event that happened, feelings that I could have died." (It could have been me.) "I was supposed to sit in the seat that Roger sat in at the front of the boat." (I've done similar things.) "That could have been myself." (It could have been me.) "I felt that I—could have drowned that day." (It could have been me.) Her testimony poignantly illustrates these points.

# CRITICAL INCIDENT STRESS MANAGEMENT

The ripple effect will, without exception, occur after a major incident or accident. Recreation professionals and organizations must address how to deal with it. Mitchell and Everly (2001) cover the critical incident stress debriefing (CISD) process. The structure in this section parallels the structure that Mitchell and Everly (2001) recommend (table 13.1). For the purposes of the EAP and of general preparation, one can divide the CISD process into three phases: precrisis, incident, and postincident. An organization must address each of the phases before an incident occurs because it is often difficult to catch up with events once they begin to unfold. Also, during a time of crisis, handling the secondary victims of the incident seems

**Table 13.1** Group Crisis Interventions

| Time | Name | Target group | Event timing | Activity elements |
|---|---|---|---|---|
| Incident | Crisis management briefing | Large groups of primary victims and non-operational personnel | During or after the event; 45-75 minutes duration | Assembly, information, reactions, coping resources |
| Incident | Demobilization | Large groups of operational emergency services, rescue, and public safety personnel | Immediately after shift disengagement; 10-20 minutes duration | Introduction, information, physical, nourishment |
| Postincident | Defusing | Small groups (3-20 people) | 6-12 hours postevent; 20-45 minutes duration | Introduction, exploration, information |
| Postincident | Critical incident stress debriefing | Small groups (3-20 people) | Usually 1-10 days postevent and 3-6 weeks postdisaster; 1-3 hours duration | Introduction, fact, thought, reaction, symptom, teaching, re-entry |

Reprinted, by permission, from J. Mitchell and G. Everly, 2001, *Critical incident stress debriefing: An operations manual for CISD, defusing and other group crisis intervention services* (Ellicott City, MA: Chevron Publishing Corporation), 10.

incidental compared with meeting the needs of the primary victims.

## Precrisis Preparation

The first part of precrisis preparation is including it in the EAP. Depending on the discipline, accident scenarios and role playing are commonly used to help prepare people for times of actual emergencies. These training exercises can easily incorporate the defusing and debriefing techniques described in the next section. Incorporating these techniques into normal activities (e.g., playground, outdoor outing) and smaller incidents will help an organization prepare for larger incidents.

Recreation leaders must review the formal and informal processes that are part of the EAP with key personnel in the organization and should consider reviewing the procedures with legal counsel. Although an administration, including legal counsel, may have agreed to a plan two years ago, it is always good to refresh their familiarity with it and their commitment to follow through with it. Also, as new administrators are hired, recreation leaders should review the EAP and the postcrisis plan with them rather than assume that they are committed to the plan.

## Incident

The crisis management briefing and demobilization procedures should be in place so that an organization can implement them quickly during the actual incident. Depending on circumstances, these functions can be performed by other agencies that have expertise in implementing the procedures or can be coordinated with the organization's public information officer.

### Crisis Management Briefing

The crisis management briefing (CMB) is a large-group intervention process. Mitchell and Everly (2001) suggest thinking of the CMB as a town meeting that focuses on crisis intervention. It can easily be used with groups of 300 people. Normally, a CMB is conducted immediately after the original incident occurs and can be 45 to 75 minutes long. A CMB is often sufficient to meet the needs of people who are peripherally involved with the crisis and who have limited needs. An organization can repeat the CMB as many times as necessary.

A CMB comprises four phases: assembly, informational, reactions, and coping strategies and resources. The assembly phase brings people together. It can be conducted in an assembly hall or even on closed-circuit television. Because of the nature of the communication, it is not necessary for everyone to be in the same facility.

The purpose of the informational phase is to disseminate information about the incident in an effort to inform people and to reduce rumors and misinformation that often result from a lack of communication. People with technical competency must be involved with the process. For example, a person with suitable medical training or a doctor can present medical information, or key personnel trained in search and rescue can present information regarding search and rescue.

The focus of the third phase, reactions, is to identify major psychological themes present in the incident and discuss their implications. Again, people involved in this phase should have technical competency so that participants find them credible. For example, a psychologist or psychiatrist should present the psychological themes of the incident.

The last phase is coping strategies and resources. According to Mitchell and Everly (2001), stress-management techniques are often discussed during this phase, and participants normally leave with a handout that delineates typical reactions, coping techniques, and available community resources.

### Demobilization and Staff Consultation

Demobilization occurs during the first two or three shifts after a disaster or major incident occurs. Demobilization provides personnel involved in the early phases of the incident with information that will help them relieve stress and return to their normal duties. Because most of the personnel are trained in these areas, they normally do not require a large amount of demobilization time. According to Mitchell and Everly (2001), as the first several shifts after a disaster pass, the need for demobilization consultation diminishes. If continued too long, demobilization may even be dangerous and disruptive because the process can increase stress rather than reduce it. Because the process is predicated on ending stress, it is easy to continue the process past the point of usefulness. Also, Mitchell and Everly (2001) note that it is logistically difficult to design a single demobilization room (figure 13.4) and suggest providing two rooms, one for presentations and another for refreshments. An organization can follow up demobilization with other crisis-intervention techniques as needed.

## Postincident

The ripple effect becomes most noticeable during the postincident phase. The immediacy

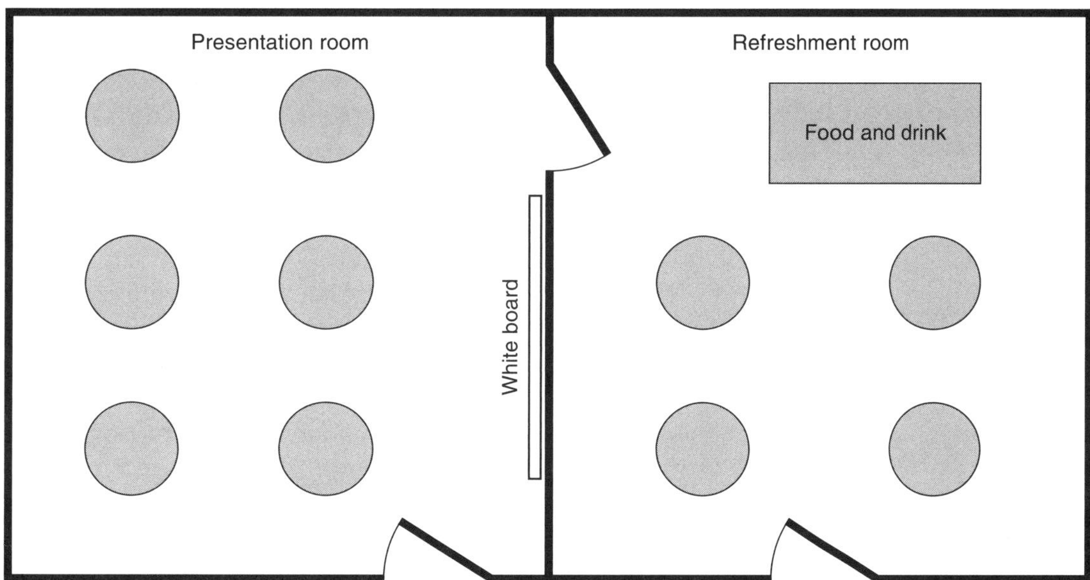


**Figure 13.4** During demobilization, rescue personnel will participate in a 10- to 15-minute meeting. After that, they move to the second room, where they will eat and rest for up to half an hour before returning to the scene of the incident.

Adapted, by permission, from J. Mitchell and G. Everly, 2001, *Critical incident stress debriefing: An operations manual for CISD, defusing and other group crisis intervention services* (Ellicott City, MD: Chevron Publishing Corporation), 109.

of the incident has passed, and people have time to think about what happened and to discuss it with others. This natural process must be channeled or directed to minimize the harmful effects on personnel and the organization. Postincident functions include defusing, debriefing, and funneling. These functions are formal processes that should be conducted by trained professionals.

## Defusing

Defusing a bomb involves removing the fuse before it detonates the explosives. The bomb in this case is the post-traumatic stress for the secondary victims of the incident. A defusing is a shortened version of a debriefing. The organization should hold the defusing in a comfortable, neutral site (e.g., church, school, living room, meeting room) any time after the incident occurs. The defusing process usually lasts for 20 to 60 minutes; the average length is 45 minutes.

According to Mitchell and Everly (2001, p. 122), "It offers an opportunity for people involved in a horrible event to talk about that experience before they have time to rethink the experience and possibly misinterpret its true meaning." A defusing sets the tone of the discussion and helps people work through and normalize the experience so that they can more quickly return to their normal routines.

Mitchell and Everly (2001, p. 129) note that the defusing process comprises three segments: introduction, exploration, and information. The purpose of the introduction segment is to introduce everyone, describe the defusing process and why the group has gathered, note confidentiality, encourage participation, and accept any questions from the group. In the exploration segment, people discuss their experience and how it affected them. They may ask about any signs or symptoms of stress that they have had since the incident occurred. Depending on circumstances, the team conducting the meeting may ask questions or the participants may provide a good stream-of-consciousness discussion. During the information segment, leaders summarize the discussion, teach practical skills for surviving stress, help people normalize and return to their normal routine, and organize a debriefing if necessary.

Assessment of those who participate in the defusing helps determine what additional steps, if any, an organization should take. Based on the intensity of the discussion, the leader or organization may conclude that they need to follow up with a debriefing. Or the discussion may suggest that the defusing was sufficient and that a debriefing is not necessary.

## Debriefing

Debriefings are usually small-group activities (i.e., 3 to 20 people) that occur 1 to 10 days after the incident occurs. Debriefings usually last for 1 to 3 hours. According to Mitchell and Everly (2001), debriefings can address the needs of peer-support personnel, mental health-support personnel, emergency personnel, and support systems for spouses and significant others. The process should be conducted by people who are trained to perform the activity.

Typically, a debriefing has seven phases: introduction, fact, thought, reaction, symptoms, teaching, and re-entry (Mitchell and Everly, 2001). Figure 13.5 shows whether each of the seven steps is cognitive, informational, or emotional. The beginning of the debriefing session addresses cognitive information, the middle of the session transitions to the emotional needs of the group, and the end of the session returns to more informational needs.

According to Mitchell and Everly (2001), the introduction phase is crucial to the debriefing process. If not done properly, it can lead to a less-than-satisfactory debriefing. The purpose of the introduction is to introduce the members of the team, explain the purpose of the meeting and the process, gain the cooperation of the participants, answer concerns and limit anxiety, and encourage mutual help. The meeting is strictly confidential, which means cell phones are turned off and no cameras or recording devices are allowed.

The introduction phase is followed by the fact phase, which includes a discussion of the incident and what happened. During this phase, the discussion transitions from the general facts of the incident to the individual.

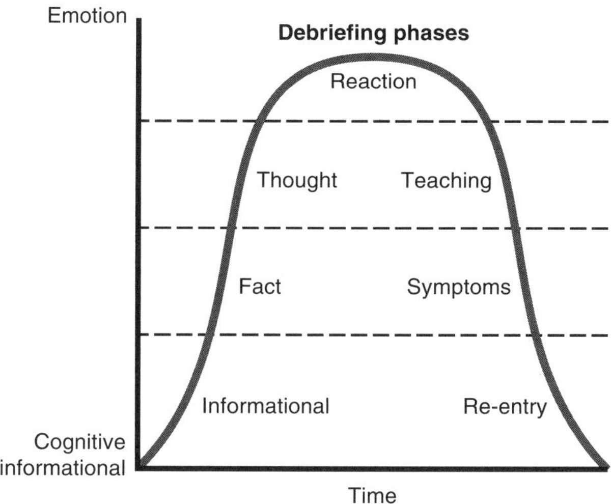


**Figure 13.5** The beginning of the debriefing session includes cognitive information, the middle of the session addresses the emotional needs of the group, and the end of the session returns to more informational needs.

Reprinted, by permission, from J. Mitchell and G. Everly, 2001, *Critical incident stress debriefing: An operations manual for CISD, defusing and other group crisis intervention services* (Ellicott City, MD: Chevron Publishing Corporation), 148.

Participants are asked who they are, what their role or job was during the incident, and what happened. They have a chance to tell their story from their perspective. Mitchell and Everly (2001) note that when participants are asked to describe the facts of the situation, they begin to express their emotions and the effect of the incident on them. They begin to transition to the thought phase and from fact to emotion. During the thought phase, the discussion moves from items that are external to the individuals to how the incident affected the individuals involved. For example, in the thought phase the facilitator may ask the participants to identify what affected them the most about the incident. In the reaction phase, they are asked how it affected them personally. It is a transition from identifying what affected them to describing how it affected them. Normally, the reaction phase is the most emotional phase.

The symptom phase is a transition back to the factual or cognitive domain (see figure 13.5). Stress affects people's behavior. It might result in withdrawal, silence, shaking hands, or the inability to make a decision. The team leaders will ask the participants if they experienced any of these effects of stress. During the teaching phase, the team leaders provide participants with instructions on how to deal with stress. Topics might include talking with one's family, exercise, diet, and rest.

The last phase, re-entry, puts closure on the debriefing and on the events that have occurred. The purpose of this phase is to answer questions, make summary statements, and return participants to their normal functions. If needed, leaders can recommend specialized counseling services such as individual crisis intervention, one-on-one counseling, pastoral counseling with a priest or minister, or family counseling.

## Funneling

Funneling is an adventure education technique that is useful in debriefing normal experiences or minor incidents in the recreation and park setting. It consists of six phases or guiding questions that help a leader direct the individual or group through the debriefing process: review, recall and remember, affect and effect, summation, application, and commitment (figure 13.6). In contrast with the more formal techniques discussed in this section, recreation leaders without significant training can use funneling techniques in their normal activities and to address minor incidents. Depending on the size of the group and the need, a funneling session can take several minutes to half an hour.

The funneling process (figure 13.7) parallels the general flow depicted in figure 13.6. It begins with the cognitive phases (i.e., informational review, recall and remember), then moves to the more emotional phases (i.e., affect and effect, summation), and then returns to the more cognitive phases (i.e., application, commitment).

If desired, one can condense the six phases of the funneling process into three general questions: "When you look back on the experience, what affected you the most?" "How did it affect you?" and "What did you learn, or what did you take away from the experience?" Leaders can modify the format and questions to meet any specific situation. It is an abbreviated form of debriefing.

## Funnel Guide Questions

**Review.** Let's talk about the [issue or topic]. Can you review for me the experience or activity we did? On a five-point scale where five is excellent, indicate how good the experience was.

**Recall and remember.** Do you remember an example of poor (or excellent) [issue, topic, or event]? Can you recall a particular time when [issue or topic] was good (or bad)? *Note:* If it was an event, they most likely have already identified it.

**Affect and effect.** Describe how [issue, topic, or event] affected you. How did it make you feel? How did this emotion affect you and the group? What influence did it have on the experience?

**Summation.** Can you summarize what you have gained from this experience? What did you learn from all this?

**Application.** Do you see a connection between this experience and your normal routine or life? Can you apply this to your job, family, and school?

**Commitment.** What will you do differently next time? On a scale of one to five where five is the highest level of commitment, what is your level of commitment?

**Figure 13.6** Funneling is a simplified debriefing process that lay people can easily use.

Adapted, by permission, from S. Priest and M. Gass, 2005, *Effective leadership in adventure programming* (Champaign, IL: Human Kinetics), 205.

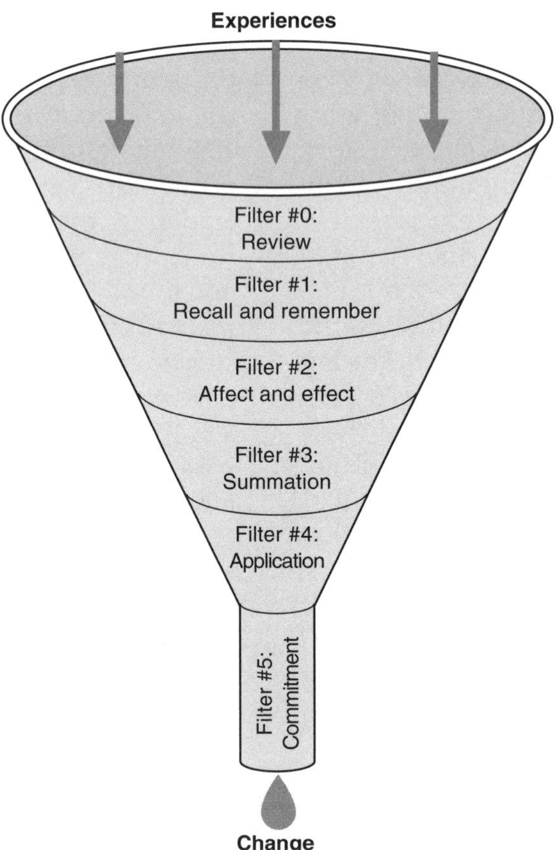


**Figure 13.7** The debriefing funnel.

Reprinted, by permission, from S. Priest and M. Gass, 2005, *Effective leadership in adventure programming* (Champaign, IL: Human Kinetics), 203.

## SUMMARY

This chapter discusses the ripple effect. An incident affects more than the victim and the victim's immediate family. Like ripples spreading outward when a pebble is dropped in water, the incident affects fellow workers, emergency personnel, and other people on the periphery. It also affects the community. The ripple effect can be subtle and, if not addressed, can disable or eventually terminate a program or lead to long-term mental health problems for participants, employees, and the community. If people do not deal with emotional stress, it can lead to severe stress, hypervigilance, shame, and guilt. However, if properly channeled, it can lead to a potential growth experience.

A recreation professional must work with the public information officer for the organization to address emotional needs and healing at the community level. Several group-dynamic functions can be used to defuse the emotional stress resulting from an incident. An organization should incorporate these functions into its EAP and planning process. Only trained personnel should lead these functions. The nature and severity of the incident will determine, in part, which functions an organization uses. Although an organization may not need to use all processes after an incident, it should plan for the worst and have all of the functions discussed in this chapter available in case they are needed.

## EXERCISES

### Exercise 1: Debriefing the Raft Trip from Hell

The purpose of this exercise is to gain experience regarding the debriefing process. Review figure 13.1. Assume that you are the raft guide for this trip and that the situation in figure 13.1 occurs, except no one drowns. The trip is over. You notice that the person who had this less-than-optimum experience is moping around the lodge. Their body language conveys that their experience was not good. You consider approaching this person with the possibility of intervening.

1. The purpose of this exercise is to explore the ethical issue regarding whether you should intervene as well as to gain experience in the debriefing process. Should you approach this person to see if you can do anything to help in terms of the trip and the experience? Explain why you should or should not approach them.
2. Review the debriefing and the funneling sections in this chapter and the debriefing steps. Using the funneling process, lay out a general approach in which you identify the steps that you will use and the questions you will ask or points you will make to the participant.
3. Jane Doe in figure 13.1 had a very bad experience and long-term repercussions, including refusing to go rafting again. Do you think you could rectify this situation or at least increase the chances that she would go rafting again? Explain why or why not.

## Exercise 2: It Could Have Been Me!

Have you ever had an "It could have been me" or "I've done similar things" experience? The purpose of this exercise is to explore how it affected you and how you handled it.

1. Briefly explain the situation.
2. Explain how the situation affected you and your behavior. Did it affect your ability to carry out your job or your assignments? If so, explain how.
3. Explain how you handled it or eventually got over it.
4. What, if anything, did you learn from this experience?

# Chapter 14

# Conducting an Investigation

The postaccident investigation helps an organization improve operations and avoid future mishaps. The organization can conduct the investigation internally using agency personnel or externally using an independent investigator. The investigation can be highly charged, like the Dzialo case (first introduced in chapter 1), or it can be as mundane as a typical research project, like the Potomac River study (discussed in this chapter). This chapter provides a basic understanding of how to conduct an investigation after an incident occurs, including tips for the principal investigator or the person who is contracting the investigation to an independent investigator. When conducting an investigation, an organization should juxtapose the investigation with legal liability concerns because any findings can and will be used by either side.

This chapter uses three very different case studies to illustrate how to conduct an investigation. The first study is an investigation of the Dzialo incident conducted by Charlie Walbridge for Greenfield Community College (first introduced in chapter 1). The purpose of the study was to determine what happened in the near drowning on the Deerfield River. It was conducted in a contentious environment. The second study is the Potomac River study (see figure 14.1). It was conducted by Dr. Kauffman for the Maryland Department of Natural Resources (DNR) after 13 fatalities occurred on the river in 1989. The third study is the case of Winding River Canoe Rentals (first introduced in chapter 1). In this case, the business owner, Janice Cody, did not conduct an investigation after the first fatality occurred, but if she had she would likely have prevented the second fatality the following year and might still be in business today. It underscores the need to conduct an investigation.

## NEED FOR INVESTIGATION

This section focuses on the benefits of or the reasons for conducting an investigation after an accident. The reasons for conducting an investigation can vary greatly in terms of purposes and benefits.

Multiple investigations can occur with the same incident. These investigations can overlap each other and conflict with other investigations. For example, in the Dzialo case, Greenfield Community College conducted its own internal study to find out what went wrong in the near drowning of Adam. Then, in an effort to address growing public concern, the college hired Charlie Walbridge to conduct a second study. He was unaware of the internal investigation until after he completed his study. Since Walbridge had conducted an investigation for the college, the assistant attorney general of the Commonwealth of Massachusetts hired this author to review the case materials and to render an opinion on the incident. Because the college was being sued by the Dzialo family, the Commonwealth was also listed as a defendant. Everything other than the college's study

## Potomac River Study

During the summer of 1989 when water levels were unusually high, 13 boating and nonboating fatalities occurred on the main stem of the Potomac River. In an effort to reduce the number of river fatalities, the Department of Natural Resources (DNR) undertook a number of safety measures, including public meetings, media coverage of the problem, and the development of the DNR pole system. The DNR issued a request for proposals to study the causes of the fatalities and to make recommendations to increase safety. The Potomac River study was conducted in response to the request for proposals.

The authors of the study analyzed the fatalities by examining accident reports and the river hydrology, conducting a user survey, and reviewing the literature (Kauffman et al., 1991; Kauffman, 1992). The study found that people drowned at moderate water levels rather than at flood levels. The survey revealed that people correctly perceived the danger of flood waters. At moderate water levels, the river gained sufficient volume, depth, and power to become a contributing factor in fatalities. People did not understand the dangers of moderate water levels because the river looked normal.

Based on these findings, the authors of the study developed the concept of the drowning trap (see figure 7.2). The authors recommended installing gauges at boating ramps and posting interpretive signs explaining the potential dangers associated with moderate water levels. The study helped the DNR to better manage the resource that was under their jurisdiction.

**Figure 14.1** This case study is typical of an investigative study used to solve a problem. The Maryland DNR commissioned the study to help determine why a problem occurred.

and Walbridge's study were provided to this author. In addition, the Dzialo family and their plaintiff's attorney most likely had their own investigation to determine what happened.

In the aftermath of this accident, there were at least four different investigations involving the same incident. Several of the reasons for conducting an investigation are illustrated by the Dzialo case and complement the needs or benefits of conducting an investigation identified by Ferry (1988) below. Walbridge's study was essentially a duplication of the college's investigation, as was this author's investigation of both of their investigations. Although they were essentially duplications, they had very different purposes. The school's study was motivated toward identifying whether the school needed to make administrative changes to improve their program. Walbridge's study was motivated by the public for an independent study. This author's investigation was conducted to independently verify Walbridge's findings for the Commonwealth.

Adapted from Ferry (1988, p. 4), the following points are often cited as the benefits of completing an investigation. They also help to frame the nature and extent of the investigation, including the selection of the investigator and whether the investigation is conducted internally or externally.

*Find out what happened.* The primary reason for conducting an investigation is to find out what happened. This is often the simplest and most obvious reason. This was the purpose of Charlie Walbridge's investigation for Greenfield Community College, and it was the purpose of the Potomac River study.

*Prevent future incidents and accidents.* This is the logical result of finding out what happened. An investigation can often help prevent future incidents. In the Cody case, the second fatality could have easily been prevented if an investigation had been conducted. By her own admission in her deposition, Janice Cody, owner of Winding River Canoe Rentals, did not conduct any form of investigation or do anything that could have prevented Melanie Carlson's death one year later. Had she conducted an investigation, she would have noticed that trees in the water were forming strainers and would have identified the danger of Yates Dam at moderately high water.

*Improve operations and procedures.* Once an organization finds out what happened, the next step is to improve operations and procedures. This is not the same thing as determining negligence, where one seeks to find a breach of standard of care. People often say "I can't fix that now because that will show we were wrong." It does not. If an organization is in a lawsuit and it makes changes because of the accident, the court cannot interpret those changes as admitting negligence. The courts want to prevent future accidents. Regardless, an organization may want to work with a lawyer so that the changes do not inadvertently suggest culpability.

*Make program decisions.* Management can use an investigation to make decisions on current and future programs. If no study is conducted, it can sometimes lead to the wrong decision. For example, an outcome of the Potomac River Study was the implementation of gauges at river put-ins to warn users of potentially hazardous river conditions. Although Winding River Canoe Rentals didn't make the wrong decision, they didn't make any decisions or changes that could have increased the safety of their livery. In discussing risk management plans in chapter 8, the Reassessment of Policies and Practices section provides recommendations that could easily have resulted as part the formal recommendations from an investigation.

*Help reduce the ripple effect.* An investigation allows people to tell the story of what they did. This discussion itself can be therapeutic. In addition, an investigation allows people to voice their concerns and see progress toward solving the problem. (See chapter 13 for a discussion of the ripple effect.)

*Help management make risk management decisions.* An investigation can often help an organization make risk management decisions or help the industry create risk management standards. For example, the long-term study by Project Adventure of initiative courses resulted in the discontinuation of the electric fence (Collard, 2001; Project Adventure, 1995; Rhonke, 2005). The industrywide study revealed a trend among seemingly unconnected occurrences of people spraining or breaking an ankle on the electric fence initiative. The Potomac River Study can lead to additional investigations on other rivers and lead to management recognizing the importance of moderate flows in river fatalities.

*Help protect against litigation.* According to Ajango (2005), 20 percent of lawsuits in the health care industry occur because people simply want to find out what happened or what is going on. Conducting an investigation can help protect against litigation because it keeps people informed of what happened and assures them that someone is doing something about the problem. The incident described in figure 12.1 illustrates this point.

*Meet insurance requirements.* In determining whether to settle or go to court, the insurance company may require an organization to conduct an investigation. Often, an investigation of this nature is involved with litigation.

*Satisfy media interest.* Depending on the visibility of the incident, an investigative report allows the media to disseminate the correct story. However, the report may prolong the life of the story because it is another topic for the media to report. Walbridge conducted his investigation separately from the internal study that the school had already conducted. He was unaware of the internal investigation when he began his investigation. Walbridge's study, the results of which were similar to those of the internal investigation, was conducted in response to the college's attempt to alleviate community and media pressure. His study continued media interest in this highly charged case.

## INTERNAL OR EXTERNAL STUDY

After determining the need for an investigation, the organization should determine whether to conduct the study internally or externally. An internal investigation is conducted by someone within the organization, and an external study is conducted by someone outside of the organization. Often, the organization will not have a

## Tips for the Investigator

Greenfield Community College asked Charlie Walbridge to conduct an independent investigation to determine what happened in the Dzialo incident. The following tips for conducting an investigation are gleaned from an interview with him (Charlie Walbridge, personal communication, 2010).

**1.** *Know the purpose of your study.* The purpose of a study determines the focus of the study and its eventual outcome, particularly if interactions between the parties involved become contentious. The purpose of the investigation could be to determine what happened (e.g., the Dzialo incident) or to improve operations and procedures, or it could be another purpose as decided by the group hiring the investigator. Walbridge knew the purpose of his investigation, which was to determine whether the college did anything wrong.

**2.** *Assume that the investigation will be contentious.* The investigator should not be surprised or unprepared if a seemingly straightforward study becomes contentious. Walbridge's study started and ended in a contentious environment.

**3.** *When interviewing people, let them tell their story.* Ask questions about who did what or when things happened. This is the simplest but most effective interview approach, particularly if one is new at conducting investigations. It helps establish rapport with the people being interviewed. The investigator should save trick questions and cross-examinations for the lawyers.

**4.** *Differentiate between factual information and opinion or nonfactual information.* Examples of factual information include "I saw this..." or "I did this...." This information goes in the report. Examples of opinion include "I believe so and so did this..." or "Sam told me that this is what happened...." The investigator should ask Sam whether he saw or did the act in question. If Sam confirms that he did, the information is then fact rather than opinion.

**5.** *If you are an independent, objective investigator, be sure that you are independent.* If the group for whom you are doing the study forbid an investigator from interviewing someone or fail to give the investigator total access to the information that he needs, the investigator is no longer an independent investigator. The investigator's request for information is framed in terms of the "charge" or the purpose of the study. The investigator should consider not doing the study or being more assertive and demanding the necessary information. As Walbridge notes, it may be difficult to be assertive with the president of the college or the college's lawyers.

**6.** *Consider consulting with a lawyer, even if the group for whom you are doing the study does not want you to do so.* Consulting with a lawyer offers protection to both the investigator and the client. The investigator does not want to write a report that inadvertently makes the client culpable or that has a technical, legal meaning that is different from lay interpretation. Consulting with a lawyer does not affect an investigator's objectivity. In the Dzialo case, the college did not want Walbridge to consult with a lawyer. Although he acquiesced, he regrets it and believes that it affected the quality of the final report.

**7.** *Have everyone involved with the draft review the draft before submitting the final report.* The investigator should ask everyone involved to review the draft to verify that the information is factually correct and that their story is accurately depicted. This review does not affect the investigator's objectivity, and the investigator still decides what to include in the report. In the Dzialo case, the college wanted the people interviewed to fact check Walbridge's report.

**8.** *Regardless of the agency, the more tragic the accident, the more likely it will reach the top administrators.* A fatality or near fatality reaches the president's office very quickly. For this reason, an organization must review the emergency action plan with top administrators before an incident occurs and review the plan with new personnel. In the Dzialo case, the college had a good emergency action plan until the college's new lawyer instituted a "no comment" policy.

choice and external factors will determine that the organization must conduct the study externally. Organizational capability and perceived objectivity can influence whether the organization conducts the study internally or externally.

### Organizational Capability

Organizational capability includes having the resources necessary to conduct the investigation and the desire to do so. Most recreation programmers are experts at conducting programs, but often they do not have the technical expertise to perform the study. Contracting out the study enables the organization to find people with the expertise to help solve the problem.

Even if an organization has the internal capability to complete an investigation, it may not desire to do so because conducting the investigation would divert personnel from their normal jobs. If the investigation were to extend over several months, this reallocation of resources could be considerable. For this reason, it may be more practical to subcontract the investigation externally.

The Potomac River study investigated the fatalities on the Potomac River in order to devise a system to warn river users of the dangers. Conducting the study would be a difficult task for the Maryland DNR. A comprehensive study of the fatalities, river hydrology, and user profiles would require several months of work. In addition, the study required developing recommendations for devising a warning system to inform river users when the river was dangerous. Even if the DNR had the internal resources to conduct the study, it would not want to do so because conducting the study internally would divert a significant amount of resources away from normal functions. The DNR wisely chose to perform an external study.

### Perceived Objectivity

Generally, people perceive external studies as being more objective than internal studies because staff may have agendas or territory to protect. In most organizational structures, injury, damage, or loss is viewed as a result of someone doing something wrong. In terms of careers and advancement, staff often have an incentive for being less than forthcoming or a motivation to minimize the impact of the incident and hope that it will not happen again. In the Winding River Canoe Rentals incident, Cody minimized the problem and hoped that it would go away. It did not.

Normally, an investigation conducted by an external investigator should correct these problems. Unfortunately, an external study and investigator are not exempt from many of the same problems as an internal study in terms of objectivity. External investigators can be influenced by politics and by the organization paying them. They may seek to please the source of their funding with results that please, or they may attempt to moderate their finding in an effort not to offend anyone. This is when reviewing the past performance and the references of the investigator becomes important in selecting an investigator who will avoid these problems.

## SELECTING AN INVESTIGATOR

Selecting the right investigator is probably the best indicator of the eventual success of the study as well as its acceptance. This is true whether the study is conducted internally or externally. When selecting an investigator, an organization should consider his competency, familiarity with the problem, ability to suggest viable solutions, and ability to deliver the final product. Enthusiasm and desire to complete the investigation are important considerations as well. The organization should also consider the credentials of the individual investigator to assess his objectivity.

### Competency

Competency is the investigator's ability to perform and complete the study. For the purposes of the investigation, competency can include the ability to understand the problem, expertise in the discipline or content area, experience in conducting similar investigations, experience in the content area so that he has the ability to suggest viable solutions, the ability to deliver the final product, time to complete the study, and enthusiasm to do the study (Ferrara, 1995).

• **Ability to understand the problem.** The investigator needs to understand the problem as well as the environment and context associated with the problem. He must not simply reflect the request for proposal or echo conventional wisdom. The investigator needs to be able to collect the appropriate data and analyze it.

• **Ability to suggest viable solutions.** Viable recommendations will reduce the likelihood of incidents in the future. The organization should review the findings of previous investigations conducted by the investigator. If the investigator was able to provide viable solutions in those investigations, he will most likely be able to do the same in the current investigation.

• **Ability to deliver.** The investigator needs to have a demonstrated ability to deliver the final product. Most often, the final product is a written report (figure 14.1). However, it may also include formal presentations to the community involved in the incident. Ability to deliver the final product includes the investigator's past record, the investigator's previous experience with similar tasks, the staff resources needed to complete the study, and the sufficiency of the funds requested. These principles apply equally well to both internal and external investigators.

• **Enthusiasm for the study.** In noncontentious studies, the investigator should have an enthusiasm or desire to complete the study. In contentious studies, which most people are probably leery of taking on because they would rather avoid the conflict, the focus should be on the investigator's commitment. The organization should examine the potential investigator's track record in terms of his ability to complete projects of a similar type.

## Objectivity

In both internal and external investigations, the organization should consider the credentials, including the previous record and the credibility, of the individual investigator. Determining objectivity can sometimes become problematic and can be challenged. In the Dzialo case, Walbridge was chosen to conduct the investigation by the college because of his national prominence, his importance in the field, and his previous commitment to and involvement in safety. Based on his previous cases, most references would recommend him as objective. Regardless, the Dzialo family challenged Walbridge's credibility as an investigator by questioning whether "someone who had never had kids himself or worked with them extensively [could] judge the situation properly" (Ajango, 2005, p. 16). A better attack on his credibility would have focused on the fact that in virtually all of his expert witness cases, he worked for the defense, and in this case he was once again working for the defense. This example demonstrates that even a person of impeccable credentials can easily be questioned regarding their credentials. Regardless, he was a good choice for the study because of his importance in the field and because of his overall commitment to safety.

## INVESTIGATION MODEL

The model in figure 14.2 depicts the basic research process normally used in investiga-

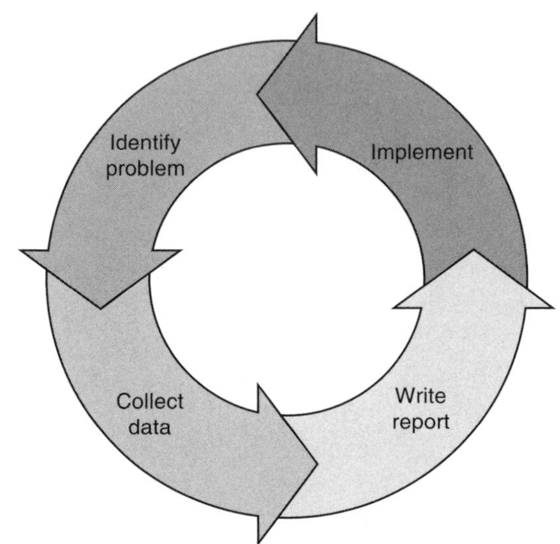


**Figure 14.2** Similar to the basic research model, the investigation process involves identifying the problem, collecting data, writing the report, and implementing the findings. The Potomac River study follows this basic model.

Adapted from B. Jackson et al., 2004, *Protecting emergency responders: Safety management in disaster and terrorism response* (Cincinnati, Ohio: National Institute for Occupational Safety and Health [NIOSH]).

tions. It is a variation of the basic research model. The model consists of four phases: identify the problem, collect the data, write the report, and implement the recommendations.

The investigation process differs slightly from the basic research model. Rather than starting with a hypothesis and then collecting data that either support or refute it, the investigator collects data that address problems and lead to recommendations or hypotheses that are then implemented. The hypotheses are often a result of the findings rather than a result of the problem being studied.

## Identify the Problem

In the investigation model, identifying the problem is the first phase in the investigation process. First, there is a need to identify that there is a problem in need of investigation. This may not be as obvious as it seems. An underlying strand interwoven through the fabric of many of the topics discussed in this book is the impact of the management culture on the safety culture in an organization. It is the attitude within organizations that accidents are an aberration and occur infrequently. It is often easier to "move on" and not deal with them (see the discussion of HROs in chapter 4). For whatever reasons, Winding River Canoe Rental did not conduct any type of investigation after the Joe Miranda fatality in the year before Melanie Carlson's fatality. Subsequently, they went out of business. Apparently, they did not think there was a problem that needed to be addressed.

Second, there is a need to frame the problem to facilitate the appropriate answer. The charge, or the question to be addressed, is important in framing the question for the investigator. In the Dzialo incident, Walbridge was charged in a letter from the president of Greenfield Community College to investigate the accident on behalf of the college. Walbridge included the letter in his final report because his investigation and report answered the charge. The charge from the letter follows. Closer examination of the charge indicates that his investigation had wide latitude in its scope.

> Greenfield Community College seeks to discover all relevant information that will help prevent a similar accident from occurring not only on the Deerfield River but on other recreational rivers across the country.

In the Potomac River Study, this author was charged with studying the main stem of the Potomac River from Cumberland to where the river became tidal below Chain Bridge. The study was delimited to this 186-mile (300-km) segment of the river. Any fatalities that occurred above Cumberland were not included in the study, nor were any fatalities on the tidal portion of the river. Because they weren't part of the charge, they weren't included in the study.

Third, a key component of identifying the problem is the proper selection of the investigator. It is important to obtain an investigator who knows enough about the content of the topic area to adequately investigate the incident. In re-reading the charge to Walbridge, it is clear that he could pretty much do whatever he deemed appropriate. The college was really relying on his expertise, knowledge of the field, and knowledge of how to complete a study.

In summary, it is important to identify that there is a problem in need of investigation. Next, it is important for the agency requesting the investigation to develop an appropriate charge for the study. Last, it follows that the investigator responds by answering the charge.

## Collect and Review Data

Collecting and reviewing data is the second step in the investigation process, regardless of whether the study is conducted internally or externally. This section discusses some basic investigation techniques and procedures (Ferry, 1988, pp. 252-255). A recreation professional serving as a liaison between the organization and the investigator is responsible for monitoring the investigator's job performance. The information in this section will help the professional fulfill that role.

## Integrity of Evidence

On any accident site, the investigator must maintain the integrity of the evidence and the chain of custody of any evidence examined. Integrity refers to preventing contamination of the evidence, and the chain of custody refers to passing the evidence from one person to the next. The contents and everyone handling it must be documented. Often, these are minor issues because most investigations in the recreation field occur long after the actual incident has occurred. Regardless, an investigator who is dealing with evidence should know the procedures for handling it (Ferry 1988).

## Photos and Diagrams

Photos and site diagrams help the reader of a report visualize the site where the incident occurred. For example, figure 1.4 is a photo of the site on the Deerfield River where the Dzialo near drowning took place. The photo orients the reader to the spatial layout of the site. A good site photo or diagram complements a discussion of where the victim was located and other aspects of the incident and rescue.

Investigators should consider taking shots in tandem. The first shot is a location shot that shows the general scene. The second shot is a close-up shot that shows details of what is important. The position of the close-up shot in the location shot should be obvious. For example, a close-up shot might show five exposed bolt threads on the piece of playground equipment where an incident occurred. This shot would be accompanied by an overall shot of the piece of playground equipment in question with the previous shot nestled in the larger photo. Figure 14.3 shows a location shot and figure 14.4 shows the close-up shot of the signage on a park trail.

Including scale in diagrams and photos can help orient the reader to the scene of the incident. Natural objects such as doorways (seven feet tall), automobiles, people, or stairs can help the reader understand the size of the objects in the picture. This is particularly true for close-up shots. If a high level of accuracy is important, the photographer can include a ruler or an object of known dimension in the shot. In figure 14.3, the trail and signs provide a sense of scale as do the fence and backhoe.

Photo courtesy of Robert B. Kauffman.

**Figure 14.3** Trail head of Patapsco Park trail in Baltimore, Maryland. The photo shows the general location of the close-up photo (the right portion of the photo).

Photo courtesy of Robert B. Kauffman.

**Figure 14.4** Close-up photo of the trail head of Patapsco Park trail in Baltimore, Maryland.

Some question whether still photos or videos are better. The final product usually determines the medium used. A paper version of a report still requires the use of photos. Traditionally, the photos have been black and white, although investigators are increasingly including color photos in reports. It is easy to convert color photos into quality black-and-white photos for the report using image processing software. On the other hand, one can easily include video in PowerPoint presentations. If one has the appropriate software, it is not difficult to export still photos of reasonable quality from a video.

The investigator should keep a photo log of who took the photo, when the photo was taken, what the picture shows, where the shot taken from (i.e., a diagram of where the camera was located when the photo was taken), and the camera settings. Much of this information can be stored in the metadata of digital photo files, but it is helpful to keep a separate log that includes when and where each picture was taken.

A single photo or diagram can effectively convey a great amount of information. For example, a user survey was conducted as part of the Potomac River study. The tables in the report show that 100 percent of the canoeists and kayakers wore life jackets, that only 7 percent of the tubers wore life jackets, that children in the innertubes wore life jackets, and that 40 percent of the tubers admitted to consuming alcoholic beverages while on the river. Although the statistics are necessary and useful in the report, the photo of river users in the final report poignantly makes the same conclusion by graphically depicting the essence of at least four tables and several major conclusions of the text regarding river users (see figure 14.5).

## Interviewing Witnesses or People Involved

Often, an investigator will need to interview witnesses, participants, and support personnel. The simplest and most effective approach is to simply let the interviewee tell his or her story (see "Tips for an Investigator" earlier in this chapter). The investigator should leave the trick questions and the cross-examination to the lawyers because, unless he is trained in these techniques, he will most likely find them counterproductive.

Generally, people will provide two types of information: first hand and second hand.

Photo courtesy of Robert B. Kauffman.

**Figure 14.5** A photo can show instantly what might otherwise be conveyed over several tables. This photo conveys a lot about safety on the river. Canoeists and kayakers wore life jackets, whereas adult tubers did not. The children in the innertubes wore life jackets. A cooler inside one of the tubes contains lunch and, most likely, adult beverages.

Examples of first-hand information include "I saw this…" or "I did this…." The information is not necessarily correct, but it is first-hand knowledge. Examples of second-hand knowledge, or opinion, include "I believe so and so did this…" or "Joe knows about that…." When receiving second-hand information, the interviewer should either interview Joe and corroborate the information—their corroboration makes it a primary source—or treat it as hearsay and not include it in the report.

### Legal Implications

Anything an investigator finds, says, or does can be part of the discovery process in a potential lawsuit. Depending on the nature of the investigation, the investigator may wish to consult with a lawyer. The investigator must not suggest culpability where none exists. If an investigator is not sure whether something could be legally damaging, he will often equivocate in his writing by using hedge words and phrases. This can make the findings and conclusions less clear. In the Dzialo case, Walbridge indicated that he wishes that the college would have permitted him to consult with a lawyer because it would have strengthened his report and potentially avoided this problem. In the Potomac River study, it was not necessary to consult with a lawyer because the environment was not contentious and the probability of litigation was very low.

## Report

Writing the report is the third step in the investigation process. The report is the document that the investigator submits that summarizes the findings of the investigation. The investigator should consider several points when writing the report. The investigator must not say anything in the report that he would be unwilling to include in a testimony under oath in a court of law. If he assumes that the case could go to court and writes the report accordingly, then he will be prepared.

The investigator should answer the charge of the study and avoid answering questions that were not asked. This is why the investigator must understand the purpose of the study and the original charge. The purpose frames the study and the findings.

The accident model that an investigator uses may bias the results (Dekker, 2006). Often the bias can be subtle. If the investigator subscribes to the domino model, then he will organize his thoughts in terms of this model. Models are important because they help simplify the world into understandable components, but models may also influence how one approaches the problem.

This section provides some techniques for organizing the final report. The basic layout of the report is derived from Ferry (1988, p. 235). The report is a stand-alone document. Whoever reads the report will have all the information necessary to understand what is going on. The charge explains why the investigator is doing the study, the chronology explains when things occurred, the text explains what happened and who was involved, and the appendixes present the investigator's credentials.

## Title Page

A well-written title page reads like an abbreviated sentence. It provides the who, what, where, and when. Normally, the title is centered horizontally and vertically on the first page. Figure 14.6 shows a typical title page.

Using figure 14.6 as an example, the following title strings the items together to make a sentence; the words in italics were added to make it read better as a sentence: *The* Report on Adam Dzialo's Near Drowning for the Board of Trustees, Greenfield Community College, Greenfield, Massachusetts, *was Conducted* by Charlie Walbridge *from* Bruceton Mills, West Virginia, *and Submitted on* November 2, 1998.

**Report on Adam Dzialo's Near Drowning**

for the

Board of Trustees
Greenfield Community College
Greenfield, Massachusetts

by

Charlie Walbridge
Bruceton Mills, West Virginia

November 2, 1998

**Figure 14.6** The title page reads like a sentence and describes the who, what, where, and when: The title (what) was conducted for whom (who) and by whom (who) on the date of the study (when). Location information (where) is usually included in the title and in the addresses of the person who created the report and the people for whom it was written.

## Body

The body of the report contains information about the investigation. The body includes the inside title, charge, synopsis of the problem, chronology, text, and findings.

**Inside Title** The inside title helps make the report a stand-alone document. Normally, the inside title is an abbreviated version of the title page and lists the title of the study and who performed the study. It is centered horizontally at the top of the page.

**Charge** The charge provides the introduction to the report. The charge is the directive. Essentially, it includes who authorized the study, what they wanted to study (the problem), and any restrictions to the study (anything that was off limits or that the person authorizing the study did not want studied).

Often the charge is written in the form of a letter to the investigator. The investigator can include a copy of the letter as a figure in the text or the appendix, or he can include only the charge from the letter in the report. If the charge was written in an e-mail or other communication, the investigator can indent it and include it in the text. If needed, the investigator should provide in this section additional clarification about who is doing the study and why it is being done. The reader must be able to follow what is occurring in the report.

As noted, Walbridge received a letter from the college president authorizing him to conduct an investigation of the accident with fairly wide latitude. In the Potomac River study, the author did not study the lower tidal and the upper reaches of the river because the author was not charged to do so in the study.

**Synopsis of the Problem** The investigator should write a brief, two- or three-line synopsis of what happened. The synopsis should not include investigative actions or conclusions. The focus is on what happened, not what the investigator is doing. Think of the actual incident and transfer of energy. In terms of event charting (figure 5.4), "six youth stepped off a gravel ledge" while swimming (wading) is an accurate description of what happened. Add to the incident that five of the swimmers drowned and the investigator has a synopsis of the problem.

**Chronology** The chronology is a time line of the incident or mishap. Again, the investigator should stick to the chronology of the incident and avoid detailing the investigation of the incident. Most lay investigations simply list or chronicle the events that led to the accident. A good alternative or addition is to use *event and causal factor analysis* described in chapter 5 and illustrated in the *accident sequence* described in figure 5.4. The advantage of using event and causal factor analysis is that it directly leads into fault analysis, MORT, and other accident investigation techniques. If desired, the investigator can use both a simple chronology of events and the more sophisticated charting technique. They can complement each other.

**Text** The text refers to the body of the study. It answers the charge or problem being addressed. The text provides linear continuity throughout the document. Photos, graphics, maps, and other elements support the text. The investigator should include facts, analysis, conclusions, and recommendations that are consistent with the charge and the problem being studied.

Often, when an investigator uses an evaluation instrument, he can use the main headings on the form as topic headings in the report. For example, if an investigator reviews a playground, the *Dirty Dozen* brochure (National Playground Institute, 1994; http://tinyurl.com/DirtyDozenBrochure) can provide the topic headings (e.g., surfacing, fall zones, inappropriate equipment, age-related equipment) for his report. If the investigator uses a model as part of the organizational structure of the report, he should indicate so in the text.

An investigator can use the analytical tree methods discussed in chapter 5 as part of an analysis. If he uses the accident sequence model in the chronology, he can define the conditions affecting the items listed on the chronology. In addition, he can use barrier analysis and fault tree analysis for his analysis and as a structure for his report. Also, many disciplines have developed these types of specialized instruments. For example, the matrix of Meyer and Williamson (2008) discussed in chapter 6 is a convenient and commonly accepted tool with which one can analyze mountaineering incidents. It could readily be adapted to other outdoor and general recreation situations.

**Graphics** Graphics should support the text and help make the report a stand-alone document. The study usually should include a site diagram to help visually orient the reader. The investigator should avoid including filler graphics or anything that is extraneous to the report.

In technical writing, the text and graphics can be viewed as two different content streams, with the text used to link the graphics. When approaching the writing of the report, consider the use of the following strategy. First, determine the basic structure or outline of the report. Second, develop a graphic, table, or figure that clearly and concisely presents the information. By their very nature, graphics, tables, or figures tend to focus the information into a clear and concise presentation. Third, use the text to write about the highlights of the graphic, table, or figure. Using this approach when writing the report, the graphic, table, or figure comes first and the text follows, not the other way around.

For example, consider the chronology section of the report. As noted earlier, it is structurally included in the report and is normally located at the beginning. Second, the investigator develops either a simple chronology (table or figure) or an accident sequence as depicted in figure

5.4. The accident sequence presents a clear and concise presentation of the chronology of events. Actually, the investigator has developed the accident sequence as part of the investigation prior to writing the report. Regardless, the chronology merges seamlessly into the report. Third, it becomes a relatively simple matter of interpreting the findings depicted in the accident sequence figure when writing about the chronology of events in the report.

**Findings and Recommendations** In the findings and recommendations, the investigator should briefly restate or paraphrase the charge. This helps frame the findings and helps those who immediately turn to the findings without reading the rest of the study understand the study. Whoever reads the finding will have all the information that they need without having to page through the document.

The findings state what the investigator found in his investigation. The findings should be written in clear and concise statements. They should directly relate to the charge and should not address questions or issues that were not in the charge. As a general rule, one provides new information in the text section rather than in the findings section. The findings summarize what was previously discussed in the text.

Recommendations indicate what an organization should do or change in the future based on the findings. The recommendations should be cost efficient, practical, and feasible. If an investigator wants to expand his recommendations beyond the original charge, he should check with those who gave him the charge to determine whether it is okay. If the investigator has no recommendations, he should state so.

### Appendixes

The appendixes normally include supplemental documents, instruments used in the analysis, and supportive analyses. Supplemental information complements and supports the main text. For example, Walbridge included his resume and credentials after the main report. These supplemental documents do not directly contribute to the accident sequence. However, they go toward establishing his credibility and competency to perform the investigation, important supplemental information. Supplemental materials can include in-depth analysis that complements a topic presented in the main text. Walbridge included an in-depth chronology completed by another study in his appendixes. This author provided a detailed analysis of the drownings (which complemented the discussion in the main study) and an expected rewards analysis (which was used to develop an instrument to assess user groups on the Potomac River).

## Implementation

The last phase in the investigation process is the implementation of the recommendations. Implementation will result, in part, from the need for and the purpose of the study. The study and its results can provide the organization with leverage with which to implement the recommendations and can help the organization justify increasing resources such as funding and personnel.

The purpose of Walbridge's investigation of the incident at Greenfield Community College was to find out what happened in Adam Dzialo's near-drowning incident. In part, it was a reaction to media pressure and the pressure from the Dzialo family to find out what happened. The investigation served its purpose and helped to strengthen the program. In the end, the program survived.

Several recommendations came out of the findings of the Potomac River study. One recommendation was the installation of gauges at the major boat ramps to warn users of dangerous water levels (figure 14.7). The Maryland DNR implemented most of the recommendations in the study. However, they did not implement the accompanying signs that interpreted the gauge reading for the different user groups. The study found that different user groups (e.g., tubers, waders, canoeists, and motor boaters) had different management and information needs when visiting the river.

# LEGAL IMPLICATIONS

Depending on circumstances, it may be important for an investigator to consider the

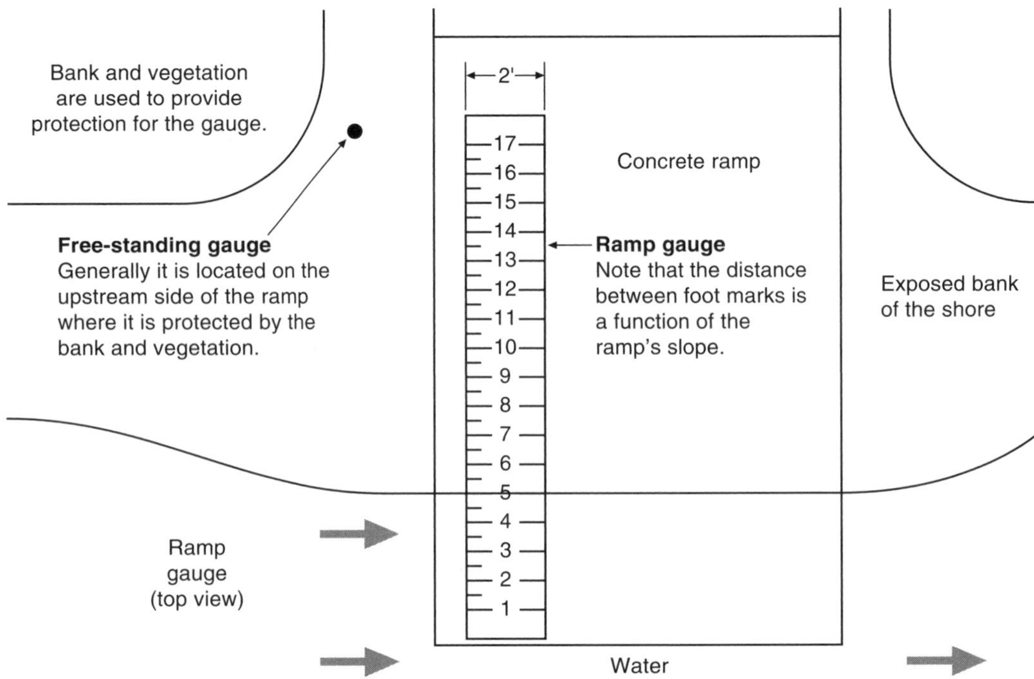


**Figure 14.7** As a result of the findings of the Potomac River study, the Maryland DNR installed gauges on all of the major boat-launch ramps.

Reprinted from R. Kauffman, S. Taylor, and R. Price, 1991, *A recreational gauging and information system to alert Potomac River users of dangerous water levels* (Annapolis, MD: Department of Natural Resources, Boating Administration, Planning and Policy Program).

legal implications of his report because it can overlap with any litigation that is occurring. As discussed in chapter 1, proving negligence involves determining a breach of standard of care and linking the omission or commission through proximate cause to an injury, damage, or loss. In contrast, one of the main purposes of an investigation is to find out what happened and to improve an organization's operations.

An investigation assumes that an organization is operating within the normal parameters of common practices in its industry. As long as an organization is operating within the range of common practices, there is likely no breach of the standard of care. The organization is merely using the investigation to improve its operations. It is a question of what the organization can do to improve its operations, not what did it do wrong. Walbridge's investigation found that the Deerfield River site was an ideal location for the college to conduct the activity. The bottom of the river was cobblestone. It was not a likely place to find a foot entrapment. Walbridge's investigation also found that, for the most part, the college conducted the activity correctly and within normal parameters. In terms of negligence, a question regarding supervision existed because one of the instructors had temporarily escorted several students off site, leaving one instructor on site to conduct the activity. In the end, the study found that the program was operating consistently with the common practices. However, the study made some programmatic recommendations in the future that if one of the leaders temporarily leaves the site they need to cease the activity.

In contrast, the Potomac River study uncovered new knowledge. It found that people died at moderate water levels rather than flood levels (Kauffman, 1991, 2002; Kauffman et al., 1991). At flood level, people correctly perceived the dangers present on the river and acted accordingly. However, at moderate water levels, people did not perceive the risks. The study found that most fatalities occurred on the Potomac River at moderate flows when the river had sufficient depth, flow, and power to become a contributing factor in fatalities (see figure 7.2).

In terms of legal liability, this finding was new knowledge. Because the importance of moderate flows in river fatalities was not common knowledge in the industry, no common practices in the industry existed regarding moderate water levels. In terms of the standard of care, no breach of the standard of care occurred because the dangers of moderate flows were not commonly known.

If an investigator discovers a potential breach in the standard of care, he should include it in the report. He should assume that the potential breach will be discovered if a lawsuit ensues because normally both sides will discover everything that there is to know about a case. Also, mitigating circumstances might exist. For example, a maintenance issue is directly involved in an incident on a playground. Reporting the maintenance issue does not mean that a breach of standard of care occurred. One must consider when the last inspection occurred, how much use the playground receives, what the weather conditions were, and whether this maintenance issue was foreseeable. The answers to these questions may help to determine whether a breach of standard of care actually occurred. Regardless of whether a breach occurred, the broken playground equipment should be fixed immediately. In fixing the equipment, the owner of the playground does not assume negligence. Rather, fixing the equipment prevents further injury.

## SUMMARY

This chapter outlines the basic procedure for investigating and reporting an incident. The environment and circumstances surrounding an incident often affect the investigation and dictate its outcome. This chapter discusses three very different postincident investigations. Janice Cody, owner of the Winding River Canoe Livery, did not conduct an investigation after the first fatality and subsequently went out of business after a second fatality. Her situation underscores the importance of conducting an investigation because had she done one, the second fatality might have been prevented and she may have remained in business providing a recreational service. The investigation of the near drowning of Adam Dzialo at an event affiliated with Greenfield Community College is an example of an investigation conducted in a contentious environment. It demonstrates that multiple investigations can be conducted on the same situation for different purposes and that the investigations can easily overlap and duplicate each other. The Potomac River study is an example of a noncontentious investigation that was more like a typical research study.

Next, this chapter discusses how to conduct an investigation and it provides a step-by-step process regarding how to conduct the investigation. This dovetails with the first point. As noted in the Dzialo situation, sometimes an investigation involves more than the mechanics of conducting a study; it also involves a political and public dimension.

# EXERCISES

## Exercise 1: Investigative Report—Mt. Hood Incident

The purpose of this exercise is to analyze available data and write an investigative report. Use the newspaper account of the Mt. Hood incident in appendix A as your source of information. Suppose that you are hired as a recreation expert by the Oregon Episcopal School in Portland, Oregon, to conduct an investigation. Submit a report on the incident and recommend changes that they could make to improve the program in the future.

## Exercise 2: *Decide to Return*

The purpose of this exercise is to analyze available data and write an investigative report. Watch the video *Decide to Return* (2007) or, if you are not able to watch the video, use the script in appendix B as your source of information. Differences may exist between the script and the actual video, but the two are reasonably close. Suppose that you are hired as a recreation expert by the two participants in the video. Write a report that includes your findings and recommend changes that they should make to improve their sea kayaking trips in the future. Consider all aspects of their trip, including trip planning, decision making, and human, environmental, and equipment factors.

## Exercise 3: *Cold, Wet, and Alive*

The purpose of this exercise is to analyze available data and write an investigative report. Watch the video *Cold, Wet, and Alive* (1989) or, if you do not have access to the video, review the *Cold, Wet, and Alive* narrative in figure 6.5 and appendix C. Imagine that Dean hires you as a recreation expert to investigate their river trip. Write a report that includes your findings and recommend changes that they should make to improve their trip in the future. Consider all aspects of their trip, including trip planning, decision making, and human, environmental, and equipment factors.

## Exercise 4: Castlewood State Park

The purpose of this exercise is to analyze available data and write an investigative report. Review the discussion of the Meramec River incident in chapter 5. Image that Castlewood State Park hires you as a recreation consultant to investigate the beach situation and river conditions. Make recommendations to improve safety of the beach users. *Hint:* Chapter 5 provides several recommendations that you might want to consider.

## Exercise 5: Fault Tree Analysis

The purpose of this exercise is to integrate fault tree analysis (see chapter 5) into an accident investigation. Review the discussion of fault tree analysis in chapter 5, specifically figure 5.14, and use the *Cold, Wet, and Alive* (1989) narrative in figure 6.5 and appendix C as your source of information. Imagine that you have been called in to investigate the incident in which David lost his boat. Apply fault tree analysis to the canoe trip in *Cold, Wet, and Alive.*

# Appendix A

# High Achievers' Climb to Death

The following newspaper article is an account of an accident that occurred to a youth group climbing Mt. Hood. It is used as the source material in several chapter exercises and in the discussion of the concepts and principles in several of the chapters.

High Achievers' Climb to Death: Disappointment, Then a Fight to Survive Mt. Hood's Brutal Winds

T.R. Reid and Don Phillips

*Washington Post* Staff Writers

Mount Hood, Ore.—The eager climbers had trekked less than halfway up the cold, snowy south slope of this deceptively gentle mountain when the first signs of trouble appeared.

With a brutal wind in their faces and wet snow clinging to their legs, five members of the highly competitive wilderness class from Oregon Episcopal School in Portland announced that they could go no farther. With considerable disappointment, one of the five teenagers said later, they left 10 schoolmates and three adults to push for the summit.

The five disappointed students turned out to be the lucky ones.

The remaining climbers hiked into a tortuous ordeal that left three frozen on the mountainside and eight others, six found too cold to be revived, jammed for three days and nights in a makeshift snow cave about the size of a compact car. Two climbers staggered off the mountain under their own power, and two others remain hospitalized, one with both legs amputated below the knees, after being airlifted to safety following an intense three-day search.

The excursion that began before dawn that Monday has prompted extensive questioning here about what went wrong. Why didn't the hikers—warmly dressed in wool sweaters, long-johns, and waterproof outer garments and led by two experienced climbers—turn back sooner? Why didn't they leave a tall marker in the snow when they dug their cave? Should they have been better prepared for bad weather on this glacial peak that, in good weather, lures about 10,000 climbers each year?

The less ambitious set out in midmorning for a brisk walk along the gentle rise near the base. Those determined to reach the 11,245-foot summit come hell or high winds start their hike just after midnight, aiming to reach the summit when the sun is high, take in the view of the

Cascade range, and scramble down before the harsh afternoon winds begin to build and ice and rock begin to fall from cliffs.

The hikers who died here last week were among the latter.

They were mainly 10th-graders taking part in the "Sophomore-Ascent," an important annual ritual at the school, an exclusive academy on a lush campus beside the sixth fairway of the Portland Golf Club. Its students tend to be high achievers—National Merit finalists and debate champions expected to go to prestigious colleges.

The school, like several others in environmentally conscious Portland, runs a four-year outdoor program designed to give the students a sense of accomplishment. In a letter of recommendation last fall for one of the students on last week's trip, the school noted that the student "had an intense drive to complete well whatever she begins particularly in her [mountain] climbing."

To make sure they would complete the ascent of Mount Hood well, the 15 students and three adults set off at 2:30 a.m. on May 12 after a midnight bus trip to Timberline Lodge about 5,000 feet below the summit. For days, the weather had been unstable and unpredictable, and the forecast was for freezing rain or snow and falling temperatures.

Clackamas County Sheriff's Lt. Don Vicars said the students from Oregon Episcopal were the only climbers on the mountain that day, not unusual for a weekday. The cold wind and cloudy sky with which they began gave way to kinder conditions after dawn, then returned as the afternoon wore on and the temperature fell.

The party pressed on but was short of the summit when its professional guide, Ralph Summers, and its faculty leader, the Rev. Thomas Goman, told the exhausted students that they must turn back. To the pain of cold and exhaustion thus was added the disappointment of failure. They knew now that they would not make it to the top. They did not know that most would not make it to the bottom.

At midafternoon, the 13 climbers suddenly were enveloped in a white haze of snow and cloud so thick they could not see one another or tell uphill from downhill. A rescue worker later said the sensation is "like walking inside a Ping-Pong ball."

In decent weather, Summers said later, the hikers could have made it back to the lodge in two hours or so. But after the group had struggled for about an hour against winds up to 50 mph, one student showed signs of hypothermia, extreme exposure to the cold. He was disoriented, lethargic, too tired to go on.

Somebody had a sleeping bag in a backpack, and the youth was wrapped in it while the others waited an hour in the driving snow for him to revive. Finally, Goman picked him up, and they set out again. With the sun beginning to sink, word was relayed from the lodge to the students' parents that they were late. But the weather at the lodge and in Portland was mild, if gray, and there was no apparent alarm.

By 5:30 p.m., after 15 hours of trudging, Goman and Summers decided that the climbers would have to dig a cave in the drifting snow and huddle there for the night, hoping for a break in the weather. Two hours of digging produced an opening barely large enough for the hikers to pack themselves in, one atop the other, leaving their gear outside. There they spent a painful, mostly sleepless night, Summers said later.

The students had practiced for this. Goman, who had climbed Mount Hood 18 times, headed the school's advanced climbing team of juniors and seniors. Each year, a sophomore was assigned to a senior for training in climbs, and cave digging, on the mountain's lower slopes. The advanced team had climbed Mount Hood in January, when temperatures were colder, the snow drier, the footing firmer.

U.S. Forest Service officials said this week that Summers was not registered, as required, as a Mount Hood guide. Outward Bound officials say he is an 11-year mountain instructor in the Northwest, trained more rigorously than government standards require. They report that he does not have a telephone, and he has not been reached for comment. School officials and families are politely shielding the climbers who turned back and those who survived from outsiders' questions.

With the mountain dark and the climbers nowhere in sight, Charles Reynolds, the bus driver who had brought the climbers to Timberline, called the Clackamas County sheriff's office at 9:30 p.m. Desk officer Damien Coates took the call—routine, so far, for authorities so close to a popular mountain where climbers often break ankles or tumble into crevasses.

Coates alerted the usual groups: the Forest Service, mountaineering clubs that regularly participate in searches and rescues, and the Air Force Reserve's 304th Aerospace Rescue and Recovery Squadron. When Summers and one of the students arrived at the lodge Tuesday morning, a large contingent of rescuers was standing by.

Summers and senior Molly Schula, at 17 the oldest student climber, had set out at 5:30 a.m. on Tuesday, straying off course in the storm. Had they walked straight down, they would have been an hour or two from Timberline. Instead they moved laterally, emerging at Mount Hood Meadows ski slope to the east where they called the lodge and waited for rescuers to drive them down the slope and back up to Timberline.

The other climbers remained stacked in their cave, the heat of their bodies melting the snow beneath them so that those on the bottom of the pile lay in a puddle of frigid water. Summers told rescuers that when he and Schula left the six teenagers, Goman, and dean of students Marion Horwell, they were cold, tired, and scared but healthy.

High winds prevented close-in use of helicopters. The sheriff's office, fearing avalanches, rejected volunteers' offers to rappel into the area where the climbers were believed to be. Men on foot inched their way up and across the mountain, but systematic rescue efforts were stymied.

But for the rescuers, morale was high. Master Sgt. Richard Harder of the 304th told reporters at the lodge—most of them local—that if the weather cleared Wednesday, they would find the students by 7 a.m. and throw "a hell of a party by 7:30."

Wednesday dawned bright and sunny, helicopters went aloft, and three bodies were spotted in the snow at about 8,300 feet. Whether because they were cramped or confused from cold, the three had left the cave. Hypothermia experts say that when body temperature drops below 86 degrees, shivering ceases and a pleasant sensation of warmth sets in. At this stage, disoriented victims may do irrational things, such as undressing or lying down in the snow.

The bodies of Erin O'Leary, Erik L. Sandvik, and Alison Litzenberger, all 15, were flown by helicopter to Emanuel Hospital in Portland, where doctors began to thaw their bodies from inside out by connecting their circulatory systems to bypass machines and returning their warmed blood to their bodies. Erik's heart beat for four hours. Neither Erin, who was running for student body president against another climber on the trip, nor Alison ever responded.

Summers had taken an azimuth reading before leaving the cave, guessing at the relative locations of the cave and the lodge on his map of the mountain and at the angle between. Rescuers set out from the lodge at that angle, but Summers had had no altimeter to pinpoint the cave's height. There was no sign of the cave where the first three bodies were found, and rescuers did not know whether or how far they had wandered from the cave. The landscape had been so changed by blowing snow that Summers could help rescuers only by instinct.

Through Wednesday night and into Thursday afternoon, mountaineers pushed 12-foot aluminum probes into the snow, working down the mountain in teams beginning at 10,000 feet. German shepherds sniffed the snow for human scents and listened for the heartbeats they are specially trained to hear. A Bell JetRanger helicopter hovered a few feet above the snow, probing with infrared scanners that detect small temperature changes.

By Thursday afternoon, hope faltered but was not abandoned. "The chances of finding them, to be honest, are just about impossible," an exhausted dog handler said. But Clackamas County deputy Russ Williams, his eyes a little glazed, told reporters, "We're hoping to find a cave with eight people real glad to see us."

"Never have I seen one so difficult to get a finger on," said Hood River deputy Bill Bryan, a leather-faced 40-year veteran of Mount Hood rescues.

Many family members who had gathered at the lodge returned to Portland to wait. Those who stayed turned sullen or talked optimistically or simply stared at the mountain. "That mountain's so close, I feel I can reach out and touch her," said Donald Penater, Horwell's brother.

At 5 p.m., clouds moved in from the west, and a cautious command station radioed the 17 exhausted rescuers still on the mountain that they had better get ready to come down.

"I'd be lynched if I tried to get them down now," a team leader radioed back.

"We're looking in a promising area," another voice said.

The base station did not know that Summers, aloft in a helicopter, had a hunch. "This looks familiar," companions quoted him later. "It's gotta be the place."

"It sort of felt right," he told reporters later.

Master Sgt. Charlie Ek moved ahead of the probers to look for hidden crevasses. Secured by a rope, held by a fellow rescuer, he leaned over cliffs to probe innocent-looking snow that might hide deep holes. At about 5:20 p.m., Ek's pole hit something soft: a backpack just beneath the surface.

As searchers converged on the area, other packs and equipment were uncovered. Then came the feeling that everyone had hoped for with every push for three days: Ek's probe broke through to open space. Beneath four feet of new snow, they dug into the snow cave, only five feet from where one of three bodies was found.

"There was noise," Ek said. "They were moaning and groaning. That's all we need to hear—life." There are several versions of what Ek said when he emerged from the cave, but according to Harder, it took a moment for everyone to believe him.

"He said, 'They're talking to us,'" Harder said. "I wanted to beat him up for joking about it."

Harder radioed, "We have patients."

Parents and friends at the lodge hugged and broke into sobs as Harder radioed, "The patients are conscious. They're not alert, but they're conscious."

Gradually it became clear that the families' elation was premature. For what seemed a long time, Harder mentioned only two patients, ignoring questions about the others.

At one point, as the base asked again for the number of patients and their conditions, Schula looked up at a reporter listening on a small scanner and said, "He won't answer that."

Unable to get needles of heart-stimulating lidocaine into the climbers' collapsed veins, unwilling to risk having thermometers snapped off by their stiff jaws, and unable to get an answer to his demands for advice on whether to move them, Harder radioed, "Forget it. We're moving the patients on my medical expertise. Two minutes—you can set your watch."

The base answered quickly, "The doctor says get them out of there." More than an hour later, when all eight climbers had been moved to the helicopter staging area nearby, Harder reluctantly radioed, "We have two alive for sure. I don't think I have anyone else conscious and breathing."

Helicopters raced the eight frozen hikers to Portland hospitals. Some were pronounced dead within minutes of arrival. Others were kept alive—in a clinical sense, at least for several hours. Brinton Clark, found in the middle of the pile, and Giles Lewis Thompson, a solidly built athlete found on top of Clark, survived.

Dr. Robert Long, who treated Thompson at Providence Medical Center, said Thompson owed his survival to his strength and rubber climbing leggings that, unlike wool, shed wet snow. Nonetheless, the dead tissue in his legs eventually threatened his life, and they were amputated below the knees.

Long said that when Thompson came around, hours after his midnight flight to the hospital, he told his doctors and family that the last thing he remembered was being in the cave, expecting to die.

# Appendix B

# Decide to Return: A Strategy for Safe Sea Kayaking

The video *Decide to Return* is the story about Katie and Jack taking an ill-fated kayak trip along the coast. It illustrates how nondecisions can become decisions. In portraying this theme, it depicts the typical accident process. This appendix contains the script for the video. The video is used as the source material in several chapter exercises and in the discussion of the concepts and principles in several of the chapters.

*Opening scene: Small dock along the coastline and fading to Jack's bedroom where he is awakened by the phone ringing. Katie narrates the story sitting on the coast with the ocean in the backdrop.*

Katie: I'd like to tell you about a kayaking trip I took with my friend Jack. We made a lot of decisions that day: some good, some not so good. It's a day I'll never forget.

*Brief cut to Lobsterman*

Lobsterman: *Moving traps on his boat.* That gal is lucky to be alive.

Jack: This better be good.

Katie: *Standing next to kayak loaded on the roof rack of her car.* I got it!

Jack: The boat?

Katie: Yeah, it's beautiful. How about you give me some pointers?

Jack: Right. Look, I'm maybe like a week ahead of you.

NP: That makes you my coach. Can you drag yourself out of bed by 10 o'clock?

*Scene changes as Jack hangs up the phone. Jack and Katie are now carrying their sea kayaks down to the water and preparing to leave shore.*

Katie: Jack, this is beautiful.

Jack: All right!

Katie: Oh, my gosh, this is awesome.

Katie: Jack started paddling a few weeks ago and now I had a boat too! This cove seemed like the perfect spot to start our adventure.

*Jack begins putting on his wetsuit.*

Katie: You don't really think we're going to need that, do you? I mean, we're just going to be paddling along the shore, right? Besides, uh, I forgot mine.

Jack: It won't take long to run back and get it. I'll get the rest of the stuff ready.

Katie: The day's half over already. Besides, I'm not planning on going swimming.

Jack: Okey-dokey.

*Flash to a more ideal scenario with Katie leaving the house with her wetsuit in hand and zipping it up next to the ocean.*

Katie: Patience isn't my strong suit. I knew the water was cold, but it was slick-calm, as they say around here. And besides, the plan was to hug the shore. So that's how our adventure began. Jack dressed for the water, which by the way was only 50 degrees. I dressed for the air. It was just one of a whole chain of decisions we'd made that day, and though we didn't realize it at the time, we'd also made some, um, well, nondecisions. You know, the stuff we'd never even thought about, like what do we know about the local waters? We hadn't brought a chart, checked the weather forecast, or even told anybody where we were going or when we'd return. All these things had escaped the scrutiny of our razor-sharp minds.

*Flash to scenes of Jack and Katie packing maps, rescue equipment, a compass, radio, and other devices that may have been useful on their excursion.*

Radio: Northwest winds at 15 knots.

*Lobsterman is setting traps. Scene fades again to Jack and Katie pushing their boats into the water to begin their day without any of the safety gear shown in the flash. The pair is shown paddling and exploring along the coast.*

Katie: We paddled down the coast in clear, calm weather, and as the hours passed my confidence grew. Jack showed me some of the techniques he'd learned. The scenery was incredible. Life was good.

Jack: Hey, look at that cove over there!

Katie: Hey, that looks cool!

Jack: Wanna check it out?

Katie: Yeah.

*They pause, resting as they float in the water. They are breathing heavily, having obviously exerted themselves.*

Jack: Whoa, Katie. Guess what time it is.

Katie: No idea. One o'clock?

Jack: Try 3:30. Maybe we ought to get heading back?

Katie: I'm just starting to get the hang of this. How about we head out to that island on the way back?

*Katie points at a distant island that is just barely visible from their cove.*

Jack: I don't know; it looks kind of far.

Katie: It's a beautiful day! There's barely any wind. Come on, it'll be a piece of cake.

*Katie and Jack begin paddling toward the island, away from the shoreline. Jack pulls out an energy bar and begins to eat before he paddles to catch up with Katie.*

Jack: Piece of cake. That reminds me. Okey-dokey.

Katie: Perhaps the explorer in me was feeling the tug of the unknown, but pointing our bows at that tiny offshore island didn't seem like a big deal. It looked like only a short paddle and it was more or less on the way back. I guess we didn't really think about it.

*Flash to a scenario where Katie and Jack are able to listen to the weather forecast and see the distance of the island. A weather report from the radio plays in the background.*

Radio: Southwest winds 10 to 15 knots.

*Katie and Jack are pictured again on their original course as they paddle visibly farther from shore toward the distant island.*

Katie: As we paddled away from shore I noticed a current nudging the lobster floats. The farther out we got, the stronger it seemed.

Jack: How are you doing, Katie?

Katie: I'm good. Are we there yet?

Jack: This current's really moving. We're going to have to hurry if we're going to make it to that island.

Katie: All right.

Jack: Can you do it?

Katie: Yeah.

Jack: Let's go!

Katie: The island wasn't looking any closer when, in a matter of a few minutes, fog rolled in. It was getting hard to see the island and we could barely see where we'd been. We should have turned around then.

*Time-elapse filming shows the quick progression of fog as it rolls in and obscures the shore and island and makes seeing difficult.*

Katie: Jack, I think it's a little more to the left.

Jack: Look at the current. It's pushing us to the right. We need to adjust. Wait, do you hear that?

Katie: It's just a boat.

Jack: Yeah, but it's a boat that's getting closer.

Katie: He's not going to be able to see us.

Jack: Hey!

Katie: Hey!

Jack: Don't hit us!

Katie: We're over here!

Jack: Hey! Wow, that was close.

*Flash to a scenario in which Jack was able to sound a horn, warning oncoming ships of their presence.*

Katie: Without a horn or some kind of radar reflector, we were stealth kayaks in the fog. Completely undetectable. What's more, it never occurred to us to bring a GPS or even a compass. We didn't have the tools to find our way.

*Scene changes to the lobsterman, talking into the radio on his boat.*

Radio on ship: Hey, Archie, how's that engine of yours working today?

Lobsterman: Yeah, the alternator's still acting up. I gotta go have a look at it. I hate to do it on a day like this.

Radio: Southwest is building over here.

Lobsterman: Yeah, it's breezing up over here. It's blowing a good 25.

*Scene changes. Boat moves off into the distance and Katie and Jack are pictured again without the fog. The island appears no closer.*

Katie: As quickly as the fog rolled in, it was gone. Blown away on the afternoon breeze. We'd been paddling blind for over an hour, but now that we could see the island it didn't look much closer.

Katie: Jack, we've got to be about halfway there.

Jack: Yeah, maybe, but the wind's really picking up.

Katie: Truth be told, I was running out of steam. Jack had been snacking all day long, and I hadn't eaten a thing. It was turning into a long, hard paddle. I was beginning to wonder if we had bitten off more than we could chew.

*The water appears to become more turbulent and Katie is visibly exhausted.*

Katie: Jack, I really don't like this.

Jack: Maybe we can make it to those rocks over there.

*Jack motions toward a small outcropping of rocks just a short paddle away.*

Katie: Go ahead. I'm right behind you.

*Jack increases speed and paddles forward. There is a significant amount of distance between him and Katie.*

Jack: Okay.

Katie: It was just a bare little rock off the end of the island, but it was the only thing between us and the ocean. We were being swept out to sea by the tide. We were both a little scared. Jack hit the accelerator but I was out of gas. I got really far behind. When Jack turned to look for me, he caught a wave wrong. That's when things really fell apart.

Katie: Jack!

*Jack turns, loses his balance on a wave, and capsizes. The scene becomes black and white as Katie races to his aid, loses her balance, and capsizes as well.*

Katie: I saw Jack flip and felt a rush of adrenaline as I paddled hard towards him. I'm still not sure what happened. One minute I was fine and the next I was upside down in that icy water fighting to hold my breath. Against the current Jack couldn't pull his boat into the rocks so he just swam for it. His wetsuit made a big difference. In the frigid water he still had enough strength to make it to dry land, and that same current was quickly sweeping me away.

Katie: I'm in the water!

Katie: No way I'd ever have made it to shore.

Katie: I can't get back into my boat! Jack! Jack!

Katie: We'd really gotten ourselves in a jam. Jack couldn't help me. I couldn't help myself, much less Jack. There wasn't another boat in sight, it would be dark in a couple hours, and I was floating toward Spain in a frigid sea. Kind of a one-person Titanic. If only we'd known about these tides and checked the forecast. If only I'd practiced some of those self-rescue techniques I'd learned about. If only we'd stayed closer together so we could have helped each other. If only. The funny thing, I wasn't even struggling. I now know I was in the initial stages of a condition called hypothermia. Without a wetsuit or drysuit to help insulate me from the cold water, my body was losing heat faster than it could produce it. My cold muscles lost any coordination and strength they might have retained after a long day of paddling with almost nothing to eat or drink. My cooling brain was sluggish at best. My life jacket was the only thing keeping me afloat. Even so, every minute in that chilly water was bringing me closer to death. Eventually I'd lose consciousness and the end would be certain.

*Flash back to a scenario where Jack and Katie stay together, aid each other in self-rescue, and have the proper gear to save themselves.*

Katie: Looking back, I could see we'd set ourselves up for this. Eager novices, we'd paddled away without the skills or equipment we needed. That, and some sketchy decisions we'd made during the day. We'd made ourselves really vulnerable! Then all it took was a minor mishap like a capsize and we were sliding down that slippery slope that ends in tragedy. We could no longer help ourselves, and if it hadn't been for a lobsterman on a route he hardly uses, well . . . As you can see, I really shouldn't be here. I got a miracle. I'm not counting on another. Next time, I'm counting on a better plan. For sure we'll be sea kayaking again, but the next paddling adventure we'll be better suited in the skills, paddling, equipment, and experience that we have. And, I'll think hard about those little decisions along the way to make sure we're not setting ourselves up for a really bad day.

*The lobsterman and his boat spot Jack signaling from the rock and rescue him before beginning to search for Katie. The scene closes with Jack spotting Katie and reaching down into the water to save her.*

Lobsterman: Gotta keep this old engine running, you know. Gotta make a dollar. It's the only reason I went that way.

[Credits]

Appendix C

# Cold, Wet, and Alive

*Cold, Wet, and Alive* is a video about hypothermia. Its secondary theme is about the accident process. In this regard, the video is useful for discussions about how accidents occur and in leadership discussions regarding how future leaders would do things differently to avoid the mishap. The individuals and the group made decisions regarding their trip that, like a series of dominos, resulted in David's loss of his boat (injury, damage, or loss). The two themes parallel each other and the two messages complement each other in a 20-minute video that is more complex than it first appears. This appendix contains the script for the video. The video is used as the source material in several chapter exercises and in the discussion of the concepts and principles in several of the chapters.

*Note:* In the video the thermographs are contained in a box. They are in an insert within the video.

Thermograph: A series of thermographs appear as graphic inserts that show what is going on internally inside David's body as he begins to develop hypothermia.

The video (DVD) *Cold, Wet, and Alive* is available from the American Canoe Association in Fredericksburg, Virginia.

Opening scene: *The group's car is driving through a rural setting and across the bridge at the lunch stop. The group is inside the vehicle.*

Radio announcer: Come on, all you late sleepers. It's Saturday. Weather service is calling for a high near 70. Sunday looks like it's back to normal—you guessed it, cold and rainy. Normal high for this date is 49 degrees. You're tuned to WTSR FM.

Dean: Whoa, it looks like it's really moving. *Referring to the river.*

David: Oh, man, it looks great. Oh, I am so ready for this.

Lisa: Did you bring the dry clothes?

Michael: Right, and you have the lunch?

Lisa: Uh, yes. And the keys.

Michael: *Relieved sigh.*

Put-in scene: *Riverside, the group is unloading boats and preparing to get on the river.*

David: Well, hey, there. My name's David, and I'd like to tell you about a canoe trip I took with some friends. For so early in the spring I don't think you could have asked for a better day. Oh, that's Dean.

Michael: How about this day?

David: There's Michael, and Becky. Me, again. And, good ol' Lisa. Some of us had a pretty rough time, but it sure didn't start out that way.

Reprinted from American Canoe Association, 1989, *Cold, wet, and alive* (Fredericksburg, Virginia: American Canoe Association). www.americancanoe.org.

Narrator: It's easy for us to take our body for granted. Without so much as a conscious thought it can synchronize the workings of 10 trillion cells. *David trips and catches himself.*

---

Thermograph: *Thermograph of David's body showing core and extremity temperatures.*

Time: 10:54 a.m.

Air temperature: 64°F.

David's body temperature: Normal (98.6°F).

Narrator: Yet as warm-blooded creatures what our cells do, our strength, our coordination, even our thinking is done best only when we stay warm. David begins the trip with a normal body temperature. There's a core region containing vital organs like the heart, lungs, and brain that's about 98.6 degrees. In fact, David's entire body is near 98.6 and so he is said to be in his optimal thermal state.

---

David: Huh, it must've been near 70 degrees by the time we got to the river. Even so, Becky decided to wear a wetsuit. Dean too!

Dean: Boy, it's been a while. I sure hope this thing still fits.

David: Wow, are you going to be ripe in that thing; it's so warm today.

David (narrating): Well, I guess I have a tendency to dress for the moment.

Michael: Lisa, you're gonna sink the boat with all that stuff.

Lisa: You're gonna be glad I brought it later.

Michael: And a thermos too?

Lisa: Yeah, and a thermos too.

Becky: Dad, do we really need all this stuff?

Dean: Well, it's a long day.

David (narrating): *It seems like these guys were bringing a ton of stuff.*

Becky: I felt the water and it's cold.

David (narrating): *I just wanted to get on the river.*

Lisa: *Shrieks.* I didn't know I was going to get my feet wet!

Dean: All right, here we go. One, two . . . *fades into background noise.*

Becky: Here we go.

River scenes: *The group begins to navigate down the river. Different scenes show the group having fun and being playful on their river trip.*

Narrator: An optimal thermal state is that warm-to-your toes feeling and is difficult to maintain. Mostly, our surroundings are cooler than 98.6 and so we lose heat. David, with his wet cotton short sleeves, is losing heat the fastest. He feels fine because he is also the most active. Lisa and Michael have managed to stay dry so their cotton warm-ups keep them comfortable. Dean and Becky have the least heat loss. Wet or dry, their wetsuits are effective at keeping heat in. So, each paddler has made his own preparations for the day, each has his own vision of what the day holds, but will events unfold according to plan? And if they don't, what margin of safety can these boaters fall back on?

Roll scene: *David rolls his kayak. Still early in the day, the group is very playful and enthusiastic.*

Dean: Hey, David, what about that fancy new roll of yours?

Lisa: Yeah, show it to us!

David (narrating): Well, they didn't have to egg me on much. I practiced in a pool over the winter and I was wondering if I could do it on the river. But, man, when my head hit that water . . .

*Group is pulled over on shore while David successfully rolls his kayak.*

---

Thermograph: *Thermograph of David rolling his kayak and heat loss of at least 25 times faster in the water than in the air.*

Time: 11:25 a.m.

Air temperature: 64°F.

Water temperature: 46°F.

David's body temperature: Normal.

Narrator: David has just given his body a real thermal jolt. Water conducts heat from the skin much faster than air. In fact, the river is drawing away heat at least 25 times faster than the air would. Luckily, David's immersion is only a momentary shock to his senses.

---

Michael: Let's go get him! Come on!

River scenes: *The group re-enters the current and continues downstream.*

David (narrating): That quick dunking was invigorating, to say the very least. Even though I warmed up right away, I decided that would be my last demonstration.

Narrator: David is having a different day than his companions. He's been charging up and down the river, pushing the whole time. He's generating a lot of heat and promptly losing it with wet, exposed skin. He's struck a kind of thermal balance between the heat he produces and the heat he dissipates. The others have found a balance, too. On the warm rocks their heat loss is minimal, so they don't need to work at all at staying warm.

*The group is pulled over again, warming and sunning on a group of rocks while David paddles in the current.*

Michael: David, you don't know when to stop, do you?

---

Thermograph: *Scene shows a person converting into a machine that consumes and gives off energy.*

Titled: Metabolism.

Narrator: But where does all this heat come from? Where does David get his energy? The warmth that David achieves by hard paddling is a natural by-product of metabolism. That's a technical term for the chemical process by which our cells burn the food we eat. In a sense, food is fuel for a complex engine that runs at different speeds but never stops. Our bodies must have fuel in order to produce work and heat.

---

Snacking scene: *Transition into group resting and passing snacks while David continues to paddle.*

Becky: Thanks!

Lisa: Any raisins left?

Narrator: Food can be stored in our bodies almost like gas in a tank. By eating high-energy foods throughout the day, we keep the tank topped off. In this group, however, the one driving the fastest has the lowest tank.

David comes out of his boat: *David is paddling and begins to visibly lose balance in a turbulent section of water. He capsizes, is unable to roll upright, swims from the boat, and performs a successful self-rescue.*

David (narrator): I passed up on the munchies and it even seems to me that I was so anxious to get on the river that morning I'd skipped breakfast. But hey, empty stomach or not, I was having a blast. No words can express the shock I felt coming out of my boat and feeling icy water head to toe. I remember gasping for breath, the cold was so intense.

---

Thermograph: *David swimming in cold water.*

Time: 3:05 p.m.

Body temperature: Core temperature is still normal; extremities and skin are cooling.

Narrator: A warm body exposed to cold water is thrown out of thermal balance. Metabolism quickens, but the heat loss is so great the balance persists. Sensing a crisis, the body reacts. Changes in blood circulation occur within seconds. Vessels near the skin and in the limbs restrict, reducing the flow of warm blood to these cooling regions. But no longer is David's body 98.6° throughout. Now, ideal temperature is maintained only in the core region. This is the body's game plan for dealing with cold stress: Conserve precious heat for the core, and let the limbs get cold.

---

David (narrator): Well, needless to say, the little dip in the creek had its effect for sure. I was beginning to lose my sense of humor. And that spray skirt, it was almost too much for my aching fingers.

River scenes: *The group continues their trip down the river.*

Lisa: Straighten out, Michael, straighten out!

Narrator: In sports that demand agility, these adjustments the body makes to cold can spell trouble. David needs a warm core for his body to function properly, but he also needs warm, coordinated muscles to get down the river safely. To satisfy this double demand, David boosts his heat production, draining his energy reserves even faster. Of course, everyone is depleting their store of energy, but at vastly different rates. As the day wears on, clothes get wet. Maybe the sun goes in. Energy is expended. Fuel reserves dwindle. Unnoticed, the margin for error shrinks.

Lunch stop scene: *Group pulls over at the base of a bridge. They pass around snacks and beverages from the thermos. David continues to paddle in the current. They have a decision to make whether to continue their trip or take out here and hitchhike to the car. They choose to continue their trip.*

Becky: Hey, Dad, there's the bridge we crossed this morning.

Dean: Yeah, let's pull over here on the right and get the water out of the boat.

David (narrator): It was past four when we got to the halfway point.

Michael: I'm hungry.

Dean: And I think this is the last we're gonna see of the road. Canyon starts just up around the bend.

David (narrator): Now, paddling hard was the only way I could feel warm. I didn't want to stop.

Lisa: Hey, David! You want something to eat? We have plenty.

David: No, thanks. I'm not hungry.

David (narrator): Actually, I was starved. But what I wanted more was to finish that run and get to someplace warm.

Lisa: Is anybody else getting cold?

Dean: You know, we still have a ways to go. We could call it a day. We could probably hitch back to the car from here.

Michael: Look, I know it's late, but if we keep up the pace, we'll keep warm.

Lisa: Let's see how David feels.

Dean: Hey, David, you good to keep going?

David: Yeah, yeah, we came to paddle. Let's keep going.

Continues trip scenes: *David begins having difficulty staying upright. He, Michael, and Lisa all have difficulties. Scenes depicting these difficulties. The group is focused inwardly. They are no longer playful in their behavior.*

David (narrator): That decision was kind of a turning point. It was late, it was getting colder, and we did have a chance to bail out at the bridge. We didn't take it, and that's when our real problems started. The fatigue was beginning to work on my mind. I would go over, and I wouldn't even try to roll.

Lisa: Turn the boat, turn the boat.

David (narrator): Then Michael and Lisa began to have problems. It seemed like one or the other of us was always in the water.

Michael: Are you all right?

Lisa: Yeah, I'm all right.

Michael: Pull the boat up.

Narrator: Any insulating value Michael and Lisa's clothing had is now gone. Even if they manage to stay upright, they'll feel the chill of rapid heat loss.

Michael: Your hands are so cold.

Lisa: I'm freezing. What do you expect?

---

Thermograph: *Hypothermia. (Note: This is the first mention of hypothermia in the film.)*

Time: 5:15 p.m.

Air temperature: 54°F.

Water temperature: 46°F.

David's body temperature: 95 to 96°F.

Narrator: But David's problem is more than comfort. He's exhausted. With the fuel gauge nearing empty, he can no longer warm himself by exercising. The body's first line of defense, activity and higher metabolism, can't hold out indefinitely. David begins to shiver. By late afternoon, he passes a critical point. The heat that David can generate and retain is no longer sufficient even to keep the core at 98.6. Slowly, insidiously, the core temperature drops. At first, it's just a few degrees. Often accompanied by shivering, this low temperature condition in the core is called hypothermia.

---

Gorge scene: *The sky darkens and raindrops begin to fall. Dean and Michael's canoes pull over to scout the drop. The water in the gorge is rising.*

David (narrator): In the gorge we noticed the water was rising. We came to a drop that Dean thought maybe we should portage around.

Dean: So much for the weather forecast.

David (narrator): And just when I was thinking things couldn't get much worse, to show you how messed up I was, the river was actually starting to feel warm.

Dean: Where's David?

Michael: He's coming.

Dean: Let's take a look.

Michael: Hey, Lisa, do you want to take a look?

Lisa: *Shakes head.* No.

David (narrator): Well, the water had gotten pretty atrocious. I was falling behind. We were all drawing inward, thinking about ourselves. We weren't a group anymore. Hmm, I guess that explains a lot of what happened next. Chalk it up to my foggy brain, but I thought Dean was waving me on.

*David approaches the rest of the group. Dean is waving David to shore to scout, but David continues to approach the drop. David capsizes and swims.*

Dean: David! Pull over!

Becky: He's going on through!

Dean: Oh, no! He's rolled over! Let's go!

Michael: What are you guys going to do?

Dean: We're going to go after him. He's in trouble.

Michael: I guess we'll go, too!

*The canoes follow David and all of the boaters capsize. Everyone makes it to shore except for David, who is caught in an eddy behind a rock and trying to hold on.*

---

Thermograph: *Death scene. This graphic shows what happens if there is no intervention in the hypothermia process.*

Time: 6:08 p.m.

David's body temperature: 95°F and dropping.

Narrator: It took a whole, long day of little mistakes to lay this trap. Now, pressed into a course of action for which no one is really prepared, the trap closes swiftly. Like falling dominoes, one error leads to another. The group unravels. Without assistance, David's swim will be a long one, with the seconds literally ticking away his life. Their blood flow now sharply reduced, limbs become numb and weak, making swimming, or even holding on to a boat, nearly impossible. Yet, the body has one last defense. In a desperate attempt to preserve life, it continues a systematic shutdown. As core temperature falls, shivering stops. The body just cannot afford the expenditure of energy. Pulse and respiration slow as the heart and lungs cool; blood becomes thick and septic. The heart strains to continue. As his brain cools, David's speech becomes slurred, his judgment clouded. Eventually, he loses consciousness. In time, his heart may falter. More likely, he will drown first.

---

Rescue scene: *The camera pans over a pinned canoe and scattered gear before focusing on Dean as he runs up the short and locates David. Hypothermic, David clings to a rock in the middle of the river while Dean rescues him. The rest of the group is on the shore watching.*

David (narrator): That's how the day might have ended. We were like debris, scattered along the river, and it was largely my fault. Lisa's condition was following close behind mine, and my luck had almost run out. Almost, but not quite.

Thanks to the wetsuits, Dean and Becky were still functioning.

Dean: David, are you okay? Are you okay? Get out of the water! You've got to get out of the water. Come on!

*Dean swims to save David as Michael follows them downstream. Michael and Dean help David onto shore.*

David (narrator): I tried to climb onto the rock but my arms were useless. Without a life jacket, I would have drowned for sure. But, yeah, Dean was turning out to be a real hero. I don't remember much about the swim, but Michael says he chased us forever.

Michael: Come on, we've got to get you out of the water.

Dean: Get him on the rock here.

David (narrator): What I do remember is not being able to get out of the water on my own. I'm not sure if I cared one way or another. Looking back, that's what scares me the most.

*Becky runs to Dean, Michael, and David with dry clothing and other supplies. The group dresses David in dry clothes and places a pad under his seat to stop further heat transfer. David is given a hat and other survival gear. Becky runs to locate Lisa and ensure she is also doing well. The group starts a fire.*

Narrator: David's shivering is actually a good sign. It means his core temperature is still above 93°. If heat loss can be staved off with dry clothing or shelter from the wind, his body will rewarm itself, but extreme care must be taken. Even though outwardly he may just appear wet and miserable, the life systems of a hypothermia victim are in a precarious state. Blood circulation patterns have adjusted to cold stress, and jostling disturbs these patterns and endangers the heart. Heat loss must be reduced in every way possible. A sleeping bag works well, but in a pinch use anything that insulates. Be sure to cover the head and neck, areas of high heat loss. Also, talk to the victim. His degree of awareness is a clue to the degree of severity of his hypothermia. And don't forget others in the party. If one person is having a problem, it's likely that they are not alone.

Dean: We gotta get off this river.

Michael: Maybe I could find a way back to the bridge?

Dean: Yeah, we gotta get David looked at.

Narrator: David's hypothermia was mild. He only needs to get shelter and nourishment, and he should get checked by a doctor.

David: Well, I think I'll survive.

Dean: You feeling better?

Narrator: But what if Dean hadn't been so quick to respond? What if David had spent longer in the river and his core temperature had dropped more than a few degrees? David's hypothermia would have then been severe. Any chance of survival would have required careful rewarming in a hospital setting, not in gathering darkness and growing desperation on the river bank.

*Flashback to dragging David from the river.*

David (narrator): Well, Michael found a trail and we all walked out just before dark. I lost my boat, of course, but all in all I feel pretty lucky. I'm alive, and a lot smarter.

Closing scene: Group gathered around fire on riverside. Credits begin.

# Bibliography


Ajango, D. (2005). *Lessons learned II.* Eagle River, AK: Safety Education for Outdoor and Remote Work Environments.

American Canoe Association (Producer). (1989). *Cold, wet, and alive* [Video]. Fredericksburg, VA: American Canoe Association.

American Canoe Association (Producer). (2007). *Decide to return* [Video]. Fredericksburg, VA: American Canoe Association.

Beck, L., and Cable, T. (2002). *Interpretation for the 21st century—Fifteen guiding principles of interpreting nature and culture.* Champaign, IL: Sagamore.

Berg, R. (Producer), and Butler, R. (Director). (2004). *White mile* [Motion picture]. New York: Home Box Office.

Bird, F., and Germain, G. (1985). *Practical loss control leadership.* Loganville, GA: Institute Publishing.

Bittenbring, C., and Paczan, P. (2000). *Crisis management.* Fairfax County, VA: Fairfax County Park Authority.

*Bronson v. Dawes County, NB.* (2006). 722 NW 2d 17.

Buys, J., and Clark, J. (1995). *Event and causal factors analysis.* Idaho Falls, ID: Technical Research and Analysis Center, Scientech.

California State Association of Counties. (1999). *Working with media.* Sacramento, CA: California State Association of Counties.

Campfire Girls. (1993). *Management of risks and emergencies: A workbook for administrators.* Kansas City, MO: Camp Fire.

CAPRA. (2009). *National accreditation standards.* Ashburn, VA: Commission for Accreditation of Park and Recreation Agencies, National Recreation and Park Association.

*Estate of Melanie Carlson v. Janice Cody d/b/a Winding River Canoe Rentals and Dawne Kabold.* (2002). Deposition of Janice Cody. Circuit Court of Macomb, Michigan. Case No: 02-3319 NO, 1-94.

Carpenter, P., Walker, T., and Lanphear, F. (1975). *Plants in the landscape.* San Francisco: W.H. Freeman, Cooper.

Collard, M. (2001). The "reasonable man" test: Or how do we know what you did was safe? *Australian Journal of Outdoor Education,* July, 67-69.

Colorado Nonprofit Association. (2010). *Working with the media—Nonprofit toolkit.* Denver: Colorado Nonprofit Association.

Cox, W., and Love, J. (1996). 40 Years of the US interstate highway system: An analysis: The best investment a nation ever made. *Highway & Motorway Fact Book,* The Public Purpose, June. Available: www.publicpurpose.com/freeway1.htm#safety.

Csikszentmihalyi, M. (1975). *Beyond boredom and anxiety.* San Francisco: Jossey-Bass.

Curtis, R. (2005). *The backpacker's field manual.* New York: Three Rivers Press.

Dekker, S. (2006). *The field guide to understanding human error.* Burlington, VT: Ashgate Publishing.

Dorfman, M. (2008). *Introduction to risk management and insurance* (9th ed.). Upper Saddle River, NJ: Pearson Education.

Eck, J. (2002). Paying the price for rescue. Available: www.traditionalmountaineering.org/News_Rescue_Charges.htm.

Ellis, M. (1973). *Why people play.* Englewood Cliffs, NJ: Prentice-Hall.

Everly, G. (2000). Crisis management briefings (CMB): Large group crisis intervention in response to terrorism, disasters, and violence. *International Journal of Emergency Mental Health,* 2(1), 53-57.

Ewert, A., and Hughes, J. (2005). Physical resource management. In van der Smissen, B., Moiseichik, M., and Hartenburg, V., *Management of park and recreation agencies* (p. 251). Ashburn, VA: National Recreation and Park Association.

Ferrara, C. (1995). *Writing on the job.* Englewood Cliffs, NJ: Prentice Hall.

Ferry, T. (1988). *Modern accident investigation and analysis.* New York: Wiley.

Gantt, H. (1919). *Organizing for work.* New York: Harcourt, Brace, and Howe.

Garrett College. (2009). *Emergency action plan (EAP).* McHenry, MD: Adventure Sports Institute.

Gullion, L. (2007, November). *Effective elements of emergency action plans (EAP).* Handout presented at the meeting of Association for Experiential Education, St. Paul, MN.

Haddon, W. (1973). Energy damage and the ten countermeasure strategies. *Human Factors Journal,* August, 355-366.

Hale, A. (1983). *Safety management for outdoor program leaders.* Unpublished manuscript.

Hardee, J. (2003). An overview of empathy. *Health Systems,* 7(4), 29-32.

Harvey, J.B. (1974). The Abilene paradox: The management of agreement. *Organizational Dynamics,* Summer, 63-80.

Harvey, J.B. (1988). *The Abilene paradox and other meditations on management.* San Francisco: Jossey-Bass.

Heinrich, H., Peterson, D., and Roos, N. (1980). *Industrial accident prevention—A safety management approach.* New York: McGraw-Hill.

Henry, R. (2000). *You'd better have a hose if you want to put out the fire.* Windsor, CA: Gollywobbler Productions.

Herman, M. (2009). *Ready… or not—A risk management guide for nonprofit executives.* Leesburg, VA: Nonprofit Risk Management Center.

Hickson, G., Clayton, E., Githens, P., and Sloan, F. (1992). Factors that prompted families to file medical malpractice claims following perinatal injuries. *Journal of the American Medical Association,* 267(10), 1359-1363.

Hoffman, J. (2004). *Keeping cool on the hot seat—Dealing effectively with the media in times of crisis.* Highland Mills, NY: 4Cs.

Howard County Department of Recreation and Parks. (2006). *Howard County Department of Recreation and Parks risk management plan.* Howard County, MD: Howard County Department of Recreation and Parks.

Hubbell, F. (2005). *Wilderness first aid.* Conway, NH: TMC Books.

Hudson, S. (Ed.). (1992). *Manual of U.S. cave rescue techniques.* Huntsville, AL: National Cave Rescue Commission.

International Association of Landscape Ecology. (2004). Activity waiver and release of liability form. Available: www.cof.orst.edu/org/usiale/lasvegas2004/forms/waiver.pdf.

Jillings, A. (2005, November). *What's new in accident theory?* Presentation at the AEE International Conference, Tucson, AZ.

Johnson, W. (1973). *MORT: The management oversight and risk tree.* Washington, D.C.: U.S. Atomic Energy Commission.

Kaiser, R. (1986). *Liability and law in recreation, parks, and sports.* Englewood Cliffs, NJ: Prentice-Hall.

Kaiser, R., and Robinson, K. (2005). Risk management. In van der Smissen, B., Moiseichik, M., and Hartenburg, V., *Management of park and recreation agencies* (pp. 593-616). Ashburn, VA: National Recreation and Park Association.

Kauffman, R. (1991). *Potomac River on-site survey.* Annapolis, MD: Boating Administration, Department of Natural Resources.

Kauffman, R. (1992). The drowning trap: On the Potomac River most people drown well below flood level. *Trends Magazine,* March.

Kauffman, R. (1995). *Boating fundamentals: A manual of boating safety.* Ashburn, VA: National Recreation and Park Association.

Kauffman, R. (2002, April). *The drowning trap.* Paper presented at the International Boating and Water Safety Summit, Daytona Beach, FL.

Kauffman, R. (2003). The rescue curve. Paper presented at the International Boating and Water Safety Summit, Las Vegas.

Kauffman, R. (2004, November). *A new use for the movie* Cold, Wet, and Alive. Paper presented at the meeting of Association of Experiential Education, Norfolk, VA.

Kauffman, R. (2005, August). *The accident process—How to effectively use the video* Cold, Wet, and Alive *to teach risk management and the accident process.* Paper presented at Paddlesport Leadership School and Encampment, Quantico, VA.

Kauffman, R. (2006, November). *Beyond the last buoy/Did you plan to return.* Paper presented at the meeting of Association of Experiential Education , St. Paul, MN.

Kauffman, R. (2007, March). *Depicting the accident process with the new ACA sea kayak video.* Paper presented at International Boating and Water Safety Summit, San Antonio, TX.

Kauffman, R. (2010). *Career development in recreation, parks, and tourism: A positioning approach.* Champaign, IL: Human Kinetics.

Kauffman, R. (2011). *Cold, wet, and alive* (transcript). Unpublished document, Department of Recreation and Parks, Frostburg State University, Frostburg, MD.

Kauffman, R., and Carlson, G. (1992). The rescue curve—A race against time. *American Canoeist,* March, 10-13.

Kauffman, R., and Councill, E. (2005a). Whitewater woes—Paddling through the river rental business can be challenging for any business. *Parks and Recreation (Ashburn), 40*(5), 34-38.

Kauffman, R., and Councill, E. (2005b). Working with paddlesports rental businesses: Safety and contracting issues. *Parks and Recreation Magazine,* May.

Kauffman, R., Taylor, S., and Price, R. (1991). *A recreational gauging and information system to alert Potomac River users of dangerous water levels.* Annapolis, MD: Boating Administration, Department of Natural Resources.

Keller, V., and Carroll, J. (1994). A new model for physician-patient communication. *Patient Education Counseling, 23,* 131-140.

Koester, R. (2008). *Lost person behavior.* Charlottesville, VA: dbS Productions.

Krakauer, J. (1997). *Into the wild.* New York: Anchor Books.

Krakauer, J. (1998). *Into thin air.* New York: Anchor Books.

KTVI Fox News. (2012). Teens rescue 2 kids from Meramec in Castlewood State Park. Meramec River. June 26. Available: http://fox2now.com/2012/06/26/river-rescue-underway-at-castlewood-state-park-2/.

Kübler-Ross, E. (2005). *On death and dying.* New York: Travistock/Routledge.

Lakoff, G., and Johnson, M. (1980). *Metaphors we live by.* Chicago: University of Chicago Press.

Law.com. (2012). Dictionary. Available: http://dictionary.law.com.

Lewis, H. (2007). *Bids, tenders and proposals—Winning business through best practice* (2nd ed.). Philadelphia: Kogan Press.

Lowry, J. (2007). Why people sue hospitals and health care professionals. Available: www.strasburger.com/p4p/publications/why_people_sue_hospitals.htm.

Mack, A., and Rock, I. (1998). *Inattentional blindness.* Cambridge, MA: MIT Press.

Martin, P., and Priest, S. (1986). Understanding the adventure experience. *Journal of Adventure Education, 3*(1), 18-21.

Meyer, D., and Williamson, J. (2008). Potential causes of accidents in outdoor pursuits. Available: www.nols.edu/nolspro/pdf/accident_matrix.pdf.

Mitchell, J., and Everly, G. (2001). *Critical incident stress debriefing: An operations manual for CISD, defusing and other group crisis intervention services.* Ellicott City, MD: Chevron.

Moray, N. (2000). Culture, politics and ergonomics. *Ergonomics, 43,* 858-868.

Moss, J. (2008). Serious disconnect: Why people sue. Available: http://recreation-law.com/2008/03/08/serious-disconnect-why-people-sue-2/.

National Mental Health Association. (2010). *Working with the media.* Alexandria, VA: National Consumer Supporter Technical Assistance Center, National Mental Health Association.

National Playground Institute. (1994). *The dirty dozen: Are they hiding on your playground?* Ashburn, VA: National Playground Institute.

National Safety Council. (2009). *Injury facts—2009 edition.* Itasca, IL: National Safety Council.

Noordwijk Risk Initiative Foundation. (2009). *NRI MORT user's manual—For use with the management oversight and risk tree analytical logic diagram.* AG Delft, Netherlands: Noordwijk Risk Initiative Foundation.

Oakley, J. (2003). *Accident investigation techniques.* Des Plaines, IL: American Society of Safety Engineers.

Oliver, B. (2004). *Managing facility risk—10 steps to safety.* Washington, D.C.: Nonprofit Risk Management Center.

Patterson, J., and Oliver, B. (2004). *The season of hope—A risk management guide for youth-serving nonprofits.* Washington, D.C.: Nonprofit Risk Management Center.

Penn, S. (Producer), and Penn, S. (Director). (2007). *Into the wild* [Motion picture]. Hollywood, CA: Paramount.

*John M. Percheski and Fern C. Percheski, his spouse, per quod, v. Lehigh River Rafting, LTD., et al.* (January 18, 1991). Deposition of Thomas Mills. Superior Court of New Jersey Law Division—Middlesex County Docket. No. W-001468-89, 65-67.

*John M. Percheski and Fern C. Percheski, his spouse, per quod, v. Lehigh River Rafting, LTD., et al.* (April 19, 1991). Deposition of Thomas Ebro. Superior Court of New Jersey Law Division—Middlesex County Docket. No. W-001468-89, 65-67.

Peterson, J.A., and Hronek, B. (2003). *Risk management—Park, recreation, and leisure services.* Champaign, IL: Sagamore.

Pines, A., and Aronson, E. (1981). *Burnout: From tedium to personal growth.* New York: Free Press.

Platt, F. (1992). Empathy: Can it be taught? *Annals of Internal Medicine, 117*(8), 700.

Political Subdivision Tort Claims Act, Neb. Rev. Stat. sect. 13-910 (2012).

Priest, S., and Baillie, R. (1987). Justifying the risk to others: The real razor's edge. *Journal of Experiential Education, 10*(1), 16-22.

Priest, S., and Gass, M. (2005). *Effective leadership in adventure programming* (2nd ed.). Champaign, IL: Human Kinetics.

Project Adventure. (1995). *Twenty year safety study.* Hamilton, MA: Project Adventure.

Raffan, J. (1984). Images for crisis management. *The Journal of AEE, 7*(3), 6-10.

Reason, J. (1990). *Human error.* Cambridge, UK: Cambridge University Press.

Reason, J. (2008). *Managing the risks of organizational accidents.* Hants, UK: Ashgate Publishing Limited.

Reid, T.R., and Phillips, D. (1986, May 23). High achievers' climb to death—Disappointment, then a fight to survive Mt. Hood's brutal winds. *The Washington Post,* p. A1.

*River Riders v. Cathy Freeman et al.* (October 18, 2007). Deposition of [xxxx xxxxxxx]. Circuit Court of Jefferson County, West Virginia.

Robertson, L.S. (1998). *Injury epidemiology* (2nd ed.). New York: Oxford University Press.

Rohnke, K. (2005). What happened to the electric fence? *The Ripple Effect Newsletter, 27*(Fall).

Setnicka, T. (1980). *Wilderness search and rescue.* Boston, MA: Appalachian Mountain Club.

Skenazy, L. (2010). The war on children's playgrounds—By trying to make kids' spaces safe and risk-free, are we taking all the fun out of growing up? Available: www.salon.com/life/feature/2010/05/17/war_on_childrens_playgrounds.

Small, J. (2008). *Improving your bedside manner: A handbook for physicians to develop therapeutic conversations with their patients.* Austin, TX: Morgan.

Spengler, J., Connaughton, D., and Pittman, A. (2006). *Risk management in sport and recreation.* Champaign, IL: Human Kinetics.

Stephans, R.A., and Talso, W. (1997). *System safety analysis handbook* (2nd ed.). Unionville, VA: The System Safety Society.

Stephenson, J. (1991). *Safety system 2000—A practical guide for planning, managing, and conducting safety programs.* New York: Van Nostrand Reinhold.

Stewart, S. (2004). *Media training 101—A guide to meeting the press.* Hoboken, NJ: Wiley.

Stoffel, R. (2001). *The handbook for managing land search operations.* Cashmere, WA: Emergency Response International.

Strauch, B. (2002). *Investigating human error: Incidents, accidents, and complex systems.* Burlington, VT: Ashgate Publishing.

Strauch, B. (2004). *Investigating human error.* Hants, UK: Ashgate Publishing.

Tilden, F. (1957). *Interpreting our heritage.* Chapel Hill, NC: The University of North Carolina Press.

Tilton, B. (2010). *Wilderness first responder: How to recognize, treat, and prevent emergencies in the backcountry.* Guilford, CT: Falcon Guides, pp. 13-25.

Trost, W., and Nertney, R. (1995). *Barrier analysis.* Idaho Falls, ID: Technical Research and Analysis Center, Scientech.

U.S. Department of Transportation. (2000). The changing face of transportation. Chapter 3. Available: www.bts.gov/publications/the_changing_face_of_transportation/chapter_03.html.

van der Smissen, B. (1975). Legal aspects of adventure activities. *Journal of Outdoor Education, 10*(1), 20-22.

van der Smissen, B., Moiseichik, M., and Hartenburg, V. (2005). *Management of park and recreation agencies.* Ashburn, VA: National Recreation and Park Association.

Vesely, W., Goldberg, F., Roberts, N., and Haasl, D. (1981). *Fault tree handbook.* Washington, D.C.: U.S. Nuclear Regulatory Commission.

Vincent, C., Young, M., and Phillips, A. (1994). Why do people sue doctors? A study of patients and relatives taking legal action. *Lancet, 343*(8913), 1609-1613.

Vt. Stat. Ann. Tit. 12. § 5791-5795 (2011).

Walbridge, C., (1998a). *Report on Adam Dzialo's near drowning.* Greenfield, Massachusetts: Board of Trustees, November 2, p. 10.

Walbridge, C. (November 2, 1998b). *Reports prepared for Greenfield Community College Board of Trustees.* Greenfield, MA: Board of Trustees.

Walker, T., and Todtfeld, J. (2007). *Media training A-Z—A complete guide to controlling your image, message and sound bites.* New York: Media Training Worldwide.

Weick, K., and Sutcliffe, K. (2001). *Managing the unexpected—Assuring high performance in an age of complexity.* San Francisco: Jossey-Bass.

Weissmann, P., Branch, W., Gracey, C., Haidet, P., and Frankel, R. (2006). Role modeling humanistic behavior: Learning bedside manner from the experts. *Academic Medicine, 81*(7), 661-667.

Wikihow.com. (2010). How to develop a risk management plan. Available: www.wikihow.com/Develop-a-Risk-Management-Plan.

Will, G. (2009). Litigation nation. Available: www.washingtonpost.com/wp-dyn/content/article/2009/01/09/AR2009010902353.html.

# Index

*Note:* The italicized *f* and *t* following page numbers refer to figures and tables, respectively.

# About the Authors

**Robert B. Kauffman, PhD**, is a professor and chair of the department of recreation and parks management at Frostburg State University in Frostburg, Maryland.

Kauffman has more than 30 years of experience in the safety field, in particular boating safety. He has worked to bring content areas of the safety field into the mainstream of the recreation and parks field. He has produced award-winning videos and boating safety materials, including *Cold, Wet, and Alive* (the most widely used boating safety video among boating law educators in the United States), *Decide to Return*, and *Almost a Perfect Day*. Kauffman has also served as an expert witness and has used several of those cases as case studies in this book.

In 2010, Kauffman received the Outstanding Faculty Award for Professional Achievement from Frostburg State University. He received the same award for service in 1999. In 2005, he received the Citation Award from the Maryland Recreation and Parks Association for lifetime achievement, the organization's highest honor. He also received a Telly Award (2009) and three Golden Eagle Awards (2012, 1994, and 1989) from the Council for International Non-theatrical Events (CINE) for his work on the production of boating safety videos.

Kauffman and his wife, Sally, reside in Frostburg, Maryland. In his free time, he enjoys canoeing, rafting, biking, and photography.

**Merry L. Moiseichik, ReD, JD**, is a professor of recreation and sport management in the department of health, human performance and recreation at the University of Arkansas, Fayetteville. In developing and teaching the risk management course for the program at the University of Arkansas, Moiseichik gained an understanding of the challenges students have in comprehending risk management. This understanding along with her knowledge of law provided important insight into the writing of *Integrated Risk Management for Leisure Services*.

Moiseichik also works with communities to evaluate risk within all areas of their recreation departments and has served as a consultant to commercial recreation agencies in evaluating risk for insurance company reporting. She is also a National Recreation and Park Association (NRPA) certified playground safety inspector.

A frequent presenter at state, national, and international conferences, Moiseichik has published over 15 journal articles, edited 3 books, and authored 7 book chapters. Moiseichik also serves as a reviewer for the *Journal of Legal Aspects of Sport*.

In 2006, Moiseichik received an Honor Award from the Sport and Recreation Law Association and a Research Award from the University of Arkansas College of Education and Health Professions. She is a past president and a current member of the Sport and Recreation Law Association.

Moiseichik resides in Fayetteville. In her free time she enjoys camping, canoeing, biking, and playing board games.